The Religious Traditions
of Africa: A History

The Religious Traditions of Africa: A History

ELIZABETH ISICHEI

Westport, Connecticut
London

Library of Congress Cataloging-in-Publication Data

Isichei, Elizabeth Allo.
    The religious traditions of Africa : a history / Elizabeth Isichei.
      p. cm.
    Includes bibliographical references and index.
    ISBN 0–325–07114–4 (alk. paper)
      1. Africa—Religion. I. Title.
   BL2400.I85 2004
   200′.96—dc22   2004017542

British Library Cataloguing in Publication Data is available.

Library of Congress Catalog Card Number: 2004017542
ISBN: 0–325–07114–4

First published in 2004

Praeger Publishers, 88 Post Road West, Westport, CT 06881
An imprint of Greenwood Publishing Group, Inc.
www.praeger.com

Printed in the United States of America

The paper used in this book complies with the
Permanent Paper Standard issued by the National
Information Standards Organization (Z39.48–1984).

10 9 8 7 6 5 4 3 2 1

Acknowledgments

W. J. Mooney drew the maps and Brett Knowles assisted with the computer layout of the chart.

For Peter Uche Isichei

And for our beloved grandchildren
Jacob Afam Mutebi
Osita
Aruka

Two loves therefore have given origin to these two cities, self-love in contempt of God unto the earthly, love of God in contempt of one's self to the heavenly.

—St. Augustine, *On the City of God,* XIV, 28
(written in Hippo, now in coastal Algeria, in 416)

There are only two categories of people in this world: those who believe in God and who are distributed among the diverse forms of religion, and those who doubt the existence of God and who are similarly distributed among the diverse forms of negation of the existence of God. . . . What is tragically ridiculous and not to the honor of the human spirit is that the believers of God war among themselves as if they did not say the same thing and attest the same truth.

—Cerno Bokar Taal, oral teachings in Fulfulde, in Bandiagara
(now in Mali) in 1933

The shrines are many; God is one.

—Karanga (Zimbabwe) saying

Contents

Note on Terminology and Orthography

Following dictionary usage, I avoid Bantu prefixes. However, I often, but not invariably, refer to Bantu languages with the appropriate prefix: chiChewa and so on. I tend to refer to colonies by their modern and more familiar designations, though there is the odd reference to "the Gold Coast" and so on. In my spelling of African words, I have tried to adopt the most familiar version—*laibon* rather than *oloiboni*. In Yoruba, I have opted for the more familiar Shango rather than Sango, which is technically more correct and consistent with my spelling of *orisa*. Unless they appear in quotations, I do not attempt to incorporate tonal markings.

I am very much aware that it is as anachronistic to talk about "the Hausa" or "the Igbo" in the eighteenth century as it is to refer to seventeenth-century Kenya or Nigeria. Where possible, I have tried to indicate the recent vintage and unsatisfactory nature of ethnic labels. But when writing of a continent, it is impossible to avoid their use.

Preface

Forty years ago I published my first book, dealing with attitudes to government and society in the work of a number of writers from the early church. I am probably the only historian of sub-Saharan Africa to have read the complete works of Tertullian. I am certainly the only one to have read the complete works of Lactantius! Occasionally I meet an early church specialist who uses this early book in his teaching and is unaware that I have written anything else since!

The study of religion, and especially of the history of religion, has been a consuming interest since my undergraduate days. In 1967, I first took up African studies as a postdoctoral fellow at Nuffield College, Oxford. My doctorate had explored a theme in Victorian religious history; I had found research an enjoyable and absorbing vocation. I changed to African studies for personal reasons—it was love, not research, which took me to Africa and kept me there. But having stumbled into the study of the African past, it became, and has remained, a consuming passion.

This is my fourth book since taking up the Chair of Religious Studies at the University of Otago in 1992. My productivity in these years reflects the fact that I have found both the department (now long since merged with Theology) and the university a most congenial working environment.

There are many synergies between my research and my teaching. I have taught the subject matter of each chapter of this book, over the years, to undergraduate or graduate classes, and have published extensively on each of the three religious traditions I explore. I acknowledge research funding in the form of Otago Humanities Research Grants with gratitude.

A number of experts in various fields have responded generously to specific inquiries, as has a Muslim colleague. Any list must be both lengthy and incomplete, so I borrow the words of the nineteenth-century stateman and scholar Abdullahi dan Fodio. "I cannot now number all the sheikhs from whom I acquired knowledge. . . . May God reward them all with his approval."

My rainbow family has been the main source of happiness in my life. When they were young, and people asked me how I managed to combine my academic life with five children, I would say that the children were a break from my work and my work was a break from the children. They are adults now, and there is another generation, mirrored in the dedication, bright and beautiful children of the Igbo diaspora, and citizens of New Zealand and the world. Jacob, indeed, is as much a muGanda as he is an Igbo. This book is for them and for Peter, for whose sake I went to Africa in the first place.

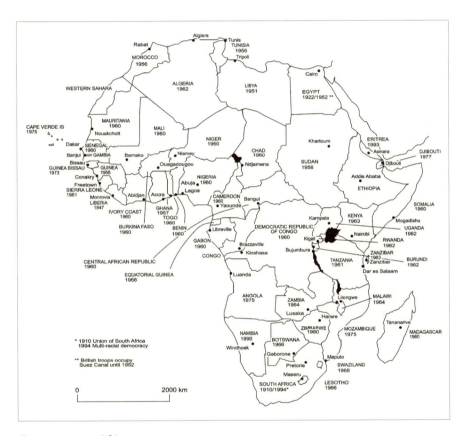

Contemporary Africa.

PART I
Religion to 600 C.E.

Chapter 1

The Study of "Traditional" Religion

> To appreciate a masked dancer, you must see him [*sic*] from every direction at once.
>
> —Igbo Proverb

This book is a historical introduction to the major religions of Africa, a task that has not been previously attempted. The vast majority of Africa's peoples are and have been either Muslims, Christians, or "traditionalists," and accordingly, these three strands compose the dominant themes of this book, with approximately equal attention paid to each. However, there were perhaps a million Jews in Egypt at the beginning of the Common Era (C.E.), and the Falashas of Ethiopia have preserved the tradition of African Judaism into modern times. Gnosticism and Manichaeanism proved less enduring, but both flourished, for a time, in Roman Africa and, of course, elsewhere in the world.

There is no separate section for any of these movements. The history of Africa's gnostics belongs with that of the early Christian church, of which they were part. The Falashas are discussed together with Ethiopian Christianity, with which their history is closely connected. The Shi'ite Indian merchants of colonial and postcolonial East Africa are mentioned only in passing. The Hindus who first reached Natal as indentured laborers enter the story only when a minority of their descendants join Bethesda, a Christian church. The rest are invisible, as are South Africa's Jews, who have never composed more than 1 percent of its population, but have made a disproportionately significant contribution.

"TRADITIONAL RELIGION" IN SUB-SAHARAN AFRICA: THE PROBLEM OF STUDYING CHANGE

Historical writing about religion in Africa, as distinct from ethnography, has tended to be dominated by books about Christianity and Islam, at the expense of Africa's many "traditional" religions. It is easy to see why this was so: both Christianity and Islam are Religions of the Book and have generated abundant written records. Antedating both, and beyond their changing frontiers, was a vast mosaic of ethnic religions that are usually called "traditional." It is far from being an accurate term—for instance, the traditional religion of Morocco is Islam—but there is no really satisfactory alternative, though some advocate "primal" or "preliterate." These religions still survive, though only a small and aging group in any African population would identify themselves first and foremost as traditionalist. "Traditional" religions survive, above all, in the hearts of Christians and Muslims; the *zar* spirit cult of Somalia and the Republic of Sudan is an example of the latter, and the persistence of witchcraft fears among African Christians, of the former.

No one has ever tried to write the history of Africa's multitude of ethnic religions, partly because there are so many of them. Although they are far more ancient than the Religions of the Book, the available historical and ethnographic data date mainly from the twentieth century. The arrangement of this book reflects one possible response to this difficulty. It begins with a chapter on approaches to the study of "traditional" religion and a case study of an ancient example. It ends by exploring these religions' twentieth-century transformations and some earlier ones.

African languages had no word for "religion." Often, the closest synonym was something like "the way of the ancestors." This is also true of "traditional" religions outside Africa. The relevant episode in the television series *The Long Search* was titled "The Way of the Ancestors"; the case study was an Indonesian "traditional" religion. In African communities, religion was part and parcel of daily life. *Christ Stopped at Eboli* is a famous book about a village in south Italy in the 1930s. Its author wrote, "In the peasants' world . . . there is no room for religion because to them everything participates in divinity." These words are quoted in an account of religion in ancient Egypt,[1] but they are equally true of sub-Saharan Africa. It has been suggested that Western missionaries, by introducing a compartmentalized attitude to religion, unintentionally contributed to secularization.[2]

Virtually all converts to Christianity in Africa have come from "traditional" religions. These religions have much in common with the culture of the Bible, including an emphasis on spiritual paths to physical and mental healing, and on dreams and visions. The detailed prohibitions of Leviticus have parallels in the ritual restrictions typical of African cultures. In the twentieth century, the Zionist or prophetic churches intuitively rediscovered these biblical elements, which had been largely lost in European and American Christianity.

In many history books, "traditional" religions are the passive, if not invisible, background to the spread of Christianity or Islam. Our knowledge of them is derived largely from the fieldwork of twentieth-century anthropologists who analyzed a particular microcosm: a "Dinka" or "Nuer" religion, which was, in practice, the religion of a particular subgroup or clan. Often, this religion was described in static terms, as if it had remained unchanged from time immemorial. When historians attempted to fill the gap, they found—often, but not always—that because these societies were for the most part preliterate, it was impossible to reconstruct the patterns of religious change in the remote past. There is, however, abundant evidence of ongoing transformations in the twentieth century and, to a lesser extent, in the nineteenth.

For earlier periods, we must rely either on highly speculative reconstructions or on glimpses in travelers' accounts, oral traditions or art, or sometimes in patterns of linguistic change. The fragmentary source material for the origins of West Africa's masking cults provides a good example.

Secret male masking cults are a very widespread feature of "traditional" West African religions. Masked figures appear in the pictures painted on rock surfaces in the northern Sahara that date from a time when there was enough rainfall there to sustain settled life, before about 2500 B.C.E. A different kind of evidence about early masking cults comes from Ife, a sacred city of the Yoruba of western Nigeria, which is famous for its classic bronze and terracotta sculptures. Traditions about its early history (which may, of course, date from long after it was founded) tell of enemies disguised in raffia masking costumes. The earliest European picture of a mask dates from the Gambia, in the late seventeenth century. It is obvious that masking traditions are ancient and widespread, but it is impossible to base a history of the West African mask tradition on fragments of this kind.

We can compare our limited knowledge of the history of masking with the successful reconstruction of the history of a cult in the Congo basin. Lemba was first mentioned in the mid-seventeenth century, as a royal cult on the Loango coast. It spread, in time, over a much larger area; those who joined were elite individuals, such as long-distance traders and diviners, who were suffering from "Lemba sickness." This condition seems to have been rooted in the fear that because of their prosperity, they would be accused of being witches. Lemba died out in the 1920s, largely because of the attacks of Christian prophets, such as Kimbangu. Lemba members were often slave traders, but paradoxically it was the victims of the slave trade who carried the cult to Haiti, where it still survives.[3]

"Traditional" religions are sometimes distinguished from the "world religions," but this terminology is misleading. If by "world religion" we mean a belief system found among different ethnic groups, this is equally true of many African mask societies and spirit possession cults. African religions span the Atlantic—one scholar has written of "the Black Atlantic"[4]—and flourish in New World forms such as Candomblé in Brazil, voudoun in Haiti, and Santería in Cuba. Immigrants have brought these religions to the United States, and one of the best studies of vodoun is set in New York.[5]

"Traditional" religions do, however, differ from Christianity and Islam in a number of important respects. They are not historical religions. Christians and Muslims look back to a historical founder and regard history as normative. For example, Christians who oppose the ordination of women point out that the twelve apostles were all men, while those who support it note that

Phoebe was in charge of a congregation (Romans 16:1–2). Both sides take it for granted that the experience of the early church should guide the practice of Christians in the contemporary world.

Like the religions of ancient Greece, with which they have much in common, African "traditional" religions begin with the "true fictions" of mythology. Christianity and Islam are Religions of the Book, regarding the Bible and the Quran, respectively, as divinely revealed texts. There is no equivalent in "traditional" religions, even in Egypt, where there was an ancient tradition of literacy. Ancient Egypt generated numerous sacred texts, such as the Pyramid Texts found in the tombs of early pharaohs, or the later, more widely distributed, Coffin Texts. These were ritual formulas that helped the spirit of the dead to enter the world to come. They were not a source of revealed wisdom.

Religions of the Book have tended to be exclusive in their truth claims—often, though not always, this exclusivity went with a strong missionary impulse. "Traditional" religions were relativistic and sought no converts. Their underlying philosophy was the idea that God is unknowable, and that each people has its own religious way, inherited from the past. A mid-nineteenth-century ruler of a Niger Igbo town said that he regarded all religions as equally true. In 1870, in distant Zimbabwe, the Ndebele king Lobengula said

> he believed in God, he believed God had made all things as He wanted them. He had made all people, and He had made every country and tribe just as He wished them to remain. He believed God made the Amandebele as He wished them to be, and it was wrong for anyone to seek to alter them.[6]

Christianity and Islam emphasized rewards and punishments in a life to come. "Traditional" religions typically offered blessings in this life: long life, good health, children, prosperity. A number of Igbo personal names and proverbs make their relative importance clear: *Nwakaego* (child is greater than money); *Ifeyinwa* (What is like a child?). Pragmatism and relativism encouraged receptivity to change. The Kalabari of the Niger Delta say, "When a spirit becomes too violent, they will tell him the stick he was carved with." In the mid-nineteenth century, they abandoned the cult of a powerful shark spirit because sharks were becoming too dangerous.[7] Village elders were willing to incorporate aspects of Christianity into their religious practices—there was a Kongo hunting charm in the form of the cross—but this kind of eclecticism was unacceptable to missionaries. In the mid-nineteenth century, Presbyterians visited a town on the Cross River, on the southeastern border of Nigeria:

> Mr. Goldie expounded the laws and exhibited the grace of God. At the close, old *Asuqa* said that they would think of what had been told them, and we must return the next morning, and tell them again all things God liked and did not like; and then they would tell us what things they could agree to, and what not; and as far as they could keep them, they would take oath to that effect. . . . Their plan of choosing and rejecting among God's laws we could not sanction.[8]

This is a good example of an encounter between two incompatible worldviews.

The ethnographer Robin Horton suggested that "traditional" religions fulfill the same functions as science in the Western world: explanation, prediction, and control.[9] The explanation of misfortune, in particular, is a central preoccupation. This explains the prevalence of witchcraft accusations and the popularity, in the colonial era and later, of witchcraft eradication movements. One might well ask why traditional forms of explanation, prediction, and control continue to flourish when Western medical science "works" more efficiently. The answer is a complex one.

Traditional therapies have their own built-in protective mechanisms. A diviner may tell a sick person that her illness is caused by a neglected ancestor, who must be placated with a sacrifice. If the offering is made, and the patient is no better, perhaps the offering was not made correctly. In Africa, as in the West, psychosomatic factors often aid healing. In the treatment of mental illness, especially, traditional African therapies may well be more effective than their drug-based Western counterparts. There is, for instance, a powerful and effective Yoruba ritual used when someone who has suffered from mental illness is restored to the community:

As this river can never flow backward,
May this sickness never return.

Part of the answer to the question of why traditional forms of explanation, prediction, and control continue to flourish lies in the nature of illness itself. Some sicknesses are self-limiting or, like arthritis, go into unexplained remissions. In such cases, the therapist, whether physician or diviner, is likely to get the credit. Some diseases cannot be cured by Western medicine, though it offers important palliatives. New drugs delay the onset of AIDS, but they are not available to Africa's poor. It is no coincidence that the spread of AIDS has led to an increase both in witchcraft accusations and in recourse to diviners. *Far and Beyon'*, a novel by Unity Dow, a distinguished lawyer from Botswana, gives a vivid picture of this at the grassroots level.

There was an intrinsic vulnerability in a worldview that sought this-worldly benefits and did not compensate for the reverses of this life with promises of Heaven. The life to come, in African traditional religion as in other comparable religious systems, tends to be shadowy and unattractive, and many early converts were drawn to Christianity by the promise of eternal life. Idigo, the first king of the Igbo polity of Aguleri, was a late-nineteenth-century ritual specialist. He was prosperous and successful but became a Christian because his powers were unable to preserve the lives of his own children. A celebrated oral text, *The Myth of the Bagre,* collected from the LoDagaa of northern Ghana, expresses a sad pessimism about the ultimate efficacy of ritual:

These things we do,
though they can't banish death.
But this our matter [ritual],
I had thought that
it was able
to overcome
death.
It can't do that.[10]

Robin Horton developed an influential model to explain conversions to Christianity or Islam. He suggested that local nature gods were well suited to the microcosm of village life; when people became part of a wider world, they tended to turn to universal religions.[11] The fact that long-distance traders have often been Muslims seemed to support this. Horton's seminal article was written in 1975. Much that has happened since then, or was already happening, seems to disprove this pattern, such as the spread of spirit possession cults and witchcraft accusations. But in some cases, one can discern a pattern of enlargement of scale *within* traditional religions.

The people who acquired a new identity as the Ndebele left Natal in 1822 and finally settled in Zimbabwe. Their religious ideas underwent an interesting change. In a sense, this was inevitable; having left their ancestral home, they could no longer make rain at the royal graves. They retained their older beliefs but also came to worship Mwari, the supreme God of Zimbabwe's indigenous people, who acquired a new corporate identity as the Shona.

DEBATES ON THE STUDY OF "TRADITIONAL" RELIGIONS

While anthropologists studied the microcosm, the local society, African theologians, reacting against European prejudice, and especially against those missionaries who rejected traditional religion as demonic, tended to concentrate on those aspects of the religions of the past which seemed most compatible with Christianity, such as the widespread belief in a High God. In the 1960s, African Christians, such as Bolaji Idowu in Nigeria or John Mbiti in Kenya, interpreted traditional religions as an African Old Testament. Parrinder was a prolific British scholar who wrote similar books, with titles such as *African Traditional Religion*. This bred a vigorous reaction. As the Ugandan scholar and poet Okot p'Bitek pointed out, to see traditional religion through Christian glasses is not to enhance it but to impoverish it, creating "a distorted and pale picture of African religious beliefs, their deities buried under thick layers of the prejudices of the students of African societies."[12] Books such as Parrinder's *African Traditional Religion* were condemned for their "stamp collecting" approach: a catalog of traits, illustrated by examples taken out of context. It should be remembered, however, that Parrinder's book appeared in 1954, when colonialism and colonial attitudes still flourished and it seemed of paramount importance to defend African civilizations from racist stereotypes.

But, as p'Bitek recognized, the "Christian" interpretation of traditional religions distorted them. Idowu applied the term "diffused monotheism" to Yoruba religion, with its rich proliferation of divinities, and described Ela, a figure in the Ife tradition, as comparable with Christ.[13]

Judeo-Christian spectacles[14] have long since been discarded, but the question of making valid generalizations about African religions remains a complex one. There are both continuities and differences in this vast body of ethnic religions, and there are exceptions to every statement. In a very real sense, no such thing as "African traditional religion" exists, as I tell my students who have just enrolled in a course on the subject. Mudimbe, a brilliant philosopher from Congo/Zaire, wrote an influential book titled *The Invention of Africa*, its title echoed by many who have not actually read it. "African traditional religion" is an invention of this kind. In a sense, these are ethnic religions, but even "Igbo religion" is an invention; it reifies and essentializes aspects of the experience of over 2,000 distinct "Igbo" communities that in precolonial times spoke different (though related) languages and had little, if any, sense of common identity. A researcher gave a literate Atuot woman (from the southern Republic of Sudan) a book on her people's religion. When she saw the title, she said, "Oh, I never knew Atuot had a religion."[15]

The very analysis of "belief" has been condemned as Eurocentric. It has been suggested that the fact that African languages have no word for belief means that the concept is absent, and that "participation" and "knowledge" are more important. Sacred knowledge is often secret, acquired by initiation or some kind of apprenticeship.[16]

A specialist in Egypt in late antiquity makes a similar point, suggesting that even in Christian history, doctrine has been overemphasized. "In paganism what is central is action, the cult. The religion *is* the sum of the dedications, the sacrifices, the rituals."[17]

The most detailed and insightful studies of Africa's "traditional" religions have been written by ethnographers. In recent years, many questions have been asked—mainly by ethnographers—about the whole ethnographic enterprise. We have already noted one aspect of the debate: criticisms of the once common absence of a historical dimension. We see particular societies through the eyes of a white—usually male, often Christian—visitor, who stayed with them for a year or so. Sometimes a younger researcher revisits a previously studied people and points out both patterns of later change and weaknesses in the first account: the invisibility of women in Evans-Pritchard's work on the Nuer and in Lienhardt's on the Dinka, for example:

> Regional variations of culture and history are likewise played down in favor of a generalized image of a timeless social order. More striking is the absence of alternative voices—particularly feminine voices—in his [Evans Pritchard's] portrayal of Nuer social experience.[18]

Ethnographers have often produced a picture that members of the society they studied would not have recognized, and to which most of them have

no access anyway.[19] Turner acknowledged that his interpretation of Ndembu
ritual symbols was significantly different from those provided by the Ndembu
themselves.[20] Mary Douglas wrote of her own account of the pangolin cult
among the Lele of Congo/Zaire:

> There are no Lele books of theology or philosophy to state the meaning of the
> cult. The metaphysical implications have not been expressed to me in so many
> words by Lele. . . . No one member of the society is necessarily aware of the
> whole pattern.[21]

Does this mean that Douglas and Turner understand the worldview of
the Lele and Ndembu, respectively, better than those peoples do themselves?

We see given cultures through the windows provided by those who have
studied them. In the early 1930s, the French ethnographer Marcel Griaule
began producing a remarkable series of publications on the Dogon of Mali.[22]
The last of these, *The Pale Fox* (*Le renard pâle*), written with Germaine
Dieterlen, appeared in 1965, after his death. These writings revealed an ex-
traordinarily elaborate world of mythology, with mystical correspondences
between spiritual beings, sacred numbers, the body, and the material world.
They include a complex story of creation and redemption that has been summarized in many books on African religions.[23] Griaule believed that the
Dogon knew that Sirius is a double star. Since this cannot be seen by the
naked eye, some enthusiasts linked this to the story of the eight ancestors
who descended from heaven as evidence of extraterrestrial visitors. The
Dogon became internationally famous. Their alleged Sirius story and creation myth came to be so well known that they figured in popular fiction.[24]
The difficulty is that later researchers have been unable to collect these stories again.[25] Nommo, far from being the heavenly being who dies and is
restored to life, is a dangerous water spirit—or, rather, a multiplicity of water
spirits— found in each body of water.

This does not mean that Griaule made it all up. Van Beek, the Dutch
scholar who restudied the Dogon, believes that these myths and correspondences are an example of what is called bricolage (a mix of different cultures),
and grew out of creative encounters between Griaule and his informants, who
in their turn, as the Nommo story suggests, were drawing on stories from
Christian (and perhaps Muslim) scriptures.

Some important studies have been written from within a given culture and
religious tradition; Abimbola's work on Ifa divination is an example,[26] as is
Bockie's account of the religion of his own northern Kongo community.[27]
The indigenous scholar has the priceless advantage of perfect command of
the relevant language; a Western-educated African Christian, however, will
not necessarily have a particularly close acquaintance with "traditional" religion. It has become increasingly common for Western ethnographers to
participate in the rituals they study, as well as to observe them. But clearly,
one does not have to be a member of a religious group in order to study it;
some excellent studies of Islam in Africa are the work of Western Christians.

If we take all these criticisms too seriously, we shall be debarred from writing anything about traditional religions at all—like the centipede who was immobilized by questions of method:

> The Centipede was happy quite
> Until the Toad in fun
> Said, "Pray which leg goes after which?"
> And worked her mind to such a pitch
> She lay distracted in the ditch
> Considering how to run.

Scholars do not hesitate to make generalizations about, for instance, the impact of globalization or the postcolonial state. We need to be equally ready to make statements about Africa's religions, though the study of African religions proceeds, as it were, in quotation marks, and must always be tied to particular case studies. It should be noted, however, that some Continental scholars have perpetuated the tradition of studying a single variable in a vast number of African cultures. Examples include H. Abrahamsson, *The Origin of Death: Studies in African Mythology* (1951), B. Lindskog, *African Leopard Men* (1954), and A. Jacobson-Widding, *Red-Black-White as a Mode of Thought* (1979).[28] British and American ethnographers of Africa—and most historians of Africa—consider it essential to spend time in the field, and have long condemned the armchair anthropologist. *The Red Fez*, however, is a striking recent study of spirit possession by a German scholar that is based entirely on library research.[29]

CHANGE IN TRADITIONAL RELIGION: ANCIENT EGYPT

The most detailed evidence for change in traditional religion in Africa comes from ancient Egypt, where written records were created and preserved from the beginning of the third millennium B.C.E. Its religious history, while amply documented, is very different from that of sub-Saharan Africa in many respects, not least in its close linkages with the Near East and the Mediterranean world.

Napoleon's forces invaded Egypt in 1798, as part of a much wider conflict. The French occupation was short-lived, but it had important consequences, both for Egypt and for Western scholarship. The discipline of Egyptology developed rapidly; ancient sites were excavated, and their writings and inscriptions were deciphered with the help of the Rosetta stone, which had parallel texts in Greek, hieroglyphs, and the cursive script known as demotic. But Westerners tended to admire ancient Egypt while marginalizing both living Egyptians and other African peoples. The achievements of ancient Egypt—literacy, monumental architecture in stone—were easier for Europeans to appreciate than, for instance, buildings in clay or wood carvings, both of which were often ephemeral in a tropical environment.

In the colonial period, there was a tendency to see Egyptian influences everywhere in black Africa. This was totally inaccurate; Egyptian influence was confined to Nubia.[30] Even there, cultural tides flowed in two directions—at one time, Nubians ruled Egypt. Geography cut Egypt off from the rest of Africa by the inhospitable Eastern and Western deserts, and the impenetrable mass of watery vegetation called the Sudd, on the upper reaches of the Nile. The quest for Egyptian influences in sub-Saharan Africa bred a reaction, and especially an emphasis on the cultural achievements and autonomy of black Africans. Some African scholars have emphasized the African elements in Egyptian culture.

A more balanced assessment has gradually become possible. Clearly, Egypt is part of Africa. No one would attempt to write the history of either Christianity or Islam in Africa without giving full weight to the Egyptian experience. Why exclude it from a discussion of traditional religion?

About 3100 B.C.E., Upper (southern) Egypt and Lower Egypt (the Nile delta) were united under a single ruler. Lacking rain, Egypt has always depended on the waters of the Nile. The rich silt brought by its annual floods generated an agricultural surplus that sustained the pharaohs. The utilization and control of the waters needed central direction. Ancient pharaohs performed the ritual of breaching the dikes; in the nineteenth century, long after the age of the pharaohs had come to an end, the Copts were still enacting this ceremony.

Western scholars have divided the age of the pharaohs into the Old, Middle, and New Kingdoms (with intervening Intermediate Periods and a Late Period afterward). An early pharaoh built a capital at Memphis, near the apex of the Nile delta. There were several different creation legends current in ancient Egypt. In one of them, the creator-god, Ptah, creates the world from a watery wilderness. Memphis was sometimes called the House of Ptah, the ultimate origin of the words "Copt" and "Egypt."

The pharaohs were associated with particular gods, including the sun god, Ra. They were also closely linked with the falcon god of Upper Egypt, Horus, and each pharaoh had a Horus name. Sometimes the pharaoh/Horus is shown killing Set, a god of Lower Egypt, in hippopotamus form, a motif that some have linked with stories of the knight who slays a monster, such as St. George and the dragon.

The great pyramids were constructed during a relatively brief period in the middle of the third millennium B.C.E. The largest of them dates from about 2590 B.C.E., and is still the world's largest stone structure after the Cologne cathedral. They were built on the desert's edge, near Memphis—the cultivable soil was needed by the living. Historians differ in their assessment of the pyramids. It was wasteful and oppressive to expend so much wealth and energy on the tomb of one man, but the pyramids were built over a long period of time, in the farming off-season. The later pyramids were much smaller.

There were many local gods, often associated with nature; some of them acquired national importance. The regalia of the early pharaohs included symbols of a vulture goddess of Upper Egypt and a cobra goddess of Lower

Egypt. The rulers of the Middle Kingdom came from Thebes (Luxor), in Upper Egypt; it was the center of the cult of the sun god, Amon, who became correspondingly important. An obelisk taken from his temple stands in the Place de la Concorde, in Paris. Other great divinities included Osiris, originally a corn god, then lord of the dead, with his cult center at Abydos, a hundred miles north of Thebes. Thoth, depicted with an ibis head, was the patron of writing, and Hathor, shown with a cow's head, was the goddess of love. The names of some of them are preserved in the Coptic calendar: Tut from Thoth, and Hatur from Hathor.[31] Why did the Egyptians depict their divinities with bird or animal heads? Animals have become symbols of eternity, because the species endure. In the Late Period (1070–332 B.C.E.) there were vast cemeteries for mummified sacred crocodiles, falcons, and so on. The English poet John Keats wrote of a (very mortal) nightingale: "Thou wast not born for death, immortal bird."

A New Kingdom pharaoh, who ruled in the mid-fourteenth century B.C.E., attempted to introduce monotheism, in the form of the worship of the Aten, the visible disk of the sun. He changed his name to Akhenaten, the Splendour of the Aten, and wrote a great hymn of praise to this divinity, but his new religion did not survive him.

The worship of Osiris and Isis grew ever more important. By the Christian era, the cult of Isis had eclipsed that of Osiris. Its center was at Philae, now covered by the waters of the Aswan Dam. A myth explained these changes: the sun god, Ra, was bitten by a serpent, and turned to Isis, the healer, to assuage his pain. The payment she required was the knowledge of Ra's secret name, the symbol of power over him. Osiris, his sister and wife, Isis, and his brother, Set, were thought to be the children of Nut and Geb, Sky Mother and Earth Father. (This reverses the much more common pairing, Earth Mother and Sky Father.)

In time, Osiris and Isis were thought of as a human king and queen. Set, out of jealousy, plotted his brother's death. Isis restored Osiris to life and conceived the child Horus. When Horus grew up, he slew his uncle, Set, and Hathor became his bride. The hieroglyphs for "Isis" and "throne" are the same.

Apuleius, who came from Roman North Africa, wrote a celebrated novel, *The Golden Ass*, in the mid-second century C.E. The hero, Lucius, is turned into a donkey, but Isis releases him. The book includes a famous prayer to Isis, in which she is explicitly equated with other ancient goddesses, such as Aphrodite. The cults of Isis and Osiris were mystery religions; devotees, such as Apuleius, went through secret rituals, hoping for eternal salvation. There were many such religions in the ancient world.

In 331 B.C.E. the Greek conqueror Alexander the Great founded the Egyptian city that bears his name, Alexandria. He visited the oasis of Siwa, sacred to the sun god, Amun, where an oracle conveniently declared that he was Amun's son. Alexander died young, and his empire was divided among his generals, one of whom, Ptolemy, founded a Greek dynasty that ruled Egypt until 30 B.C.E. Cleopatra was the last of this line, and when she died, Egypt became a Roman colony.

Under the Ptolemies, a new cult was introduced that was intended to make Egyptian religion more acceptable to the Greeks, who laughed at mummified crocodiles. Osiris was identified with the sacred bull Apis and became a new god, Sarapis. Despite the apparent artificiality of the process, Sarapis came to be extremely popular.

In Roman Egypt and Roman North Africa, in times of persecution Christians were sometimes ordered to offer a sacrifice to the divine emperor. This was the state religion, a symbol of political allegiance, but there was also a complex, varied, and changing world of popular belief and practice. Ancient Egyptians were obsessed with death, and the practice of mummification continued well into the Roman era. However, in a monumental inscription from the first century B.C.E., a dead woman advised her husband:

> Cease not to drink, to eat, to get drunk, to enjoy sex, to make the day joyful.
> . . . The West land is a land of sleep and darkness, a place where inhabitants lie still.[32]

The Nubians worshiped Egyptian divinities such as Amun and Isis, as well as one with no Egyptian equivalent, a many-armed lion god. Herodotus visited Egypt and its environs in 440 B.C.E. and paid tribute to the piety of the Libyan women of Cyrenaica who worshiped Isis.

Religious belief in the Maghrib was influenced by the presence of a foreign enclave, the Phoenician settlement of Carthage, founded early in the first millennium B.C.E. and sacked by Rome in 146 B.C.E. The Carthaginians were notorious for the cruelty of their religion, and leading families sacrificed their own small children to their implacable divinities, Baal, Melkart, and Tanit. Modern archaeologists have uncovered their tiny skeletons. The name Hannibal means Honoring Baal. Baal, originally a rain god, was equated with the sun god Amun in the religion of the indigenous Libyans.

Carthage was rebuilt as a Roman city where Tunis now stands. Baal and Tanit became Saturn and Caelestis; Melkart became Hercules. They inspired much terror, and even Christians referred to Saturn by a euphemism: *senex* (the old man). Gradually, in Roman Africa, Christianity replaced these divinities; the last inscription to Saturn dates from 323. They were still worshiped beyond the boundaries of Roman rule.

It is not, of course, intended to imply that the religions of Mediterranean and sub-Saharan Africa were similar, let alone that any continuity exists between them. We have explored the religion of ancient Egypt for two reasons. First, there are ample materials from which to reconstruct patterns of change in "traditional" religion, including the spread of particular religious configurations among different nationalities and ethnic groups. Second, it provides a background for the account of the early church in chapter 2.

Chapter 2

The Early Church in Northern Africa

There is but one river of truth, but many streams flow into it.
—Saint Clement of Alexandria (ca. 150–ca. 215)

By 600 C.E., there were flourishing Christian churches in North Africa, Egypt, Nubia, and in Aksum, near the Red Sea, in northern Ethiopia. The North African and Egyptian churches, in particular, had sustained a brilliant intellectual life, and their debates had helped shape the core beliefs of Christendom. Both Mediterranean North Africa and Egypt had been ruled by Rome, but for historical reasons the official language of the church in the former was Latin, while the language of scholarship in Egypt was Greek. There were also other major differences in thought and emphasis between them.

The Coptic Church of Egypt has survived as the faith of a small minority in an overwhelmingly Muslim nation. The Ethiopian church also survives, and was for many centuries central to national identity. The churches of North Africa and Nubia came to an end at different points in time after the Arab invasions. Much has been written on why some churches survived and others did not, but the answer is, to a large extent, a mystery.

Religious diversity flourished in northern Africa in the first six centuries of the Common Era. There were large Jewish communities in Egypt and Cyrenaica. Christians were often divided, as we shall see, forming both separate churches (such as the Donatists in North Africa) and "heretical" movements, such as the many branches of gnosticism. When Saint Augustine was a young man, he was, for a time, a follower of Manichaeanism, a dualistic religion founded by a Persian. Like the gnostics, the Manichaeans considered themselves Christians. The Emperor Diocletian, who persecuted Christians, also prohibited Manichaeanism.

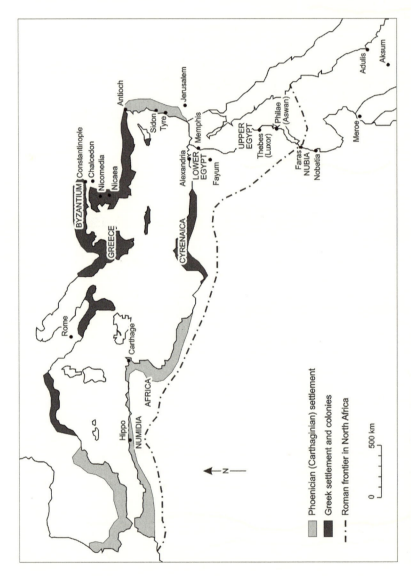

The Early Church (to 500 C.E.).

Legend:
- Phoenician (Carthaginian) settlement
- Greek settlement and colonies
- — ·· — Roman frontier in North Africa

Map labels:
Rome
Carthage
Hippo
NUMIDIA
AFRICA
BYZANTIUM
Constantinople
Chalcedon
Nicomedia
Nicaea
GREECE
Antioch
Sidon
Tyre
Jerusalem
Memphis
Alexandria
LOWER EGYPT
Fayum
CYRENAICA
UPPER EGYPT
Thebes (Luxor)
Philae (Aswan)
Faras
NUBIA
Nobatia
Meroe
Adulis
Aksum

0   500 km

N

THE EARLY CHURCH IN EGYPT AND CYRENAICA

If one should ask a contemporary Egyptian Christian when the history of Christianity in Africa began, he or she would almost certainly reply, "With the Flight into Egypt." Both Egypt's Christians and Muslims believe that the Holy Family stayed there for some time. Many stories are told of the miracles they performed, and the landscape is made sacred by these memories. For instance, a tree that grows in Bahnasa is said to have been planted by Jesus. This is myth, not history, but the way in which the past is understood and remembered is just as "real" and important as actual events. The Flight into Egypt also became of symbolic significance to many Christians in black Africa. As a group of church members from Northern Rhodesia (later, Zambia) wrote in 1958: "When Jesus was persecuted by the European Herod, God sent him into Africa; by this we know that Africans have naturally a true spirit of Christianity."[1]

Egypt had a long history of Greek and Jewish settlement. Isaiah, writing in the eighth century B.C.E., mentioned the Jews who had settled in Egypt. Jeremiah, who lived in the late seventh and early sixth centuries, blamed these Jews of the Diaspora for the fall of Jerusalem, since some of them had, in his view, provoked God's anger by worshiping the Canaanite goddess Asherah.

A Greek colony was founded in Cyrenaica in the seventh century B.C.E. From this time on, many Greeks settled in Egypt, their numbers increasing when Egypt was ruled by a Greek dynasty. Greek remained the language of scholarship and the cities, while the people of the countryside continued to speak Egyptian (or Coptic, as it came to be called). In time, the Jews of Egypt lost the knowledge of Hebrew and spoke Greek instead. In 280 B.C.E., the Hebrew Bible was translated into Greek, becoming the Septuagint, the first translation of any part of the Bible into another language. Christians would rely on it for access to its contents for centuries, though a few exceptional individuals did learn Hebrew.

Many Greeks were drawn to Judaism, and it was well established on the Arabian Peninsula. On the road between Jerusalem and Gaza, Philip met and converted a black official studying Isaiah, in the Septuagint version. (Acts 8:26ff.). He came from Kush, or Nubia, south of Egypt, in what is now the Republic of Sudan.

Greek-speaking Jews from Egypt were among the first Christians. Simon of Cyrene helped Jesus to carry his cross—the fact that his sons are mentioned by name suggests that they became Christians. Greek-speaking Jews from Egypt and Cyrene were present at the Pentecost. Apollos was a learned Jew from Alexandria who knew only the baptism of John the Baptist until he was instructed by the missionary couple Priscilla and Aquila. Missionaries from Cyrene taught at Antioch; one of the Christian teachers there was Simeon the Black.[2]

An ancient tradition claims that Saint Mark first brought Christianity to Alexandria, but we have no way of knowing whether this is true; most scholars regard it as a legend. (Venice has the same tradition about Saint Mark.)

Christian intellectuals who sought to make their faith acceptable to educated Greeks or Romans often borrowed from the work of Philo, a Jewish scholar of Alexandria, who died in ca. 50 C.E. He made a synthesis of the Hebrew Bible and Greek philosophy that had a great influence on later Christian scholars. Indeed, it may well have been more influential among Christians than among Jews. One of the ways in which he made the synthesis was by interpreting parts of the Hebrew Bible allegorically. There was also an important Jewish presence in Carthage and in Aksum/Ethiopia.

Apart from the few references in the New Testament, and the traditions about Mark, the history of orthodox Christianity in Egypt until the end of the second century is a hidden one. In the contemporary world, there is a huge diversity of Christian faith and practice, and no one should be surprised that this was also the case in the early church. In the second century C.E., Alexandria may have been the world's leading center of a branch of Christian thought, now long since almost forgotten except in the academic community, called gnosticism. (The word comes from the Greek *gnosis*, knowledge). The gnostics were influenced by Neoplatonism. The Greek philosopher Plato taught that the spiritual world is infinitely superior to the material world, and that the soul is imprisoned in its material body.

The gnostics had no desire to form a separate church.[3] They did not form a single united movement. Each gnostic teacher believed that he was the heir to a secret tradition going back to the time of the apostles. For many centuries their thought survived only in quotations in books written by their enemies. In 1945, at Nag Hammadi, north of Luxor, an Egyptian peasant discovered a collection of forty-five gnostic texts that had been translated from Greek into Coptic. They had been hidden because, by the time these manuscripts were written in the late fourth century, gnosticism had been condemned as a heresy. Partly because of this discovery, there has been a great revival of scholarly interest in the subject. Like many modern theologians, the gnostic teachers emphasized that God is completely unknowable to human minds, an insight they expressed in mythical terms. Since some texts give a central role to Sophia, Lady Wisdom, and others refer to God as both Mother and Father, gnosticism has had a great appeal to feminist scholars. Great importance was placed on Mary Magdalen; one gnostic text is called the Gospel of Mary. We should not idealize the gnostics—they condemned the material world and, in many cases, rejected the Creator God of the Hebrew Bible—but their emphasis on following the light within speaks to us still. "Abandon the search for God and the creation and other matters of a similar sort. Look for him by taking yourself as the starting point. . . . If you carefully examine these matters, you will find him in yourself."[4]

A catechetical school grew up in Alexandria, probably as a response to gnosticism. It was headed by Clement (ca. 150–ca. 215), a learned Greek convert to Christianity who studied and taught there until 203. His attempts to make Christianity acceptable to Greek intellectuals relied heavily on the work of Philo. Clement wrote, "There is but one river of truth, but many streams flow into it. The law is for the Jew what philosophy is for the Greek, a schoolmaster to bring them to God."[5]

Clement was replaced by an eighteen-year-old Egyptian, Origen (ca. 185-ca. 253). His brilliance eventually made him an international celebrity who was invited on two separate occasions to meet an emperor's wife and his mother. His adult life was divided between Alexandria and Palestine. Unlike Clement, he was never canonized, partly because he took a Gospel verse (Matthew 19:12) too literally and castrated himself as a young man. He wrote so much that he kept eight secretaries busy, but many of his works—mainly biblical commentaries—have been lost. He speculated boldly on cosmic issues, and thought that human souls existed before the body came into being and went through many lives. He was a universalist, like Clement before him; that is, he believed that all will ultimately be saved, even the fallen angels in Hell. Like many Christians of his time, he longed for martyrdom, but although he was tortured and imprisoned, he died in bed. Many of his views came to be regarded as heretical, and in the Middle Ages, scholars sometimes debated whether he could have been saved. The patterns of Clement's and Origen's lives remind us of the close links between Egypt, the Mediterrean world, and the Near East. Both intellectually and geographically, Alexandria was close to Antioch.

Between about 320 and about 450, the Christian churches of the East were deeply divided by what now seem obscure controversies about the Trinity and the human and divine aspects of Christ. These intricate debates were to have an enduring impact on Christendom, and led to the formation of new churches. In all these debates, which we can survey only very briefly in a book of this kind, the subtle intellects of Egypt played a major role.

Two of the leading participants in these debates came from Alexandria. One was Arius, who died in extreme old age in 336. He was an interesting character who popularized his theology in songs that were sung in taverns. There is much other evidence of an intense popular interest in religion. In Constantinople, later in the century, "If in this city you ask anyone for change, he will discuss with you whether the Son is begotten or unbegotten. If you ask about the quality of bread, you will receive the answer, that 'the Father is greater, the Son is less.'"[6] Arius believed that the Son, while divine, was not equal to the Father and had not existed from all eternity. However, He not only existed before the world was created but was responsible for its creation. Arius had a much more exalted idea of Christ than those twentieth-century Christian thinkers who do not, for instance, accept His physical resurrection. But his views were condemned at a council summoned by Constantine, the first Christian Roman emperor, in 325.

Earlier emperors had often persecuted Christians. Sometimes they were scapegoats for military defeats or natural disasters. Tertullian, a Carthaginian convert to Christianity, complained that if the Tiber flooded or the Nile failed to flood, there was a cry of "Christians to the lions."[7] The Coptic calendar dates from August 29, 284, the accession of Diocletian, commemorating the terrible persecution late in his reign (the "Era of Martyrs"). The names of many of those who died are still remembered and honored. They include Abnub, a boy of twelve, and Dimiana, a young and beautiful woman who remains one of the most popular Coptic saints.

The Emperor Constantine was a sincere Christian, though he prudently postponed baptism until his deathbed (because it was thought to wash away all sins). He built a new capital in Byzantium that he called Constantinople (now Istanbul). From this time on, the empire was Byzantine rather than Roman. Constantine hoped that Christianity could be a unifying force in the empire, and he attempted to put an end to its divisions. In 325, he held a council at Nicaea, in what is now northern Turkey. This council condemned Arius and produced the Nicene Creed, which is still recited in churches today. Tradition ascribes the Christological formula to the emperor himself. The council also declared that the three leading sees in Christendom were Rome, Antioch, and Alexandria. (A later council, in 381, gave second place, after Rome, to Constantinople, much to the indignation of successive patriarchs of Alexandria.)

There were to be many more debates about Christ, especially about the relationship between his divine and human natures. Cyril, a patriarch of Alexandria who died in 444, argued that Christ had only one nature, which was divine. In 451, another imperial council was held, this time at Chalcedon, across the Bosporus from Constantinople. There 520 bishops met, and agreed on a formulation to the effect that Christ has two natures, human and divine, distinct but indivisible. This was unacceptable to many Eastern Christians, who felt that this was to divide Christ and lessen the glory of his divinity.

In time, five Eastern churches that are usually called Monophysite developed an independent existence. Three of them were in Africa: in Egypt, Ethiopia, and Nubia. (The others were in Armenia and in Syria [the Jacobite Church].[8]) Their continuing separate life is based not on Christology but on some 1,500 years of later history. They call themselves not Monophysite but Orthodox. A twentieth-century pope acknowledged that there is no real difference between the faith of these churches and that of the Catholic tradition.

In both Egypt and North Africa, the conversion of the mass of the population seems to have begun in about 250 and to have been almost complete by 400. Paganism survived longest in aristocratic and intellectual circles, where it was often linked with Neoplatonism.

What, in spite of persecutions, led the people of Egypt to turn en masse to Christianity? Sometimes it was the courage of the martyrs that converted them. To Christians, the mass adoption of their faith was a proof of its truth, but the same argument could be equally well applied to the spread of Islam, which would replace Christianity wholly in North Africa and Nubia, and partly in Egypt. Some historians believe that Christianity's promise of a life to come offered a refuge from the sufferings of daily life, but this was equally true of mystery religions, such as the cult of Isis. It has been suggested that part of the attraction of Christianity lay in the fact that it was international. But Isis was also worshiped throughout the Mediterranean world and beyond.

If the reason for the mass adoption of Christianity remains something of a mystery, the Coptic contribution to Christian history is clear. Copts were among the first Christian hermits and were the first Christian monks. The hermits are remembered as the Desert Fathers, though some were women and some, to complicate matters, were women disguised as men. Many attractive stories are told of the Desert People. They include anecdotes about their closeness to the wild animals that surrounded them, and insights that are true for all ages. When one of them was asked about the road to holiness he followed, he replied that he had never allowed an angry thought to stay in his heart. One of the most famous and influential of the Desert People was the long-lived Copt, Saint Antony (ca. 251–ca. 356), who as a young man followed the Gospel literally, selling his small farm and giving the proceeds to the poor. When he died, he left his cloak to his friend Athanasius, who became his biographer.

For some, however, solitary life could lead to self-absorption, eccentricity, or madness. Pakhom, or Pachomius (ca. 290–346), was converted by his experience of Christian charity while serving as a young conscript soldier, and founded the first monastery in about 320. Fifty years later, monasticism was a mass movement, and 50,000 monks attended the annual meeting of their order. Pakhom's Rule was to influence many founders of monastic orders, among them Saint Benedict.

In 570, the Coptic Church declared its independence of Constantinople. For a time, there were two patriarchs. One was Byzantine and Chalcedonian, based in Alexandria, head of a church hated by the Copts, who called its members Melkites (king's men). The Coptic patriarch was based at the monastery of Saint Macarius in Wadi Natrun in the Western Desert, where a chain of salt lakes lies in a deep valley. This unpromising environment had been home to many of the Desert People, and would, in the twentieth century, be the scene of a great monastic revival. In one of the lakes is a spring of fresh water, which tradition attributes to the Holy Family.

The Arab-Muslim invasion of Egypt, which began in 639, was a decisive turning point in Coptic history. In the short term, the Copts rejoiced at the defeat and expulsion of the hated Melkites. It was not immediately obvious that the Ishmaelites, as the Muslims were called, were not austere Arab Christians. The Byzantine aristocrats fled, and so did Cyrus, the Melkite patriarch. His Coptic counterpart, Benjamin, left the desert and came to Alexandria. It was the end of Chalcedonian Christianity in Egypt, at least until Western missionaries arrived in the nineteenth century.

The Muslims did not, at first, seek to convert their Christian subjects here or elsewhere. They protected the Peoples of the Book if they acknowledged Muslim authority and paid a special poll tax. The Peoples of the Book included not only Christians and Jews but also the Zoroastrians of Persia, whose faith, however, virtually died out in its homeland. (The Parsis of India are the world's largest Zoroastrian community, numbering 100,000.) The Copts were valued by their new rulers both as taxpayers and as the adminstrators who collected taxes and controlled irrigation. Until the nineteenth century, they were forbidden to serve in the army.

In the context of a discussion of Judaism and Christianity, the Quran (5:48) states:

> And to you we have revealed the Book with the truth. It confirms the Scriptures which came before it. . . . We have ordained a law and assigned a path for each of you. Had Allah pleased, He could have you one nation, but it is His wish to prove you by that which He has bestowed upon you. Vie with each other in good works, for to Allah you shall all return and He will declare to you what you have disagreed about.

The Coptic Church still survives, as the largest Christian community in the Arab world. It is estimated that today there are 4 million Copts in a population of 48 million.

NORTH AFRICA

In ancient times, the inhabited area of Egypt was much the same as it is now, though with a much smaller population. In North Africa, Christianity was confined to the Roman colonies of Africa and Numidia (now Tunisia and northern Algeria). (There was also a Roman colony farther west, but we know little about its early Christian history.) A local people, the Afri, gave their name to both the colony and the continent. Roman and Christian North Africa was confined to a coastal plain extending some 200 miles inland from the Mediterranean. It did not include the steppes, which merged into desert in the south, or the Atlas Mountains.

Many Romans settled in North Africa, and in Roman colonies many of the indigenous Berbers came to speak Latin. Victor, the first pope from the

African continent (r. 189–199) was also the first pope to write in Latin. Saint Augustine, who grew up 200 miles from the sea, spoke only Latin.

As in Egypt, the first decades of Christian history in North Africa are shrouded in obscurity. By the third century, the eastern Maghrib was one of three regions in the world where Christians were in a majority; the others were Armenia and modern Turkey. The Latin-speaking Christians of the Maghrib had, on the whole, little interest in the Trinitarian and Christological controversies of the East. Eastern Christians said of them that they numbered the Trinity but did not understand it. North African Christians were concerned with different issues, especially grace and salvation. Like their counterparts in Egypt, they experienced intense, if spasmodic, persecution. The first recorded event in North Africa's Christian history was the trial and execution of twelve Christians—five men and seven women—from the village of Scilli, near Carthage, in 180. One of them was carrying the writings of Paul. The judge, a kindly man, did not want them to be executed, and offered them time to think things over. They refused: "Today we are martyrs in heaven. Thanks be to God." The zeal for martyrdom was to be a hallmark of the North African church.

In 203, another small group of martyrs died at Carthage during a persecution that also drove Clement out of Alexandria. One of them, Perpetua, kept a prison diary. A recent convert, she was a young married woman, well educated and well born, with a baby son. Her father, who was not a Christian, begged her in vain to save her life. In prison she had several visions, as did one of her companions. The emphasis on visions and dreams was to be very typical of the prophetic churches of black Africa in the twentieth century. Perpetua and her companions, who included another young mother, Felicity, died bravely in the arena. An anonymous author, who may have been Tertullian, added an account of their deaths to Perpetua's journal. She is one of four women from the early church whose writings survive.

Tertullian, a Carthaginian lawyer, was an adult convert to Christianity and a prolific author. His outlook contrasts strikingly with that of his contemporary, Clement of Alexandria. Though happily married, Tertullian condemned women in extreme terms ("You are the Devil's gateway..." [referring to the Genesis story of Eve and the Fall]). Highly educated, he nevertheless condemned classical learning. ("What has Athens to do with Jerusalem?") He wrote in favor of fasting and against the remarriage of the widowed. Women should avoid cosmetics, elaborate hairstyles, and even colored clothes, because God did not "order sheep to be born with purple and sky blue fleeces." In his last years he joined an ascetic and visionary movement called Montanism, which originated in Turkey and came to be condemned as heretical, perhaps because two of its three founders were women.

Cyprian, another Carthaginian lawyer, went through a dramatic conversion in 246, when he was in his forties. A wealthy man, he gave his goods to the poor, as Saint Antony had done, and read Tertullian daily. He became bishop of Carthage; when the dreaded plague struck the city, the Christians ministered to the dying. Cyprian fled from one persecution, but died a martyr in 258, with the same words as the Scilli martyrs: "Thanks be to God."

Not all Christians, of course, welcomed martyrdom. This became a burning issue in the North African church: Should those who recanted be allowed to rejoin the church after a period of repentance? Ironically, just as persecution was coming to an end, the issue split the North African church apart. Those who believed that backsliders should not be allowed to rejoin the Christian community formed the Donatist Church, named after its austere founder, Donatus, who came, like Augustine, from southern Numidia. They looked on the church as a small body of chosen souls. Augustine was involved in long disputes with them. He thought that the church contained both wheat and tares, to be distinguished only in eternity, and that it was bizarre to suggest that God's chosen church was located in Numidia. He compared the Donatists, who thought that they were the universal church, to frogs in a pond.

A militant Donatist wing called themselves Champions; their enemies called them Circumcellions. They embarked on a peasants' revolt, attacking unjust landlords and moneylenders with the war cry "*Deo laudes*" (Praise God). Some committed suicide by leaping off cliffs, because they had been born too late for a more orthodox martyrdom.

Augustine was one of the great formative intellects of Christian history. He was born in 354, the son of a devout Christian mother, Monica, and a pagan father. When young, he was a restless seeker after truth. For nine years he was a Manichaean, adhering to a dualistic faith that largely replaced gnosticism. Its founder, Mani (216–276), was a Persian; the religion he founded lasted a thousand years. He believed that there were two opposing principles, good and evil. The great attraction of this, as of all dualist systems, is that it explains the mystery of sin and suffering, which is so difficult to reconcile with the idea of an all-good and all-powerful God. Like the gnostics, the Manichaeans considered themselves Christians but were condemned as heretics. Augustine later abandoned Manichaeanism, turning for a time to Neoplatonism.

Augustine earned his living as a teacher of rhetoric. He went to Italy, hoping for more pupils, and took with him his de facto wife, who bore him a son. (She is nameless in his autobiography.) He later sent her back to Africa, intending to marry an heiress. But before he could do so, in 386 he had a conversion experience in a garden in what is now Milan that changed his life. He returned to the devout Catholicism of his mother, and reluctantly became bishop of Hippo, an otherwise obscure town in what is now coastal Algeria. Augustine wrote his autobiography, the *Confessions*, in what he regarded as old age (he was forty-three). He produced so many books that an inscription in a Spanish library said that anyone who claimed to have read them all was a liar. He attacked the Donatists, not only in works of learning but also in posters and in popular songs, such as the "ABC against Donatists."

In 410 Rome was conquered by "barbarians." It had long ceased to be the capital of the empire, and the invaders soon left, but it was still a huge shock. Pagans blamed the catastrophe on Christianity. Augustine responded in his *City of God*, which took him fifteen years to write and is still studied in university courses on the history of political thought. He argued that the Kingdom of Heaven could not be identified with any earthly state; it consisted of those who loved God more than self, and its membership would be known only on Judgment Day.

Augustine attacked Pelagians as well as Donatists, with grave, long-term consequences. Pelagius, who may have come from Britain, rejected the idea of Original Sin. He believed that the words of the gospel, "Be ye therefore perfect," applied not only to a heroic minority of hermits and monks but to everyone, and that God would not have commanded the impossible. He thought it was unjust that all mankind should pay the price for the Fall in the Garden of Eden. His humane and optimistic teaching, which appeals to many contemporary Christians, was condemned by two successive popes. Augustine believed that we are predestined to be saved or lost, and that only a small minority of human beings escapes Hell. His profound sense of human sinfulness was probably rooted in his own sexual adventures as a young man and in his years as a Manichaean.

It is striking that the North African church seemed to feel no missionary impulse toward the peoples living south of the wall which protected the Roman colonies. They were pastoralists who still worshiped the old gods Hammon and Baal, and from time to time they attacked Roman Africa. The North African church looked inward, and Augustine was more concerned with local Donatists and Pelagians than with the pagans of the southern steppes. This was to be one of the great weaknesses of North African Christianity. In the future, the desert's edge would be the home of many Muslim saints and scholars.

Much remains of Christian and Roman North Africa: the ruins of churches, villas with mosaic floors, cemeteries, courtyards, baths, and aqueducts. But Christianity itself did not survive.

It was not Carthaginians, Romans, or Byzantines, but Arabs, who were to effect a lasting transformation in the religion and language of North Africa. The first Arab forces reached the Maghrib in the third quarter of the seventh century. The decline of indigenous Christianity was slow and obscure, but it seems to have come to an end in the twelfth century. By the ninth century, people were living in the Cyrene cathedral. The last Latin inscriptions in the Maghrib date from the eleventh century. In the ruins of Roman Hippo, Muslim visitors looked for the cathedral of "Augodjin, a great doctor of the Christian religion."

Why did Christianity survive in Egypt but not the Maghrib? In the West, it had clearly been weakened by disputes between Catholics and Donatists and by incursions of worshipers of Baal from the southern steppes. Many who fought for the Arabs were Berber allies. Conversion to Islam meant both freedom from the poll tax and the chance to share in the plunder of victorious armies, which were soon to conquer Spain. The monastic tradition, which did much to preserve Christianity in both Egypt and Ethiopia, was not entirely lacking in North Africa, but it was much weaker there.

Christianity has a later history in the Maghrib, but it is as the faith of a tiny minority of foreigners.

ETHIOPIA

Aksum, a small kingdom near the Red Sea in what is now Ethiopia, adopted Christianity early in the fourth century. It is possible that its king was influenced by news of the conversion of his illustrious counterpart, Constantine. The change from the worship of traditional gods to Christianity is reflected in contemporary royal inscriptions and in traditions recorded much later. They tell of shipwrecked Christian brothers from Tyre (in what is now Lebanon), Frumentius and Aedesius, who were welcomed at the king's court. When the king died, Frumentius became the regent for the infant heir, and later was the first bishop of Aksum, ordained by Athanasius, the patriarch of Alexandria. The head of the Ethiopian church, the *abuna* (bishop), was sent from Egypt until 1959. There was usually only one *abuna* at a time, and he was the only bishop. No one else could crown kings, ordain clergy, and bless the Ark found in all churches. When an *abuna* died, a deputation was sent to Egypt to ask for a replacement. It was sometimes years before one arrived.

Ethiopian tradition remembers Frumentius as Abba Salama (Father of Light). The links with Near Eastern Christianity continued; in the fifth century, Syrian missionaries, remembered as the Nine Saints, arrived. A number of monasteries were built near Aksum. From that day to this, the Ethiopian church has been Monophysite. The Nine Saints are said to have translated the Bible into Ge'ez (Ethiopic), which was to remain the language of Ethiopian liturgy and sacred records. The rule of Pakhom and the life of Saint Antony were translated at an early date, as were extracts from the work of Saint Cyril.

The boundaries of modern Ethiopia were finalized only in the nineteenth century, and extend far beyond the medieval state, which in its turn was much larger than Aksum. Contemporary Ethiopia includes large Muslim populations, notably the Oromo, and peoples in the south who are, or were until recently, traditionalists.

NUBIA

Nubia, now covered by the lake created by the Aswan Dam, was desert. Unlike Egypt, there was no significant flood plain, and villages were built as a line of single houses on the banks of the Nile. Farther south, the rainfall increases, and cereal cultivation is possible. This is where the kingdom of Meroë flourished from about 300 B.C.E. to 300 C.E. Its people invented their own alphabet; we know the sounds of their words, but not their meaning.

Christianity came late to Nubia in the sixth century—brought not, as one might expect, by Egyptian neighbors, but by missionaries from Byzantium. The Emperor Justinian was a supporter of Chalcedon, but his able and energetic wife, Theodora, was a Monophysite. In 543 she sent a monk, Julian, to the northern Nubian kingdom of Nobatia, instructing the Byzantine governor of southern Egypt to stop any other mission. Julian suffered greatly from the heat, seeking shelter in caves, but Nobatia adopted Christianity with a striking rapidity, which is mirrored in the archaeological record. There was undoubtedly a Greek and Jewish presence in the area already, and perhaps there were Christian traders there as well. The central and southern Nubian kingdoms were converted later in the sixth century.

Nubia, like Ethiopia, was one of the few countries of the ancient world to adopt Christianity without any experience of Roman rule. Nubians kept written records, first in Greek, later in Old Nubian, and later still in Arabic. In the 1960s, in the course of rescue archaeology in areas about to be covered by the waters of the Aswan Dam, researchers uncovered many relics of Christian Nubia, including churches with striking murals of saints and royalty.

A number of texts in Old Nubian survive. One of them, which may date from 973, is a sermon supposedly preached by Jesus before the Ascension. It includes a forty-six-line litany in praise of the Cross:

The Cross is that which strengthens the feeble.
The Cross is the physician of the sick.
The Cross is the perfection of the priests.
The Cross is the hope of the hopeless.
The Cross is the freedom of the enslaved.[9]

Muslim forces never conquered Nubia, deterred by both its aridity and the skill of its archers, but here, too, Christianity slowly declined and ultimately disappeared, as a result of successive waves of Arab immigration. In 1317, the cathedral in Dongola became a mosque. Christianity—and the

Nubian kingdoms—seem to have disappeared by about 1500, after a long period of decline. Farther south, new Muslim states grew up: the sultanates of Funj, Wadai, and Darfur.

CONCLUSION

Christianity and Islam are both missionary religions; it is one of their distinctive hallmarks among the world's great faith traditions. But where Islam has taken root it has usually, though not invariably, survived. Christianity, on the other hand, has often died out in its heartlands, not only in the African cases we have discussed, but elsewhere—for instance, the churches in what is now Turkey, to which the John who wrote Revelations sent messages. Mecca remains the center of the Islamic world. The church in Jerusalem, initially the acknowledged center of Christianity, did not survive the city's destruction in 70 C.E. The Judaic Christianity of Jerusalem was replaced by that of Hellenistic cities such as Antioch and Alexandria. Later it would be Celtic, Germanic, and Slavic peoples who played a leading role in Christendom. Nineteenth-century missionaries to Africa sometimes cited the conversion of Germany as an important precedent. Now, the dominance of Europe has faded. The center of gravity in world Christianity has moved south and east: to Africa, parts of Asia, and Latin America. Korea has been called the world's leading missionary nation.[10]

PART II
Islam in Africa

Chapter 3

The Spread of Islam in Northern Africa to 1800

The differences of opinion among the learned within my community are [a sign of] God's Grace.

—Hadith (tradition) of Muhammad[1]

The Prophet Muhammad was born in the trading and religious center of Mecca, in west central Arabia, not far from the Red Sea. The Kaaba, a sacred shrine there, was destined to become Islam's Holy of Holies. Its black rock is apparently a meteorite, an eloquent symbol of the interaction of the divine with the visible world. When Muhammad was about forty, he began to withdraw to an isolated cave to meditate. There he encountered a spiritual presence, identified as the Angel Gabriel, and was called to be a prophet. The angel began to dictate the Quran ("recitation"). Its full text was revealed to him over a period of twenty-three years, first in Mecca, then in the oasis city that came to be called Medina.

Tradition claims that the Prophet was illiterate; the Quran's text was preserved by scribes and remembrancers. The Quran is roughly the same length as the New Testament. It consists of 6,000 verses divided into 114 chapters (suras). All Muslims regard its Arabic text as divinely inspired, which is one of the reasons why "Islamic fundamentalism" is a misnomer. Memorizing the Quran, or parts of it, is an essential part of a traditional Islamic education. It is often suggested that its counterpart in Christianity, as the revealed Word of God, is not the Bible, but Jesus. It is *the* formative classic of written Arabic—one of the Prophet's opponents was converted by the sheer beauty of its language.

The Prophet did not claim to found a new religion. He believed that what was revealed to him was the fullness of a revelation that had been glimpsed by others in the past. There were two prophetic lineages decended from

Abraham, one through Isaac, culminating in Jesus, and one through Ishmael, culminating in Muhammad. Every country had had its own messenger, but their details have not been revealed. Muhammad was the Seal of the Prophets, and there would be no others. The genuineness of each prophet was attested by a miracle; Muhammad's miracle was the Quran.

Muhammad lived at a time when a considerable number of Arabs had adopted Christianity or Judaism, and when monotheism seems to have been spreading even within "traditional" religion; it is an excellent example of Robin Horton's thesis about enlargement of scale. Muhammad's father, who died when the boy was an infant, or even before his birth, was called Abdullah ("servant of God").

Many passages in the Quran are parallel to biblical narratives—stories of Adam and Eve, Noah, Abraham, Ishmael and Isaac, Joseph, Moses, and Isa (Jesus). Mary is mentioned more often by name in the Quran than in the New Testament. The two versions are similar, but not identical—in the Quran, for instance, Adam is forgiven at once, and becomes a prophet.

The core of the Prophet's message was monotheism: the unity of God (Allah). All but one sura of the Quran begin with an invocation to God the Gracious and Merciful. There is a strong emphasis on individual moral responsibility; all people are answerable for the eternal consequences of their own conduct, which will lead them to Paradise or to Hell. Like all sacred texts, the Quran requires interpretation. There are, for instance, mutually incompatible texts about whether it is permissible to drink alcohol. (The standard interpretation is that the prohibition came later and supersedes the earlier verses.)

Paradise is described in material terms, as it also is in Christian art, though in a different way. Some later interpreters saw this as allegorical, but it can also be read as an affirmation of the body and the created world—very different from, for instance, the rejection of sexuality and the body so common in the early and medieval church.

The pursuit of social justice is central to Islam. Giving alms to the poor is one of the Five Pillars of Islam that demarcate Muslim identity. The other four are the declaration that there is no God but God (Allah) and that Muhammad is his Messenger, prayer five times daily (when both rich and poor lie prostrate before God), the monthlong fast of Ramadan, when all share the privations of the hungry, and the pilgrimage to Mecca. Making war on one's fellow Muslims is forbidden.

Muhammad's first converts were members of his immediate family, including his wife, Khadija, and his cousin Ali. Other early adherents included Bilal, the Ethiopian who was to issue the first call to prayer at the Kaaba. When some Mecca notables opposed his teaching, the Prophet moved with his supporters to what became Medina ("the city," exemplar of Islamic society). The Islamic era dates from this *hijra* (Emigration). Later, Muhammad would return to Mecca in a bloodless triumph.

Much of the last decade of Muhammad's life was spent on campaign; he suffered one major defeat, at the battle of Uhud, but in general his followers' victories seemed a convincing demonstration of the authenticity of his message. The first Muslims were called Believers or Emigrants. "Islam" means submission (to Allah), and a Muslim is one who submits; the words were not used to denote the Prophet's followers until the second half of the eighth century. The word *salaam* (peace) is cognate.

Muslim men are permitted to have four wives. The Prophet, by special dispensation, after Khadija's death had considerably more, though only Khadija bore him surviving children, four daughters. (His Coptic wife bore him his only son.) All wives are to be treated equally; some modern Muslim commentators say that since this is impossible, Islam requires monogamy. Similarly, modernists state that the rule that a thief's hand must be amputated applies only in a (nonexistent) just society, where nobody needs to steal. The lending of money at interest is condemned both in the Quran and by later scholars (as it was by medieval Christians). In the modern world, Islamic banks define their transactions as profit- and risk-sharing.

Muhammad, in his lifetime, solved problems by seeking direct divine guidance. This was no longer available after his death, when the leadership of the Islamic community became of crucial importance. Abu Bakr, one of Muhammad's earliest followers and the father of his favorite wife, Aisha, became caliph, or deputy (of the Prophet). He died two years later and was replaced by another early associate, Umar. Umar was murdered in 644, and was succeeded by Uthman, who died a violent death in 656. Ali, the Prophet's son-in-law and cousin, was the fourth and last of the men later tradition looked back to as the Four Rightly Guided Caliphs. He was assassinated in 661. Later Muslims tended to remember the Medina period as a golden age, and Islamic reform has often been conceptualized as a return to its norms, even though three of the first four caliphs were assassinated.

The Umayyads, the Meccan noble family to which Uthman belonged, ruled the Islamic world from the death of Ali until 850. Their capital was not in Arabia but in Damascus.

The word "Arab" means "nomad." The bedouin of the desert were inured to hardship; the struggle for scarce resources led to raiding, and their culture placed a great emphasis on courage. From one point of view, the early expansion of Islam can be seen in ecological terms: the expansion of a desert people, newly unified by religion, into more favorable environments such as the Nile and Tigris valleys.

Between 635 and 637, Arab armies expanded into territory that had belonged to two empires already weakened by war with one another, the Byzantine and the Persian. They invaded Syria and Palestine, both under Byzantine rule, and Egypt, a Byzantine province. The Arab forces settled in a new garrison city near the apex of the Nile delta called Fustat. They went on to penetrate the Maghrib (the word means "west" in Arabic). Their numbers were augmented by Berber auxiliaries (clients, or *mawali*), who included freed captives and were, of course, only a tiny minority of the whole Berber population. In time, they became Muslims and Arabic speakers, often acquiring Arab genealogies.

In 670, the Muslims founded a new city at Kairouan (in modern Tunisia). The word means "resting place" and is cognate with "caravan." It was, for a time, the capital of the Maghrib and Muslim Spain. In later centuries, Kairouan was to be famous for its scholars—a visitor asked what people were discussing there, and was told, "the name and attributes of God." The Muslims destroyed Carthage, then founded Tunis nearby. Roman and Byzantine Africa became Ifriqiya. Uqba ibn Naf'i, the founder of Kairouan, is said to have ridden his horse into the sea on Morocco's Atlantic coast, lamenting the fact that he could go no farther.

The great mountain ranges of Morocco and the deserts to the south remained beyond the reach of any government. Many centuries later, Moroccans would distinguish the realm of government and the realm of dissidence.

Histories written much later say something of the Muslims' opponents, who included a probably legendary Berber Jewish (or Christian) queen, the *kahina*, in the Aures Mountains, west of Ifriqiya. She is said to have adopted a captive Arab as her son and to have died fighting the Muslims, after telling her sons to join them. It is probably a "true fiction," a condensed, symbolic account of an epoch.

By 710, the Muslims had reached Tangier. They went on to conquer Spain, which they called Andalus. They crossed the Pyrenees, but were turned back at the battle of Poitiers in 732. Like Nubia, northern Europe seemed an impoverished backwater, not worth the loss of Muslim lives. When the Abbasids seized power in 750, a fleeing Umayyad prince found his way to Spain and established a dynasty there, with its capital at Córdoba.

SHI'ITES AND KHARIJITES

Differences over the leadership of the Islamic world created divisions that endure to this day. Some believed that the descendants of the Prophet, through his daughter Fatima and Ali, had a unique and enduring role. The word s*hia* means "party" (that is, of Ali). Today, about 12 percent of the world's Muslims are Shi'ites. The history of Islam in Africa is almost entirely a history of the larger, Sunni branch.

Until the tenth century, both Shi'ism and Kharijism were important in the Maghrib, which offered a refuge to fleeing religious dissidents. Local people accepted Islam in the form in which they encountered it. The Barghawata, however, who lived in northern Morocco, near what is now Casablanca, had their own local prophet and their own Quran, and thus were not Muslims by any definition.

The Shi'ites are devoted to the memory of Ali and his descendants, especially his son Husein. His death at the hands of Umayyad forces in 680—transfixed with arrows, his dying baby boy in his arms—is still mourned and re-enacted by Shi'ite Muslims, in a way not unlike the commemoration of Christ's crucifixion among Mediterranean Christians.

The Shi'ites are divided into a number of different traditions, all of which trace a line of spiritual leaders (imams) from Husein's surviving son, Ali Zain. By far the largest is that of the Twelvers, or Ithnasheris, followed by the Seveners, or Ismailis, who are themselves divided into several sects. These imams were not revolutionaries, but secluded mystics living in Mecca; many, perhaps all, were put to death by the caliph of the day.

The Twelvers believe that the twelfth and last imam, who disappeared in 940, is still alive, though hidden, and will return as the Mahdi at the end of the world. Twelver Islam has been the official religion of Iran since 1501. Baha'i is a nineteenth-century offshoot, but neither Baha'is nor Muslims consider it part of Islam.

The Ismailis also believe in a hidden imam who will return as the Mahdi. They trace the same line of imams as the Twelvers until 765, when the sixth imam, Ja'far al-Sidiq (the Authentic), died. He had declared his son, Ismail, his spiritual heir, but was predeceased by him. The Twelvers believe his authority was inherited by a younger son; the Ismailis, that Ismail was the last imam. The Ismailis have influenced African history at several points, most notably in the foundation of the Fatimid empire. A smaller Shi'ite branch, the Zaidis, has ruled Yemen, with short interludes, since 892.

The belief in the Mahdi (the Expected One), who will restore the world to justice, is a core Shi'ite doctrine, but is not restricted to them. In Sunni Islam, it has tended to flourish on the fringes of the Islamic world—and, thus, in Africa.

The Kharijites ("those who secede") were puritans who believed that the head of the Islamic community should be determined by popular choice, and that Muslim sinners, including rulers, should be treated as unbelievers. Ali was killed by a Kharijite—the faction had originally supported him, but deserted him when he agreed to submit to arbitration. Not surprisingly, the Kharijites were divided into sects and, also not surprisingly, it was the most moderate of these, the Ibadites, that lasted longest. Oman, a state on the Persian Gulf, is officially Ibadite.

Kharijite teachings took root among some of the Berbers of the Maghrib, and provided the ideology for several extensive but unsuccessful revolts. There was a major rising, led by a water carrier, in 740–743. Two centuries later, another great insurrection was led by Abu Yazid (the man with a donkey). The victorious Fatimids inflicted gruesome punishments on him.

A number of small Kharijite states, such as Tahert, were founded in the Maghrib and later were defeated by the Fatimids. There is still a small Ibadite

Berber enclave at Mzab, in the Algerian desert, which traces its history to Tahert.

Kharijism and African history interacted in another very distant and different context. Large numbers of black slaves toiled in the swamps of southern Iraq. They revolted on several occasions, most notably in the great rising of the Zanj in 869. Their leader was a Kharijite.

THE ABBASIDS

In 750, the Umayyads were overthrown by the Abbasids, whose name reflects the fact that they claimed descent from Abbas, Muhammad's uncle. The first great age of expansion had ended, and the Islamic world extended from Lisbon to Samarkand. The Abbasids built the palace-city of Baghdad, near the former capital of Persia. The caliph Harun al-Rashid (d. 809), best known in the West through *A Thousand and One Nights*, was an Abbasid. The Abbasids' effective power lasted only until 945, when Baghdad fell to a dynasty from the Caspian Sea, though puppet Abassid caliphs survived much longer.

In the Medina period and under the Umayyads, the entire Islamic world formed a single caliphate. Under the Abbasids, the unity of the Islamic world was permanently lost—we have noted the Umayyad state in Córdoba. Independent dynasts founded separate states in Ifriqiya and Egypt. After an unsuccessful revolt in 786, a descendant of the Prophet named Idris fled Arabia and founded a small state at Fez, in northern Morocco. Fez was to have a long history as a capital and seat of learning, and claims to sharifian descent, usually through Idris, have remained of great importance in Morocco. (A sharif is one who claims descent from the Prophet through his daughter Fatima.)

"Caliph," as we have seen, means "deputy" (of the Prophet), and the name denotes a divinely sanctioned role. "Sultan" means "man of power," and refers to the realities of political authority.

THE TRADITIONS AND THE LAW

It was not only the Shi'ites who felt disillusioned with the later caliphs, or with the wars between rival claimants that took place from time to time. In the eighth and ninth centuries, certain devout scholars sought to establish a guide to right action by collecting hadith, traditions of the Prophet's life and teachings. The customs enshrined in the hadith are known as the *sunna* (hence Sunni Islam). Their work led to the formation of four Sunni law schools, each dominant in a different geographic area. The differences between them are minor.

Perhaps the greatest architect of Islamic law was al-Shafi'i, who was born in Syria but taught in Egypt, where he died in 820 and is still revered as a saint. The school that bears his name flourished in Arabia and was taken to East Africa. The Malikite school, founded by al-Shafi'i's teacher, Malik ibn Anas, (d. 795), a scholar of Medina, prevails in the Maghrib and was taken from there to West Africa. A third school was founded by Abu Hanifa (d. 767) in Iraq and was adopted by the Ottoman Turks, and therefore in those parts of North Africa that came under Ottoman rule. A fourth bears the name of Ibn Hanbal (d. 855), but was formalized as a school much later, when it was adopted by the Wahhabi of Arabia in the early nineteenth century.

Islamic law is based, in descending order of importance, on the Quran, the hadith, community consensus, and analogy. When coffee first made its appearance in the thirteenth century, it was consensus which decided that its consumption was lawful. (Some regarded it as a prohibited stimulant, like alcohol.)

In the ninth century, there was a major dispute as to whether the Quran was created or uncreated. The latter viewpoint became Sunni orthodoxy; the advocates of the former, the Mu'tazili, had a considerable impact on nineteenth- and twentieth-century modernists. They said that to claim the Quran existed from all eternity, like God, was blasphemous, and that parts of it, such as anthropomorphic references to God, must be understood allegorically.

ARABIC

Under the later Umayyads and the Abbasids, whole populations turned to Islam—it was no longer necessary to become an Arab client. The frontiers of Islam and the Arabic language are not the same. Ultimately, while Arabic remained the sacred language of Islam, and a lingua franca over vast areas, Arab Muslims came to be outnumbered by Persians, Turks, and others. Coptic Christians have long spoken Arabic, and many Muslims in Algeria, Morocco, and the Sahara still speak Berber, the original language of the area, which is related to Ancient Egyptian. ("Berber" was a name imposed by [Roman] outsiders and adopted by the Arabs, as Barbar; it has been replaced in recent years by Imazighen for the people and Tamazight for the language.)

Arabic gradually became the first language of vast areas, as a result both of successive waves of Arab immigration and of the adoption of Arabic by Berber communities, a change often accompanied by the adoption of Arab genealogies. Arabic continues to advance, despite a current Berber cultural revival. Today, Berber languages are spoken by about 1 percent of the people of the Maghrib, mainly in Kabylia and the high mountains of Morocco, significantly fewer than at the beginning of the twentieth century. In the vast but thinly populated Sahara, the language of the Tuareg also belongs to the Berber family.

THREE EMPIRES

Between the tenth and the thirteenth centuries, three successive Islamic empires were founded, each of which included the Maghrib but extended far beyond it. The first relied on Berber supporters; the second and third were ruled by Berbers. They arose beyond the margins of Roman or Arab Africa, either in the high mountains or among the camel nomads of the western Sahara. Each had a distinctive ideology— it has been said that they began as sects and ended as empires.[2]

The Fatimids (909–1171)

The Fatimids, whose name reflects their claim to be descended from Muhammad's daughter Fatima, were Ismailis. Islam was often spread by holy men, clerics and sharifs, but only the extreme Shia branches created what one might call an organized missionary movement. The Ismailis operated a secret network of this kind. One of its members, a Syrian named Abu Abd Allah, was spectacularly successful in winning support among the Berbers of the Aures Mountains in western Ifriqiya. He summoned the man who claimed to be the Mahdi, who took the name Ubayd Allah (and later put his benefactor to death). By 909, the Fatimids, with the help of their Berber supporters, had conquered Ifriqiya and had built a new coastal capital, al-Mahdiya. They made war on the small Kharijite polities. The rulers of Andalus, in defense of Sunni orthodoxy, took the title of caliph.

The Fatimids sought to establish not a kingdom in Ifriqiya, but a universal caliphate. In 969, they conquered Egypt, which became the heart of their empire, leaving Berber lieutenants behind them in the Maghrib. In due course, these former followers established an independent dynasty in Ifriqiya. For a time the Fatimids ruled Damascus and were the guardians of Mecca and Medina. They built a new capital, called Cairo ("the victorious"), a reference to the planet Mars; it is the largest city in the Islamic world. They also founded the mosque university of al-Azhar ("the fair," one of Fatima's praise names), which would remain a great center of learning. Gradually, their power declined. Ismaili doctrines were confined to the court, and their subjects remained Sunni Muslims. Shi'ites were disappointed that the Fatimid regime seemed much like any other.

In 1171, Salah al-Din, a Kurdish general in the service of the Turkish ruler of Damascus, reestablished a Sunni government in Egypt, founding a dynasty that lasted for only fifty-seven years after his death, when it was overthrown by its own soldiers, the Mamluks. To the Crusaders, the opponent they knew as Saladin was a byword for chivalry and generosity, though some modern scholars have questioned this idealized portrait.[3]

After Baghdad fell to Mongol forces in 1258, Cairo became the center of the Islamic world. Mystical poetry in Arabic flourished there; the great

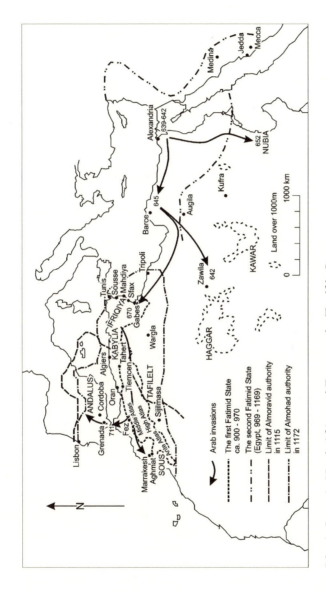

Islamic States in North Africa and Egypt to the Twelfth Century.

poet Ibn al-Farid (d. 1235) was born and died in Cairo. Colleges (*madrasas*) were founded to teach higher levels of Islamic scholarship.

The Fatimids added several further strands to the complexities of Shi'ite sectarianism. To the Druze of Lebanon, the caliph al-Hakim, who died in 1021, is divine. When the caliph al-Mustansir died in 1094, a child, al-Mustuli, was proclaimed his heir. He is the founder of a line of hidden imams. The followers of his adult brother, Nizar, based in Persia and Syria, continued the revolutionary traditions of earlier Ismailis. For a time they were called the Assassins and ruled a state in Syria, but later became a quietist and mystical movement. In the nineteenth century, their imam adopted the title Aga Khan and shifted the center of the movement to India. Ismailis and Twelvers were prominent among the Indian merchants of colonial East Africa.

The Almoravids (1042–1148)

The camel reached the Sahara at the beginning of the Common Era. In the often quoted words of the Quran, it was the ship of the desert. The unifying effect of Islam helped create a vast international network of trade routes, some of which crossed the Sahara. Towns such as Sijilmasa and Awdaghust grew up at their northern and southern termini. The gold of the western Sudan encouraged merchants to make a crossing that was always dangerous and sometimes fatal.

From the early tenth century on, Islam spread first in the Sahara, and then in the western Sudan—a striking contrast with the way in which North African Christianity had had no impact south of the Roman frontier.

The Almoravids were Sanhaja, Berbers of the desert, camel-owning aristocrats who derived a livelihood from Saharan trade. They were called People of the Veil—their men, but not their women, covered their faces, which seemed to Muslims from other cultures to be an inversion of the natural order of things. Their modern descendants are the Tuareg of the central Sahara and the Arabized Moors of Mauritania.

The explosion of the Almoravids from the Sahara is strikingly similar to that of the first generations of Muslims from the deserts of Arabia. There was a clear ecological dimension; they began by conquering the northern and southern termini of the desert trade routes. In the words of one source, "their country suffered a famine so Ibn Yasin ordered the weaker ones to go out to the Sus [in Morocco] . . . they gathered for themselves something of value and returned. Then they found the desert restricting."[4]

The great historian Ibn Khaldun suggested that the Almoravids conquered the kingdom of Ghana, in the western Sudan, though some modern scholars have questioned this. They certainly had large supplies of gold, and they issued fine gold dinars inscribed with a text from the Quran.

The movement began in 1035, when a Sanhaja aristocrat went on pilgrimage and came to realize his people's imperfect understanding of Islam. He looked for a teacher and found one in Ibn Yasin, a fiery ascetic from the Atlas Mountains who was devoted to the Sunni orthodoxy taught in Kairouan. Ibn Yasin is the title of sura 36 of the Quran, so Ibn Yasin was the Son of the Book. However, Ibn Yasin's own understanding of Islam was imperfect—his regime was so harsh that it alienated many. In 1059, he died while making war on the Barghawata. The new leader was another Sanhaja aristocrat, Abu Bakr; After a time he handed over power to his cousin, Yusuf ibn Tashfin, and returned to the desert. Ibn Tashfin went on to conquer Fez and invade Spain. The southern Moroccan city of Marrakech was founded by the Almoravids, ca. 1062.

From the time of Ibn Tashfin, the Almoravids, like the Almohads after them, were deeply involved in a Spanish civil war between Muslims and Christians. The Christian kingdoms of northern Spain, founded in the ninth century, had embarked on the long process they called the Reconquista. In 1085, they took Toledo, which had once been the capital of Spain. The caliphate of Córdoba had disintegrated, and the fragmented states that had succeeded it could not stem the Muslim advance. They became part of the new Almoravid empire.

Ibn Tashfin, who called himself not caliph but Commander of the Faithful, became the leader of a vast but short-lived state with its capital at Marrakech, far outside the boundaries of Roman, Byzantine, or Arab Africa. Sunni orthodoxy became the norm in the western Maghrib. However, the Almoravids were overthrown, soon after the long reign of Ibn Tashfin's son and successor ended, by the Almohads. The great historian Ibn Khaldun was to write of the veiled men of the desert:

> Those of them who founded an empire in Morocco and Spain . . . were consumed by the exercise of authority, swallowed up in vast territories and destroyed by luxury until finally the Almohads annihilated them.[5]

The Almohads (1148–1269)

Almohad is a Spanish form of an Arabic name that means Proclaimers of the Unity of God. All Muslims proclaim the unity of God; the name reflects one aspect of its founder's teachings. The Almohads, like the Almoravids, were Sunni Muslims. Their leaders criticized the legalism of their predecessors, and were influenced by the growth of Sufism. The movement began in 1122, in the High Atlas, not far from Marrakech, with another returning pilgrim, in this case the learned Ibn Tumart, who built up support among his own people, the Masmuda Berbers. He not only preached in Berber but also wrote his books in it (they were later translated into Arabic).

Ibn Tumart's teachings were orthodox, except for the fact that he claimed to be the Mahdi. He died in 1130, and it was his disciple Abd al-Mu'min who founded an empire and claimed the title of caliph (deputy [of Ibn

Tumart]). Far from being a kinsman or clansman, Abd al-Mu'min came from northwestern Algeria. His forces captured Marrakech in 1147, and then invaded Ifriqiya. For the first and last time, North Africa was ruled by a single authority. Abd al-Mu'min's son invaded Muslim Spain. Afterward, the empire had two capitals, Seville and Marrakech. Both were centers of scholarship, but Seville played a special role in the transmission of Arab learning to Europe. The Andalusian philosopher Ibn Rushd, whom the West knew as Averroës, wrote his commentary on Aristotle there. The Almohads, like their predecessors, were committed above all to a jihad against Christian Spain, but paradoxically, Seville was the gateway through which a great deal of Greek and Arabic learning passed to Europe.

The Almohad empire was short-lived; its forces suffered a crushing defeat in 1212, at the battle of Las Navas de Tolosa. By 1276, all Spain was ruled by Christians except for the city-state of Granada, which fell in 1492. The empire collapsed because of its failure in Spain, because of succession disputes, and because of its size. Its distinctive religious teachings—the claim of Ibn Tumart to be the Mahdi—like those of the Fatimids, left no permanent imprint on Maghribi Islam.

The Almohads were succeeded by three smaller states. Portugal and Spain carried the Reconquista to North African soil, beginning with the former's capture of Ceuta in 1415. They conquered a few coastal enclaves, in some but not all of which their control was ephemeral.

The word Almoravid is the Spanish form of *murabitun* (men of the *ribat*, or fortification). There were *ribat*s on the Mediterranean coast and the northern edge of the desert, but *ribat* can also mean a spiritual fortress, and *murabitun* became a general term for Muslim ascetics. In francophone West Africa, the word survives as "marabout," a Sufi or teacher. The city that would become the modern capital of Morocco, Rabat, was founded by the first Almohad caliph, who called it the Ribat of Victory.

The most important long-term consequence of these short-lived empires was that Sunni orthodoxy was firmly established in the Maghrib. In Morocco, a link was forged with Sufism that has lasted ever since.

THE SUFIS

A small but influential minority of Muslims chose—or were chosen by—the mystical way. They are known as Sufis, after the rough wool garment some of them wore, the garment of the poor in the Prophet's day. They emphasized the love of God, a personal relationship with God, and the transitory and illusory nature of this world's satisfactions. Some had a great love for Isa (Jesus). Typically, they practiced asceticism; the early Sufis had a great deal in common with the (Christian) Desert Fathers.

The early history of Sufism is one of inspired charismatic individuals. One of them, Dhul Nun al-Misri (the Egyptian), was a Nubian. When he died, in 860, legend claims that these words appeared on his forehead: "This is the friend of God, he died in love of God, slain by God." A later Egyptian mystic, Ibn al-Farid (1181–1235), is celebrated for his mystical poetry. He was a contemporary of the greatest of all Muslim mystical poets, a Persian named Rumi.

Sometimes the early mystics fell foul of the orthodox; al-Hallaj ("the wool carder") was executed for blasphemy in Baghdad in 922. He would say, "I am the creative Truth," meaning that his own identity was lost in God. There was, for a time, a considerable gulf between the charismatic individualism of the Sufis and the scholars learned in the law. This gulf was bridged by an eleventh-century Persian scholar and teacher, al-Ghazali, who went through a great personal crisis when he came to see that knowledge about religion means little without real experience of the divine. He became a wandering Sufi, and later wrote a book that did much to reconcile the two traditions. The Almoravids burned his writings, but Ibn Tumart, founder of the Almohads, revered them.

Sufism took root in the Maghrib under the Almohads, and both Sufi families and Sufi brotherhoods were to be of great importance there. The *ribat*s were replaced by lodges called *zawiya* (a nook), which were often located near the tomb of a holy man and were run by his descendants. Sustained by alms, the *zawiya* trained disciples, provided hospitality to travelers, and acted as mediators in local disputes.

Distinctive prayers and the founder's *baraka* (blessedness, supernatural power) were passed down from one generation to the next. Each initiate received a *wird* (litany), and Sufis tended to collect as many of them as possible. A saint of Baghdad, Abd al-Qadir al-Jilani, who died in 1166, is remembered as the founder of the oldest Sufi order, the Qadiriyya, which later had a major impact in Africa.

The earliest well-documented Maghribi Sufi was Abu Madyan (1126-1190), a Spaniard who settled in Tlemcen in western Algeria. His disciples included al-Shadhili (ca. 1196–ca. 1256), founder of a very extensive brotherhood that still flourishes today. Houari Boumédienne was the head of state in Algeria from 1965 to 1978; the following year, he was succeeded by Chadli Benjedid. Their names are those of these medieval Sufis.

The Sufi lodges completed the Islamization of North Africa. In the Sahara, whole clans came to identify themselves as clerical, tracing their descent from a Sufi saint (as distinct from military clans of Arab origin).

MIGRATION AND GENDER

It was the informal but long continued immigration of bedouin that slowly led to the Arabization and Islamization of Nubia. Other bedouin settled in the Nile valley, contributing to the Arabization of Egypt. Those who reached the Maghrib, in a long process extending over centuries, were collectively called the Banu Hilal. Migration reshaped the human geography of much of Muslim Africa. When one of the Fez sultans who succeeded the Almohads went in procession, he was escorted by a Berber on the one hand and an Arab on the other.

It is a male-dominated history. Where women enter the story, it is often as the mother or wife of a scholar or saint. A fifteenth-century Moroccan woman was called "the ninth copy of the Quran" in her family, because she knew it so perfectly.

In Africa, as elsewhere, a few exceptional women entered the historical record. One of the most celebrated mystics of the early Islamic period was Rabiah (d. 801), a freedwoman of Basra, in what is now southern Iraq. In Egypt a sultan's widow who died in 1479, at the age of eighty, was remembered for her feisty interventions in affairs of state—a parallel to several equally redoubtable queen mothers in medieval (Christian) Ethiopia.

The early Islamic history of Northern Africa can be understood only in a wider, international context, as is equally true of the early church. Fez was founded by a sharif from Arabia. It is located on a river, one bank of which was called Kairouan and the other, Andalus. The Fatimid empire was founded by Syrians, and the Kharijite imams of Tahert were of Persian descent. The Almoravid and Almohad empires belong as much to Spanish as to North African history.

IBN KHALDUN

The great historian Ibn Khaldun (1332–1406) was born in Tunis, wrote his book in western Algeria in the 1370s, and died in Egypt—a good example of the international character of the world of Islamic learning. His life's work was a world history, first written in 1374–1378 and revised repeatedly until he died. Its book-length introduction, *Al-Muqaddimah*, remains one of a handful of true classics of world historical writing. Ibn Khaldun reflected on the world around him, and especially on successive waves of Arab migration to the Maghrib, which he saw as destructive, a view scholars now question. He compared this with the advance of the Turks and Mongols, horse nomads from the steppes of Central Asia, toward the Caspian Sea and beyond. His basic theory was that a conquering group initially had a strong sense of solidarity. When they became a ruling elite, they were weakened by a comfortable lifestyle and internal conflicts. Inadequately responsive to the needs of the ruled, they were vulnerable to a new group of vigorous invaders.

THE TURKISH DIMENSION

Relations with states ruled by Turks, first the Seljuks and later the Ottomans, form an important theme in the history of Northern Africa. It would, however, be misleading to write of a Turkish phase in its history. The cultural imprint of the Turks was as evanescent as that of the Vandals and, as was true of the Vandals, their language did not take root in Africa. Many who called themselves "Turks" were members of other ethnic groups. For instance, Algiers, though part of the Ottoman empire, was founded by Muslim Greeks from the island of Lesbos.

The Seljuk Turks took their name from an ancestor who was converted to Islam in 956. They invaded Iran, Iraq, and Syria, capturing Baghdad in 1055 and driving a wedge between the Fatimid and Byzantine empires. They conquered eastern Anatolia and called it Rum, after Rome and Byzantium. The Seljuks declined after the end of the eleventh century, and by 1200 they ruled only Rum. However, the danger they posed had induced the Byzantine emperor to appeal to the pope for aid. The result was the First Crusade (1095–1099). Muslims called the Crusaders "Franks," to distinguish them from Greek Orthodox Christians, and the Crusaders in their turn called Muslims "Saracens." The Crusaders were mainly younger sons of the nobility who hoped to acquire lands of their own and win the favor of God in the process. They sacked Jerusalem with frightful bloodshed and founded four military states: the kingdom of Jerusalem, the counties of Edessa and Tripoli, and the principality of Antioch. All proved ephemeral; Saladin reconquered Jerusalem in 1187.

Jerusalem was and is as sacred to Muslims as to Jews and Christians. (The Dome of the Rock was erected there in 691, becoming a model for mosque construction throughout the Islamic world.) In modern times, Muslims have often felt that the rapacity and brutality of the Crusaders foreshadowed later imperial and neocolonial conquests.

The Ottomans also took their name from an ancestor, Uthman, and were at first the princes of a tiny state in Anatolia. They later became the rulers of one of the world's great Islamic empires. They conquered Constantinople (now Istanbul) in 1453. The capture of the Byzantine capital was of immense symbolic significance, and the Ottomans became the acknowledged leaders of the Islamic world. Much of their success was due to their slave soldiers, the janissaries, who formed a disciplined infantry, and to their early adoption of firearms.

Greece and the Balkans, which had always been outside the Islamic world, were also part of the Ottoman empire. The ethnic and religious conflict that ravaged the Balkans in the early 1990s sprang partly from folk memories of events like the death of the Serbian prince Lazar, at Ottoman hands, after the battle of Kosovo Field in 1389.

EGYPT'S MAMLUKS

From 1250 to 1517, Egypt was ruled by Mamluks, an institution peculiar to the Islamic world.[6] Some modern Egyptian women have reclaimed the memory of Shajar al-Durr, a concubine of the last sultan of the preceding dynasty and wife of the first Mamluk ruler, who, in this version at least, "ruled over Egypt and Sham [Damascus] and who victoriously fought against the Crusaders."[7]

The word Mamluk means "owned," and is sometimes translated as "slave soldier." Mamluks were indeed recruited by the enslavement of non-Muslim children, but they were freed at the age of eighteen. They were brought up as Muslims and trained as horse archers, becoming a military elite. Their children, though privileged, could not be Mamluks. In the thirteenth century most of Egypt's Mamluks were Turks. Later, a majority came from the Caucasus, though some were Kurds or Slavs. Egypt's Mamluks were often at war among themselves, but they ruled a powerful state that for a time included Syria and Palestine. They came to power in the context of the Crusades; forces led by Saint Louis, the king of France, were entrenched in the Nile delta and seemed likely to conquer Egypt, but were defeated by the Mamluks in 1249. It was the Mamluks who finally expelled the Crusaders from Palestine, with terrible loss of life, in the capture of Acre in 1291.

The Mongols, like the Turks, were warlike horse nomads who exploded out of the steppes of Central Asia. A king who called himself Genghiz Khan (lord of the world) created an empire that stretched from coastal China to Persia. After his death in 1227, it was divided into smaller states, but the advance continued. The Mongols accompanied their progress with great destruction: although they had become Muslims, they sacked Baghdad in 1258 and Damascus in 1260. The mystic and poet Rumi, founder of the so called whirling dervishes, was a refugee from the Mongols. When they invaded Syria, it was the Mamluks who stemmed their advance in 1260, at the battle of Goliath's Spring.

THE OTTOMAN EMPIRE IN NORTHERN AFRICA

Egypt, which had been ruled by so many different foreigners, became part of the Ottoman empire in 1517. Later in the sixteenth century, three coastal states owing allegiance to Istanbul were founded farther west: the regencies of Algiers (1518); Tripoli, now coastal Libya (1551); and Tunis (1574). The Ottoman link was confined in practice to the sending of tribute and the periodic arrival of officials and troops from Istanbul. Tunisia became an independent kingdom in 1705, and its last bey was deposed in 1957. Tripoli was an independent kingdom from 1711 to 1835, when the Ottomans reasserted control. Algiers was a military oligarchy until 1830, when it became the nucleus of a French conquest state.

By the early sixteenth century, the power and prosperity of Egypt had declined. In 1498, Vasco da Gama reached India, having sailed around the Cape of Good Hope. It was once thought that the development of the sea trade to India impoverished Egypt by undermining its middleman role in the spice trade. More recent studies point to the adverse effects of plague—the Black Death—and to the fact that Ottoman troops used firearms, whereas the Mamluks were horse archers. Despite this, the Mamluk system survived in Ottoman Egypt until the early nineteenth century, when Muhammad Ali massacred their last representatives.

The Ottomans were primarily a land-based power, and their naval activities were confined to the Mediterranean, where they continued to use galleys propelled by captive oarsmen rather than by sail. The regencies were founded by corsairs who attacked foreign shipping under an Ottoman flag, in much the same way that Francis Drake preyed on Spanish galleons. Each regency was a coastal enclave that looked toward the sea and had little impact on inland peoples.

MOROCCO

Morocco was never part of Ottoman Africa. After a period of fragmentation following the fall of the Almohads, Morocco was reunified in the early sixteenth century by a dynasty that, like the Almoravids, came from the south—not, in this case, from the Sahara but from the desert edge. Like the Almoravids, they made Marrakech their capital; they ruled there until 1613. They claimed to be sharifs, and were called the Banu Sa'ad (Sa'adians). Some have thought the name came from their enemies, to imply that they were descended not from the Prophet but from his foster mother, Hamila al-Sadiyya. It may be a corrupted form of a word for Sufi that was chosen by the Sa'adians themselves.

Like the Almoravids, the Sa'adians were committed to jihad against the Christians of Spain and Portugual, who had come to control a chain of settlements on the North African coast. In 1502, Spanish Muslims had been given a stark choice: become Christians or go into exile. Those who chose exile went to the Maghrib, taking with them an enduring bitterness. In 1609, the New Christians were exiled from Spain as well.

In 1578, King Sebastian of Portugal invaded Morocco; he was defeated and killed at the Battle of al-Qasr al-Kabir, sometimes called the Battle of the Three Kings. The sultan died of a heart attack at the moment of victory. His younger brother, Ahmad, who ruled until 1603, took the title al-Mansur (the victorious). In 1591, he sent an expedition across the Sahara that defeated a great Islamic state, Songhai. The soldiers, 4,000 in number, were Spanish and, originally, Christian. For a short time, gold poured into Morocco, but Timbuktu, a major center of the Songhai empire, soon became a small, independent state. No government has ever succeeded in maintaining a regime that stretched both north and south of the Sahara. When al-Mansur died, his sons fought over the throne, and the kingdom fell apart. In 1660, another dynasty of sharifs from the south, the Alawites, established their rule in Morocco. They rule it to this day.

The area actually controlled by the central government covered perhaps a third of the country, the coastal plains. In the High Atlas, many of the functions of government were filled by local holy men, often Sufi sheikhs, This was also true in the rest of the Maghrib away from the coastal towns.

CHRISTIAN–MUSLIM RELATIONS

Muslims and Christians from Africa were involved in many wars of religion. Both the Almoravids and the Almohads were committed to the Spanish civil war between Christians and Muslims. Later, Spaniards and Portuguese carried the Reconquista to the Maghrib. Tripoli became an Ottoman outpost only after it was reconquered from the Knights of Malta. Both Saladin and the Mamluks fought the Crusaders. In the early sixteenth century, the Ethiopian kingdom and the Muslims of the adjacent lowlands were locked in conflict. The Portuguese and the Swahili city-states of the East African coast also were often at war.

But there was also a tradition of mutual tolerance and peaceful coexistence. The Coptic Church survived as a minority faith in Egypt. The Ottoman empire had a policy of toleration toward foreign merchants, which the latter often exploited. The regencies were founded by corsairs, but each had a resident community of Christian traders who had their own churches and clergy.

Of much greater long-term significance than these conflicts was a gradual shift in world resources, to which we return in a later chapter.

Chapter 4

The Growth of Islam in Sub-Saharan Africa

There were *mallam*s and holy men in the country in such numbers that
God alone could count them. But their history is not known because
no one has written books about their country.

—Muhammad Bello (1813)[1]

The edge of the Sahara is known as the Sahel, a word related to Swahili (both
are based on an Arabic word for "shore"). Bilad al-Sudan means "land of
the blacks." The western Sudan and the Swahili coast were on the frontiers
of the Islamic world; the faith had crossed the desert in the first instance,
and the Indian Ocean in the second. Because of the superior efficiency of
water transport, the Swahili coast stayed in relatively close contact with the
Islamic heartland. There was a Muslim presence there much earlier, but it
was between about 1200 and 1500 that Islam was firmly established. In striking contrast with the West African experience, it did not penetrate inland
until the nineteenth century.

THE WESTERN SUDAN

We have noted the spread of Islam in the Sahara, and the way in which
the Almoravids burst out of their desert home. The desert and desert edge
were thinly populated; the savanna was to be the demographic heartland of
West African Islam.

Whereas in the Maghrib the initial spread of Islam was linked with political conquest and state formation, it penetrated the western Sudan through
a long process of osmosis. It was introduced by North African traders and
religious teacher-scholars, roles sometimes, but not always, combined.

By 1500, every known ruler of a state in the western Sudan was a Muslim.
But both then and long afterward, Islam and traditional religion coexisted

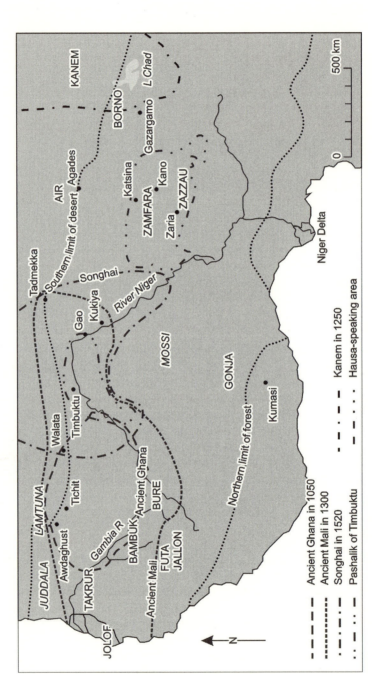

Islamic States of the Western Sudan to ca. 1600.

in intricate permutations. Usually, Islam was first established at court, although then and for some time to come, elements of the traditional religious culture survived. Some scholars spent their lives at court, while others formed rural communities of disciples and from this vantage point criticized the shortcomings of kings. In the jihads of the eighteenth and nineteenth centuries, some of them seized, or attempted to seize, political power. They are sometimes referred to as "clerics," but the word is unsatisfactory because there are, of course, no priests in Islam. The Arabic term is *ulama* (sing., *alim*); the Hausa word, *mallam*, is derived from this.

Al-Bakri was a Córdoba scholar who never visited Africa. He collected information from travelers and from earlier authors, and in 1068 wrote an account that provides a striking picture of the state of Islam in the western Sudan at the time.

Ghana was a state of the Soninke, a northern branch of the great Mande language family, that was famed in the Arab world as a land of gold. "The richest gold mine on earth is that of Ghana. . . . Deserts and fear of the Sudan bar the way to it."[2] The gold came from regions farther south, where it was purchased by Muslim merchants called Dyula. In the words of al-Bakri:

> The city of Ghana consists of two towns situated on a plain. One of these towns, which is inhabited by Muslims, is large and possesses twelve mosques. . . . There are salaried imams and muezzins as well as jurists and scholars.[3]

The king was not a Muslim, but his "interpreters, the official in charge of his treasury and the majority of his ministers are Muslims." There was a mosque near the court for their benefit.

A mid-twelfth-century writer suggested that the process of Islamization was completed when the state was conquered by the Almoravids in 1076:

> They turned Muslim in the days of [the Almoravids] and became good Muslims. . . . They . . . have scholars, lawyers and Koran readers and have become pre-eminent in these fields.[4]

Some modern scholars have questioned whether such a conquest did in fact take place.[5]

In another Soninke state, according to al-Bakri, the people worshiped a sacred snake. The Soninke still have traditions about an ancient state they call Wagadu, where a snake provided gold and rain in return for the annual offering of a young girl. But one year, the girl's lover killed the snake, and the rain and gold departed. The story is a "true fiction," a condensed, symbolic account of the decline of traditional religion (as a result of the coming of Islam) and of the degeneration of the environment. Today the long abandoned capital of ancient Ghana lies on the desert edge. Perhaps rainfall declined over the years, the wells were neglected, and the land was over-grazed—or perhaps the state was weakened by its reliance on gold from outside its boundaries.

In eleventh-century Takrur, generally thought to have been on the lower Senegal, the king was a zealous Muslim. Its people

> were previously, like all the other Sudan, pagans . . . until Warjabi b. Rabis [d. 1040/1041] became their ruler. He embraced Islam, introduced among them Muslim religious law and compelled them to observe it.[6]

In Malal, there was a terrible drought. There was a Muslim at court, and the king agreed to become a Muslim; the rains fell, and "the king ordered the idols to be broken." Thenceforth the royal family was Muslim, while the common people remained traditionalist.[7]

By the middle of the thirteenth century, Ghana had declined. It was a state of the Sahel. Its successor, Mali, was a vast empire in the savanna, its heartland among the Malinke, southern Mande speakers. One tradition suggests that Bilal, the black companion of the Prophet, was the ancestor of the royal line. The oral epic of Sundiata, which bards called griots still sing today, tells of a hero who led his people to independence from a Susu overlord and probably lived in the early thirteenth century. He and his forebears were Muslims, but he is remembered as a magician, his powers derived from traditional religion. Later kings were devout Muslims. Mansa Musa (1312–1337) was an internationally famous pilgrim king who spent so much money in Egypt that the gold dinar was devalued. His image dominates a famous Catalan map drawn in 1375. He returned home with a poet-architect from Andalus, Abu Ishaq al-Sahili, who built a royal palace and the Great Mosque in Timbuktu. Abu Ishaq lies buried there. After Mansa Musa's reign, the empire began to decline, weakened by provincial revolts and the struggles of rival princes. The Mali heartland survived the rise and fall of imperial Songhai, becoming a relatively weak state south of the inland delta of the Niger.

The Songhai empire began as a state on the Niger, with its capital at Gao. Its people were originally fishers and river farers who spoke a language quite unrelated to the Mande speech of ancient Ghana and Mali. By the middle of the eleventh century, the capital consisted of twin towns, one royal and one Muslim. The king was a Muslim, and was given a copy of the Quran on his accession; the people remained traditionalists.[8] For a time, Songhai paid tribute to Mali, until a national hero arose who led his people to independence.

Sonni Ali (1462–1492) was the architect of Songhai's imperial greatness. He conquered the desert trading towns of Walata and Timbuktu; the Songhai link with rivers is reflected in the fact that he attempted to build a canal to Walata. Timbuktu became a de facto capital, though the court stayed at Gao.

Sonni Ali, a Muslim with strong links to traditional religion, persecuted the scholars of Timbuktu.

After his death, which was followed by a period of civil war, a man remembered as Askia Muhammad seized the throne. Only three years later, he went on pilgrimage, and the parallels with Mansa Musa are striking. Like Mansa Musa, Askia Muhammad spent a fortune in gold during the journey. He was deposed by his son, in extreme old age, in 1528, and Songhai subsequently was weakened by the struggles of its princes. In 1591, it was conquered by an army of 4,000 mercenaries from Morocco, a victory of firearms and military training over traditional weapons and levies. For a short time, Morocco acquired vast amounts of gold but was unable to maintain control of its distant dominions. Timbuktu became an independent *pashalik*, ruled by the descendants of the original invaders.

Much of our information about the history of these states comes from Arabic sources written by travelers or by scholars who collected reports from others, though there are also major local histories: the *Tarikh al-Sudan* and the *Tarikh al-Fattash*, both written in the seventeenth century.

Far to the east, another great state grew up in Kanem, northeast of Lake Chad. In the tenth century, it was said, "Their religion is the worship of their kings, for they believe that they bring life and death, sickness and health."[9]

Umme Jilmi, who reigned in the late eleventh century, is remembered as the first Muslim king:

> At night a warrior on a coal-black horse; but when day dawns he is to be seen with his Koran in his hand.[10]

There had been a Muslim presence in Kanem much earlier. According to al-Bakri, a group of Umayyads, fleeing from the Abbasids, had found refuge there.

Umme Jilmi's son and heir drowned in the Red Sea while on his third pilgimage. These pilgrim kings, who risked their lives on the perilous desert crossing and their thrones during their long absences, were men of heroic faith, as were their humbler, and now forgotten, fellow pilgrims from the far-flung edges of the Islamic world.

Abu Ishaq Ibrahim ibn Yaqub al-Kanimi was a distinguished poet from Kanem who lived at the court of Marrakech and died in Spain in 1212. (The trans-Saharan brain drain flowed in two directions.)

In the fourteenth century the ruling dynasty, the Seyfawa, migrated to the south, to Borno. It was a movement from sahel to savanna, and perhaps we need look no further than ecology for an explanation. Ancient Ghana, Mali, and Songhai have long since disappeared, but Borno survived until colonial times and was ruled by the Seyfawa until the early nineteenth century.

West of Borno were the smaller but still considerable states of Hausaland (now in northern Nigeria or just over its borders). Because they were not directly involved in trans-Saharan trade, we lack the Arabic travelers' and geographers' accounts that are such a rich source for other places. The traditional history of one of them, The *Kano Chronicle,* written much later, tells of power struggles between early (pre-Islamic) kings and the custodians of the sacred grove on a local hill. In the mid-fifteenth century, Muslim clerics from Mali, the Wangara, wise men from the west, brought Islam to Kano. Those who rejected the new religion attempted to defile the mosque, and God punished them with blindness.

Muhammad Rumfa, king of Kano from 1463 to 1499, is remembered as a Muslim king. He introduced purdah and the celebration of Id al-Fitr, but he stood between two worlds, and is said to have had a thousand wives.[11] One of his successors gave up the throne to follow the path of religious devotion.

In all these states, there was a tension between Islam and the continuing power of traditional religion that had many facets. Often, the king and his court were Muslim, but traditional belief flourished in the countryside. Even at court there was tension, because traditional religion was one of the monarch's sources of power. A mysterious story tells of a thirteenth-century king of Kanem who opened a sacred object called the *mune,* and of troubles that followed. The object was a heavily wrapped Quran.

The famous traveler Ibn Battuta visited Mali in 1352–1353. Born in Tangier, he was the North African equivalent of Marco Polo. He traveled in Asia and East Africa, and his visit to the western Sudan was his last great journey. He disapproved of some aspects of Mali's court culture, such as the bards, who wore bird masks, but also found much to praise: "One of their good features is their lack of oppression. They are the farthest removed of people from it, and their sultan does not permit anyone to practise it . . . . Another is their assiduity in prayer and their persistence in performing it in congregation."[12] Some parents went so far as to fasten chains on their sons until they learned the Quran.

Al-Maghili was a famous scholar from Tlemcen, in western Algeria, who died in 1504. He visited Gao, Kano, and Katsina, and wrote books to guide their rulers both in their religious duties and in practical affairs of state. The jihadists of the early nineteenth century would overthrow the Hausa kings of their day, accusing them, among other things, of syncretism. They often quoted al-Maghili.

The history of Islam in the western Sudan is also that of its scholars, who are at least as central to it as its kings. In Timbuktu and Jenne, southern termini of Saharan trade, the wealth generated by commerce sustained celebrated communities of the learned. By the mid-sixteenth century, there were 150 Quranic schools in Timbuktu. A scholar from Arabia is said to have recognized the inadequacies of his own knowledge when he arrived there, and to have gone to Fez for further study. When the economy of Timbuktu declined, it proved impossible to sustain so many teachers. Local scholars blamed the Moroccan invasion, but this has been questioned.

When did Sufism reach the western Sudan? Tradition claims that the Qadiriyya was introduced there by al-Maghili. He may well have initiated individuals, but it is thought that the spread of the Qadiriyya dates from the mid-seventeenth century, later than in the Sahara (where it was closely linked with the Kunta).

The Kunta were a merchant family of sheikhs based in the western Sahara, who were famous for their learning and piety: "After acquiring a substantial grounding in the religious and mystical sciences, they would concentrate on accumulating wealth."[13] Some members held the advanced Sufi title of *qutb* (pole), about 1400, one of them began a family tradition of long preaching tours in the desert. In the mid-fifteenth centuy, Sidi Ahmad was called "the Weeper" because of the tears he shed for humanity's sins. Sidi al-Mukhtar (1729–1811), a contemporary of Uthman dan Fodio, was the most famous of the clan, a Sufi saint whose teachings paved the way for the great expansion of the Sufi brotherhoods in the nineteenth century and later.[14] He opposed the jihad of the sword, and said Islam should spread by attraction, especially by drawing new members into the brotherhoods. A later member of the family warned al-Hajj Umar: "Jihad leads to kingship, and kingship to oppression."[15] A Fulfulde proverb makes the same point: "The cleric gives birth to the chief, and the chief to the pagan."[16]

THE DYULA

The Dyula, or Wangara, were Mande-speaking Muslim merchants who obtained the gold exported by ancient Ghana and Mali by trading with non-Muslim peoples to the south. They are apparently mentioned by al-Bakri.[17] The Dyula diaspora continued, and by the early nineteenth century, they were present at the court of the Asantehene in Kumasi, where they ran a secretariat in Arabic. Kong was an independent Dyula city-state. In the nineteenth century, it was sacked by a Dyula empire builder, Samori, who was from a farming background and had begun his career as a soldier of fortune, a reminder that not all Dyula were traders or, indeed, devout Muslims.

Farther west, the Jakhanke operated a similar trading network in the Senegambia. Their lifestyle was similar to that of the Dyula. Both groups revered a great teacher who probably lived in the early sixteenth century, al-Hajj Salim Suwari. He is said to have gone on pilgrimage seven times. He spent his early life at Ja (Diakha) in Massina, near the Niger River bend; later, he settled in Bambuk, on the upper Senegal at Jahaba (Diakhaba, "great Ja," the source of Jakhanke).

Al-Hajj Salim Suwari, like the Kunta, opposed the conversion of unbelievers by force of arms, saying that Muslims should preach to them by their example, and by continued study keep their own religious practice free from error. A recourse to arms was permissible only in self-defense. In the eighteenth and nineteenth centuries, the jihad of the sword would dramatically change the political geography of the western Sudan. It is important to remember that there was also a very different tradition.

MORAL GEOGRAPHIES

The Muslims of the western Sudan had a strong sense of their distance from the Islamic heartland. Muhammad Bello wrote in 1812, "I am living on the fringe of the Sudan—the Sudan where paganism and dark ignorance prevail."[18] Some went on pilgrimage to Mecca, and some Egyptian, Maghribi, and other scholars made the reverse journey. The people of the western Sudan also created symbolic linkages with the Islamic heartland. We have noted the tradition that the royal family of Mali was founded by the prophet's companion, Bilal. The Seyfawa took their name from the tradition that the dynasty was founded by Seyf, a hero from Yemen. A comparable narrative suggests that the founder of the Hausa states was a prince from Baghdad who slew a snake (symbol of traditional religion) in a well and married a local queen. By the nineteenth century, the Fulbe claimed descent from the Arab invader Uqba ibn Nafi. There are many traditions of this kind. We have noted the prevalence of Arab genealogies in the Maghrib, and the same pattern is true of Somalia. In the colonial period, colonial officials tended to regard these myths as real history, a record of creative "white" invaders from the north with whom they unconsciously identified. They are now universally regarded as legends, an attempt to link the Islamic periphery with the Islamic heartland.[19]

We should not, of course, idealize Islam, in Africa or elsewhere. Al-Maghili's memory is tarnished by the role he played in the massacre of the Jews of Tuat. African peoples who chose not to adopt Islam were sometimes marginalized, enslaved, or displaced to adverse environments—and this was later equally true of the southern neighbors of the jihadist states. The words of an eleventh-century geographer bring out something of all this. A (mythical) Egyptian Muslim prince who took an army to West Africa is said to have made war on the Damdam (one of the generic terms Muslim writers used for non-Muslim peoples). Their king "proceeded to fight very bravely, but then al-Rayan defeated him. They retreated into marshes, jungles, caves and rugged mountains, where al-Rayan could not follow them."[20] This is a good example of a "true fiction."

THE SWAHILI COAST

A distinctive Islamic civilization grew up along a vast expanse of the eastern coast of Africa, in a chain of small trading towns stretching from southern Somalia to Mozambique. Linked with each other by water transport, they developed a common culture and sense of identity, and saw the people of the interior, from whom they were separated by natural barriers, as the Other. They have sometimes been interpreted as foreign (Arab) enclaves, but this is misleading.

The Swahili are black Africans whom Arabs called the Zanj, a word preserved in Zanzibar. Swahili belongs to the Bantu language family and is closely linked to the languages spoken by neighboring peoples. It has many Arabic loanwords, but most of these were added in the nineteenth century, and none date from before the seventeenth. The Zanzibar dialect of Swahili is the official language of Kenya and Tanzania, but it is far more widely spoken than this. In the nineteenth century, Swahili spread inland more rapidly than Islam—it is spoken, for instance, in Shaba, in the eastern Republic of Congo.

The Swahili coast was part of a world of international trade long before the Islamic era and long before the proto-Swahili settled there. It is described in a mariner's guide written in Alexandria in 100 C.E. There is a ninth-century account of East Africa written in Chinese, and a painting of a giraffe is part of the corpus of Chinese art. Madagascar was settled by immigrants from Indonesia at the beginning of the Common Era.

It was trade, especially in gold and ivory, that drew foreigners to the East African coast. Ivory found its way to Europe and to India, where it was used for the bangles of Hindu brides. Since the bangles were cremated with their owners, the demand was never ending. The proto-Swahili settled on the coast at various points in time in the second half of the first millennium C.E. They seem to have been drawn, initially, less by foreign trade than by the other resources of the coast, such as fish and turtles.

In 915, the traveler al-Masudi visited East Africa while returning to Oman from China. His account includes the first recorded identifiable Swahili word (*mfalme*, "king"). He said that tyrannical kings were deposed, and spoke warmly of the local religion: "The Zanj have an elegant language and men who preach in it. One of their holy men will often gather a crowd and exhort his hearers to please God in their lives and to be obedient to him."[21] Perhaps contact with Islam was modifying traditional religion, or this may be an example of the tendency for monotheism to become more dominant in a context of cultural encounter. According to al-Masudi, there was a Muslim community on an offshore island called Kanbalu (probably Pemba), where a tenth-century mosque has been excavated.

The Swahili towns were always small; some, such as Kilwa, Shanga, Pemba, and Pate, were located on islands. They developed a rich, distinctive culture in which Islam and literacy in Arabic script (and later in Swahili as well) played an important role. Their rulers issued silver coinage, and the elite built houses of coral blocks and decorated the walls with porcelain from China. They looked toward the Indian Ocean and had closer cultural, religious, and economic links with those who arrived from the sea than with the peoples of the African interior.

The interplay of indigenous and foreign elements is reflected in local traditions of origin. The Swahili, like their neighbors, have a tradition of migration from Shungwaya, in southern Somalia. There are also widespread traditions of state founders or ancestors from the Shiraz, in Persia, though ascertainable cultural contacts seem to have been Arab, not Persian. The first king of Kilwa is said to have been a Shirazi; by the mid-fourteenth century the ruling family were sharifs (which implies, of course, a claim to Arab descent), and there were many sharifs at court. This has been variously interpreted. It is possible that the emphasis on Shirazi descent emphasises a non-Arab ancestry in the Muslim heartland—perhaps in a reaction to elite families that claimed Arab descent.

In 1331, Ibn Battuta visited Mogadishu (now in Somalia) and the Swahili states of Kilwa and Mombasa, all of them by this time fully Islamized. Kilwa had grown rich by exporting the gold of the Zambezi valley: "Kilwa is one of the most beautiful and well-constructed towns in the world. . . . The chief qualities are devotion and piety." The king, who claimed sharifian ancestry, astounded even the much-traveled Ibn Battuta by his piety and generosity.[22]

Vasco da Gama reached the East African coast in 1498. In 1505 the Portuguese sacked Kilwa and Mombasa. By establishing trading posts on the Zambezi, they cut off Kilwa from its hinterland. Soon, European shipping established a rival network of Indian Ocean trade. In 1598, the Portuguese built Fort Jesus at Mombasa. Like the forts built by slave traders on the Gold Coast, or the Crusader castles in Palestine, it fossilizes the militarism and rapacity of the past.

Today, most of the ancient Swahili towns, including Kilwa, are remote and impoverished backwaters. Portugal, however, was a small nation with its resources and people spread too thin over a world empire, and its Indian Ocean administrative center was in Goa. Mombasa, though repeatedly attacked, continued to flourish, and Malindi allied with the foreigners. In 1698, the Portuguese were driven from the coast north of Mozambique by an alliance between the Swahili states and forces from Oman, which had expelled its own foreigners in 1650.

Its written literature was one of the glories of the Swahili coast. The oldest surviving manuscripts date from the eighteenth—or perhaps the seventeenth—century, but the tradition was an older one. Here, as elsewhere in Muslim Africa (including Madagascar), Arabic characters were used to transcribe a local language. Swahili poets included both women and men. The most famous poem is a lament for Pate, written by Sayid Abudallah, who died in 1820:

How many rich men have you seen
Who shone like the sun?

The possessors of the tools of internecine war,
Gold and silver they had stored up.
Their dwellings brightly illuminated
With lamps of crystal shell and copper;
The nights stayed as light as the days,
Beauty and fortune surrounded them . . .
The wall-niches in the houses, inlaid with porcelain bowls
Now little birds nestle in them. . . .[23]

This is a reflection on the brevity of life, the transience of wealth and luxury. Pate flourished in the eighteenth century, and what led to its downfall was not foreign aggression, but civil war.

THE NINETEENTH CENTURY IN EAST AFRICA

From the western Sudan, Muslim merchants carried their wares and their faith far to the south, but in East Africa, it was inland peoples such as the Yao of southern Tanzania who pioneered trade to the coast, where they sold ivory and slaves. The Yao in time adopted Islam, but this happened long after these trade routes were developed.

In the nineteenth century, Islamic influences intensified and expanded. In 1840, the sultan of Oman moved his court to Zanzibar. The Omanis were Ibadites, but made no attempt to spread Kharijite teachings among African Muslims.

Swahili and "Arab" merchants (the latter often Swahili or part Swahili, or long settled on the coast) began to trade in the interior, establishing settlements there. One Zanzibari founded a small state on the western shore of Lake Malawi, where he flew the red flag of Zanzibar and a school taught both Swahili and the Quran.[24] But in general, the religious influence of these merchants did not extend beyond their immediate entourage.

At the court of Buganda, however, a situation of remarkable religious debate developed. The first Muslim traders arrived in the 1840s, in the reign of Suna (d. 1856). Their leader risked his life when he rebuked Suna in the name of Allah the Compassionate. The next king, Mutesa (1856–1884), wore Muslim dress and kept Ramadan, but as Islam spread at court, he began to be apprehensive, fearing the effects of a higher allegiance. In 1875–1876, he put a thousand Muslims to death, ten times as many as the more famous Christian martyrs of 1886. The first Christian missionaries arrived in 1877. In the years that followed, there was a unique ongoing debate among traditionalists, Muslims, Catholics, and Protestants. The establishment of a British colony, after a war of religion, did much to encourage the spread of Western education and Christian missions, but Muslim Ganda, like their Christian counterparts, carried their faith far afield.

SOUTH AFRICA

Islam came to South Africa as the faith of Asian Muslims who were slaves, convict laborers brought to work on the harbor and fortifications of Cape Town, or political exiles. The first cargo of slaves landed in 1658; initially they came from other parts of Africa, but in time an increasing number were brought from Asia, especially the Malay Peninsula and what is now Indonesia. Muslim leaders from the Dutch East India Company's Asian possessions were sometimes exiled to the Cape, just as at a later date many African Muslims would be exiled by colonial powers to a great variety of destinations. Perhaps the best-known Muslim exile in South Africa was Sheikh Yusuf, a pious scholar who had taught at court in Java. He reached the Cape in 1694, age sixty-eight, with an entourage of forty-eight people.

It was not until 1798 that Muslims were allowed to build a mosque. It still stands in Cape Town.

Chapter 5

New States in the Western Sudan: The Nineteenth Century

Thus it is related that at the beginning of every century God sends men a scholar who regenerates their religion for them. There is no doubt that the conduct of this scholar . . . in enjoining what is right and forbidding what is wrong . . . will be in contrast to the conduct of the scholars of his age. . . . He will be an odd man out among them. . . . Then will it be plain and clear that he is one of the reformers . . . because of the saying of the Prophet . . . , "Islam started as an odd man out and thus will it end up, so God bless the odd men out."
—al-Maghili of Tlemcen to Askia Muhammad of Songhai (ca. 1498)[1]

INTRODUCTION

Three themes dominate the history of Islam in nineteenth-century Africa. The first is a movement that began in the late seventeenth century, a quest for political renewal and reform in the western Sudan. A succession of Muslim teachers judged the society in which they lived by the standards of early Islam and the writings of their earlier counterparts, especially the fourteenth-century scholar al-Maghili, and found it wanting. They turned to holy war, jihad, to create new states where the practice of Islam and social justice might flourish. (War and state formation, however, are only one aspect of a history that has many other dimensions.)

The growing power of an industrialized Europe was not unknown to them. A North African visitor to the court at Sokoto in 1827 brought a warning: "By God, . . . they [Europeans] eat the whole country—they are no friends: these are the words of truth."[2] But no one dreamed that less than a century later, the great caliphate of Sokoto would be part of a British colony.

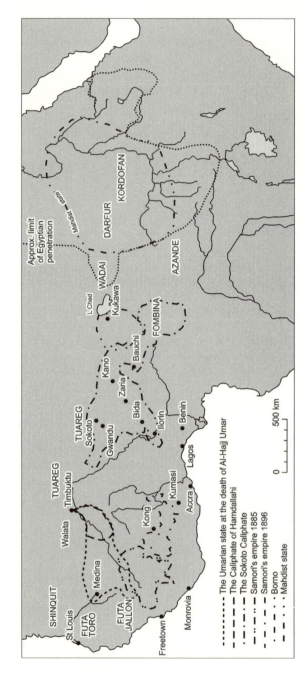

The Western and Central Sudan in the Nineteenth Century.

Between 1673 and 1880, the jihad of the sword led to the creation of a number of new states. Some of them lived on, with attenuated powers, in the new colonial order. A great deal of academic attention was devoted to them in the 1960s and 1970s—not only were they well-documented cases of African state formation, but they reflected, in varying degrees, a desire to realize ideals of social justice. As in resistance studies, there is now a greater awareness of the social costs that jihadist and other wars exacted. These states were sustained, to varying degrees, by raiding and enslavement. There is also now a greater awareness of the existence of a different, peaceful tradition, outlined in the previous chapter.

From the eighteenth century on, Sufi orders became centralized organizations owing allegiance to a head who in turn appointed regional deputies, *khalifa*. Some of the latter would play an important role, first in resisting colonial encroachment and later in collaborating with colonial regimes. The rise of neo-Sufism on the one hand, and of modernist and other critiques of Sufism on the other, is a recurrent motif in the chapters that follow.

The second theme focuses on those who attempted to assimilate what seemed worth borrowing from Europe while remaining true to Islam. Their numbers included both statesmen and theorists who wrote on how best to reconcile an Islamic heritage with modernization and Westernization. It was the states of the Mediterranean littoral, geographically closest to Europe, that experienced these pressures first. One of the most interesting motifs in their nineteenth-century history is found in the way in which, to varying degrees, they embarked on a quest for modernization. Muhammad Ali's attempt to modernize and industrialize Egypt is the classic example. In many respects the problems he and his successors experienced anticipated the experience of postcolonial sub-Saharan Africa. The responses of Muslim intellectuals to these challenges, whether in Egypt, Turkey, or elsewhere, are part of an absorbing international history of ideas. All this forms the theme of the next chapter.

Colonial encroachment led, inevitably, to armed conflict, the third dominant theme. Some wars were fought to prevent the initial imposition of colonialism, and others to overthrow it after it was established. Some of the longest struggles with colonial regimes were waged by Muslims. There is an intrinsic connection between Islam and government that was forged in Islam's earliest history. In Africa and elsewhere, Islam had an indelible historic connection with military conquest and state formation. (In non-Muslim areas, wars of resistance against colonialism often derived both their leadership and their ideology from neotraditional religion.)

In the western Sudan, as in Christian Ethiopia, the pressure of colonial encroachment—and often of hostile neighbors—meant that the acquisition and maintenance of modern firearms became of overwhelming importance, the area par excellence where modernization was sought and achieved.

Muslim leaders such as Abd al-Qadir in western Algeria, al-Hajj Umar or Samori in the western Sudan, the Mahdi in the eastern Sudan, Muhammad Abdallah Hasan in Somalia, and Abdelkrim in Spanish Morocco shaped their political strategies in terms of the imperative of resisting colonialism. The states they founded were distorted and imperiled by this context. We cannot know what shape they might have taken in different circumstances, or how they might have developed later. Each was defeated by colonial forces. By 1914, the political map of Africa had been redrawn—only Ethiopia and Liberia remained independent.

In histories written in the 1960s and 1970s, there was also a tendency to idealize resistance, which seemed to anticipate a later victorious nationalism. It is now recognized that all these wars exacted a great human cost, and that rulers who chose to cooperate with the new overlords won significant benefits for their people. But those who took up arms did achieve a measure of success. Colonial governments were haunted by the fear of risings, especially of a Pan-Islamic rising, and this proved to be a most effective restraint in the exercise of power.

THE JIHADIST STATES IN THE WESTERN SUDAN

It is one of the paradoxes of nineteenth-century Islamic history that some of the most striking manifestations of a reforming impulse were found on the periphery of the Islamic world and were a response to local conditions. Some have contrasted this vitality with "decline" in the Islamic heartland. We should not, however, equate the weakness of political institutions, such as the Ottoman empire, with religious decline.

The most important legacy of the jihadist states was to be not new frontiers, but the growth of Islam in the general population, the spread of Islamic schools and legal structures. Literacy became more widespread, including literacy in local languages written in Arabic script. New cities were founded, but not all of them survived. The Sufi brotherhoods expanded, becoming, in time, a genuinely popular movement.

It is often suggested that in previous centuries, Islam had been the faith of the court and of a minority of merchants and scholars. The evidence is contradictory, and the situation clearly varied over space and time. The Hausa have been Muslim for centuries, but traditional religion was still flourishing in the countryside well into the twentieth century.[3] But it was a critic who wrote of nineteenth-century Borno: "Indeed there are not to be found in those countries ordinary people more scrupulous than they in reciting the Qur'an and reading it and memorising it and writing it out. And the ordinary people did not cease to be thus down to the beginning of this jihad."[4]

THE FULBE DIMENSION

Almost all the jihads in the western Sudan were led by members of a single widely dispersed ethnic group, the Fulbe (called Fula in Sierra Leone, Fulani in Nigeria, and Peul in French). The Fulbe were cattle nomads; their original home was in Senegal, and their language, Fulfulde, is related to languages spoken there, such as Wolof. They moved across the western Sudan in search of fresh pastures, a gradual process that took centuries. Some got as far as Chad, where they met another nomadic people, the Baqqara, who had gradually migrated westward from what is now the Republic of Sudan, through central Africa. In the early nineteenth century, most Fulbe still practiced a pastoral lifestyle and had varying degrees of allegiance to Islam. The strict practice of religion often took second place to the all-important business of caring for the herds. In Fombina (the south land), in northeastern Nigeria, on the eve of the jihad, thirty men fasted for one day each during Ramadan, on behalf of the community.

A few Fulbe became noted scholars and teachers. When they called the faithful to jihad, many of their pastoral kin followed them. In time, the Fulbe came to see themselves as a chosen people, and Fulfulde as a sacred language, second only to Arabic.

THE EARLY JIHADS

The earliest jihad was led not by a Fulbe, but by a scholar from the desert of Shinqit (now Mauritania). Shinqit's highly stratified society had two noble castes that had much in common. Both spoke the Hassaniya dialect of Arabic and were nomadic pastoralists. The warrior caste, the Banu Hassan, looked on themselves as Arab. The scholar caste, *zawiya*, were originally of Sanhaja descent.

Nasir al-Din was a cleric of the *zawiya* who denounced the oppressive rule of Senegal's Wolof kings in words that speak to us still: "The people were not created for the benefit of kings, but rather kings for the benefit of the people." [5] He condemned the export of slaves. His followers, called the Penitents, won several victories, but in 1674 Nasir al-Din was killed in battle. The movement did not survive him, but many of his adherents preserved the tradition of Islamic reform. Their descendants were among the founders of Futa Toro.

Three more relatively small early jihadist states were established later. Bundu, between the headwaters of the Gambia and Senegal Rivers, was founded by Malik Sy (d. 1700). The standard history of this state is called, significantly, *Pragmatism in the Age of Jihad*.[6] Futa Jallon is an upland region in Guinea where a jihad began with a meeting of nine clerics in 1726; the process of state formation took until 1780 to complete. Both Bundu and Futa Jallon were areas of ethnic mixture that were ruled by a new Fulbe elite who prospered through the labor of domestic slaves and the Atlantic slave trade. Here and elsewhere, it was slave labor that made a life of study possible, and Futa Jallon became an important center of Islamic education. Al-Hajj Umar spent some time there before going on pilgrimage.

The jihad in Futa Toro, on the Senegal River, was led by the Torodbe ("seekers"). The Tukulor, the people of Futa Toro, were sedentary Fulbe. The Torodbe were a clerical Tukulor caste. They soon became a propertied elite, though initially the export of at least Muslim slaves was banned. The leader of the jihad, Sulayman Bal, died in battle. Abdul Qadir Kan became the first *almami* (imam) of Futa Toro; he was a devout man who prayed for his own death, afraid that his eminence might endanger his salvation. He died in 1807. The later history of Futa Toro, which was conquered by the French in 1890–1891, was one of political division, but a strong commitment to Islam and to Islamic education remained characteristic. Many of al-Hajj Umar's supporters came from Futa Toro.

These states were small, and in some respects drifted far from their original religious ideals. The jihad that created the Sokoto caliphate however, has been called "the most important event in nineteenth century West Africa."[7] It began in 1804 and had succeeded in the old Hausa kingdoms by 1810, though the caliphate continued to expand, through the foundation of new emirates on the southern frontier, until the 1850s.

UTHMAN DAN FODIO AND THE SOKOTO CALIPHATE

Uthman dan Fodio (1754–1817) was a Fulbe scholar-saint who led a rural community of disciples in Gobir, the northernmost Hausa kingdom. He lived simply, owning only a single turban and gown, and earned his living by rope making. He longed to go on pilgrimage, but never did so:

Is there a way for me to Tayba [Medina] swiftly
To visit the tomb of the Hashimite, Muhammad?[8]

Uthman was a member of the Qadiriyya, and it was the founder of the order who, in a vision, bade him to take up the Sword of Truth. He is, however, an example of an older pattern of Sufism: the personal devotion of individuals rather than a large, centralized organization. He combined the roles of scholar and Sufi, a common pattern in the western Sudan. He wrote over a hundred works, of varying length, including poetry in Arabic and his mother tongue, Fulfulde, and, on a smaller scale, in Hausa. (Later on, Hausa, written in modified Arabic script, would become the language of popular religious education.) Uthman said, "A man without learning is like a country without inhabitants." He denounced the Hausa kings for syncretism, rapacity, and unjust taxation. His precepts, if followed, would have changed the history of independent Nigeria: "One of the swiftest ways of destroying a kingdom is to give preference to one particular tribe over another."[9] He believed that he was the *mujaddid* (Renewer) of his time.

Uthman advocated the education of women, criticizing teachers who "leave their wives, their daughters, and their captives morally abandoned . . . without teaching them what God prescribes should be taught."[10] Six of his daughters were the authors of religious literature. The best-known of them, Nana Asma'u, wrote religious poetry in Arabic, Fulfulde, and Hausa, like her father, whom she revered. A wife and mother, she built up a network for women's religious education from the seclusion of her home. Her memory lives on in Hausaland, like her father's.[11]

In time, Uthman dan Fodio came into conflict with the sultan of Gobir. His supporters included both devout disciples and pastoral Fulbe; despite some reverses, the victories of the Fulbe archers over the heavily armed cavalry of Gobir seemed a clear indication of God's approval. The Shehu—as Uthman is known in Hausaland—was the spiritual head of the movement, while political and military leadership were shared between his brother, Abdullahi, and his son, Muhammad Bello, both of whom also wrote a great deal of religious literature. In 1812, the new state was divided between them. Muhammad Bello was the first caliph of Sokoto and had a clear primacy.

The caliphate was a group of provinces, or emirates. All but one of the first emirs were Fulbe. Some of the emirates, such as Kano, replaced existing Hausa kingdoms; others, such as Bauchi, were new political entities. Sokoto was a new city, like Hamdullahi. The Shehu chose to live outside Sokoto, a symbol of his rejection of worldly things:

> People came to him from east and west. He disseminated knowledge. He drove away unhappiness. . . . He made men to know things which it is difficult to know.[12]

The jihad did not succeed in Borno, though jihadist states were carved out of its western provinces and al-Kanemi, a scholar not unlike the jihadist leaders, came to power, replacing the thousand-year-old dynasty of the Seyfawa. He engaged in a notable debate with Muhammad Bello, who accused Borno of failures in religious faith and practice. Al-Kanemi replied that no state on earth realized its religious ideals completely: "If praying and the giving of alms, knowledge of God, fasting in Ramadan and the building of mosques is paganism, what is Islam?"[13] To a remarkable extent, this exchange between two rulers on the edge of the Islamic world foreshadows late-twentieth-century debates between Islamists and their Muslim critics.

Despite the religious devotion of the Shehu and many of the emirs, the gap between ideal and reality was, of course, as true of the caliphate as of the kingdoms it overthrew. Even before the fighting was over, Uthman dan Fodio's brother (who was also his biographer) warned the jihadists about the love of power and property. About 1850, a Hausa poet wrote:

Do not despise the people of this world,
People of the bush and of the scattered villages,
Do not practise confiscation as the courtiers do,
Galloping, galloping upon their ponies,
They seize by force from the peasants . . .[14]

On the southern frontiers of the caliphate, there was much enslavement, partly through raids and partly through the exaction of tribute. The emirate of Kontagora was founded about 1857 by one of the Shehu's grandsons, who was known as the Destroyer. Another southern emirate, Nassarawa ("victorious") overthrew the Ebirra kingdom of Panda. Its refugee king told a visitor

> that he would never go to Panda again. . . . He said that if they complied and paid one hundred slaves one year, in the next they would require two hundred, and where were they to get them? and that they detested war, trade being their chief employment.[15]

The British invasion of the caliphate began in 1897. Partly because of poor communications and the great distances involved, its component emirates did not provide a united resistance. The emirs had a choice between resistance, the migration sanctioned by the example of the Prophet, and accommodation to the invader. The choices they made were shaped in large part by religion. The emir of Kano wrote, "I have found no more useful plan for all Moslems than . . . that we leave this country all of us."[16]

The last independent caliph, who had just ascended the throne, embarked on *hijra*, followed by people from all walks of life. The British pursued him, rejecting his request to become a solitary pilgrim, and he died in battle. Some of his followers continued on to the eastern Sudan, where their descendants still live. His vizier sought the advice of theologians, who told him that it was permissible to make peace with unbelievers. When he was sure that the British would permit the free practice of Islam, the vizier returned to Sokoto.[17]

HAMDULLAHI

The caliphate of Hamdullahi (the name means "Praise God") was founded in 1818, in Massina, on the bend of the Niger River, by a Fulbe cattle herder named Ahmadu (d. 1845).[18] He lacked the learning of the other jihadist leaders, and this and his economic restrictions (he prohibited trade in tobacco) earned him the hostility of the scholars and merchants of Timbuktu. He initially obtained a flag, the symbol of legitimation from Sokoto, but later abandoned this link and declared himself caliph (not the first caliph of Hamdullahi but the twelfth caliph of Songhai, dated from the pilgrimage of Askia Muhammad). Much smaller than the Sokoto caliphate, Hamdullahi was perhaps the most purely theocratic of all the jihadist polities. Ahmadu is said to have invited a hundred scholars to write an essay on Islamic government; the authors of the forty most acceptable ones were given seats on his council. The state he founded was conquered in the reign of his grandson and namesake, not by a colonial invader but by the forces of another jihadist leader, al-Hajj Umar. The city of Hamdullahi did not survive.

AL-HAJJ UMAR

Al-Hajj Umar Taal (ca. 1794–1864) came to found an empire as the consequence of a vision of the Prophet in 1852, when he was fifty-eight. (Uthman dan Fodio also embarked on jihad after a vision; perhaps they felt able to take such a momentous step only after a specific divine command.) Originally a Tukulor from Futa Toro, al-Hajj Umar spent much of his adult life as a pilgrim and was the only jihadist leader from the western Sudan to visit Mecca. Before leaving home, he joined the Tijaniyya, a Sufi brotherhood or *tariqa* (pl., *turuq*) recently founded by Ahmed al-Tijani (d. 1815). Al-Tijani was a Sufi from the desert of southwestern Algeria who came to settle in Morocco. He made exalted claims for the new movement and for himself. He stated that he was the Seal (the last) of the Sufi sheikhs. His followers were forbidden to join other brotherhoods (it was quite common for the devout to join several).

Al-Hajj Umar spent some years at Mecca and Medina and became the head of the Tijaniyya for the western Sudan. His return journey took nine years, six of them spent at the Sokoto court. He also visited Hamdullahi; no other leader had such an extensive firsthand knowledge of the other jihadist states. On his return, al-Hajj Umar founded a community of scholars, not in his native Futa Toro but in Dinguiray. For some years he concentrated on teaching and writing before turning to the jihad of the sword in 1853. His defense of Tijaniyya teachings, *The Spears of the Party of the Merciful against the Throats of the Party of the Damned*, despite its ferocious title, is considered authoritative, and has been called one of the most widely read books ever written by a West African scholar.[19]

In the last twelve years of his life, al-Hajj Umar created an empire, mobilizing supporters through the Tijaniyya. Other jihadist leaders sought to replace an imperfect local Muslim government with one closer to the ideals of Islam, but al-Hajj Umar had a wider aim: to conquer pagan states and extend Islamic frontiers. In particular, he sought to overthrow the Bamana (Bambara) kingdoms of Kaarta and Segu. Both had a substantial Muslim minority and a strong symbolic identification with traditional religion.

His initial victories in the small kingdom where Dinguiray was located attracted many supporters. They were equipped with firearms that al-Hajj Umar had acquired through trade with Europeans on the coast. Kaarta fell in 1856. His advance led to conflict with the French, who were moving inland from their coastal enclaves in Senegal. Al-Hajj Umar was the first jihadist leader to make opposition to European encroachment part of his mission. In 1857, his forces besieged the French fort of Medina (the name is deeply paradoxical). It was under the command of an officer of mixed European and African descent who erected a banner that read "Long live Jesus, Long live the [French] Emperor."

Al-Hajj Umar then moved to the east, away from the French, and challenged Segu. These wars had an ethnic as well as a religious dimension: Tukulor against Bamana. He conquered Hamdullahi because its ruler supported Segu. He was well aware of the tragic irony of this conflict between two jihadist states, and felt it necessary to write a defense of his actions. He captured Segu in 1861, but the Fulbe of Massina revolted, and he died a fugitive. He is remembered in Senegal as a patriot who fought the French; what is remembered in Mali is the bloodshed caused by his wars.

Al-Hajj Umar's reliance on the Tijaniyya reflected the fact that he was surrounded by jihadist states: Futa Toro, Futa Jallon, and Hamdallahi. It was difficult to accuse them of syncretism and unbelief, as Uthman dan Fodio had done farther east. His role in the Tijaniyya gave him a new and independent source of spiritual authority.

After his death, al-Hajj Umar's sons and nephew fought over his inheritance, and there were many local revolts. His short-lived empire was divided into smaller states that fell to the French between 1890 and 1893. In 1893, his eldest son, Ahmadu, migrated eastward, choosing the path of *hijra*. He died on the journey to Sokoto. Another son became an ally of France.

Because of its multiethnic character and an extensive use of firearms, what is often called the Segu Tukulor empire was once regarded as a prototype of the modern nation. It is now seen as a state sustained by war and the capture of slaves. In 1890, the ruler of a town near Segu complained, "We [have nothing] but weariness and poverty . . . we have nothing in our hands but hunger."[20]

SAMORI TOURÉ

The Dyula, as we have seen, were Muslim merchants with a strong commitment to peace. But, as the career of Samori Touré illustrates, human realities are far more complex than even the best-informed generalizations. Samori, a Dyula from a nominally Muslim background, was born in about 1830 in what is now the Republic of Guinea. He became a soldier of fortune and created first a small state and then, by 1881, an empire with its capital at Bissandugu.

Samori became a devout Muslim and learned to read in middle life; he fostered education and renounced the traditional title, *fama*, for the Islamic one, *almami*. He said that it was his aim to create a world in which a woman could travel safely to Freetown (Sierra Leone) on her own. In 1886, he attempted to make Islam compulsory for his subjects. This led to a widepread revolt in 1888, and he was forced to abandon this policy. In other circumstances, he would be remembered as one of the western Sudan's great state founders, similar to Sundiata. But beginning in 1882, he came into conflict with the expanding forces of European imperialism. He attempted to deal with the French threat by diplomacy, signing a treaty in 1886. But the French began to foment rebellion within his borders and gave arms to his enemies. In 1891–1892, they launched an invasion, capturing the capital. Samori followed a scorched-earth policy, and the French were forced to withdraw. It was, however, a Pyrrhic victory.

Samori then decided to relocate his entire empire hundreds of miles to the east, again destroying villages and foodstuffs as the French advanced. His forces went as far as northern Ghana. The advance of both British and French forces from the south meant that there was nowhere left to go. He was captured by the French in 1898, his forces decimated by hunger, and died in exile two years later. His empire did not survive him. He was not a jihadist, but he founded a vast, if short-lived, Islamic state.

Like al-Hajj Umar, Samori has sometimes been seen as a prototype of modern nationalism and modernization; for example, his elite troops were armed with modern repeating rifles. In 1887, a French visitor to Bissandugu emphasized his love of Islam, his support of education, and his construction of mosques. But in his latter years, the survival of the state he had founded became an end in itself. Much of his state revenue came from the capture of slaves, and his scorched-earth policies caused untold suffering. Though he was a Dyula, al-Hajj Umar destroyed the prosperous Dyula city of Kong because its people did not support him. Fifty-odd years after his death, his namesake, Sekou Touré, the first leader of independent Guinea, was asked, as he drummed up political support, "You will not sell us into slavery?"

CONCLUSION

The jihads created new states, some of which did not survive. Others, such as the Sokoto caliphate and its component emirates, lasted into the colonial period and beyond, though their role was transformed by these changes. Islam became more widely and deeply rooted. Although the practice was not new, this process was reflected in the way many West African towns were named after the holy places of the Islamic heartland, such as Medina, a sacralization of local landscapes. Pilgrimages to the tombs of West African saints, such as Uthman dan Fodio, increased. The practice of keeping women veiled and in seclusion expanded. Like the studies of the learned and school attendance, it was facilitated by an extensive use of slave labor.

More children came to attend Quranic schools. A mid-nineteenth-century visitor described "about fifty little boys repeating with energy and enthusiasm the verses of the Koran which their master had written for them on their little wooden tablets."[21]

Much religious literature was produced, either in Arabic or in local languages using Arabic script. The Quran itself was not translated, because it was believed to be divinely revealed and therefore untranslatable. Elementary education consisted of memorizing it, or parts of it, but it was not necessarily understood. Even the Shehu's brother wrote of himself as "humble, speaking Arabic incorrectly, non-Arab in tribe."

In very many ways, Islam was profoundly indigenized in sub-Saharan Africa. But the Gambian scholar Lamin Sanneh has argued that the insistence on Arabic weakened local understanding and true acculturation. He quotes the nineteenth-century Liberian Edward Blyden, who called the Quran

a poetical composition . . . its ideas and the language in which they are conveyed cannot well be separated. . . . The . . . Mandingoes, Foulahs [Fulbe] etc. speak in their "own tongues wherein they were born" but read the Koran in Arabic.[22]

Chapter 6

Northern Africa in the Nineteenth Century

The West surely seeks to humiliate us, to occupy our lands and begin destroying Islam by annulling its laws and abolishing its traditions.
—Hasan al-Banna (1906–1949)[1]

Most of the jihads in the western Sudan were fought against Muslims whose religion was thought to be adulterated by indigenous religious practices. In the eastern Sudan, the Mahdi urged his fellow Sudanese to fight against Egyptian (Turkish) rule because these (Muslim) overlords were "enemies of the faith and infidels."[2] But the dominant challenge to northern Africa's Muslims came from Europe, both in the form of colonial encroachment and in its closely associated technological supremacy.

By 1800, a great change had taken place in the economic and military resources of the Islamic world vis-à-vis the West. The maritime revolution of the late fifteenth and sixteenth centuries had had enormous economic and political consequences. European nations would come to dominate a web of international trade, including the slave trade. Although the precise linkages are disputed, the mercantile revolution paved the way for the Industrial Revolution. There was a close link between industrial capitalism, with its need for markets and raw materials, and imperialism. The armaments revolution of the nineteenth century, which did so much to facilitate colonial invasions, was a by-product of industrialization. It relied both on vast amounts of high-quality steel and on a number of technological innovations. Even before the establishment of colonial jurisdictions, the economic and political power of Europe shaped the history of northern Africa in many ways, reducing its rulers' choices and their real autonomy.

In the tenth century, Muslims had led the world in various branches of scientific knowledge, such as mathematics, astronomy, and medicine. By the nineteenth century, the Western world had a commanding advantage in science and technology, built in part on knowledge originally obtained from Muslims.

In 1700, the world's largest Islamic states were the Ottoman and Moghul empires. In 1529, the former had laid siege to Vienna. This was to be the high point of the Ottoman empire; by the nineteenth century, it was called the Sick Man of Europe. From the eighteenth century on, British forces gradually conquered the Moghul empire in India, a process completed when the last caliph was deposed after the unsuccessful Indian Mutiny of 1857. In 1876, a Christian woman, Queen Victoria, became empress of India; as a missionary pointed out, she had more Muslim subjects than the Ottoman sultan had had. An old aphorism, which was originally a comment on the transitory nature of this world's pleasures, acquired a new meaning: "This world is the prison of the believers and the paradise of the unbelievers."[3] Nevertheless, throughout the nineteenth century and beyond it, many Muslims, especially those living in remote areas such as the High Atlas, still led lives virtually untouched by the Western world.

Napoleon invaded Egypt in 1798. He saw it as a strategic stepping-stone to British India. Algiers sent forces to assist Napoleon in his conquest—a reminder that colonialism existed only because of its local supporters and allies, and that there were many determinants of policy other than religion. Though France ruled Egypt for only three years, the episode was of great symbolic significance. The French conquest of Algiers in 1830 would lead to the creation of the vast colony of Algeria, which in 1962 regained its independence after a protracted armed conflict. Tunisia was a French protectorate from 1881 until 1956. The Ottomans regained control of Tripoli, the nucleus of the future nation of Libya, in 1835. It was ruled by Italy from 1911 on, and regained its independence in 1951. The conquest of Morocco began in 1907 and was complete by 1912; it was unequally divided between France and Spain, the latter acquiring an enclave in the north and an expanse of desert in the south. Morocco returned to independence in 1956. Egypt became a "veiled protectorate" in 1882 and regained a limited autonomy in 1922.

Islamic responses to colonial encroachment could take the form of armed resistance or withdrawal (*hijra*) or various attempts to reconcile an Islamic inheritance with European-style modernity. Not all reformists were responding to Western challenges. The learned sultan of Morocco, Muhammad ibn Abdullah (r. 1757–1790), personally collated different versions of the hadith, in an attempt to ascertain and apply the most authentic form of Islamic teaching. His son, Mawlay Sulayman (r. 1792–1822), was a critic of popular Sufism, though he welcomed al-Tijani, whom he saw as a reformer. Twentieth-century Moroccan reformers looked to these sultans as precursors.

The creation of colonies in which Muslims were ruled by Europeans who were Christians, or had no religion at all, created a religious as well as a political crisis. Egypt and the Maghrib (excluding Morocco) had been largely ruled by foreigners for centuries, but never by non-Muslims. Al-Nasiri, a Moroccan historian who died in 1897, lamented:

> Know too that during these years the power of these Europeans has advanced to a shocking degree and has manifested itself in an unparalleled manner. The progress and improvement in their condition have accelerated at an ever growing pace. . . . Indeed, we are on the brink of a time of corruption.[4]

The editor of an Egyptian magazine was asked what the various countries grouped as "the Orient" had in common. After a period of reflection, he decided, "There is one thing that unites us all in the Orient: our past greatness and our present backwardness."[5] Because of Islam's historical links with state formation and conquest, it was easy to believe that its political decline was due to religious failure.

Christian missionary activity had almost no long-term impact in Muslim Africa, but was a direct affront to Muslim sensibilities. Colonial conquest often went hand-in-hand with racist stereotypes; one is fossilized in the word "wog" ("wily Oriental gentleman"), which was first recorded in Egypt. A British official in India said that "a single shelf of European books [is] worth the whole literature of India and Arabia."[6]

Some intellectuals were enthusiastic in their admiration of all things Western. Al-Tahtawi (d. 1873), one of Muhammad Ali's translators, wrote a book on Paris and a poem in honor of the steamship.[7] In India, Sayyid Ahmad Khan (d. 1898), founder of Aligarh College, was a great admirer of British accomplishments.

Many North African Muslims, however, believed that Western education and technology and their Islamic inheritance were inherently incompatible. When Moroccans were sent for military training in Europe, it was said, "They want to learn how to fight to protect the faith, but they lose the faith in the process of learning how."[8] There were parallel debates in the Ottoman empire after Greece's successful war of independence. As in the western Sudan, some chose the path of *hijra*. In 1911, 800 Muslims left western Algeria for Syria in order to avoid living under colonial rule. A more common form of withdrawal was to avoid contact with modernity, living in self-chosen seclusion or rejecting its products (the path chosen by some Sufi sheikhs). In 1930, a poet in northern Nigeria warned his hearers against all foreign imports, including flashlights, suits with buttons, and the English language:

> Towels and washing-blue, and powder, whoever uses them,
> Certainly on the Last Day the Fire is his dwelling.[9]

SUFISM AND ITS CRITICS

The Wahhabi movement, launched in Arabia in the mid-eighteenth century, stressed the need to return to Islam in its original form. After initial successes, the first Wahhabi state was overthrown in the early nineteenth century by Muhammad Ali's forces, fighting on behalf of the Ottomans. The dynasty that rules Saudi Arabia today was founded by a later Wahhabi imam. The Wahhabi are best seen as one manifestation of a much wider quest for renewal and reform, rather than as its inspiration.

Sufism was central to Islamic identity in Egypt and the Maghrib, but many, including the Wahhabi, were critical of it, partly because the *turuq* (sing., *tariqa;* way) did not exist in the first Islamic centuries. They condemned the cult of Sufi saints, pilgrimages to their tombs, and so on.

Many Muslims deplored some of Sufism's popular manifestations. An Egyptian decree of 1881, which never went into effect, banned practices that included "the use of swords, needles and other instruments for self-mortification, the eating of live coals, serpents and glass."[10]

The rejection of Sufism led to a reaction, a Sufi revival, which in turn led to the creation of new *turuq,* such as the Tijaniyya, and the revival of old ones, such as the Qadiriyya. *Tariqa* is conventionally translated as "Sufi brotherhood," but women joined the Tijaniyya and Rahmaniyya, and sometimes headed the latter's lodges.[11] These new *turuq* were actually or potentially mass movements, a development facilitated by their traditions of unquestioning obedience and devotion to one's sheikh. They were frequently critical of the older orders.

Often, support for an anticolonial struggle was mobilized by old or new brotherhoods; the Qadiriyya in western Algeria, the Sanusiyya in Libya, and the Salihiyya in Somalia are examples. However, one of North Africa's most significant sheikhs, the Moroccan Ahmad ibn Idris (1750–1838), had no involvement in war or politics and never founded a brotherhood, preferring to remain in the Shadhiliyya. His disciples included men who would have a huge impact on the history of their times, including the founder of the Sanusiyya and Muhammad Abdallah Hasan, who led a major resistance movement among the Somali. Another disciple, Muhammad Uthman al-Mirghani, founded the Khatmiyya in the Sudan, so named because, like al-Tijani, he claimed to be the Seal (*Khatim*), that is, the last of the founders of Sufi orders.

Ibn Idris left Morocco for Arabia in 1798 and never returned. He urged Muslims to turn directly to the life and teachings of the Prophet for inspiration and guidance, thus bypassing the huge body of complicated scholarly teachings and commentaries that had grown up in the intervening period. At the heart of neo-Sufism is an intense mystical devotion to the Prophet: al-Tijani's litany was taught to him directly by Muhammad, in a vision. From within the Sufi tradition, Ibn Idris advocated a reformist Islam not unlike

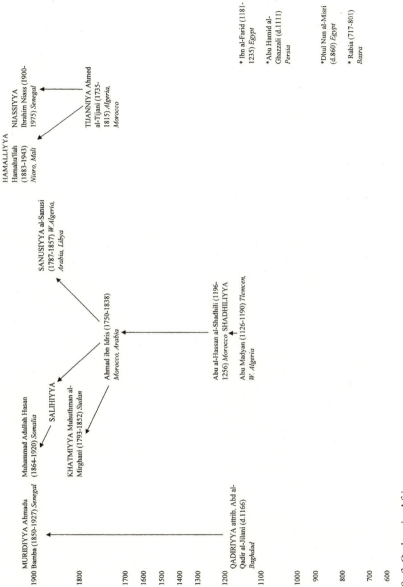

Sufi Orders in Africa.

that of the Wahhabi or the modernists. Critics saw in neo-Sufism, and especially in the Tijaniiyya, a tendency to exalt the Prophet to a point where he took on some of the attributes that belong only to God.

THE SUFI ORDERS AND COLONIAL RULE

Abd al-Qadir (1807–1883), a sheikh of the Qadiriyya, succeeded, for a time, in establishing what was virtually an independent theocratic state in western Algeria. It was ultimately conquered by French forces. Abd al-Qadir surrendered in 1847 and spent the rest of his life in exile. Later Algerians called his wars "jihads" and hailed him as a national hero, a precursor of the war of independence.

There was only one year between 1830 and 1871 when there was no rising against the French in Algeria. They found the financial and human cost so great that a total withdrawal was sometimes contemplated. The last great revolt broke out in 1871, in Kabylia in eastern Algeria. It was led by a traditional Berber leader and by a sheikh of a recently founded *tariqa*. The reprisals, in fines and land alienation, were such that they have been said to constitute the second conquest of Algeria. There would be no more large-scale risings until the bloody war of independence that began in 1954.

As we have seen, a common religion did not necessarily lead to concerted action, though this is what colonizers always feared: "Our enemies, aided by the fanatical religious orders, such as the Sanusiya . . . are organizing from Tripolitania to Morocco a vast anti-French conspiracy."[12] This was an illusion, but a salutary one. Rulers who fear revolt tread carefully.

The pattern of interaction between the Sufi orders and the government was an intricate and changing one. Partly because of an earlier clash with the Qadiriyya, the leaders of the Tijaniyya submitted to French authority in Algeria, a striking contrast with the career of al-Hajj Umar. In Morocco, the authority of Sufi sheikhs sometimes seemed to rival the sharifian sanctity of the crown. Abd al-Hafiz, the last sultan of independent Morocco, wrote a book condemning the Tijaniyya. After his abdication, he joined the brotherhood and wrote poetry in honor of the mystical way.

The modern history of Libya is inextricably entwined with that of the Sanusiyya. Sidi Muhammad ibn al-Sanusi (1787–1859) was a sharif who was born in western Algeria and died at a desert oasis on the Libya-Egypt border.[13] He spent less time in North Africa than he did at Mecca, where he studied under Ahmad ibn Idris. Al-Sanusi's enduring impact reflects his charismatic personality and the services rendered by the order he founded, first in Cyrenaica and then in the Sahara. His sons, who led the movement effectively after his death, shifted the order's center deep into the desert. They were moving away from European encroachment, but paradoxically, the trade on which they depended was, in a sense, an extension of Western industrial capitalism. *Turuq* flourished where they met a social need. In this case, the Sanusiyya arbitrated disputes among the warlike men of the desert, and their *zawiya* provided lodgings for travelers.

Al-Sanusi probably had little interest in politics, though he is said to have foretold the Italian invasion of Libya. The Sanusiyya were missionaries, not empire builders or statesmen, but events were to lead them into a military and political role. The Grand Sanusi's grandson, Idris, would become first the head of the Sanusiyya, and then the first and last king of Libya, overthrown by Mu'ammar al-Qaddafi in 1969.

THE MODERNIZING RULER: MUHAMMAD ALI

It was Muhammad Ali (1769–1849) who made the most radical attempt in nineteenth-century Muslim Africa to adopt the knowledge and technology of the West. Nasser was to claim him as a precedent. Like all rulers of Egypt since the pharaohs, he was a foreigner. He reached the country in 1799, as an officer in an Albanian regiment that was part of the Ottoman army. By 1805, he was the Ottoman governor of Egypt, and he confirmed his personal supremacy when he massacred the last Mamluks in 1811. Although Muhammad Ali was a Muslim, his motives were essentially secular. His life's ambition was to make his family the ruling dynasty of a strong and independent Egypt. The scholars had initially supported him, but he confiscated much religious property; they were weakened as a class and, not surprisingly, became hostile to Westernization.

Muhammad Ali was a modernizer but not a democrat, and the establishment of a strong modern army and an efficient civil service were his key priorities. Rather than adding new courses in existing Islamic schools, he created a parallel system of Western schools, whose graduates had far more employment opportunities. Many Egyptians were sent to study in Europe, and there was a great influx of foreign advisers. Muhammad Ali also set up translation bureaus, to make the knowledge of the West more accessible.

Muhammad Ali's grandson, Ismail, who ruled from 1863 until his deposition in 1879, had the same admiration for the Western world and Western education. During his regime, railroads and canals were built, Alexandria's harbor was improved, and the educational system was expanded. He introduced a representative assembly and hoped to become prime minister, less because he was convinced of the merits of democracy than because he wished to win the support of Western governments.

However, Ismail plunged deep into debt, borrowing money on extremely unfavorable terms. Some was spent on development projects, but much was squandered: the extravagant celebrations that marked the opening of the Suez Canal, constructed on terms disastrous from an Egyptian point of view, are an example. Ismail purchased the title of khedive, at great expense, from the

Ottoman sultan. But his indebtedness destroyed his independence and led to his deposition. Soon afterward, Egypt became in fact, though not in name, a British colony.

In the years of optimism that followed the return to independence in most African states, there was a tendency to idealize modernizers such as Muhammad Ali and Ismail. It is now recognized that their innovations exacted a great human cost, increased the gap between rich and poor, and led to the creation of privileged foreign enclaves. Foreign debt eroded the states' independence, a sadly familiar theme in postcolonial Africa.

In 1882, for a moment, Egypt came close to democratic government. Egyptians who studied in Europe, or read the classics of British and French political theory, were naturally drawn to democracy. But as in so many later regime changes in independent Africa, the key role was played by army officers with career grievances (in this case, the exclusion of Egyptians from the higher ranks, which were open only to "Turks"). Their leader was Urabi Pasha. Critical of the waste and mismanagement of the court, he came to voice an early form of national consciousness. In 1882, there were riots in Alexandria, which led to the city's bombardment by British forces. Urabi Pasha went into exile, and a period called "the veiled protectorate" ensued, during which Egyptian ministers were unable to defy the instructions of British officials without losing their posts, and Egyptian revenues paid not only accumulated foreign debt but also the costs of British administration. At the very time when a substantial class of Western-educated Egyptians had developed, Egypt became a virtual colony.

THE MAHDIST STATE IN THE EASTERN SUDAN

Mahdism is central to Shia Islam, but in the Sunni tradition, it has tended to flourish only on the margins of the Islamic world. Muhammad Ahmad was not the only African Muslim to be acclaimed as the Mahdi. Some candidates were obscure, but this claim was made for the founders of both the Fatimid dynasty, in the tenth century, and of the Almohads, in the twelfth.

The origins of the contemporary Republic of Sudan are to be found in the colonizing ambitions of Muhammad Ali. His forces had invaded the Sudan in 1821, in the quest for gold and soldiers. Both hopes were largely disappointed—so many Sudanese died in Egypt that Muhammad Ali turned to the conscription of the Egyptian peasantry. Often, these conscripts died of an incurable disease. It was called homesickness.[14] A conquest state survived in the Sudan, with its capital at the new city of Khartoum. In 1881, a leader arose who challenged the regime locally known as the Turkiyya. His forces reconquered much of the Sudan, and the new state survived until its army was crushed by an invading power in 1898.

Muhammad Ahmad ibn Abdullah, the son of a Dongola boatmaker, was a devout and ascetic Sufi sheikh. He attacked the "Turks," much as Uthman dan Fodio had condemned the Hausa kings, as oppressive rulers who had strayed from the teachings of Islam. His message was welcomed as "Kill the Turks and cease to pay taxes." He believed that he was much more than a reformer or military leader, and claimed to be the Mahdi, the Awaited One, who would restore the world to justice and whose coming would herald the Endtime.

It was thought that the Mahdi would come at the end of an (Islamic) century, and Muhammad Ahmad made his proclamation in 1298 A.H. (Anno Hijra). Initially, following the example of the Prophet, he called his followers to emigration (*hijra*) rather than war, but conflict with the Turkiyya was unavoidable. Armed only with spears and clubs, Muhammad Ahmad's forces won a series of victories over the Egyptian forces, which seemed a clear sign of divine approval and enabled the Mahdi to incorporate the captured firearms and soldiers into his own army.

In 1884, General Charles Gordon was sent to Khartoum to organize the evacuation of government troops. Instead, he embarked on a heroic but ill-conceived defense, dying when the city fell in 1885. His death became part of the mythology of empire. The Mahdi died later in the same year, at the age of forty-four. He had not set out to create a modern nation—he believed his mission was international—and his successor attempted to invade both Ethiopia and Egypt. The Mahdist state, however, had much the same boundaries as the modern Sudan. It included many different ethnic and linguistic groups, and was destined to be fatally polarized in the colonial situation, into north and south.

By the time he died, the Mahdi's state had a well-developed organization, a system of taxation, and its own mint. Disliking Khartoum, the Madhi had lived at the nearby village of Omdurman. He consciously emulated the Prophet and his companions, calling his troops ansar Helpers, the name given to the Medina Muslims who, after the Hijra, welcomed their fellow believers from Mecca. He named his closest associates after the Rightly Guided Caliphs who succeeded Muhammad. One of these associates became caliph (*khalifa*) after his death. His state was called the *umma* (Islamic community).

British forces embarked on the invasion of the Sudan in 1896, building a railway through the Nubian Desert, where the Nile makes a great loop to the southwest, a classic instance of the way in which technological resources aided the subjugation of Africa. At the battle of Omdurman, in 1898, the invading army numbered 25,800 men, only a third of whom were British. Eleven thousand Sudanese were killed in the battle, mowed down by machine guns. There were forty-nine fatalities on the Anglo-Egyptian side. The caliph escaped and continued the struggle, dying in battle the following year.

The Mahdi had said that the day of Sufi orders had ended, but after his death, the Mahdiyya came to resemble a *tariqa*. Many Sudanese, then and later, admired his patriotism and piety but could not accept him as Mahdi.

They remembered him as Renewer and as a patriot, Abu'l Istiqlal (Father of Independence). In the 1950s, as independence neared, Sudanese politics was dominated by two parties: one of Mahdists, led by the Madhi's descendants, and one comprising their long-standing opponents, the Khatmiyya. The Mahdi's great-grandson, Sadiq al-Mahdi, would serve twice as prime minister.

The relative ineffectiveness of Egypt's nationalists contrasted with the success of the Mahdist state. The latter, however, was conquered in 1898, while the nationalist tradition survived.

REFORMIST INTELLECTUALS

In Egypt, as elsewhere, those who became familiar with Western education and technology inevitably absorbed Western political concepts as well. The Indian poet Muhammad Iqbal addressed a poem to England that referred to political freedom:

> It was the scent of the rose that drew the nightingale to the garden:
> Otherwise the nightingale would not even have known that there was a garden.[15]

Jamal al-Din al-Afghani (1838–1897) had a great influence on several men who were to have a major impact on Egyptian nationalism. Despite his name, he was a Persian who had lived in Afghanistan and had first encountered Western ideas in India. He spent some years in Egypt. He was deported in 1879 and finally died in Constantinople, where he was under house arrest because one of his followers had assassinated the shah of Persia.

Al-Afghani exercised a formative influence over the Egyptian Muhammad Abduh (1849–1905), who has been called "modern Africa's most important intellectual."[16] Abduh met al-Afghani at the mosque university of al-Azhar. For a time he, too, was an exile, but he ended his career as minister of education and grand mufti of Egypt.

In his teachings and writings, Abduh insisted that Islam in its early, pure form—the religion of the Quran and the well-attested hadith—was perfectly compatible with science and reason. Sufism was an unnecessary later accretion. Democracy could be understood in terms of the Islamic principle of *shurah* (consultation). He advocated monogamy and condemned archaic punishments, such as amputation. The curriculum of traditional Islamic educational institutions should be broadened to include modern science. He made use of the work of Western critics of Christianity, such as Ernest Renan, to show that this was a superstitious faith, less compatible than Islam with pure reason. This modernist or reformist movement was called the Salafiyya (from *salaf,* ancestor).

In the early 1890s, a Syrian named Rashid Rida (1865–1935) read a periodical published by al-Afghani and Abduh, "and every number was like an electric current striking me."[17] In his turn he published his own journal, *al-Manar* (the lighthouse), which had a huge impact in the Islamic world. In 1899 and 1900, Qasim Amin, another disciple of Abduh's, published two books on the position of women: "Look at the eastern countries; you will find woman enslaved to man and man to the ruler."[18]

Al-Afghani's main emphasis was Pan-Islamic, but Muhammad Abduh was above all an Egyptian nationalist. He had a considerable influence on the future leader of Egypt's Wafd (Delegation) Party, Zaghlul (1857–1927). His works were widely read by the Egyptian and Maghribi politicians of the interwar period, though their interests were predominantly secular. His writings influenced intellectuals and the middle class—he made no attempt to mobilize widespread popular support for his ideas.

In the fourteenth century—a time of great social dislocation—there was a general agreement among scholars that the gates of *itjihad* (independent judgment on religious issues) had been closed, and that in future, one should rely on precedent. The nineteenth-century modernists reopened these gates.

CONCLUSION

The impact of colonialism was enduring—especially, perhaps, in terms of the national boundaries it created and of the distribution of European languages. (Often, in elite Algerian or Tunisian circles, French was preferred to Arabic.) These boundaries sometimes led to future conflicts. But in a sense, what is most striking is colonialism's brevity and fragility. El-Mokri was grand vizier of Morocco in 1912, when it was divided into French and Spanish protectorates. He lived to see its independence, at the age of 105.[19]

Chapter 7

Northern Africa in the Colonial Era

I wanted my people to know that they had a nation, as well as a religion.
—Abdelkrim, in exile[1]

The tradition of armed resistance did not come to an end with the establishment of colonial rule. Two of the best-known anticolonial struggles waged by African Muslims, one in Somalia and one in Spanish Morocco, date from the early twentieth century.

SOMALIA

The last African jihad led by a Sufi sheikh was fought in Somalia, from 1899 to 1920, under the leadership of a scholar who was also a member of the Salihiyya, Muhammad Abdallah Hasan (1864–1920). He is known as the Sayyid, a title that, like sharif, reflects a claim to descent from the Prophet.

Islamic brotherhoods reached Somalia in the late nineteenth century, and then spread rapidly. They included the ancient Qadiriyya, as well as several that had been recently established, such as the Salihiyya, which belonged to the cluster of orders founded by followers of Ibn Idris. Their expansion was part of a general Islamic resurgence in the area, and their leaders represented a new effective authority in a time of crisis.[2]

The Sayyid was distinguished for his learning while still a teenager. He studied in Arabia and joined the Salihiyya in Mecca, returning to Somalia as its *khalifa* (local representative.) The *tariqa* later disowned him. His message was an austere one: he condemned coffee, tobacco, and *qat*, a mild drug popular in the area. In 1899 he moved inland to the desert, and began to attract followers and acquire firearms. He called for a jihad against Ethiopians, Europeans, and those Somali who cooperated with the colonial powers, whom he called unbelievers.

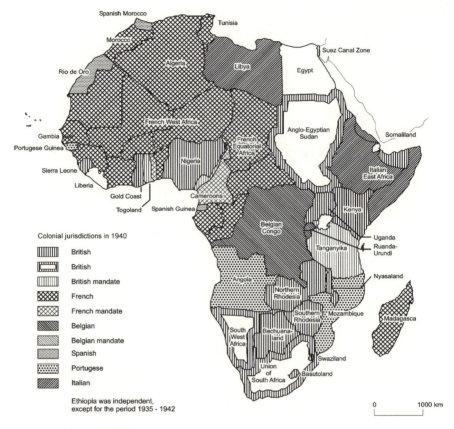

Colonial jurisdictions in 1940

‖‖‖‖	British
⊞	British
‖‖‖	British mandate
⊠	French
⊠	French mandate
⧄	Belgian
▨	Belgian mandate
▦	Spanish
⋰	Portugese
⧄	Italian

Ethiopia was independent,
except for the period 1935 - 1942

0   1000 km

Colonial Africa to 1940.

The Sayyid's first major battle was an attack on an Ethiopian settlement in the Ogaden. Between 1901 and 1905, the British sent annual expeditions against him. Their personnel reflected the resources of an empire. Their failure reflected the difficulty of defeating highly mobile guerrilla forces in desert terrain. The First World War, during which the Sayyid sought an alliance with the Turks and Germans, delayed the inevitable final conflict. In 1920, a British expedition decimated his followers, using aircraft mounted with machine guns. The Sayyid died of illness soon afterward, at the age of fifty-six.

He had hoped to unite all Somalis in a theocratic state that followed the principles of Islam as he interpreted them. Like the Mahdi (in the Sudan), he is remembered as the founder of Somali nationalism. In a nation that reveres the composition of oral poetry, he is acknowledged as the greatest poet. The British called him the Mad Mullah, perhaps confusing poetic expression with insanity. The Sayyid and his followers were sometimes guilty of great cruelty, especially in his last years. One of his associates wrote:

> Again and again the Sayyid made war and people helped him;
> Thousand upon thousand, all with white turbans. . . .
> But what brought his downfall was the day he destroyed the Khayr people.[3]

In the coastal town of Brava, another Somali Sufi lies buried. The long-lived Dada Masiti, who died in 1921, was enslaved as a child of six and taken to Zanzibar. Her family redeemed her ten years later. She became a noted Sufi scholar and poet; her poetry is still recited and her tomb is still honored.[4]

THE REPUBLIC OF THE RIF

A very different rising, under a very different leader, in the 1920s led to the creation of an independent Berber republic in the mountains of the Rif, in Spanish Morocco. It will always be associated with the name of Abdelkrim (Muhammad ibn Abd al-Karim al-Khattabi, 1882–1963), a well-educated man who had worked for the Spanish. Ironically, he had been made a Knight of the Order of Isabella, the Castilian queen who in her will had told her heirs that "they should not cease in the conquest of Africa." He had studied at the great mosque university of Fez; his brother was a Spanish-trained mining engineer.

Abdelkrim was a beneficiary of colonialism who sacrificed his freedom to oppose it. In 1921, he was asked what he was seeking. He replied, "a country with a government and a flag."[5] In 1922, he proclaimed the existence of a new nation, the Republic of the Rif. For a time its forces enjoyed a high level of success, but inevitably the tide turned. In 1926, Abdelkrim's headquarters was captured, and he surrendered to the French; the movement collapsed, and he was exiled to Réunion. In 1947, he escaped, and settled in Cairo. He was invited to come home as a national hero in 1958, but chose to wait until all colonialism in the Maghrib had ended. He died in 1963, as he was about to return.

In the years of its existence, the Rif Republic was the only independent Islamic state in Africa.

ISLAM, NATIONALISM, AND THE NATION-STATE

In one hugely significant respect, the colonial period meant a radical transformation of the interface between Islam and government. The territorial state replaced the Islamic "community" (*umma*) as the unit of political action. There were, of course, alternatives, above all the Pan-Islamism advocated by al-Afghani and others. Late nineteenth-century Ottoman sultans claimed the title of caliph, hoping to spearhead Pan-Islamic aspirations, but a dynasty in decline had little hope of achieving this. The Organization of the Islamic Conference was founded under Saudi leadership in 1969. Modeled on the United Nations, it now has fifty-five member states, whose heads meet periodically to debate matters of mutual concern, but each preserves its own sovereignty.

In the twentieth century, there was a great diversity of theory and practice regarding the relationship between Islam and the state. At one extreme was Turkey, after the First World War. The last sultan was deposed. A former military commander who took the surname Ataturk led Turkey toward a resolute secularity. There was an emphasis on Turkish language and culture, and the Western alphabet and Western dress were adopted. The Pahlavi shahs who ruled Persia from 1925 to 1979 also adopted secular policies. (The name Iran was adopted in 1935.) At the other extreme were the theocracies—Iran under the Ayatollah Khomeini and Afghanistan under the Taliban.

A key issue for nationalists in northern Africa was whether to emphasize Islamic or Arab identity. Educated Egyptians had tended to see themselves as heirs of ancient Egypt rather than as "Arab." But in a country that included a substantial Christian minority, it made sense to emphasize the Arab dimension. Pan-Arabism seemed more attractive than a foreign and imperfectly realized model of national democracy. In 1944, the Arab League was formed, with its headquarters in Cairo. It now has twenty-two members.

Gamal Abdel Nasser was the most influential advocate of Pan-Arab socialism. Its heyday was in the 1960s, and it came much closer than Pan-Islamic movements to being put into practice. But the United Arab Republic (Egypt and Syria) lasted only from 1958 to 1961, and did not, as was hoped, attract additional member states. It failed because the Syrian elite were unwilling to relinquish their own role in government. Understandably, no national leadership has been willing to be submerged in a wider political entity. In the contemporary world, both governments and their challengers, in Islamic countries as elsewhere, in practice work within a national framework.

The impacts of colonialism and the gamut of possible responses were very diverse, as the following four case studies—Egypt, the Sudan, Algeria, and Morocco—demonstrate.

FOUR CASE STUDIES

Egypt

In Egypt, the "veiled protectorate" became an open one during the First World War. The khedive took the title "sultan," to emphasize Egypt's inde-

pendence from the Ottoman empire. In 1922, after extensive popular unrest, Egypt regained its independence, the first nation in Africa to do so.[6]
Egyptian Muslims and Copts united in this independence struggle. "Muslim ulama preached in Christian churches, and Christian priests gave Friday
mosque sermons. . . . A new national flag appeared, with the Christian cross
where the star within the Muslim crescent had been."[7] After the rise of
Islamism, this age of cooperation became a distant memory, and in the 1990s,
there were recurrent attacks on the Copts and their churches and property,
which were reciprocated.

It was a qualified independence, for Britain retained extensive rights until Nasser's rise to power in 1956. The new constitution, based on that of
Belgium (!), made the sultan a king, with a real political power he had hitherto lacked.

The years from 1922 on were a time of incessant conflict between Egyptian politicians, British officials, and the king. Partly because they were obsessed with challenging the powers still in British hands, successive
governments did little to introduce social reforms.

In the 1920s, elite Muslim women embarked on a symbolic rejection of
the veil, which the poor had never worn, and which many of a later generation would embrace once again. They turned to philanthropy, much like their
counterparts in Victorian England, and achieved much in spheres such as
education and health; in a sense they were filling some of the gaps left by
the politicians.

The remarkable blind Egyptian scholar, Taha Huseyn (1889–1973), obtained his doctorate at the Sorbonne. He wrote *The Future of Education in
Egypt* in 1938. He emphasized that Egypt has always been part of the Mediterranean world, and must consider itself part of Europe: "We must follow
the path of the Europeans so as to be their equals and partners."[8] But in
the end the liberal nationalist tradition was discredited by its failures and
shortcomings. It was challenged on the one hand by Islamism, and on the
other by the secular Arab socialism of Nasser.

The Sudan

In 1899, an Anglo-Egyptian condominium (in practice, a British colony)
was established in the Sudan; it lasted until the country became independent, in 1956. Its boundaries were approximately those of Turco-Egyptian
rule. (The new regime was often referred to as "the Turks.") The Mahdists
in general lost their revolutionary millennarianism, and in 1916, the Mahdi's
posthumous son became an ally of the government.

The most damaging legacy of colonialism was the creation of a north and
south—the former, Arabic in speech and putative genealogies, and Muslim
in religion; the latter, largely traditional, with a mission-educated Christian
elite. The fear of Muslim insurgency led the British to exclude Arabic speech,

Islam, and even Islamic dress from the south. From a Muslim point of view, this prevented the gradual, peaceful spread of Islam that continued to take place elsewhere in Africa. After independence, the divisions between north and south were to lead to an appallingly destructive and protracted conflict.

Algeria

By 1954, there were 1 million French settlers living among 9 million Muslims in Algeria. Settlers were always in a minority, but they owned much of the best land and exercised cultural, economic, and political dominance. Algeria was governed as if it were part of France (France *outremer,* overseas France). It was said that the Mediterranean divided France as the Seine divides Paris.

Algerians who attended French schools came to form a new salaried francophone elite. They could become French citizens only by renouncing *sharia* law, a step that few Muslims were prepared to take. (In Tunisia, in the 1930s, Muslim French citizens were refused burial in Muslim cemeteries.)

In 1931, Abdulhamid ben Badis (1889–1940) founded the Algerian Association of Ulama. A member of the traditional urban Muslim elite, he was claimed as a precursor by both Islamists and nationalists; however, as its name suggests, this association was not a political party. Ben Badis's goal was to foster a revived Islam in the face of French and Christian cultural imperialism. He was inspired by the Salafiyya movement and was hostile to the Sufi orders. He founded schools where Arabic was taught to both boys and girls. Whereas the Western-educated elite sought the full rights of Frenchmen, Ben Badis said, "We have discovered that the Algerian Muslim nation does exist. This Algerian Muslim nation is not France, cannot be France, does not want to be France."[9] His most famous saying has resounded in Algerian consciousness ever since: "Algeria is our homeland, Islam our religion and Arabic our language." (But it is not, of course, the language of the Berbers of eastern Algeria.)

Because of the size of its settler population and the extent of French investment there, Algeria won its independence only after a protracted war marked by much bloodshed and cruelty on both sides, an experience very different from that of its neighbors, Tunisia and Morocco. What has been called the Savage War of Peace began in 1954, less than thirty years after the fall of the Republic of the Rif, and ended in 1962. In the course of it, a million indigenous Algerians died. At its end, virtually the entire settler population left the country.

In a country with so many sources of division—francophone Berbers and Arabic speakers, competing Sufi orders—a generalized reformed Islam was accepted as the nation's ideology. The war of independence was called a jihad.

Morocco

In the interwar period, protonationalist movements tended to be moderate in their aims, and limited to a small urban elite. In Morocco, as in Algeria, there was a large Berber minority, so that religion, not language, was what all Moroccans had in common. In 1930, there was an outcry when it was proposed to exclude Berber communities from Islamic law. It was seen as an attack on Islam and national unity, and helped to forge nationalist consciousness.

The Istqlal (Independence) Party was founded in 1943 by Allal al-Fasi, but it was the successive kings who dominated Morocco's postindependence history. Morocco and Swaziland are the only two African nations to retain a regnant king. In Morocco, this reflects the way in which the sultan, with great foresight, threw in his lot with the nationalist cause in the 1940s. In 1953 he was deposed and exiled to Madagascar. In the popular mind, he became a saint and martyr—many believed they could see his face in the moon. One of the nationalist rallying cries was "Sidna" (Our Lord). In the year of independence, the sultan was reinstated as King Mohammed V. A dream of advancing beyond the boundaries inherited from colonialism was important to the Moroccan independence movement. Allal al-Fassi stated in 1956, "Our independence will only be complete with the Sahara! The frontiers of Morocco end in the south at Saint-Louis-de-Senegal!"[10]

Hassan II succeeded his father in 1961. The invasion of Spanish Sahara began in 1975. It led to a long war that contributed to a vast external debt, and that has been seen as an attempt to deflect popular discontent away from domestic inequities and, in particular, to absorb the energies of the army, the main focus of opposition to royal power. Hassan died in 1999 and was succeeded by Mohammed VI.

The Moroccan monarchy has often been challenged, by failed army coups and by an increasingly miltant Islamist movement, and has survived in part through the skillful manipulation of a very large number of political parties.

THE DECLINE OF SUFISM

Traditionally, much of the Maghrib lay beyond the sphere of any government, and it was the local holy man, a member of a respected Sufi lineage, who filled many of the functions of government: "Here there is neither sultan nor *makhzan* [government]—only God and Sidi ben Daoud."[11] In the colonial era, the impact of government was more widely felt, and the role of the local sheikh was correspondingly eroded. Many rural people left the countryside to seek work in the towns or become laborers on settlers' farms. The role of the marabout was local; colonialism created a consciousness that was national. Inevitably, the Sufi orders, sooner or later, made their peace with colonial authority. At the time of independence, this meant that they were sometimes marginalized as collaborators.

THE DAWN OF ISLAMISM

The Muslim Brotherhood was founded in Egypt in 1928 by a school-teacher, Hasan al-Banna (1906–1949). Its growth reflected popular dissatisfaction with elite politics in Egypt and the hardships inflicted by a worldwide depression. It soon became an international movement, though each national branch is independent, and it remains the largest Islamist organization. Initially, the Brotherhood ran schools and hospitals, and only a tiny minority of its millions of members have engaged in terrorism.

In some ways, Al-Banna's ideas were very similar to those of the modernists. Both sought a return to the Islam of the Quran and best-attested hadith, were hostile to Christian missions, and were critical of Sufism. Al-Banna and his followers were far from hostile to Western education or technological innovation. They differed from the modernists in certain major respects. The members of the Brotherhood were committed to a transformation of society from the grass roots up, whereas the modernists wrote largely for the Westernized elite. The Islamists, as they would come to be known, had a radical vision of a society entirely subject to God, a submission symbolized by the adoption of *sharia*. In 1943, believing himself in danger of exile, Al-Banna wrote a farewell message:

> My Brothers, you are not a benevolent society, nor a political party, nor a local organisation having political purposes. Rather, you are a new soul in the heart of this nation to give it light by means of the Qur'an.[12]

He was assassinated six years later.

DIVISIONS

"'Modernization' had no impact . . . on the attitudes and mentality of the masses."[13] These words were written of Egypt, but apply equally well to the rest of northern Africa. Colonialism created new horizontal divisions between a Western-educated and often secularized elite and a rural population whose lifestyles and ideas had changed little. It also created divisions between a traditionally educated, Arabic-speaking elite and those who had embraced Western education and who tended to monopolize salaried positions in the modern sector.

Among the legacies of colonialism were parallel Muslim and secular judicial and educational systems. When Algeria won its independence, many of the educated elite were francophone Berbers, a situation that led to a lasting rivalry between French and Arabic speakers. In the early 1960s, 60 percent of the teachers in Algeria, 40 percent of those in Morocco, and 25 percent in Tunisia were French.[14] Where attempts were made to make Arabic the major vehicle of education, they ran into difficulties, including the same reliance on foreign teachers. In this case, the teachers often came from Egypt, and were frequently members of the Muslim Brotherhood who were fleeing Nasser's persecution.

OBSCURE LIVES

Because Islamic history is inextricably entwined with state formation and government, there is a tendency for any account of it to focus on the Big Men whose names loom so large in political narratives. The Sayyid's impact on Somalia is mentioned in any history of twentieth-century Africa, but who outside Brava has ever heard of Dada Masiti?

Holy women become invisible, and so do holy men. The mountain guerrillas who fought for the Rif Republic appear anonymously and collectively in general histories, but not the Rifi pilgrims who walked for weeks to sit at the feet of a revered teacher.

In 1920, a French doctor formed a friendship with an Algerian sheikh, Ahmad al-Alawi (b. 1869), who headed the Shadiliyya from 1909 until his death in 1934. The doctor was an agnostic, but often visited Ahmad's *zawiya* on the Algerian coast. The *zawiya* was built by unpaid volunteers, some of whom came from a great distance. The sheikh, an austere mystic and writer of mystical poetry, told him, "You are nearer to God than you think."[15]

Marcel Carret wrote of the volunteers:

I was specially struck by the most humble of them all, the Riff mountaineers, who had been travelling for a whole month, going on foot from hamlet to hamlet. . . . Their quest was purely spiritual. . . . They were happy, in complete accord with themselves, in the Presence of God.[16]

Chapter 8

Northern Africa since Independence: The Islamist Challenge

Sin does not make anyone a pagan when he has confessed his faith. . . .
Acts of immorality and disobedience without number have long been
committed in all countries. Egypt is like Borno, or even worse. So is Syria
and all the cities of Islam. . . . No age and no country is free from its
share of heresy and sin. If therefore they all become pagan, then surely
their books are useless.

—Al-Kanemi, in Borno, ca. 1808[1]

The governments that came to power at independence[2] identified with mod-
ernist/reformist Islam to varying degrees, less because of the personal con-
victions of their members than because, to the average Moroccan, Tunisian,
or Algerian, Islam was a fundamental part of his or her individual and national identity. (Egypt, of course, has a Christian minority.) The nature and
degree of this identification varied; it was strongest in Morocco's sharifian
monarchy and weakest in Tunisia.

The constitutions of Somalia, Tunisia, Morocco, and Algeria named Islam as the state religion, but politicians assumed that the state should be
essentially secular. Taha Huseyn had claimed, indeed, that this was part of
Muslim tradition: "From earliest times, Muslims have been well aware of the
now universally acknowledged principle that a political system and a religion
are different things."[3] Secularity seemed to be an intrinsic part of modernization, and was becoming increasingly evident in daily life. In the words of
a book published in 1966: "The mosques are poorly attended, public prayer
is rarely seen, many educated North Africans admit they have abandoned
most of the required ritual of Islam."[4] In Tunisia, Habib Bourguiba, head
of state from independence until 1987, tried, unsuccessfully, to end the
Ramadan fast, claiming it was an obstacle to development. Both the attempt
and its failure are significant.

Few would have predicted that a time would come when the central challenge to the governments of northern Africa would be an Islamist one, a challenge all the more damaging because it was from Islam that these regimes derived at least part of their legitimacy. Much of the support that Islamism attracted was due to disillusion with the fruits of independence, which were seen to benefit only a ruling elite. In some ways, it was like a second nationalist movement. In Algeria, the name of the Islamic Salvation Front (*Front Islamique du Salut*, FIS) echoes that of the National Liberation Front (*Front de Libération Nationale*, FLN), which played the leading role in the war of independence and was the ruling party until 1990. The success of the Iranian revolution in 1979 seemed to show that even a powerful regime could be overthrown.

A crisis was deferred by the discovery of mineral wealth and, in the era of the Cold War, by various forms of aid, which tended to dry up when that era ended. In 1986, oil prices fell. The outlines of a profound social and economic dislocation became evident, caused in part by an ever burgeoning population. Young people moved from the countryside to increasingly overcrowded cities. Education expanded, though schools and universities were seriously overcrowded. Often those who attended them were the first in their families to have this opportunity. Instead of joining the middle class, as they expected, they found themselves faced with unemployment. In Algeria, the unemployed were called *hittistes* (from the Arabic word for wall; that is, they had nothing to do but prop up a wall). In Cairo, suppliants left letters at the tomb of the eighth-century jurist al-Shafi'i: "I am the breadwinner of a large family but cannot provide the bread for lack of an income. . . . I have no one to go to but you."[5] A Tunisian peasant complained, "The workers have become beggars. The sun shines on everyone."[6] The sufferings of the poor were made intolerable by the contrast with the wealth of the few, the corruption of those in power, and the governments' intolerance of dissent. Morocco's king is among the world's richest men, but the World Bank estimated in 1980 that over 40 percent of his subjects lived below an absolute poverty line.[7]

There was a widespread perception that the governments of northern Africa had failed to meet the needs of their citizens, and Islamism provided a focus for this anger. Underlying this discontent was an entirely new set of expectations of government. Uthman dan Fodio had criticized the Hausa kings for syncretism and oppressive taxes. In 1988, the rioting crowds in Algeria, who tore down the flag and replaced it with an empty couscous sack, were complaining about what pediatricians call a failure to thrive.

This entirely new set of expectations of government—that it would further "development" by providing better and more schools, universities, hospitals, roads, and jobs—was one of the truly revolutionary consequences of colonial rule.[8] Colonialism was justified in different ways at different times. Initially, despite the bloodshed that accompanied its imposition, it was interpreted in terms of "law and order" and what the French called "a civilizing mission." Increasingly, from the 1940s on, it was justified in terms of development. Nationalists criticized colonial regimes for a lack of development—what was called *immobilisme* in French—and for creating dependent and distorted economic structures. In Ghana, Kwame Nkrumah revised a verse of the Bible: "Seek ye first the political kingdom, and everything else will be added unto it."

Development meant building a better future. But at the same time, no one wanted to devalue or lose sight of the past. The assumption of colonial officials and missionaries that theirs was a superior religion and culture encouraged Muslims to affirm the civilization and achievements of their predecessors.

SAYYID QUTB AND THE RISE OF ISLAMISM

An Egyptian, Sayyid Qutb (1906–1966), was one of the most influential Muslim thinkers of the twentieth century. He is sometimes called the Father of Islamic Fundamentalism, but the word "fundamentalism" is a misnomer. If it refers to the sacred authority of the Quran, then all Muslims are fundamentalists. It is a term that Muslims reject; hence the use here, as is now general, of "Islamist."

Qutb was initially an advocate of Westernization and modernization, but during a visit to the United States, he became critical of its shortcomings. He wrote in words with which many Americans would agree:

> . . . nervous tension devoured their lives despite all the evidence of wealth, plenty, and gadgets that they have. . . . Many times I thought it was as though the people were in a grinding machine that does not stop day or night.[9]

He joined the Muslim Brotherhood in 1953 and was imprisoned by Nasser's government, with thousands of his fellow members, the following year. He spent much of the rest of his life in prison, smuggling his writings out. He was released in 1964, but the publication of a further book led to his re-arrest. He was executed in jail, a fate that gave his life and writings the halo of martyrdom.

Qutb was much influenced by the Pakistani thinker Sayyid Mawdudi (1903–1979), from whom he absorbed the idea that everything which lies outside Islamic ideals is *jahiliyya* (an age of ignorance), the expression that Muhammad applied to pre-Islamic Arabia. Mawdudi saw not only secularism, but also democracy and nationalism, as enemies of Islam because they do not acknowledge the absolute sovereignty of God in human affairs. If necessary, the Muslim must realize the ideal society, ruled by God's laws, by having recourse to jihad.

Qutb had the same polarized vision of the world:

> There are two kinds of culture: Islamic culture based on the fundamentals of
> the Islamic world view and the *jahili* culture which manifests itself in a variety
> of systems, all of which can be explained by one principle . . . that of elevating
> human thought [to the status] of a God.[10]

The errors of capitalism and communism spring from the fact that they
exalt human intelligence over the eternal mandates of God.

Qutb advocated the duty of jihad against rulers such as Nasser, who were
at least nominally Muslim but whom he regarded as apostates, just as Uthman
dan Fodio had led a jihad against the Muslim kings of Hausaland. He saw
Christians and Jews as enemies: "It is the eternal doctrine which we see veri-
fied in every time and place. . . . This is the reality of the battle which the
Jews and the Christians initiate in every land and at all times against the Islamic community."[11] This is a departure from the Prophet's tolerance of
other Religions of the Book. Qutb justified this by stating that only in a just
(that is, truly Islamic) society would people have a real freedom of religious
choice.

Islamic rulers had usually, but not always, practiced tolerance of other
religions. In a position of relative weakness, this tradition was lost—terrorism has been called the warfare of the weak. Qutb advocated jihad but was
in a sense an advocate of peace, for wars fought for any other reason had
no justification.

Like the modernists, from whom in many ways they are so different, Islamists often call themselves *salafiyya*. What they have in common with reformists such as Abduh is their conviction that religion is of paramount
importance, their insistence that Muslims should return to the religion of
the Quran and hadith, and their hostility to the Sufi orders.

Islamists vary in the details of their thought, in particular, over the issue
of whether to seek the violent overthrow of a regime or attempt to work
within the system, but some general principles are characteristic. They are
far from hostile to modern science and technology. The use of radio, cassettes, videos, and so on has greatly facilitated the spread of their ideas, and
many of them are highly educated. They reject the idea that religion and the
state should be separate. They are critical of Western democracy as the rule
of man rather than of God. Nineteenth-century modernists justified democracy in terms of the Quranic concept of *shura* (consultation). The current
head of the Muslim Brotherhood in Egypt, like other Islamists, sees *shura*
as a preferred alternative:

> In my opinion, those who support democracy in the sense that the West does,
> that is, free from any restrictions imposed by religion . . . I regard as outside
> the regulations of the Sharia.[12]

Islamists tend to condemn the government of, for instance, Egypt, not as an imperfect one but as part of the realm of ignorance. There are echoes of the debate between Uthman dan Fodio and al-Kanemi. To all Islamists, the litmus test of a truly Islamic state is its official adoption of *sharia*. In precolonial times, as O'Fahey says of the Sudan, "the law that prevailed in any given Muslim country was in practice a compromise between divine law, local custom, and the fiat of the rulers."[13] *Sharia* was usually followed in personal matters such as marriage, inheritance, and divorce. This remained the case in the colonial era, but the imposition of secular law codes in other areas seemed to be a dimension of cultural and religious imperialism.

To Islamists, the restoration of the *sharia* is part of a return to the more perfect religious practice of the distant past, an assertion of the supremacy of Divine law in every aspect of daily life. There are many difficulties, however, in its imposition, not the least of which is that men and women are not equal before it. It is unacceptable to non-Muslim minorities. Issues surrounding imposition of *sharia* have been a major cause of war in the Sudan and have underlain much Muslim-Christian conflict in Nigeria. Many Muslims and all non-Muslims oppose the introduction of harsh penalties for *hudud* (forbidden acts), such as the amputation of a hand for theft. Saudi Arabia has become notorious for these penalties, and they were imposed with great brutality in the last years of Nimeiri's rule in the Sudan. There is also a fundamental contradiction between *sharia* and Western democracy, because it limits the powers of the legislature to make or change laws.

It is clear that there is a widespread move to a more fervent practice of Islam and adoption of the *sharia* as a rule of life, sometimes symbolized by women's adoption of the veil. In the words of a book published in 1983:

> The personal aspect of the Islamic revival is reflected in increased emphasis upon religious observances (mosque attendance, Ramadan fast, outlawing of alcohol, and gambling), religious programming in the media, the proliferation of religious literature . . . the vibrant *dawah* (missionary movements).[14]

There are various reasons for this, including the shaping of opinion through the use of modern technology, but there is also a fear of condemnation by Islamists. Algerian-born Marnia Lazreg condemns Islamism as coercive. Religion ceases to be a matter of personal devotion and choice: "Algerians have been Muslims since the eighth century—whence comes then this ostentatious display of religiosity? . . . Now [religion] is not only a public matter, but judging by the violence that has erupted since 1992, it is also coercive."[15] Islamists condemn the modern state of Algeria as the heir of colonialism, but to Lazreg, they are "recolonizing" Algerian consciousness.

Whereas the nineteenth-century modernists felt that Islam was in need of revival, and sought to absorb what was best in the Western world, Islamists

are critical of the West's materialism and secular spirit, and of the unjust global distribution of resources. They see its history as centuries of military
aggression, beginning with the Crusades and including colonial wars. The
conflicts of recent years are sometimes called "the Crusade" (*al-Alibiyyah*).
Whereas the modernists believed that Muslims could learn much from the
West without compromising their faith, the Islamists condemn the West. The
Western world is not a model to be emulated, but a failure.

While all deplore the bloodshed and suffering caused by violence, Western scholars vary in their interpretations of Islamism. Some regard it as re-
actionary, because of its insistence on *sharia* and its perceived tendency to
subordinate women. Some, on the other hand, see it as a response to suffering and oppression, and to the political and cultural violence of colonialism. They claim that Islamists have been forced to turn to violence by
repressive governments. Islamists see themselves as part of a succession of
Renewers, like Uthman dan Fodio, whom the Prophet foretold would appear every century. Muslim critics often compare them with the Kharijites.

Some consider that violent struggle is a transitional phase which is already
giving way to an era of "post-Islamism" marked by the adoption of democratic processes.[16] The election of the reformist Khatami as president of Iran
in 1997 was hailed as an example, but in 2004, conservative clerics resumed
control of Iran's government.[17] Some Egyptian members of the Muslim
Brotherhood have left it to form a political party, al-Wasat (the Center), committed to the democratic process. It is very small, with 200 members, and
has not yet been officially recognized, but it has both women and Coptic
Christians among its members and reminds us that there are many
Islamisms.[18] The policies of the Muslim Brotherhood in Egypt since the mid-
1980s are another example.

There is currently a tendency for Islamists and Western political leaders
to demonize each other: "Axis of Evil," "the Great Satan." Inevitably, in the
aftermath of September 11, Americans tend to see Islamists as the enemy,
just as they once saw Communists. But it is important to remember that in
recent years Muslims have also been the victims of terrible crimes, such as
"ethnic cleansing" in the Balkans and mob attacks in India. Only a tiny number of Africa's or the world's Muslims are involved in radical movements,
and of these, only a few are engaged in terrorism.

GOVERNMENT AND RELIGION

The interactions between religion and government in northern Africa are
complex and varied. Somalia is a country that has been torn apart by civil
war, though all its people are Muslims and speak the same language. (The
same is true of Catholic Rwanda.) Islamist movements have not played a
major role there. Somalia's wars have essentially been a continuation of
precolonial clan struggles over scarce resources, especially water, in an era

of sophisticated weaponry. The account that follows, outlines four contrasting case studies.

Egypt

Nothing did more to radicalize Muslims, in Egypt and elsewhere, than the creation of the state of Israel. A disastrous attempt to invade Palestine in 1948 was one of the nails in the coffin of Egypt's discredited monarchy. Later, Nasser in his turn was weakened by the Six-Day War, which Muslims remember as The Disaster, when Israeli forces captured Sinai, Gaza, the Golan Heights, the West Bank, and East Jerusalem.

Britain's role in Egypt began and ended with popular discontent. In 1882, riots in Alexandria led to British bombardment and the "veiled protectorate." In 1952, there were mysterious riots and arson outbreaks in Cairo. Soon afterward, a group of Egyptian army officers staged a coup that led to the fall of the monarchy and the departure of the British. They were patriots, critical of the corruption and ostentation of the court, and anxious, like Muhammad Ali before them, to establish a strong economic and industrial base as a prerequisite for true independence. It was the first time Egypt had been ruled by native Egyptians since the time of the pharaohs. By 1954, one of these officers, Gamal Abd al-Nasir, or Nasser (b. 1918) was supreme. The constitution of 1956 gave him vast powers as president, a position he retained until his death in 1970.

In 1956, Nasser sought to borrow money from the United States to build the Aswan Dam, in order to create the power supplies essential for a program of industrialization. When this fell through, because of his policy of nonalignment, he nationalized the Suez Canal. Britain and France tried to reverse this by military action, but failed. The symbolism of these events was far-reaching, and Nasser became a hero in colonized countries everywhere, and especially in Africa. Although he was a Muslim, Nasser's primary commitment was to Pan-Arabism and socialism. (We have noted the short-lived union of Egypt and Syria.) Nasser's Arab socialism inspired both Qaddafi in Libya and Gaffar Nimeiri in the Republic of Sudan.

The Muslim Brotherhood initially supported the 1952 coup, but its leadership lost confidence in Nasser when it became evident that he did not intend to create an Islamic state. After an apparent attempt on Nasser's life, thousands of members were imprisoned, among them Qutb. Some, like him, were executed. The movement went underground and was, inevitably, radicalized. The Society of Muslim Sisters, led by Zaynab al-Ghazali, cared for released prisoners and their families.

Nasser was succeeded by Anwar al-Sadat, who was president from 1971 to 1981. He attempted to dissociate himself from Nasser by projecting an image of personal devotion—"the pious president"—but he profoundly alienated many Muslims by embarking on negotiations with Israel. The Camp

David Accords were signed in 1978. The rest of the Arab and Islamic world severed diplomatic relations in protest. In 1981, Sadat, who was by now extremely unpopular, was assassinated by a member of an Islamist group, Al-Jihad.

African-American Christians have often claimed the Exodus story; an example is the spiritual "Let My People Go." Egypt's Islamists came to identify the nation's rulers with Pharaoh. At his trial, Sadat's assassin said, "I have killed Pharaoh and I do not fear death!"

Sadat's successor, Husni Mubarak, is still (2004) in power. He has attempted to follow a middle-of-the-road policy, which predictably has pleased neither liberals nor Islamists. Gamaa Islamiyya (the Islamic Group) has attacked both Coptic Christians and foreign tourists. The Muslim Brotherhood has avoided violence and has concentrated on providing social services, as it had done initially. It has cooperated with small political parties, a good example of a transition to "post-Islamism" and of the need to distinguish different "Islamisms."

Algeria

Islamists have often embraced the political process if this is open to them—which, sadly, has not always been the case. In Algeria, the National Liberation Front (FLN) had monopolized political power since independence. Islamists had emerged as the main critics of the government since the early 1980s. In 1989, President Chadli Benjedid introduced multi-party democracy, hoping that he could enhance his own power by manipulating small parties. In 1990, the Islamic Salvation Front (FIS) won an overwhelming victory in local elections. It went on to win the first round of national elections to the legislature in 1991. However, a different Islamist faction believed a just society could be achieved only by jihad, and initiated violence.

There was an army coup, and thousands of FIS leaders and members were interned or fled into exile. Once more, Islamists were radicalized by injustice, and the Armed Islamic Group (*Groupe Islamique Armé*, GIA) embarked on a violent campaign. A civil war followed, which left perhaps 100,000 dead and lasted for seven years. Acts of terror were committed on both sides, and the GIA's attacks on journalists and intellectuals brought worldwide criticism. By 1997, the Islamists were defeated. Many Algerian Muslims who had initially supported them had been alienated by years of bloodshed.

Libya

Libya was a former Italian colony that gained its independence in 1951. It was ruled by the grandson of the founder of the Sanusiyya, who became King Idris. In his first year in power, he abolished political parties. At the time Libya was one of the poorest countries in the world, a situation trans-formed by the discovery of oil in 1959.

In 1969, the eighty-year-old king was deposed in a coup led by a soldier from the southern desert, Mu'ammar al-Qaddafi. His initial image was that of a reforming Muslim: he banned alcohol and closed churches and night-clubs. He had replaced a king whose legitimacy depended on his religious credentials, and he was initially supported by the (non-Sanusiyya) *ulama*.

Qaddafi's religious views became increasingly idiosyncratic, to a point where they became "heretical" to many Muslims. Between 1975 and 1979, he published the three volumes of his *Green Book*. The title suggests that it was meant to be a Muslim counterpart to Mao's *Red Book*, but it has almost nothing to say about Islam, other than to deplore sectarianism. The primary emphasis is on nationalism and socialism, the bases of "The Third Interna-tional Theory." (The first two international theories were Marxism, rejected for its atheism, and capitalism.) Qaddafi took to an extreme the belief in *itjihad* (ongoing religious interpretation). He revised the Islamic calendar, denied the authenticity of many hadith, and stated that pilgrimage to Mecca is not obligatory.

Like the Saudis, Qaddafi used oil revenues to promote Islam in many countries in Africa and elsewhere. In time, African governments came to fear his destabilizing political influence, and broke these links. On the world stage his regime was isolated by its association with terrorism. Libya is now (2004) coming in from the cold, and the United Nations has ended eleven years of sanctions.

Qaddafi is the ruler of a state with about a million people. His high in-ternational profile has been due partly to the political and economic impor-tance of Libya's oil and partly to the attention paid him by Western media.

The Sudan

When the Sudan regained its independence in 1956, three Muslim groups were a force in politics: the followers of the Mahdi's family; members of the Khatmiyya order, who were their traditional opponents; and the Muslim Brotherhood, which reached the Sudan in 1940 and emerged as an open political force in 1954. In 1969, Colonel (later General) Gaffar Mohamed Nimeiri (b. 1930), came to power in a coup with left-wing support. When the left attempted to overthrow him in 1971, he began to identify strongly with Islam, a change that is variously interpreted.

An accord in 1972 ended the civil war between the north and the south, at least for a time. A leading member of the Muslim Brotherhood, Sorbonne-educated Dr. Hassan al-Turabi, has been a major force in Sudan politics ever since. In 1983, decrees established both *sharia* and Islamic banking. To southerners, this abrogated the accord, and the civil war began again.

Islamists felt that Nimeiri's identification with their cause was opportunistic, and that his policies did not go far enough. He was toppled in a coup in 1985. Another army officer, Umar Hassan al-Bashir, led a successful coup in 1990, and has been in power ever since (as of 2004). His government, which was supported by the Muslim Brotherhood, reintroduced *sharia* and introduced a dress code for women. In 1987, Turabi published the Sudan Charter, a document that has influenced Muslims far beyond the Sudan. It insists that a Muslim head of state and *sharia* are essential.

The Sudan experience is distinctive in several respects. Islamists, as represented by the Muslim Brotherhood, have played a major role in the creation of governments and the shaping of their policies. The state's essential dilemma is the incompatibility of Islamist policies with the demands of southern leaders for a high level of regional devolution in a secular state. This conflict has overshadowed the Sudan since independence, and remains unresolved.

GENDER

The relationship between Islam, Islamism, and gender relations is a complex and disputed one. The words of Algerian-born Marnia Lazreg, quoted earlier, are an example of a feminist critique of Islamism. To outsiders, the veil sometimes seems to be a symbol of subjection. Sometimes it is freely chosen, sometimes imposed by a father or husband. Many veil-wearing women study at secular universities and embrace a variety of professions. Islamist styles of dress tend to be found mainly among urban and middle-class women. Much has been written on the subject:

> It is often said that "veiling" represents the most dominant form of resistance to Western cultural and political hegemony. . . . [I]t is difficult to say where wearing clothes as an expression of Muslim identity and lifestyle ends and the force of fashion or social control takes over.[19]

Undoubtedly, women have often suffered in Muslim theocracies. A recent film from Afghanistan explores the terrible problems faced by households without men during the rule of the Taliban, when women were forbidden to work.[20] However the example of a distinguished Egyptian woman, who is almost unknown in the Western world, may stand for countless others who grew up in a conservative milieu and found their own way and created their own identity. Aisha Abdul-Rahman (1913–1998) was not allowed to attend school. Despite this, she became a scholar and journalist who always wrote under a pseudonym, "Daughter of the Shore." She wrote newspaper articles on social issues as well as Quranic commentaries, studies of early Islamic literature, and a novel, dealing with the sufferings of women in the countryside, that was made into a film. None of her works have been translated into English.

There are many other themes one might explore, including the story of the North African Muslims of the diaspora and their descendants. There are 5 million of them in France alone. To borrow the words of a sixteenth-century Borno historian that are equally applicable to the rest of this book, "We have mentioned a very little, passing over much in the fear of being lengthy and verbose. But the sensible reader will understand that beyond the stream there is a big sea."[21]

Chapter 9

West Africa since 1900

The light of Truth . . . is a darkness more brilliant than all lights combined.

—Cerno Bokar Salif Taal (1933)[1]

It is not always realized that the colonial period was one of the great ages—perhaps the great age—of the extension of Islam in sub-Saharan Africa. It has been called "the period of the greatest expansion of the Muslim presence in Africa."[2] This spread was reflected in the widespread adoption of Muslim dress, the long, flowing gown.

Because of constraints of space, this chapter concentrates on West Africa. Good recent surveys for eastern, central, and southern Africa have been written by others.[3] I omit these vast regions with regret— "beyond the stream there is a big sea."

It has been suggested that Islam spread faster in West Africa in the colonial period than Christianity did at the same time, with more people becoming Muslims than during the previous nine centuries.[4] This was also true elsewhere. In Tanzania, Islam spread inland from the Swahili coast, with the result that Muslims constituted 40 percent of the population at independence, even before the union with Muslim Zanzibar.

In 1966, when an astute and well-informed observer described the decline in religion and rise in secularism in the Maghrib, another scholar suggested, quite independently, that the same thing was happening in tropical Africa. Islam, he suggested, was undermined from within "by the increasing secularism of modern Muslim states and the general recognition that secular aims and politics are more important in the modern world than common religious interest."[5] As in the Maghrib, things were to turn out very differently.

COLONIAL ALLIANCES

Colonial jurisdictions fossilized the states that existed at the moment of conquest, irrespective of whether they were ancient or of relatively recent vintage. The British established a close alliance with the traditional rulers of northern Nigeria. Some of these rulers were devoted and outstanding men, like the "devout and upright" Hassan, sultan of Sokoto from 1931 to 1938, and Yahaya of Gwandu, the north's first Western-educated emir, who was noted for his simplicity of life, receptivity to change, and "deep compassion for his fellow man." It was said of Ahmadu, who succeeded to the small emirate of Misau in 1926, "His Emirate, admirably governed, must be one of the happiest states on the face of the earth."[6] Not all emirs were so satisfactory, but British officials working in the north tended to shield both the system, and those in it, from every breath of criticism. They could appreciate Islamic civilization more readily than the traditionalist cultures of the south. They warmed to its ancient tradition of literacy, its architecture, the pageantry of its court, the superb cavalry. They hoped to protect the Muslim north from the winds of change, and thus insulated it, very largely, from the encounters with modernity that had begun much so earlier in Egypt and the Maghrib. The governor of northern Nigeria told a London audience in 1911:

> We want . . . no transmogrification of the dignified and courteous Moslem into a trousered burlesque with a veneer of European Civilisation. We do not want to replace a patriarchal and venerable government by a discontented and irresponsible democracy of semi-educated politicians.[7]

Traditional rulers had often fought against the imposition of colonialism. The Western-educated had tended to welcome it. But, as in India, the British were hostile to the latter. The very existence of a Western-educated class challenged the rationale with which colonizers justified their conquest states. The British allied with "traditional" rulers, whose role, of course, was fundamentally changed. But when democracy finally arrived, half a century later, it was the Western-educated who were in a position to take advantage of its glittering opportunities. Some independent nations, such as Guinea and Tanzania, abolished traditional rulers entirely.

In Nigeria, a system that survived colonialism came to an end after it, when the powers of what had come to be called Native Authorities were stripped away. With some modifications, *sharia* had been retained in northern Nigeria. It was in 1960, the year of independence, that a new penal code was introduced.

In the vast expanses of French West Africa, colonial officials tended to ally with the Sufi orders. The leaders of the Umarian branch of the the Tijaniyya and many other Sufi leaders worked closely with the French, though some celebrated sheikhs were exiled.

During the First World War, local notables in French West Africa were loyal to the colonial government. Previously the French had been haunted by the possibility of a Pan-Islamic revolt. Afterward, these alliances flourished. Whereas the British sought to protect Islamic states from modernity and change, the French had a different basic philosophy, *la mission civilatrice* (the civilizing mission). The result of this policy was the *évolué*, the product of an excellent French education who was thoroughly fluent in French. Only a tiny number could become *évolués*, and many parents, for religious reasons, chose not to send their children to government schools. Inevitably, the *évolués'* knowledge of Islamic learning tended to be limited, and their outlook secular. However, the teachings of the Sufi Cerno Bokar are preserved only because an *évolué* disciple wrote down his Fulfulde discourses in French.

WESTERN EDUCATION AND THE CREATION OF NEW ELITES

Vast numbers of pupils attended Quranic schools, but it was the Western-educated who came to dominate the affairs of independent states. Inevitably, they were more employable in the modern sector than those with a traditional Islamic education.

In the western Sahara, in precolonial times, it was the Moors (Arabized Berbers) who were politically and culturally dominant. Black *harratin*, a despised caste, worked as cultivators in the desert oases. Black Mauritanians welcomed Western education and became a ruling elite at independence. In Mali and Niger, farther east, there have been a number of separatist risings among the desert Tuareg. These are not wars of religion, for the black elite they reject are Muslim as well. They are an attempt to regain a vanished dominance or, at least, independence.

With at least 40 million Muslims (some would say far more), Nigeria has one of the largest Islamic populations in the world. When Nigeria became independent in 1960, there was a great imbalance between the numbers of Muslims and non-Muslims with a Western education. One should not, of course, equate the south with traditionalist religion or Christianity. Many Yoruba were, and are, Muslims. But the non-Muslim peoples of the south, such as the Igbo and many Yoruba, gave Western education an unequivocal welcome. Christian missionaries were prevented from working in Muslim areas, though a few managed to do so. They established a vast network of schools in the south.

Nigeria's colonial government had established a small number of elite Western educational institutions in the north. Their graduates found, like their *évolué* counterparts, that no one could do justice both to a standard Western curriculum and Islamic learning. The first premier of northern Nigeria, Ahmadu Bello, a devout Muslim, was more fluent in English than Arabic, for which he needed an interpreter. "[T]raditional Islam depends on a vast corpus of learning . . . the acquiring of this learning, for which a flu-ent knowledge of classical Arabic is essential, consumes a lifetime."[8]

Muslims tended to embrace Western education most enthusiastically when they lived in the same area as Christians—for instance, in Lagos or Freetown. The Ahmadiyya was founded in 1899 by a Punjabi Muslim, Mirza Ghulam Ahmad (d. 1908); his basic teaching was that of a continuing revelation. He claimed to be a prophet, a claim totally unacceptable to all other Muslims, because Muhammad is the Seal (last) of the Prophets. After Ahmad's death, the movement split into two branches, one of which was closer to ortho-doxy.

Ahmadiyya missionaries from India reached Lagos in 1921 and then went on to the Gold Coast. They laid great emphasis on Western education, and the Quran was studied in English translation. They had some success in Lagos and the southern Gold Coast. Their Western-type schools were attractive and their heterodoxy not always realized. They had no impact in the regions far-ther north, which had been Muslim for centuries, apart from a single town, Wa, in the northern Gold Coast. The Ahmadiyya are not regarded as Mus-lims in Pakistan, and the Saudi government forbids them from making the pilgrimage to Mecca.

The stimulus of the Ahmadiyya schools and the influence of Salafiyya ideas were among the factors leading to the establishment of Muslim as-sociations to promote Western education. Ansar Ud-Deen (Helpers of the Faith) was founded in Lagos in 1923. Its founders described its purpose thus:

> Education on Western lines; by this means alone can Islam be better studied and understood; as lack of proper knowledge of the essence of Islam and fail-ure to grasp its spirit and correct teaching have been the greatest cause of the backwardness of the Muslim.[9]

This was followed by similar organizations in other Yoruba cities. The Ijebu Ode Muhammedan Friendly Society, founded in 1927, defined its aims as "the support of Islam, education and the Motherland" [which was not Nigeria, but Ijebu Ode].[10]

Many students were and are involved in both the Muslim and the West-ern educational systems. Sa'adu Zungur started out as an outstanding Quranic student and went on to attend first government schools and then Yaba College (in fact, though not in name, Nigeria's first university).

In 1960, as independence approached, there was a widespread fear in the north of perpetual domination by Western-educated Christian southerners. A Hausa poet wrote:

> Without any doubt the men of the South will sit
> In the saddle of Nigerian rule.[11]

Nigeria had a federal constitution, but lacked the essential element that makes federalism workable: the equal size of its component parts. The demographically and geographically dominant Northern Region was headed by a descendant of Uthman dan Fodio, Sir Ahmadu Bello, Sardauna (Prince) of Sokoto. He established an umbrella organization for Nigerian Muslims—at first, specifically for northern Muslims—the Jamaat Nasril al-Islam (the Society for the Victory of Islam). He felt a duty to foster the expansion of Islam in what was then known as Nigeria's Middle Belt, seeing this as a peaceful continuation of dan Fodio's jihad. His death at the hands of southern Christian army officers in a coup in 1966 shocked and embittered his co-religionists.

Northern and southern Nigeria were created by colonialism. What was at first an artificial line for administrative purposes became part of popular consciousness. Later governments of Nigeria, by the creation of ever more states, have attempted to break down this harmful and dangerous polarity.

THE BROTHERHOODS

The brotherhoods declined in North Africa, where they were once so strong, especially after independence, but they flourished in sub-Saharan Africa, contributing both to the spread of Islam and to the intensification of faith and religious practice. Sometimes similar factors in different regions are cited to explain different outcomes. Thus, the improvement of communications is said to have undermined the role of *zawiya* in providing hospitality to travelers in the Maghrib. In West Africa, improved communications and expanding trade networks are said to have aided the spread of Islam: "Becoming a merchant in the [twentieth century] Malian context meant becoming a Muslim."[12]

Originally, a Sufi or Sufi family would adopt the *wird* (litany) of one or more orders, though some followed the Sufi way without taking this step. Uthman dan Fodio was personally devoted to the founder of the Qadiriyya, but did not see it as a potential mass movement. The mobilization of large numbers of people in a centralized organization, with regional *khalifa*, was a later development. The *turuq* cut across class lines and in theory, though not always in practice, ethnic differences. In the twentieth century, they became mass movements. In a sense, of course, a mass movement of Sufis is a contradiction in terms, and most members were not mystics, though they were faithful to a regime of additional prayer beyond what is required of all Muslims. The definition of Sufism in Hausaland is "being good."

The Muridiyya

The Muridiyya (Mourides) of Senegal, an offshoot of the Qadiriyya, are an interesting example of adaptation to new social conditions. *Murid* means a student or disciple of a Sufi brotherhood. Ahmadu Bamba, a member of a marabout family, was a saintly figure indifferent to wealth, drawn to solitude, and devoted to prayer and writing. He had a vision in 1891, in a place that came to be called Touba (repentance). He began to attract disciples, some of whom were former warriors who, in a colonial situation, found themselves out of a job. The French, fearing his influence, deported him first to Gabon and then to Mauritania, but finally allowed him to return.

Legends grew up around Bamba's exile. It was said that when the French ship's captain forbade him to pray on board, he spread his prayer mat on the water. By 1912, he had 70,000 followers. The French soon realized how much they gained from the industry and discipline of the Mourides, who have also been closely associated with the governments of independent Senegal. Central to Bamba's teaching was the necessity of absolute obedience to one's sheikh; a perfect submission would lead to salvation. Work and prayer were paramount, but the responsibilities were divided. The disciples devoted themselves to work rather than prayer and study, which were the duties of the sheikh.

Bamba was opposed to anticolonial wars, telling those who thought differently that jihad was justified for "times which differed from yours, and whose men differed from yours." Instead, he advocated "a holy war on souls."[13] When the First World War broke out, Bamba and his associates recruited Mouride soldiers for the French army. They fought against Turkish Muslims in the Dardanelles, and Bamba was given a decoration by the French.

Largely self-taught in Arabic, Bamba wrote 30,000 lines of Arabic didactic poetry, some of which the Mourides still sing regularly, and 4,000 lines of prose. When he died in 1927, he was buried at Touba, which remains the center of the order. Its mosque, to which the Mourides make an annual pilgrimage, is the largest in black Africa.

It was Bamba's first disciple, a former soldier named Sheikh Ibra Fall, who organized the practical application of Bamba's teachings. The Mourides devoted themselves to the cultivation of peanuts, Senegal's main export. When they began to run out of land, they colonized the western edge of the inland desert. This practice was pioneered by groups of men who, after ten years of unpaid seasonal work, were given their own plots and were able to settle down with their families. In 1970, there were over half a million Mourides in Senegal, twice as many Tijaniyya, and a third of a million Qadiryya.

In 1970, the peanut market collapsed, and the Mourides turned to new forms of economic enterprise. In Europe and the United States, disciples worked as street traders. With their profits they bought textiles or electronic goods, which their fellow Mourides sold in Dakar's main market. Some African-Americans have joined the order.

It is a paradox that a man so unworldly founded an order in which the labors of the many support perhaps a hundred "saints" in luxury.[14] A distinctive branch, Bay Fall, founded by Ibra Fall, carries the doctrine of work, rather than prayer and fasting, even further. Its members sport dreadlocks and wear bright patchwork clothes, and have a predilection for alcohol and cannabis. They carry heavy clubs, like the Donatist Circumcellions in fifth-century North Africa.

Sokhna Magat Diop, a revered woman sheikh, inherited the position from her father. She avoided a public role, which she entrusted to her sons, and spent her time in prayer, fasting, and seclusion, much like the order's founder.

The order flourished because it filled important social and psychological functions. It gave economic security to the landless; the early disciples included many former slaves and members of marginalized artisan castes. In a society where indigenous governments had been overthrown by French colonialism, the Muridiyya created an alternative and independent social order. There was also a valued emphasis on protection from evil and witchcraft. Senegalese took pride in the fact that the Muridiyya was an indigenous order: "Arab Muslims come and play games with us, saying that Muhammad was an Arab. . . . There are some Arabs, although they are Muslims, who scorn the Africans even more sordidly than do the French."[15]

New Branches of the Tijaniyya

Though founded in the Maghrib, the Tijaniyya was most successful in the western Sudan, initially through the agency of al-Hajj Umar, in both peace and war. During his long stay in Sokoto, Umar introduced the Tijaniyya there, and later, Hausa traders carried the order to the Gold Coast and elsewhere.

By the early twentieth century, there were several branches of the Tijaniyya that traced their origin to al-Hajj Umar. It was, however, a new branch that was destined to attract far more adherents.

The Community of Grace[16]

Ibrahim Niass (1900–1975), another Senegalese, founded a branch of the Tijaniyya that is sometimes called Reformed, as opposed to Traditional. (Another branch, the Hamalliyya, is also called Reformed, though in both cases the adjective is misleading, implying that the older order is in need of reform.) It is often known as the Niassiyya, but its members call it Jama'at al-Fayda (the Community of Grace). Niass's father was a sheikh of the Tijaniyya, but the family came from an artisan caste of ironworkers who were despised in Senegal. Many recruits were former slaves or caste members.

Baye Ibrahim (Father Ibrahim) was a charismatic figure. Like the founder of the Tijaniyya, he had a passionate devotion to Muhammad, and wrote mystical poetry in his honor. His headquarters was in Medina-Kaolak in Senegal (another example of the way in which place-names sacred to Islam were transferred to Africa).

At the age of thirty, Ibrahim declared that he was the Savior of the Age, a Sufi title that implies supernatural powers. Large numbers accepted this claim, including the emir of Kano and his son and heir. On a visit to Fez, the head of the Tijaniyya is thought to have transferred his own role to him. Ibrahim had a vision in which he received an infusion of grace (*fayda*). His followers believed that Ibrahim could share this gift of grace, and that his prayers would assure their prosperity in this life and, above all, their salvation in the next, so that they would be transported to Paradise on the mythical beast that carried the Prophet through the seven heavens to the throne of God.

In the 1940s and 1950s, Baye Ibrahim visited a number of West African cities and was received with great enthusiasm. Part of his attraction, in the days when nationalism was a growing force, lay in the fact that he was an African spiritual leader. The organization's message was spread far and wide on radio and through sermons recorded on cassettes.

By the mid-1960s, 55 percent of adult males in the northern Nigerian city of Kano were members of the Niassiyya. Only 5 percent belonged to the older version.[17] Kano had especially strong Tijani links, but far to the south, at the confluence of the Niger and Benue Rivers, over 80 percent of Muslim men are Tijaniyya, and nearly all of them are Niassiyya. The order was introduced there in 1949.[18] It has spread far and wide in Africa, and has a number of *zawiya* in the United States.

The Hamalliyya[19]

The Hamalliyya (sometimes referred to as Hamallism) is another branch of the Tijaniyya. It was founded by Hamahu'llah (ca. 1883–1943), who came from Nioro in Mali. It is also called the Tijaniyya of the Eleven Beads. Hamahu'llah taught that the Tijani 100-bead rosary should begin and end with a cluster of eleven, not twelve, prayers. In the 1930s and 1940s, this was a matter of intense controversy. In the same way, congregations have come to blows over whether to pray with their arms crossed over their chest (the practice of the Tijaniyya) or at their sides.

Hamahu'llah was a saintly mystic, devoted to prayer, who spent much time in solitude and shunned contact with Europeans. His aloofness and the hostility of other Sufi leaders—Tijani leaders in particular—made him suspect to colonial authorities. In 1925 he was exiled, first to Mauritania, then to the Ivory Coast, where he started using the abbreviated daily prayers permitted in time of war. He was able to return to Senegal in 1935, but in 1940, a group of his followers, led by his sons (who were later shot), were involved in a bloody local clash. The sheikh repudiated this use of violence, but was exiled once more, and died in France after a hunger strike.

In the period after the Second World War, the Hamalliyya became closely linked with the main opposition party in French West Africa. In 1970, Alexandre wrote of its post-independence history, "On the whole it seems to have lost most of its significance," but added that its teachings were preserved in some villages in Niger, Upper Volta (now Burkina Faso), and Mali. In contemporary Burkina Faso, there are self-sufficient Hamallist villages, centered around their sheikhs, still living out Hamahu'llah's rejection of the world.[20]

The attraction of all three—Bamba, Ibrahim, and Hamahu'llah—lay partly in the fact that they were, in their different ways, all great indigenous spiritual leaders.

The Qadiriyya

In response to the challenge of the Tijaniyya, the Qadiriyya became more of a popular movement in Nigeria during the colonial period, and its various branches united. However, the links with the traditional ruling class continued (though the emirs of Kano were Tijani), and when Nigeria became independent, the order supported the Northern People's Congress, founded by a descendant of Uthman dan Fodio.

> We pray God the Glorious, the King of Truth
> That NPC may rule Nigeria,
> For the sake of the Lord 'Abd al-Qadir al-Jaylani,
> May your rule [O Sardauna] last until the coming of the Mahdi.[21]

The Tijaniyya were linked with the smaller, radical, Kano-based opposition party, NEPU (Northern Elements Progressive Union).

Reformists

The countries of the Maghrib and Egypt were in constant contact with each other, so that the Salafiyya in Morocco and Egypt had much in common. In West Africa, there was much less contact of this kind, and reformist/Salafiyya-type movements emerged in different countries at different times and with different names. Like the Salafiyya, they were hostile to Sufism. They had similar concerns about education, though what troubled their leaders was less the power and technology of Europe than their situation vis-à-vis local educated Christians. This was, as we have seen, the problem of the Helpers of the Faith in 1920s Lagos.

Some West African Muslims encountered these teachings on pilgrimage to Mecca, or through contact with Egypt's Muslim Brothers. In the independence era, the Saudis used oil revenues to extend their influence in sub-Saharan Africa; students were given scholarships to study at a Saudi university, and after their return home were financed as missionaries. Nasser encouraged African Muslims to study in Egypt, and sent Egyptian teachers to many African countries. As in the Maghrib, they were often Muslim Brothers fleeing Nasser's persecution. Links with Egypt are reflected in French West Africa by the fact that the movement was often called Subbanu, after the Egyptian Society of Muslim Youth (*shubban*). Its founders included men who had returned from the mosque university of al-Azhar in Egypt. Typically the Subbanu and their counterparts are either young and well-educated or prosperous merchants. Two case studies, Mali and Nigeria, shed more light on their role.

Mali

An anti-Sufi movement began in French West Africa in the late 1940s and 1950s, and has expanded greatly since then. Its members are often called Wahhabiyya, but they reject the name, and call themselves the Community of the Orthodox (*ahl al-Sunna wal-jama'a*, or Sunni). The difficulty with this is the fact that it is also the name of the vast body of Sunni (as distinct from Shi'ite) Muslims. The Subbanu, as they are conveniently called, criticized the "traditional" Islam of the *turuq*, though the name Sunni implied a return to Islam's most ancient traditions. They condemned what they called *maraboutisme* or *maraboutage* (the choice of a French neologism is significant) and were hostile to polygamy. The Sufi orders, for their part, called the Subbanu "Rejecters," echoing passages in the Quran (21:50 and 23:69).

The Subbanu have been responsible for a number of development initiatives, including the construction of clinics; their primary schools educate a quarter of Mali's children. They have also founded more advanced colleges (*madrasa*) where Arabic is taught, and graduates go on to study either in national universities (usually in religious studies) or in Arabic-language institutions abroad.

The conflict once so evident between rival Sufi orders and between Sufi orders and the Subbanu is gradually becoming a thing of the past: "[A] new ethic of disagreement has emerged. . . . According to this doctrine, the enemy resides within oneself, and the Muslims must act on the basis of their unity rather than differences."[22] Among the Mandinka, this rapprochement is reflected in a use of the joking relationships originally applied among some categories of kin. Most Tijani now regard both Eleven Beads and Twelve Beads as acceptable. Despite this entente, mosques have proliferated, built both by competing brotherhoods and by the Subbanu. Many consider this is a tragic waste of resources in a country as poor as Mali.

Nigeria

In northern Nigeria, the Wahhabi/Sunni call the members of Sufi orders "Innovators." The "innovations" they condemn include what they regard as an excessive veneration of the Prophet, devotion to holy men, and the addition of Sufi litanies to the standard daily prayers. A Hausa Tijani poet ripostes:

Protect me from the rascally rejecter,
Who will die away there in unbelief.[23]

The pioneer of Wahhabi/Sunni ideas was the poet, nationalist, and NEPU member Sa'adu Zungur (1915–1958). He was a critic of Sufism, an advocate both of popular education and of the education of women, and an opponent of purdah and polygamy.

Abubakar Gumi (1924–1992) became the undisputed leader of the movement. He was closely associated with the Sardauna of Sokoto until the latter's murder in 1966. He was the Sardauna's interpreter in his dealings with Arab states, and became Grand Qadi (chief *sharia* judge) of the north. After his patron's death, Gumi worked for the unity of Nigerian Muslims. Like Zungur and the Sardauna, he looked back to the days of Uthman dan Fodio for inspiration. Unlike dan Fodio, however, he wished to eradicate the Sufi orders, which he saw as divisive and sectarian. He believed they advocated a withdrawal from the world, whereas what was needed was to work for the creation of a truly Islamic society. Gumi's voluminous popular writings in Hausa, including many articles in the press, and his speeches and sermons on radio and television, did much to shape Muslim opinion. He translated the Quran into Hausa, completing a task begun by Zungur. By the 1980s, supporters of Sufism, not surprisingly, had become equally vocal in the media.

In 1978, Gumi and his associates founded the movement known as 'Yan Izala (Jama'at Izalat al-Bid'a wa Iquamat al-Sunna, the Society for Suppressing Innovations and Restoring the Sunna). Its headquarters is in central Nigeria, at Jos. It members include both men and women. It is hostile not only to the Sufi orders but also to corruption, luxury, and ostentatious spending, including expensive religious celebrations. Gumi was critical of the emirs of the late twentieth century: "They had brought back to life all the corrupt practices against which Sheikh dan Fodio went to war with the former Hausa rulers. They had become kings with big palaces, full of servants and courtiers."[24] This was equally true, of course, of the politicians.

There have been many violent clashes between Tijaniyya and Qadiriyya. Their local names, *kabalu* and *sadalu*, refer to their different views on the position of the arms during prayer, which symbolize their other differences. Since 1978 there have been many clashes between Sufi supporters and 'Yan Izala. Again, mosques and imams proliferate, since each group insists on having its own place of prayer. In recent years, conflict between Muslim groups has waned, and it has been Christian-Muslim violence that has repeatedly threatened life and property in northern and central Nigeria.

MUSLIM–CHRISTIAN CONFLICT IN NIGERIA

The Nigerian civil war (Biafran War) of 1967–1970 has sometimes been interpreted as one between Muslims and Christians. It did have some religious overtones, but the alignments were primarily regional and ethnic. General Yakubu Gowon, Nigeria's head of state at the time, was a Christian from central Nigeria.

The First Republic, discredited by tribalism and corruption, was overturned in a coup in 1966. The Second Republic, destined to be equally discredited, began with the elections of 1979, after thirteen years of military rule. It ended in a coup four years later, which led to another extended period of military rule.

From the late 1970s on, religion replaced ethnicity and regionalism as the main source of division in Nigerian society. Christians became more organized and militant, a change partly linked with the growing strength of the "Born Again" movement. The Christian Association of Nigeria (CAN) was founded in 1976 as an alliance of churches rather than of individuals. Its members, among whom people from central Nigeria, and especially from Jos and Kaduna, were prominent, felt the need to respond to militancy with militancy. They feared northern and Muslim political dominance, in particular the possibility that Nigeria might become an officially Muslim state. Muslims perceived CAN as a body that sought to destroy Islam and achieve southern political dominance. From this time on, two powerful movements, CAN and 'Yan Izala, confronted one another head-on. CAN opposed government subsidies to pilgrims and advocated recognition of Israel.

Muslims claim that three-quarters of Nigeria's population is Muslim; CAN, that 71.4 million out of an estimated 117.3 million Nigerians are Christians.

Two issues in particular polarized Christians and Muslims and acquired immense symbolic significance. In the constitutional debates that preceded the Second Republic, the issue which dominated discussion above all others was the proposal to introduce a Federal Sharia Court of Appeal. To Muslims, it was important that *sharia* be entrenched in the national constitution, not simply a regional provision. To Christians, a secular state where all religions are on an equal footing was non-negotiable. The issue was defused when the proposal was withdrawn.

In 1986, the government secretly joined the Organization of the Islamic Conference. There were economic advantages to be gained, and African members included "such unlikely candidates as Benin, Gabon and Uganda, in all of which Muslims constitute only a tiny minority,"[25] but the move provoked a furious Christian backlash.

In 1987, rioting broke out in the central Nigerian town of Kafanchan. It began at the local Training College; Muslim students were enraged both by a sign that referred to "Jesus' campus" and by the Christian preaching of a former Muslim who made comments on the Quran. Eleven died, many were injured, and much property was destroyed, including a church and a mosque. Muslims in other centers mounted reprisal attacks. There were other such clashes in the years to come, some with much greater loss of life.

Maitatsine

A conflict of a quite different kind exploded in Kano in 1980, when the police attempted to arrest some followers of a man known as Maitatsine and were attacked with "hatchets, bows and arrows, swords, clubs, dane-guns, daggers and other . . . dangerous weapons."[26] Maitatsine ("anathemizer") was the nickname of Muhammad Marwa, a religious teacher and preacher originally from Cameroon. The uprising was quelled only when the army was brought in. According to official figures, over 4,000 were killed, including Maitatsine. Despite his death, the "fanatics," as they were always called in the Nigerian press, launched further uprisings that horrified Christians and Muslims alike; the last was crushed in 1985. The total death toll was at least 10,000. Much has been written on these uprisings.[27]

Maitatsine arrived in Kano in 1945. He was deported in 1962 but managed to return four years later. He had a number of brushes with the law, of the "disturber of the peace" variety, but by 1980 he had 6,000 followers in Kano alone; they occupied a whole section of the city.

Interpretations of the uprising vary, and it is not easy to disentangle fact from rumor. It is evident that Maitatsine was remarkably successful in attracting followers, and that they fought to the death fearlessly They were poor, and hence receptive to his attacks on modernity and the rich. The late 1970s was a time of great social tension; the country was flooded with oil revenues, and some accumulated vast fortunes, but the poor who flocked to the cities in search of a livelihood struggled with inflation, food shortages, and unemployment. Maitatsine condemned not only cars but even bicycles, "preaching that anyone wearing a watch, or riding a bicycle or sending his child to the normal state schools was an infidel." His followers were told to regard the rich, including rich Muslims, "with extreme abhorrence and contempt."

The Kano rising greatly embarrassed the state and national governments, both of which were dominated by Muslims. Muslims of all shades of opinion hastened to repudiate the movement—Gumi called Maitatsine "Satan." There is some evidence that Maitatsine claimed to be a prophet. This would be unacceptable to all Muslims, and it seems surprising that he could found a mass movement on this basis in a city where Islam had been firmly established for centuries. It is possible that this claim was attributed to him later, to justify the deaths of his followers.

Nigeria is a vast country, and one should not exaggerate religious violence. I lived in the northern city of Zaria in 1971 and 1972, and in Jos, in central Nigeria, from 1976 to 1985. Though I am a Christian, I had friendly relations with Muslims at the university and in many other walks of life. I knew and cared little about CAN or 'Yan Izala; my research had a completely different focus. I never experienced Muslim-Muslim or Muslim-Christian violence, though I was sometimes alarmed by rumors that proved untrue.

ISLAM AND THE POLITICIANS

North-South or Muslim-Christian conflict was far from universal. In some countries, a Christian head of state ruled for long periods over a predominantly Muslim nation.

Tanganyika became independent in 1961. Julius Nyerere, a Catholic, was its president until he chose to retire in 1985. In 1964, an African uprising overthrew the Arab ruling class in Zanzibar, which then united with Tanganyika to form Tanzania. Nyerere insisted on the exclusion of religion from the political sphere. He was succeeded by a Muslim Zanzibari, Ali Hassan Mwinyi. In 1995, when his term of office ended, Mwinyi was succeeded by a Christian. There has been a resurgence of Islamic activism, especially in Zanzibar, a Muslim island dominated by the mainland, with its strong Christian/"traditionalist" presence. But independent Tanzania, with roughly equal numbers of Muslims and Christians, has been remarkably stable, despite its overwhelming economic problems.

In Senegal, where 95 percent of the population is Muslim, another Catholic, Léopold Senghor, was president from 1960 to 1980. He formed a close alliance with Muslim leaders in general and the Sufi brotherhoods in particular:

> To respond to Muslims' expectations, a French/Arabic curriculum was offered in primary schools and classical Arabic in secondary schools, along with Latin. . . . [T]here were countless new mosques, Muslim associations and publications.[28]

Like Nyerere, Senghor was succeeded by a Muslim, Abdou Diouf.

A third Catholic, Félix Houphouet-Boigny, president of Ivory Coast from independence in 1959 until his death in 1993, also ruled in close association with the Muslims, who constituted more than half the population. After his death, a Catholic from the south, Henri Bédié, and a Muslim from the north, Alhassane Ouattara, vied to succeed him. The latter was excluded by laws, passed the following year, preventing those whose parents were not born in Ivory Coast from seeking the presidency. Ouattara's father was born in Burkina Faso, and his family was part of the Dyula diaspora. Inevitably, Ivory Coast Muslims were radicalized.

A Muslim, Sékou Touré, was head of state in Guinea from independence in 1958 until his death in 1984. Initially, his outlook was left-wing and strongly secular, hostile to any organizations, including Islamic ones, that seemed to challenge the hegemony of the ruling party. Citizens were urged to "war against the hustlers and swindlers licensed as 'marabouts'; against charlatanry, and other forms of mystification and exploitation linked to those obscurantist entities."[29] By the 1970s, Touré had become a strong supporter of Islam, a change of heart rather like Nimeiri's. He looked to Islam for legitimation, "politicising Islam and Islamicising his politics."[30] In the late 1960s, a leading Guinea politician, Dr. Louis (later Lansana) Béavogui, also became a Muslim. Albert-Bernard (later Omar) Bongo, who became president of Gabon in 1967 and is still in power in 2004, did the same in 1973.

THE WORLD WITHIN

This study has focused to a large on the relations between Islam and government, a link that has been central from Islam's beginnings, and is clearly a matter of immense importance in the contemporary world. However, at the heart of Islam is the soul's relationship with God, and there have been countless Muslim saints, both famous and unknown, who were totally indifferent to politics.

Shortly before her death in 1951, an old Hausa woman recorded the story of her life. She had married four times, but her true love was an obscure villager named Mallam Maigari:

> We made our marriage for fifteen years [1907–1922]. . . . I loved him very much, I left him because I had to—I had no children.
>   Our husband was a *malam* [scholar-teacher]; he had a school with about twenty pupils, and apart from teaching, he farmed.

In the rainy season, he worked on his farm until 2:30 P.M., when he prayed, and then held school in the "entrance hut of our compound." Boys studied there until evening, with a break for an evening meal.

> Then the elders would come and study at night. After they had gone, you would hear him come to his sleeping hut, he would light the lamp and continue studying far into the night.[31]

In the dry season, he traveled with his large household to other towns, and taught there.

Cerno Bokar Salif Taal was another village schoolmaster. He was a Fulbe (Tukulor), the great-grandson of al-Hajj Umar. He inherited the names

Cerno Bokar (Abu Bakr) from his grandfather. Cerno is a Fulfulde honorific for a learned man, like *mallam* in Hausa. He was born in Segu, but spent most of his life in the Dogon town of Bandiagara. He was a noted Sufi who ran a school and imparted spiritual teachings to disciples who included a number of *évolués* who later played a prominent role in the affairs of independent Africa. He emphasized the essential unity of all religions and warned his followers that riches are like rubbish which the wind blows from place to place.[32] When a fledgling fell from its nest and his students failed to rescue it, he blamed them for their hardness of heart.

In 1937, he made a solitary journey to Nioro, to visit Hamahu'llah, and accepted him as his sheikh. He had much to lose and nothing to gain by giving allegiance to a teacher whom the French distrusted and his Umarian relatives saw as a heterodox rival. He accepted Hamahu'llah as his teacher because he recognized his holiness. He spent his last months in isolation, and his trials shortened his life. But then truth, as he had told his students, "is a darkness more brilliant than all lights combined."

PART III

Christianity in Africa since ca. 500

Chapter 10

Christianity from ca. 500 to ca. 1800

I am a Catholic Prince and desire the accomplishment of my salvation.
—Antonio III of Soyo (a coastal province of Kongo; 1701)[1]

In the centuries that separate the world of late antiquity from the nineteenth-century missionary revival, it was only in Egypt and Ethiopia that Christianity had the continuous history characteristic of Islam. *Cuius regio eius religio* (the ruler chooses the religion) was an aphorism applied to sixteenth-century Europe that was equally true of Africa. In the two sub-Saharan states where Christianity lasted for centuries, the kingdom of Kongo in central Africa and Warri in the western Niger Delta, it survived almost entirely because of royal support.

There are many recorded debates between Christians and Muslims, Christians and traditionalists, and Western and Orthodox Christians. They are usually recorded by the Western Christian participant, and tend to be not intellectual encounters but attempts to convert the other—a book by a sixteen-century Jesuit is titled *The Primacy of Rome and the Errors of the Ethiopians*!

Frequently, Western Christians did not get the best of these encounters. In the 1820s, a British explorer visited Muhammad Bello in Sokoto and was nonplussed when he was asked whether he was a Nestorian or a Socinian! Protestant missionaries in nineteenth-century Ethiopia had similar problems. One described how an Ethiopian "put several questions to me, on the nature of God—on the manner of the Union of the Divinity with the humanity in the person of Christ, etc. but they were all questions too obscure for me to be able satisfactorily to reply to them."[2]

Virtually all those who have become Christians in Africa were previously traditionalists, not Muslims. Even in the twentieth century, when Christianity was the faith of colonial rulers and closely linked with the Western education that opened the way to life-changing opportunities, Africa's Muslims stayed true to their faith. A few Muslims have been drawn to Christianity and have made important contributions to their adopted religion. Enbaqom in the sixteenth century is an example, as is Lamin Sanneh in the twentieth.

There are parallels between Africa's Christian and Muslim histories. Mystics in the different traditions have often recognized how close they are to each other. A ruler like the sixteenth-century Kongo king, Afonso, devoting his evenings to prayer and study, has countless Muslim counterparts. In the twentieth century, women who founded prophetic churches spent their days in prayer and seclusion, while a husband or son ran the organization. The Mouride woman sheikh Sokhna Magat Diop did the same. Twentieth-century Muslim and Christian preachers attracted converts though the hope of healing and protection in this life and of salvation in the next. The traditionalists on the southern border of Christian Ethiopia and on the edge of the Sokoto caliphate had much in common, too.

CONTINUITIES: ETHIOPIA

The Ethiopian church survived, but its members found themselves in an unrecognizably different world. At the time of the Nine Saints, Aksum was part of a vast Christian continuum that included Egypt and Nubia, parts of Arabia, Syria, and Anatolia (now Turkey.) The spread of Islam left Ethiopian Christianity isolated. Aksum declined, though it kept its ritual preeminence and kings were still crowned there, but the center of gravity of the Christian kingdom was farther south.

In the 1970s, the Ethiopian church had 250,000 clergy, including not only priests but also deacons and musical specialists (*dabtara*). There were 10 million Christians, 15,000 churches, 800 monasteries, and 15,000 monks. There was one cleric for every forty Christians. The ratio in Dublin at the same time was 1:947.

Priests, but not monks, are allowed to marry, provided they do so before ordination. Their role is a ritual one: three are needed to say Mass. They are often men of limited education who earn their own living. Each church, even the smallest, is divided into three sections: one for laymen, one for women, and the Holy of Holies, where the Ark is kept (only priests may enter it).

Ethiopians keep fasts of great severity; laypeople fast 150 days a year, and the clergy, 270. On these days they eat only one meal, after noon, and abstain from foods of animal origin. Ethiopian Christians are rebaptized each year. All Ethiopians had a strong sense of the reality of evil, and the monks did battle with devils. Polygamy formerly was common, especially among the nobility, though it was forbidden to priests. Kings traditionally had three wives, a practice monks denounced regularly. Some were imprisoned or exiled for their pains.

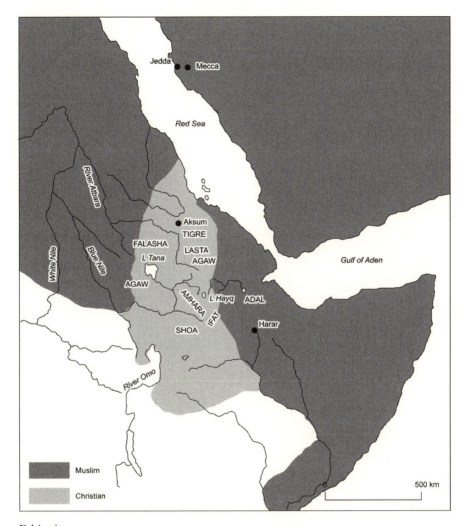

Ethiopia.

It was the monasteries that were the real powerhouse of Ethiopian Christianity, and the monks, who were celibates and ascetics, were missionaries, teachers, chroniclers, and healers. Whereas the Copts built their monasteries in the desert, Ethiopians chose mountaintops or islands. Lake Hayq was famous for its monasteries.

The monks created and transcribed a great deal of literature, including the lives of saints (who are for the most part unknown outside Ethiopia). The most popular non-Ethiopian saint was Saint George. Their labors preserved some important books that survive elsewhere only in fragments. The Book of Enoch is a Jewish source from the first or second century B.C.E.

that is quoted in the New Testament (Jude 14–15). Over thirty manuscripts survive in Ge'ez, and there are fragments in other languages.[3]

Ethiopia developed a distinctive form of Christianity with strong Hebraic elements. There was a sense that Ethiopia was the heir of ancient Israel, a chosen nation. Both the Sabbath (Saturday) and Sunday were kept holy. Each had its impassioned advocates, and a compromise was reached in the mid-fifteenth century. Ethiopian Christians followed the dietary rules of Leviticus, such as the avoidance of pork, a practice that was to be typical of many African Initiated Churches in the twentieth century. Baby boys were circumcized on the eighth day. Only Jews and Coptic Christians do likewise. Every Ethiopian church has an Ark of the Covenant, a copy of an original in Aksum.

The identification with Israel has been explained in different ways. The Ethiopians themselves believe that they were once Jews. The legend of the so-called Solomonic monarchy was first recorded in the fourteenth century, in a book called *The Glory of Kings*, which was translated from Arabic, but the tradition was much older. Solomon and the Queen of Sheba are said to have had a son, Menelik. He took the Ark of the Covenant to Aksum (the original Raider of the Lost Ark) and was the ancestor of later Ethiopian kings. Because it has the Ark, Ethiopia is Zion.

The early inscriptions of the first Christian king of Aksum, however, show that he initially worshiped the divinities of south Arabia. It is more likely that Ethiopian Christians were drawn to elements in the Hebrew Bible, such as circumcision and ritual prohibitions, that were close to aspects of their traditional culture. It is also probable that the centuries of beleaguered isolation fostered a sense of identification with ancient Israel, which had been surrounded by enemies.

The earliest Christians had different views about the relationship between the Old and New Dispensations. The Ethiopians, like the Jewish Christians of Jerusalem, argued for a high level of continuity. Zara Ya'iqob (Seed of Jacob), who was Negus Negast (king of kings, or emperor) from 1434 to 1468 and wrote eight books on theology,[4] pointed out that Jesus said he had come not to abolish the Law, but to fulfill it (Matthew 5:17–19).

Sheba is Sabaea, a historic state in what is now Yemen. Sabaean immigrants settled in Aksum from about the third century B.C.E. on. (This is why the Aksumites worshiped the gods of south Arabia.) Their language is ancestral to the Semitic languages of northern Ethiopia: Amharic, Tigre, and Tigrinya. The Solomonic legend was intended to bolster the authority of kings from this ethnolinguistic cluster, based in Shoa, who seized power in 1270. They were preceded by Cushitic-speaking kings, the Zagwe, whose base was in Lasta. The greatest of them, Lalibela (1182–1221), had eleven churches hewn out of solid rock, one of the archaeological marvels of the world. He was trying to re-create Jerusalem in his own land, 150 miles south of Aksum.

During the coronation ceremony, the new ruler was rejected when he called himself king of Ethiopia, and accepted when he called himself king of Zion.

The warrior king Amda-Siyon (Pillar of Zion; 1314–1344) was the architect of the Ethiopian state, a highland kingdom inextricably linked with Christianity, Amharic language and culture, literacy in Ge'ez, and plow cultivation. Its cultural hegemony was extended and consolidated by missionary monks. To the pagans of the south, Christianity often seemed the ideology of conquest. Zara Ya'iqob declared, "Whoever kills pagans has committed no sin." In the late seventeenth century, Yohannes devastated the Agaw countryside. "Then every Agaw who lives in the middle of Sikut . . . was terrified, took refuge at a church . . . and said . . . , 'I shall become Christian and submit to the king and pay tribute and I shall do whatever the king orders me to do.'"[5] Ironically, the Agaw now venerate the memory of Yohannes the Saint.

Some Ethiopian Christians insisted that the Kingdom of Heaven was not to be found in any earthly state, but within. A monk named Estifanos (Stephen; 1397–1444) was flogged and exiled because he refused to prostrate himself before the king, saying that this should be done only before God. He was accused of denying Mount Zion, and replied, "I do not say that there is no Mount Zion, for those who purify their hearts and bear the yoke of Christ's Gospel will find it." He opposed excessive devotion to the Cross and to Mary.[6] He had much in common with the fourteenth-century English reformer John Wycliffe.

When the Prophet said, "You will find the Christians nearest in affection to you" (Quran 5:82), he was referring to the Ethiopians who had aided some of his followers when they were fleeing from Mecca. But Christian-Muslim relations changed gradually from peaceful coexistence to a state of hostility that was at least partly ecological in origin. Muslims living in the arid lowlands near the Red Sea were inevitably drawn to the well-watered highlands. In 1529, a jihad broke out, led by a young man from Adal, the imam Ahmad, who was only twenty-three. Ethiopians called him el Gragn (the Left-handed). Devout, fearless, and a born leader, he is a good example of the way in which a single individual can rewrite history. His forces overran Ethiopia, burning monasteries and churches, including Aksum's cathedral. Many monks chose to die in the flames. The precious contents of monastic libraries were burned to ashes.

The imam set up his capital at Lake Tana and offered the king an alliance, which he declined. In 1535 the latter sent a letter to Portugal, asking for reinforcements and technical aid. A contingent of 400 soldiers arrived seven years later. The imam also called for foreign reinforcements and won an initial victory, but in 1543 he was killed in battle, and the Muslim alliance he had built died with him. The Christian kingdom was restored, the churches and monasteries were rebuilt, Christians who had become Muslims returned to their first allegiance, and the manuscripts were recopied. An enterprising monk tackled the problem of lost manuscripts by setting out for Rome, where he found printing facilities.

Enbaqom was an Arab convert to Christianity who reached Ethiopia in the 1490s and lived there for many years as a monk. He attempted to convert the imam Ahmed by writing a book in Arabic, which he later translated into Ge'ez, in which he quoted the Quran from memory. He claimed that the Christian scriptures are international, having been translated into all the world's known languages, whereas the Quran is linked solely with Arabic. He also suggested that both Jewish and Muslim sacred texts contain prescriptions for waging just war. There is nothing of this kind in Jesus' teachings, which are also morally superior because they were written for the poor.[7]

When Vasco da Gama reached India in 1498, he said that he had come in search of Christians and spices. Stories of a mysterious Christian king in Africa, called Prester John, probably grew out of meetings with Ethiopian monks and pilgrims in Jerusalem during the Crusades. Ethiopian Christians have always been drawn to the holy city, and there has been an Ethiopian church there since at least the thirteenth century. Christians from Western Europe sought an ally in a war with a common enemy, Islam. (Projects often mooted, but never accomplished, included diverting the headwaters of the Nile). But Ethiopia was treated not as an ally or an equal, but as a mission field. Ethiopia's kings were torn between the desire for European military assistance, on the one hand, and fear of the threat to their religion and independence, on the other.

Galawdewos (Claudius) succeeded to the throne in 1540, at the age of eighteen. At the age of thirty-seven, four years before he died in battle, he wrote his *Confession of Faith*.[8] Less than three pages long in English translation, it begins with a declaration of faith in Christ and the Trinity, and goes on to defend the aspects of Ethiopian church life that Catholic missionaries condemned: the celebration of the Sabbath, the avoidance of pork, and circumcision. They are, he says, simply matters of local custom and dietary preference. Had Latin Christians accepted this view, the Ethiopian church might well, like the Maronite church in Lebanon, have affiliated with Rome.

Pedro Paez was one of a band of remarkable Jesuits who realized the importance of incarnating Christianity in the local culture. Matteo Ricci, who worked in China from 1583 until his death in 1610, and Roberto de Nobili, active in India from 1605 to 1656, learned the local language, immersed themselves in the host culture, and showed a prophetic awareness of the need to separate Christianity from a European packaging. Paez was sent to Ethiopia in 1589, but was captured by pirates in the Red Sea. He toiled in the galleys for seven years, finally reaching his destination, undaunted, in 1603. He soon learned to read and write Ge'ez and Amharic, and converted King Susenyos and some of his kinsmen and courtiers. Susenyos openly declared himself a Catholic in 1622; Paez died in the same year, and his successors, lacking his tact and wisdom, opposed cultural practices that were, from a religious viewpoint, neutral (such as the prohibition of pork consumption), while insisting on the Latin calendar and liturgy. They ordered the rebaptism of all Ethiopian Christians, and the reconsecration of priests and altars. There was a huge outbreak of popular opposition, and Susenyos abdicated in 1632, having restored his people to their ancient allegiance. The missionaries were expelled, and the episode left a long heritage of mistrust of Western Christianity.

A new court was established at Gondar, near Lake Tana; it would later be the scene of protracted and impassioned Christological controversy. There was talk of a great future king named Tewedros (Theodore), who would restore strength, peace, and unity to Ethiopia.

The Jesuits paid tribute to the quality of Ethiopian religious life even while they tried to change it. One of them wrote, in the seventeenth century:

> No country in the world is so full of churches, monastries, and ecclesiasticks as Abyssinia; it is not possible to sing in one church or monastry without being heard by another, and perhaps by several. . . . The instruments of musick made use of in their rites of worship, are little drums, which they hang about their necks and beat with both their hands. . . . They have sticks likewise with which they strike the ground, . . . when they have heated themselves by degrees, they leave off druming and fall to leaping, dancing and clapping their hands. . . . They are possess'd with a strange notion, that they are the only true Christians in the world.[9]

Ethiopian higher education fell into three divisions: the House of Music, the House of Poetry, and the House of Reading. Tradition claims that Ethiopia's church music and musical notation date from a sixth-century deacon who heard a choir of angels singing and, with great presence of mind, kept a record. Poetry was always sung, and was often symbolic and elliptical, like this tribute to Takla Haymanot (Tree of Faith), who founded the Solomonic dynasty: "The tree Takla Haymanot has been sanctified because the waters cover him with the warm tears of his weeping."[10]

The Falashas, who call themselves Beta Israel (House of Israel), are black Jews who have practiced their faith in Ethiopia for many centuries. They, too, believe that their fellow Ethiopians were Jews before they were Christians, and consider themselves heirs to this ancient tradition. They first appear in written records in the fourteenth century C.E., but this does not mean, of course, that their history began then.

The Falashas were often persecuted by the Christian kings. Zara Ya'iqob's titles included Exterminator of the Jews, but some Christians joined the Falashas, and vice versa. Their faith is based on the Pentateuch, the first five books of the Hebrew Bible. They do not have the Talmud, the vast rabbinical commentary gradually compiled by the Jews of the Diaspora after the second fall of Jersusalem in 70 C.E. Like Ethiopian Christians, but unlike Jews elsewhere, they practice monasticism. By 1983, it was estimated that there were only 30,000 Falashas. In recent years, many have settled in Israel.

THE COPTIC CHURCH IN EGYPT

In the late fourth century, virtually all Egyptians were Christians. They remained a majority in Egypt until the tenth century and then declined to a minority, mainly as a result of successive waves of Arab immigration, but also in response to heavy taxes and sporadic persecutions.

Language and religion, though often linked, are quite distinct. A decree of 705 made Arabic compulsory for government records, and the Copts became bilingual. At the end of the tenth century, most Egyptian Christians still spoke Coptic. Two centuries later, the patriarch of Alexandria found it necessary to urge priests to recite the Lord's Prayer in Arabic. As Coptic gave way to Arabic, the Copts made great efforts to preserve their language and history, and built up a rich store of Christian literature in Arabic. *The History of the Patriarchs of the Coptic Church of Alexandria*, which begins with Saint Mark, was written in Arabic from Coptic sources, completed in 1102, and later updated. "Copt," which had once meant Egyptian, now meant Christian. Coptic has remained the language of the liturgy, as Latin used to be in the Catholic Church.

Nearly all of the 281 men and women listed in the Coptic *Lives of the Saints*, the *Synaxarium,* are martyrs, monks, or hermits from before the sixth century. A history by a noted Coptic Christian scholar devotes seventy-one pages to the period ending with the Arab invasion, and twenty-four to the 1,160 years from then to Napoleon's arrival. His account of the earlier period is dominated by theologians, martyrs, monks, and hermits. In the period of Muslim rule, he concentrates on government policies toward Christians and the role of Coptic administrators, tax collectors, and other professionals, such as the two architects who designed Cairo's citadel for Saladin.[11] Some individuals continued the heroics of the desert ascetics, among them Barsum the Naked (d. 1317), a man from a wealthy family who lived for twenty years on brine and beans in the damp, dark crypt of a Cairo church. Fortunately, there are other paths to God.

The Crusades were a trial for the Copts, who remained neutral. They tended to be suspect as a potential fifth column, and were forced to contribute heavily to Egyptian war costs. Their prosperity and their role as tax collectors made them unpopular with the Muslim masses. However, Muslims and Copts also joined in celebrating joyful festivals, such as the ceremonies surrounding the breaching and closure of the irrigation dams, which date back to the pharaohs. The Copts identified the closing of the dams with the feast of Jesus' baptism. In 942, the sultan ordered the bank of the island and the bank of el-Fustat to be illuminated each with a thousand torches, beside private illuminations. Muslims and Christians, by hundreds of thousands, crowded the Nile on boats, . . . or on the banks, all eager for pleasure, and vying in equipage, dress, gold and silver cups and jewellery. The sound of music was heard all about, with singing and dancing.[12]

Less than a hundred years later, Christians and Jews endured al-Hakim's dreadful persecution. The dilemma of the Copts was that they had no independent power base.

The number of bishops declined. According to one estimate, there were 100 in 600 and 40 in 1400.[13] There are now 25 in Egypt and 3 outside its borders. Of course the vitality of a church is not to be judged by the number of its sees—they reflect demography and financial resources. Monasticism, however, had been at the heart of the Coptic way, and its decline was significant, especially since nearly all bishops, including the Ethiopian Abuna, were chosen from the monks.

Copts, like Ethiopians, have a great devotion to the Cross and to Mary; in both churches, the latter has thirty-two feast days a year. Rural Copts and rural Ethiopians sometimes tattoo the Cross on their forehead or on a wrist. The Coptic Cross (al-Salib) is woven on textiles, and painted or carved on the walls of homes. In 1954, a Coptic delegation attended a meeting of the World Council of Churches in Illinois. The "newcomers," who received a warm welcome, replied that they had been members until 451, when they decided to withdraw!

CHRISTIAN KINGDOMS IN SUB-SAHARAN AFRICA

In 1443, Portuguese caravels sailing along the coastline of the western Sahara came to Cape Blanco, where the white desert sands contrasted with the vegetation of Cape Verde, farther south. In 1471, the Portuguese reached what would become the Gold Coast (and is now part of Ghana). In 1484, they anchored off the mouth of the Congo (Zaire) River. In 1498, Vasco da Gama and his men, having circumnavigated Africa, reached Goa, guided by a pilot from Malindi, on the Swahili coast. The very process of exploration was linked with hostility toward Islam: the quest for Christian allies and the desire for direct access to Asian spices, bypassing Muslim middlemen.

This journey and that of Columbus, six years earlier, marked the beginning of an era when Europeans came into direct contact with the civilizations of the Americas and sub-Saharan Africa for the first time. Their visits to Asia, hitherto confined to rare overland travelers such as Marco Polo, became far more frequent, and the economies of water transport revolutionized the visits' economic significance. European adventurers traveled in search of wealth and empire, rather than converts, but in this new world of global

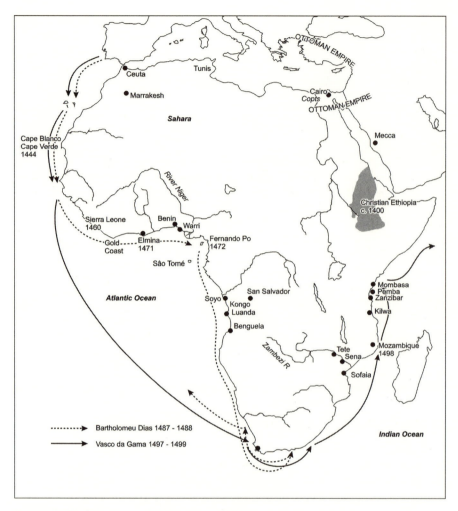

Portugal, Christianity, and Africa to c. 1600.

culture contacts, Christianity again became truly international, as it had been in its beginnings.

The religious ideas of African and Portuguese villagers had a good deal in common in the sixteenth century and, indeed, much later. There was a benevolent but remote High God, as well as a multiplicity of spiritual beings who were nature spirits or ancestors in Africa, and saints and angels in Portugal. Both groups paid much reverence to visible emblems of the sacred: crucifixes, statues, or relics in Portugal, and *nkissi* (ritual objects) among the Kongo.

Most Europeans came to Africa to trade, especially to trade in slaves; there was, of course, an inherent contradiction between converting Africans and buying them, though one of the arguments slavers put forward in their own defense was that captives would become Christians in the New World! European merchants named regions after the commodities they sought: the Slave Coast, the Gold Coast, Ivory Coast (still the name of a modern nation). The first Portuguese settlement on the Gold Coast was Elmina (the mine).

Inevitably, each European nation that became involved in ocean trade brought its own Christian and cultural tradition—Catholicism, in the case of Portugal. A papal concession of 1514, the *padroado,* which lasted into the twentieth century, gave the Portuguese crown control of the church in its overseas possessions. This was an ongoing source of weakness. Portugal, with a population of a million, could not supply clergy in adequate numbers to its far-flung possessions, and for long periods excluded foreigners, such as Spanish Capuchins. There were not yet religious orders specifically devoted to missionary work, though many of the most zealous missionaries were members of existing orders, especially the Capuchins (a reformed branch of the Franciscans) and the Jesuits.

Because of its emphasis on the sacraments, Catholicism is, like Ethiopian Christianity, especially reliant on its priesthood. In a mission field such as the kingdom of Kongo, a village would not see a priest for years, and when one finally appeared, he would conduct mass marriages and baptisms. Not all the priests were European missionaries. Some Africans, and men of mixed European and African descent, were trained in Europe or in seminaries established in São Tomé, Luanda, and elsewhere. Some Catholic missionaries were Goans from India. Would-be priests had to commit themelves to celibacy and years of study, and to master both Latin and Portuguese.

But in the two states where Christianity took deepest root and lasted longest, it did so because of the devotion of the laity, especially royals and aristocrats. They, too, learned to read and write a foreign language. In the long period of Kongo Christianity, the only book translated into kiKongo was not the Bible, but the Catholic catechism. (European Catholics at the time and much later were not encouraged to read the Bible, either.) Sanneh has argued that "Christianity in Africa has been characterised by a vigourous vernacular process from the period of the earliest Christians on the continent."[14] This was not the case in the period covered by this chapter, even in Egypt and Ethiopia, where Coptic and Ge'ez were no longer living languages. In sub-Saharan Africa, with the exception of the Kongo catechism, Christians read sacred texts in Latin or not at all.

In Africa, as in Europe, the religious adherence of the ruler was all important in determining that of his subjects. In 1623, Yusuf became sultan of the Muslim state of Mombasa on the Swahili coast. He had studied in Goa, where he became a Catholic and was baptized as Jerónimo. Later he returned to Islam, and led a revolt against the Portuguese in 1631, in the course of which a number of African and Portuguese Christians were killed. He died in exile.

In Warri and Kongo, the conversion of a king was to have lasting consequences.

Warri

Warri was a tiny state in the mangrove swamps of the western Niger Delta. In the 1570s, Catholic missionaries from São Tomé converted the heir to the throne. Baptized as Sebastian, he remained a devoted Christian for the rest of his long life. He sent his eldest son to Portugal to train for the priesthood, but the boy decided that his calling lay elsewhere, and returned with a Portuguese bride. Christianity was strongest at the court and in the capital, which was named after Saint Augustine. In 1620, it was said:

> Outside the small town of Santo Agostinho there are no other Christians: and even in the town only a minority are of the Catholic faith. Although very many of them are nominally Christian, true Christianity is almost wholly confined to the King and the Prince.[15]

For long periods, Warri Catholics had no priests. A bishop of São Tomé explained, in 1597, that this was because the area was unhealthy for Europeans and "very poor," so that "clergy would be unable to live there in reasonable comfort."[16] Nevertheless, Warri Christianity survived until the mid-eighteenth century, when a king turned against it during a long drought. But in the late eighteenth century, when the reigning king had sixty wives, there was still a chapel in the palace and a wooden cross at the crossroads.[17]

Kongo

Today there are some 3 million Kongo living in the two nations of that name (one formerly Zaire) and in Angola. Here, too, Christianity was established, and survived, because of decisive and wholehearted royal support. In 1491, the king was baptized as João. He soon returned to the religion of his ancestors, but his son, Mbemba Nzinga (Afonso), who was a provincial governor at the time, remained a committed Christian. Afonso became king after a civil war with a traditionalist brother, and reigned from 1506 to 1545. Soon after becoming king, he sent his son Henrique, who was still a boy, to study for the priesthood in Portugal. He returned as a bishop (though not of Kongo[18]), but suffered from ill health and depression, and died in his thirties. The first bishop of Kongo was a Portuguese. There would not be another black bishop in western central Africa until 1970. The Kongo capital became São Salvador.

In 1516, a Portuguese priest who knew Afonso well wrote:

> . . . his Christian life is such that he appears to me not as a man but as an angel sent by the Lord to the kingdom to convert it . . . he does nothing but study

and . . . many times he falls asleep over his books. . . . He studies the Holy Gospel and when the priest finishes the mass he asks for benediction. When he has received it, he begins to preach to the people with great skill and great charity.[19]

Outside the Islamic world, Afonso is the only sixteenth-century person from sub-Saharan Africa who speaks to us in his own voice. In a series of letters dictated to a Kongo secretary, he asked for what we would now call development aid. He laments the havoc wrought by the slave trade and states that the Kongo needs not consumer goods, to be paid for with captives, but only priests and education, including technical education. These letters are among the most moving records from the African past. The tendency to idealize Afonso has bred a reaction among some historians, but there is little real evidence to substantiate a more cynical view, and foreign observers did not praise all Kongo kings.

Christianity became deeply entrenched among the Kongo elite. They took Portuguese titles of nobility, such as marquis, and Christian baptismal names, and were literate in Portuguese.

For a long time, Christianity was largely confined to the capital. From 1645 on, Capuchins worked in the Kongo. Notable for their zeal and self-sacrifice, they did much to spread Christianity in the countryside. Many died in Kongo or were invalided back to Europe; the concerns expressed by the bishop of São Tomé were very real ones. But Christianity was sustained by the work of Kongo lay catechists.

In 1571, the Portuguese established a colony in Angola,[20] which deflected much foreign trade away from Kongo. In 1665, the king of Kongo and many of his nobility were killed at the battle of Ambuila, fighting against invading forces from Angola. Among the dead was the king's métis cousin, the Capuchin Manuel Roboredo. The kingdom never recovered from this defeat. In 1681, a Portuguese historian wrote, "We will say how our lord punished this kingdom which was so catholic. [It] is a pity and heartache to see how this new Christianity of the Kongo was retarded."[21]

In Africa before 1800, and indeed much later, "missionary" meant a male missionary. Christian history in the period covered by this chapter is dominated by men: kings, clergy, and catechists. In Ethiopia, Claudius's grandmother, Eleni, served twice as regent. His mother, Sabla Wangel, not only was active in organizing opposition to the imam Ahmad, but also tended the wounded on the battlefield. These powerful royal women served their dynasty and country well, but have no obvious place in a history of religion. Nevertheless, a Kongo woman named Vita Kimpa, baptized as Beatrice, was in some ways the precursor of women leaders in twentieth-century African Initiated Churches.

In 1704, when she was about twenty, she claimed to have died and been resurrected as Saint Anthony. (Why Saint Anthony? He was a Franciscan, like the Capuchins.) She taught that Jesus was born in Kongo and was baptized in the Congo River. Like an African Joan of Arc, she urged the king to return to his abandoned capital. When a Capuchin asked her if there are Kongo in Heaven, and if they remain black, she replied wisely that there were indeed, but that there is no color in Heaven. She was burned at the stake by the Portuguese in 1706, as was the father of her baby. The child was spared. Three years later, the Kongo king returned to his capital.

The eighteenth century was a time of decline in Kongo Christianity. This was the age of the Enlightenment in Europe, when missionary zeal was unfashionable. From 1750 to 1777, the anticlerical Marquis de Pombal was in power in Portugal; he deported the Jesuits and was actively hostile to foreign missions. Often there was only a single priest in the Kongo state, which was by now in a weakened and fragmented condition. Christianity survived through the steadfast devotion of some of the provincial rulers, and especially through Kongo catechists.

The Gold Coast

Portugal and Catholicism dominate the history of Western Christianity in sub-Saharan Africa in this period, but there was also a Protestant presence on the Gold Coast.

In 1493, the pope divided Africa, Asia, and the New World between Spain and Portugal. The dividing line was in the mid-Atlantic, 1,770 kilometers west of the Cape Verde Islands. (This gave Brazil to Portugal.) Not surprisingly, other nations disregarded this—especially, after the Reformation, Protestant nations. The Gold Coast was one of the few areas in tropical Africa where Europeans established permanent settlements, the so-called forts that were better called prisons because they were holding pens for slaves. The nations with forts in the area at different times included France, England, Holland, Denmark, and Brandenberg. Some Protestant clergy worked there as chaplains to the forts rather than as missionaries. These pockets of cultural interaction produced a small number of highly educated black Christians, forerunners of the African academics and professionals who now contribute so much in the United States, Britain, and elsewhere.

Philip Quaque, a Fante, was a protégé of Thomas Thompson, Africa's first Anglican missionary. Educated in Britain, Quaque worked as a clergyman in Cape Coast for fifty years, until his death in 1816. Christian Protten, who died in 1769, was a métis Moravian missionary, educated in Denmark. Jacobus Capitein (1717–1747) was educated in Holland; ironically, he wrote a defense of the slave trade in Latin.

These men and others like them were marginal in the African societies from which they sprang and had little long-term influence. Often, in the long years abroad, they forgot their own language or came to speak it imperfectly. They were often lonely and unhappy.

THE CHRISTIAN CAPTIVE AS ABOLITIONIST

In the early 1680s, a black or métis Brazilian named Lourenço da Silva reached Rome with a petition from an African confraternity (association of Catholic laymen) in Portugal.[22] It protested the enslavement of baptized Christians and their descendants; detailed their sufferings, which often drove them to suicide; and asked that those who bought or sold Christians be excommunicated. The Congregation for the Propagation of the Faith urged the papal nuncios (ambassadors) in Spain and Portugal to persuade the crown to outlaw the inhumane treatment of slaves. No practical consequences followed, because the vested interests that profited from the slave trade were so powerful. Lourenço was protesting the enslavement of Christians, not slavery, but he did so at considerable personal risk and sacrifice. He chose to light a candle rather than curse the dark.

Olaudah Equiano (1745–1797), a western Igbo, was kidnapped and enslaved as a child. He became a seaman, acquired an education, and ultimately saved enough money to buy his freedom. A devout Evangelical who went through a life-changing conversion experience, he settled in England, where he wrote his autobiography and became actively involved in both the antislavery movement and the plans for the Sierra Leone settlement. Another former slave living in London, a Fante named Ottobah Cuguano, was also involved in the antislavery movement, and in 1787 wrote a book titled *Thoughts and Sentiments on the Evils of Slavery.*

Twice Equiano offered to work in Africa, either as an ordained missionary or for the Sierra Leone Company. Twice, he was turned down. But his autobiography was a best-seller. It is often reprinted and is still widely read. It ends with the words "'I early accustomed myself to look for the hand of God in the minutest occurrence. . . . After all, what makes any event important unless by its observation we become better and wiser and learn 'to do justly, to love mercy, and to walk humbly before God'?"[23]

BLACK NEW WORLD CHRISTIANS

Black Christians from the New World thread their way though Africa's Christian history. The so-called Nova Scotians were originally "black Loyalists" who fought on the British side in the War of Independence, in return for the promise of freedom and land. To do this, they first had to escape from slavery. When the war ended, some were enslaved again, but others were resettled in Nova Scotia. Not only was it bitterly cold there, but often they waited in vain for their land. One of their number took their grievances to London, and they were offered the chance of settlement in Sierra Leone. Some chose to stay in Canada, but 1,190 set sail for Africa in 1792.

Their history is one of dauntless courage—they accepted the dangers inherent in escaping from slavery, fighting their former masters, and settling successively in two unfamiliar and exceptionally difficult environments. Most were ardent Christians: Methodists, Baptists, or members of a Methodist splinter group called the Countess of Huntingdon's Connection. They were not the first black settlers in Sierra Leone; they had been preceded by a small and disastrously unsuccessful settlement in 1787. Their faith gave the Nova Scotians confidence and social cohesion. In the words of the son of one of them:

> They arrived at Sierra Leone at the most trying and sickly season of the year—
> the approach of the rainy season—without the least shelter being afforded them,
> many being very sick at the time of their landing. Many died during the voy-
> age.... [T]hey all disembarked, and marched towards the thick forest, with
> the Holy Bible, and their preachers (all coloured men) before them, singing
> the hymn . . .
> Awake! And sing the song
> Of Moses and the Lamb,
> Wake! Every heart and every tongue
> To praise the Saviour's name.[24]

Many died in the first year of settlement. But the survivors created role models for the much larger number of liberated Africans who were landed in Freetown during the first decades of the nineteenth century and whose influence ultimately spread far beyond it.

By 1800, Christianity seemed almost, but not quite, extinct in Kongo. It had vanished in other places where it either had taken root or had once seemed about to do so. Foreign missionaries seldom lived long in tropical Africa, for they were exposed to a new environment with the causes and cures for its diseases still unknown. Indigenous Catholic priests had to commit themselves to celibacy and learn not one but several foreign languages. All this was equally true in the nineteenth century. What changed was that there was a major missionary revival, which was closely linked with the Evangeli-cal movement. However, most of those who spread Christianity effectively were to be not Europeans, but their African converts.

Chapter 11

Christianity in the Nineteenth Century

We accepted the Word of God in our youth . . . but we did not know all that was coming behind it.

—the Thlaping (southern Tswana; 1878)[1]

It is one of the mysteries of church history that Christians at some times and places, but not at others, have felt that it was an overriding duty to obey the precept to preach the Gospel to all nations. The Nestorian Church created a remarkable network of churches in Persia, Arabia, and beyond. Its missionaries had reached China by 635.[2] Augustine was more concerned with his (Christian) Donatist neighbors than with the "pagans" of Algeria's southern steppes.

In the sixteenth and seventeenth centuries, Catholic missionary work had flourished. The great Jesuit, Saint Francis Xavier, who died in 1552, was a missionary in both India and Japan. We have seen how Jesuits worked in Ethiopia and Capuchins in the Kongo—both orders served in many other mission fields as well, though neither was founded for this purpose. Protestant churches had relatively little missionary outreach, though there were exceptions. John Wesley advised a would-be missionary, "You have nothing at present to do in Africa. Convert the heathen in Scotland." When William Carey advocated foreign missions to his fellow Baptists, he was told, "Sit down, young man. When it pleases God to convert the Heathen, He'll do it without your help or mine."

In the eighteenth century, Catholic involvement in foreign missions declined. This was linked to some extent with a changing climate of opinion. The thinkers of the Enlightenment, such as Voltaire, glorified human reason and were hostile to religion, which they equated with superstition. The French Revolution and the wars associated with it had a catastrophic effect

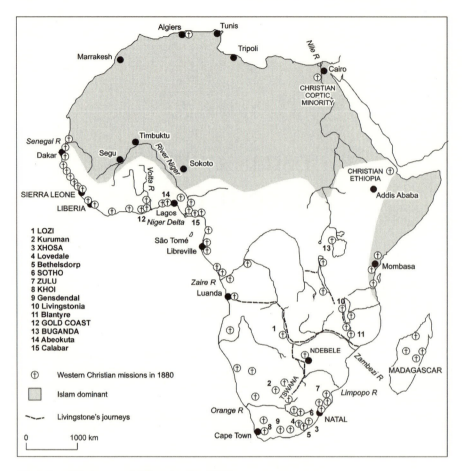

Christian Missions and Islam in the 1880s.

on the Catholic Church and the religious orders. Some orders ceased to exist, and those that survived did so with a much diminished membership. There, was, however, to be a great resurgence of missionary activity, first among Protestants, especially in Britain, and then among Catholics.

In the Protestant case, the growth of a strong interest in foreign missions was closely linked with Evangelical Christianity and the antislavery movement. What Evangelicals had in common was a belief in salvation by faith and in the necessity of a personal conversion experience, and a strong conviction that, in the words of Hannah More, a pioneer of the Sunday school movement, "Action is the life of virtue and the world is the theatre of action."

In theory, at least, the doctrine that one is saved by (Christian) faith implied that only Christians would be saved. Clearly, a belief that the heathen were in danger of perishing provided an extremely strong motive to convert them, though views of this kind did not always survive encounters with actual "traditionalists," and had become less prevalent by the late nineteenth century. There was no possible answer to the often repeated question, "My forefathers were living at the same time yours were, and how is it they did not send them word about these terrible things sooner?"[3]

An Evangelical or Catholic concern for the salvation of souls tended to go with a strong hostility to other faiths. A famous hymn by an Anglican bishop about a Ceylon he had never visited runs as follows:

In vain with lavish kindness
The gifts of God are strown,
The heathen in his blindness
Bows down to wood and stone.

The Wesley brothers wrote in a similar vein about Muslims:

The souls by that Impostor led,
That Arab-chief as Satan bold,
Who quite destroyed Thy Asian fold . . .

Exclusivism was not peculiar to Christians. Ahmadu Bamba said, "Oh, ye Jews and Nazarenes, die, and do not hope for help tomorrow."

Some missionaries were motivated by the belief that the Gospel must be preached to all nations before Christ's second coming. This is still a motivating factor in some mission circles. Not all missionaries were exclusivists. John William Colenso (1814–1883), Anglican bishop of Natal, condemned the view that non-Christians are bound for Hell, baptized polygamists, and was an ardent advocate of Zulu causes. But his enlightened views did not make him a more successful missionary—he reached Natal in 1855 and had a congregation of eighty-six by 1880.

LANGUAGE AND TRANSLATION

Whatever their views, in theory, on "traditional" religion, nineteenth-century missionaries often acquired a remarkable knowledge of African languages and cultures, in many cases despite a lack of formal education. In 1821, Robert Moffat, who was originally a gardener, founded what was at the time the African mission station farthest from the coast. He stayed there, on the Kuruman River, on the southern edge of the Tswana culture sphere, for fifty years; under his leadership, it became a solidly built village. In 1839, he printed a seTswana translation of the New Testament on his own press; he had visited Cape Town to learn the craft of printing. It was the first complete translation of the New Testament into an African language by a non-African. Today the Bible has been translated into about a hundred African languages, and the New Testament into 200 more; much of this was done between 1820 and 1920.

Sanneh has argued that the translation of the Bible brought it closer to indigenous cultures than the Arabic Quran, but we need to look more closely at the question of how many Christians actually read the Bible in their own languages. In the twentieth century, at least, the schools that taught literacy also taught the knowledge of English or French. Igbo speakers, for instance, find it easier to read the Bible in English than in Igbo, partly because of differences of dialect, but mainly because everything else they read—books, magazines, newspapers—is in English. The faith missions regarded the ability to read the Bible as essential, but not facility in English or the ability to write. Their missionaries feared a situation where people would become Christians in order to acquire useful and saleable skills. In central Nigeria, Christian members of faith missions, such as the Anaguta and Berom, tend to read the Bible in Hausa. It is a language that they speak fluently, but it is not their mother tongue.

Not all missionaries mastered local languages. Thomas Birch Freeman, another gardener, was born in England; his father was of African descent and his mother English. He is remembered as the founder of Ghanaian Methodism, but always needed an interpreter.

Some missionaries seemed to think that sheer fervor and sincerity were enough to transmit their message: "Is it possible a sensible man, like Mr. Horne, can suppose it in his power to imprint notions of Christianity through the bare medium of a language they do not understand?"[4] When Africans asked how the missionaries knew that their teachings were true, they were, not surprisingly, unconvinced when told that the Bible says so. "Does lie never live for book?"[5]

One writes of "dialogue" between foreign missionaries and African Christians. It is always the foreigner who records it. What is the language used, and who understands it? Missionary translators relied heavily on local collaborators: Nlemvo for kiKongo, William Ngidi for isiZulu, Henry Wright Duta for luGanda. Nevertheless, most translators made the odd slip. Robert Moffat wrote, "Consider the tarantulas of the field." But where a choice of words for God or Satan is involved, the consequences are momentous and impact on "traditional" religion as well as local perceptions of Christianity. The first verse of Saint John's Gospel reads, in Luo, "From long, long ago there was News. News was with the Hunchback Spirit, News was the Hunchback Spirit."[6]

CHRISTIANITY AND COMMERCE

Evangelicals were prominent in the antislavery movement, though the two did not always go together. John Newton was a slaver when he was converted. He wrote his famous hymn, "How Sweet the Name of Jesus Sounds," on the deck of a slave ship. In time he became an opponent of the slave trade, but not immediately. Critics of the slave trade often emphasized the dark side of African life, to show the harm slavery did. They tended to assume an air of moral superiority, seeing the European as reformer and philanthropist, but as a man on the lower Niger pointed out:

> When I told one, this morning, that the slave trade was a bad thing, and that White people worked to put an end to it altogether, he gave me an excellent answer. "Well, if White people give up buying, Black people will give up selling slaves."[7]

It seemed self-evident to abolitionists that the slave trade could be most effectively destroyed by developing so-called legitimate trade. "The Book says you are to grow cotton," explained Livingstone's interpreter, "and the English are to come and buy it."[8] It is now generally recognized that the products categorized in this way, such as palm oil, were mainly collected, produced, or processed by domestic slaves. It is also clear that "legitimate trade" provided raw materials for the factories of industrial Britain. Trade is shaped by the market, and "commerce and Christianity" initiatives often failed. The Sierra Leone settlement was originally planned as a Province of Freedom engaged in legitimate trade. In its initial form, it was a disastrous failure. Not all missionaries shared Livingstone's enthusiasm for "Christianity and commerce." To members of the faith missions and some others, the combination was unspiritual.

When Livingstone died, two new missions were founded in his memory, in what is now Malawi: Livingstonia and Blantyre. The former became a great educational center; its Christian graduates worked far afield in the colonial era and were often important agents of religious change. Livingstonia influenced far more African lives than Livingstone had.

THE MODERN WESTERN MISSIONARY MOVEMENT

The year 1792 is of special significance in the history of the expansion of Christianity, since it was then that the Baptist Missionary Society was founded, thanks to the initiative of William Carey, who was soon to leave for India. Other organizations followed, among them the interdenominational London Missionary Society (LMS) in 1795, the (Evangelical Anglican) Church Missionary Society (CMS) in 1799, and the Wesleyan Methodist Missionary Society in 1813. Swiss, French, and German Protestant missionary societies came a little later, starting with the Basel Mission in 1814.

These new organizations had a worldwide focus. Each developed its own mission field: the LMS in Africa, Madagascar, and the Pacific; the CMS in East and West Africa. The so-called faith missions, founded later, were interdenominational, but strongly Evangelical and fundamentalist. They were modeled on the China Inland Mission, founded in 1865. In Africa, the best-known were the Sudan Interior Mission and the Sudan United Mission.

At first, all official missionaries were men; some had wives, who, although they were expected to contribute to missionary work, were not listed as missionaries. In the 1880s things began to change, and by 1915 the CMS had 444 single women in the field, out of a total of 1,354 missionaries. Since there were also 378 wives, women had come to constitute a majority. The change reflected the changing position of women in Britain and elsewhere, as well as the important contribution they had made to the China Inland Mission.

Christianity came to nineteenth-century Africa in a great variety of cultural packages. Missionaries often found it hard to distinguish between their core message and the cultural presuppositions with which it was entangled: for instance, the preposterous but common suggestion that square houses are more Christian than round ones. To some missionaries, Western dress was an essential aspect of Christian identity. To others, when it was worn by Africans, it was a symptom of a dangerous worldliness. The churches of Egypt and Ethiopia were so deeply indigenized that Western Christians regarded them as corrupted, rather than as possible role models.

Some of the most famous missionaries—Robert Moffat, David Livingstone, Mary Slessor— belong to this period. The heroism and sacrifice of the pioneer missionaries were very real, though later research has sometimes modified the idealized portraits. Many foreign missionaries died young in Africa, or buried husbands, wives, or small children there. Those who survived often suffered from illness, isolation, and depression. After twenty-six years in Africa, Christina Coillard, a missionary wife, wrote, "I don't live here. I languish." She died in the Zambezi valley five years later. Among Catholic missionaries in Dahomey, a priest or brother survived on average for three years; a nun, for four. In all African mission fields, the single most important factor in determining an individual's success was longevity.

But the impact of all this effort and sacrifice was surprisingly limited. Moffat once said that he had fewer Christians than fruit trees, though his influence spread far beyond Kuruman. Livingstone baptized only one person, and became a full-time explorer largely because he was discouraged by his lack of success as a missionary. Slessor worked as a Presbyterian missionary in southeastern Nigeria from 1876 until her death in 1915, and became a national heroine in her native Scotland. She made a handful of converts, most of them her dependents. The first baptized Ndebele Christian had worked as a housemaid for a missionary family for twelve years. After fifty years of missionary effort, there were twelve Ndebele Christians who professed their faith openly. A Catholic order of missionary priests, the Oblates of Mary Immaculate, worked in Natal from 1850 until 1862 with no success at all.

The modern phase of Catholic mission work in West Africa was initiated by women. Sisters of Saint Joseph of Cluny reached Senegal in 1819. Three years later, their founder, Ann-Marie Javouhey, was invalided home from Sierra Leone, but the Josephites worked on. In the middle years of the nineteenth century, a number of new men's congregations were founded, some specifically to work in Africa; they included the Holy Ghost Fathers and the Society of African Missions (SMA Societas Missionum ad Afros). In 1868, the archbishop of Algiers, Charles Lavigerie (1825–1892), founded the Society of Missionaries for Africa, known as the White Fathers. Like many others before and after him, he found it impossible to convert Muslims, and the White Fathers came to run a far-flung network of missions in Uganda and elsewhere in East Africa. They became the largest male congregation founded to work in Africa. There were 1,800 of them there in the 1980s.

One of the most remarkable Catholic missionaries converted nobody at all. Charles de Foucauld (1858–1916) was an aristocratic officer in the French army who first served in North Africa and then traveled there incognito and was profoundly influenced by the example of Muslim and Jewish religious devotion. After a period in a Trappist monastery, he became a hermit in the steppes of southern Algeria; in 1905 he moved farther into the desert. Foucauld assisted the sick and poor and compiled a grammar and dictionary of the language of the Tuareg. He was killed by raiders in 1916.

Catholic and Protestant missionaries tended to be hostile to each other and often engaged in a race for a particular territory, much like the race between the representatives of colonizing powers. In 1879, the Baptists and Holy Ghost Fathers reached San Salvador, where they confused the king with their conflicting claims: "You white men, you perplex me with your different teachings. I do not know how to choose between you."[9] Bishop Crowther, however, gave a newly arrived Catholic mission a plot of CMS land: "I acquired this land for God's cause, take it."[10]

The Tswana kings in southern Africa permitted only one mission in each kingdom (usually the LMS) and prohibited independent churches. "If the two religions, the Catholic and Protestant, are the same, we clearly need only one of these two. If they are different, there will be constant conflict between them and they will cause division among my subjects."[11]

Protestant missions working in the same area tended to see each other as rivals rather than as allies. (The Catholics, with their strong tradition of obedience to central authority, were allocated different mission fields.)

Nineteenth-century missionary biographies tended to depict their subjects in a heroic and idealized light; Africans, whether hostile or grateful or responsive, became the passive background for their achievements. It is now generally accepted that Christianity was largely spread by Africans, not only by famous individuals such as Samuel Ajayi Crowther but also by countless obscure and forgotten ones. Nevertheless, foreign missionaries were the agents of change, and to understand the nature of this dynamic, it is necessary to be aware of the great human and cultural variety of the Western missionary enterprise, which one can do no more than hint at in a book of this kind.

The first missionary to South Africa was a Moravian butcher, George Schmidt, who worked among the Khoi from 1737 to 1744; he left because the local clergy questioned his right to baptize. When more Moravians arrived in 1792, they found one of his converts still alive—eighty-year-old Lena, who still treasured her Dutch New Testament. Johannes van der Kemp, who reached South Africa in 1799, at the age of fifty, was an immensely learned doctor who turned to religion when a boating accident robbed him of his family. After a brief period among the Xhosa, he turned to the Khoi. He founded a Christian village, Bethelsdorp, where he lived in radical poverty and wrote, among other books, a catechism in a Khoi language. He denounced the injustice of a slave-owning society, the first voice in an enduring tradition of Christian social criticism in South Africa. He shocked settler society by marrying a much younger woman, a former slave of Malagasy descent, and died after eleven years as a missionary. In 1849 Louis Harms founded the Hermannsburg Misionary Society, which was destined to work in Natal. It was supported by a single German village.

In the nineteenth century, Holy Ghost and SMA fathers tended to come from peasant stock in Brittany and Alsace. The Jesuits who worked among the Ndebele in the 1880s belonged to the upper echelons of English society, and one of them was a son of the Marquis of Lothian. While early missionaries, other than those from the Continent, were often men of little education, the (High Church Anglican) Universities Mission to Central Africa recruited only Oxford and Cambridge graduates. In a regional study, it is possible to explore the precise cultural identity of foreign missionaries. In a survey of a continent, it is clearly impossible.[12]

BLACK NEW WORLD CHRISTIANS[13]

Soon after the emancipation of the slaves in the West Indies, one of them, Thomas Keith, worked his passage back to Africa with the intention of spreading Christianity. Another Jamaican, James Keats,[14] reached Sierra Leone with the same intention. He boarded a ship bound for the Congo River. Nothing is known of the fate of either man.

Virtually all black New World missionaries were Protestant and English-speaking. There were many obstacles in their path. Missionary societies often rejected black candidates, and the members of African-American churches tended to be too poor to sponsor foreign missions. To their chagrin, those who did get to Africa as missionaries found that their white counterparts did not treat them as equals. Despite this, African-Americans and West Indians thread their way though Africa's nineteenth-century mission history. Often they worked in Liberia, where the line between settler and missionary is not easy to draw. By 1900, there were 115 African-American missionaries in Africa, 68 of whom were in Liberia.

Some interpreted the Exodus story as a call to return to Africa. Like all black Christians, they found a special meaning in Psalm 68:31: "Princes shall come out of Egypt; and Ethiopia shall soon stretch forth her hands to God." Some believed that God had permitted slavery so that Africans might bring Christianity back to their homeland. Others, a majority, believed they were called to find the Promised Land in an America largely created by their labors.

The famous Presbyterian mission at Calabar was founded in 1846 through the initiative of recently freed Jamaican Christians. White, métis, and black Jamaican missionaries worked there.[15] The initial response from the Scottish Missionary Society was that the proposal was "highly presumptuous."[16]

The first African-American missionary to Africa, if we exclude the Nova Scotians, was Lott Cary, born in slavery in Virginia in 1780. Like Equiano, he saved up and bought his freedom. An ardent Baptist, he emigrated to Liberia and played a leading role in the early days of Monrovia. In a tragically ironic accident, he blew himself up in 1828 while making ammunition to use in local wars.

Antonio (ca. 1800–1880), exceptionally, was a Catholic who returned alone to Africa without any funding or institutional support. After being taken as a slave to Brazil, he became a Catholic there, regained his freedom, and returned to West Africa. A layman, it was his intention to act as the unofficial pastor of a "Brazilian" Catholic community until white missionaries arrived. He settled in Lagos, where he built a small church, baptized babies, blessed marriages, and prayed for the dying and at funerals. When missionaries arrived in 1868, he checked their Catholic credentials and handed over his little congregation. He continued to study his catechism, asking for a new one when he lost the one he had: "I am old and more than ever I need to study to know the path to eternity."[17]

MISSION AND SOCIETY

Why were missions so much less successful in the nineteenth century than in the twentieth? Outside the areas of colonial rule and white settlement, which were very limited before the 1880s, missionaries were living on sufferance in sovereign states. Often, their first converts were drawn from the poor and marginalized, and were quite few in number. The towns on the lower Niger were exceptionally well supplied with missionaries. Successive expeditions up the great river and the books based on them had made it famous. The CMS founded its Niger mission in 1857. Forty years later, one of its staff lamented that they had influenced perhaps 1 percent of the population. In 1884, the Society of African Missions founded its first station on the west bank of the Niger. By 1900, its members had baptized 446 people,

all but eighty of them on their deathbeds. Thirty of the rest were employees of the Royal Niger Company.

In the Igbo towns on or near the Niger, the first Christians tended to be
society's rejects—old women accused of witchcraft, slaves, lepers, or mothers of twins—though there were individual exceptions. Idigo was a diviner
and a titled man. When his powers proved unable to preserve the lives of
his own children, he became a Catholic and founded a Christian village variously called Crossroads or Life Is Supreme, where he spent the rest of his
life surrounded by slaves and witches.

The Igbo lived in small village democracies. There was a different dynamic
in centralized states. Kings, even those who proved sympathetic to Christianity, were often prepared to accept missionaries primarily because of practical services they might render as diplomatic advisers, scribes, healers,
teachers, gunsmiths, or artisans. They needed assistance of this kind because
they so often faced a variety of external threats. Some missionaries, such as
Livingstone, had medical training; most did not, but this did not deter them
from treating illnesses and injuries, at which some proved to be remarkably
successful.

> The Lozi of the Zambezi flood plain debated the pros and cons of a mission-
> ary presence. "Don't we hear tell of all the black nations, all the chiefs having
> their missionaries to teach the young people and the Kings the wisdom of the
> white nations?" Others said, "No we do not need these teachers unless they
> know and teach us to make powder and such like things." One man said the
> missionaries were bad . . . and not long ago they caused the sun to rot (mean-
> ing the eclipse [sic]) and they chased away the rain.[18]

But kings had reason to fear that a new religion would prove divisive and
undermine traditional allegiances. Gradually they became aware of the sub-
versive potential of the Gospel. Robert Moffat's son, perhaps rashly, preached
a sermon to the Ndebele King Mzilikazi on human equality. The king was
furious, telling the interpreter to stop "telling the people such stuff and
lies."[19] Later, in the reign of Mzilikazi's son, it was said, "We like to learn
& hear about God & His Word but if we say openly that we belong to King
Jesus, then we shall be accused of disloyalty to Lobengula & of witchcraft
& killed."[20]

Plural marriages were a recurrent source of difficulty. Where potential
Christian men were already married to several wives, they were expected to
send away all but the eldest. The distress and injustice this caused were only
too apparent:

> "How many wives have you, Zatshuke?" "Seven."
> "Have you ever put any away?" "No."
> "How old is the eldest?" "I married her when Dingane came into power. She
> is an old woman now."

"Don't you think of putting her away, now that she is old and useless?" "I would rather say, Let us be killed together."[21]

Monogamy was especially problematic for kings, and some, but not all, Ethiopian and Kongo rulers were polygamists. Each marriage represented an alliance with a family and region. Christians soon discovered the precedent of Israel's patriarchs and kings, including the much-married Solomon. Reading the Bible with fresh eyes, they sometimes recognized problems and anomalies that had never occurred to the missionaries. Bishop Colenso was led to reconsider the interpretation of the Hebrew Bible when Ngidi questioned the number of animals in Noah's Ark, vis-à-vis its dimensions.

The so-called Christian villages were a striking aspect of nineteenth-century mission work, but died out early in the twentieth century. Sometimes they simply grew up around a mission station, as at Kuruman. Sometimes they were founded through deliberate policy, as when Catholic priests and nuns purchased enslaved children in order to free them in Christian settlements. Centers such as Kuruman offered welcome protection and security in a time of widespread war. Refugees were given a stable life in return for the loss of cultural and personal autonomy.

In Natal, where land was increasingly scarce, access to mission land was a valuable asset. In a sample of those who joined mission settlements, only 12 percent joined for "religious" reasons, 33 percent were seeking refuge, and 26 percent sought employment.[22] The failure of the Oblates of Mary Immaculate was at least partly due to the fact that they lacked land to allocate. Women were often among the first Christians and enthusiastic, if now anonymous and largely forgotten, Evangelists. The association with small communities of the poor and marginal, of course, made Christianity less attractive to the powerful and eminent.

We need to ask, of course, not only why relatively few people became Christians, but also why any did so at all. The pattern in the nineteenth century is different from that in the colonial period. Where the first converts were the disinherited—slaves, lepers, accused witches—they had little to hope for in the traditional order and were predisposed to change. Older concepts of a future life were shadowy and uncertain, and Christian ideas of Heaven and Hell were both attractive and terrifying—though it was said of the Zulu that they neither desired the first nor feared the second. "Traditional" religion promised this-worldly benefits: long life, good health, children. This gave it an immense vulnerability, since it offered no refuge against misfortune. Its adherents grappled with the insoluble moral problem of the suffering of the innocent and the too evident injustices of the world in which they lived. Too often, they found an explanation in the malice of imagined witches, the unthinkable Other.

The emphasis on rewards in this life had another implication, for the evident prosperity and power of Britain could be seen as a confirmation of the truth of the religion its people professed. This argument came readily to missionaries and others, among them Queen Victoria, who wrote to the people of Abeokuta: "England has become great and happy by the knowledge of the true God and Jesus Christ."[23]

EAST AFRICA

In 1844, Johann Ludwig Krapf, who had been expelled from Shoa, where he had buried a wife and two babies, began work at the town of Rabai, near Mombasa. It was intended to be the first of a chain of mission stations spreading across the southern border of Muslim Africa. He was a fine linguist and an intrepid explorer, but had little success: "I often prayed fervently for the preservation of my life in Africa at least until one soul should be saved."[24] The first Christians were the poor and marginal, such as the crippled Mrenge, who was baptized when he was near death. Missions would be far more successful inland, especially in Buganda.

In an earlier chapter, we noted the debates between Muslims, Catholics, and Protestants at the Buganda court from 1879 on, and the way in which both Muslims and Christians were cruelly martyred for their faith. The power of the Ganda king is mirrored in proverbs such as "The king is the lake which kills those who fish and those who do not fish alike." Mutesa (1856–1884) encouraged religious debate, and this made choice possible for others, at least for those at court. Gradually he came to understand that both Muslims and Christians now owed a higher allegiance. In 1875–1876, seventy Muslim chiefs and pages were burned at court, and a thousand elsewhere. Mutesa's son, Mwanga, persecuted Christians in 1886, killing perhaps a hundred. Thirty-one of them were burned alive in June, with "Katonda," the traditional name for God adopted by Christians and Muslims alike, on their lips.

In 1893, after civil wars of religion, Buganda became a British protectorate. What followed was "one of the most remarkable and spontaneous movements for literacy and new knowledge that the world has ever seen."[25] Ganda Christians and Muslims soon carried their respective faith far beyond Buganda. Apolo Kivebulaya (1864–1933) was apprenticed to a diviner as a child. For a time he was a Muslim and then became a Christian, adopting the name of the missionary in Acts. An Anglican, he was ordained in 1903 and worked as a parish priest in Toro. He never married, and embraced poverty. In 1921, he was drawn by a dream to work among the so-called Pygmies of the Zaire forest. When he died, he asked to be buried with his head toward the Congo and not, as was the custom, toward his birthplace.

COLONIAL CONQUESTS

The main missionary influx was between 1880 and 1920—it was no co-incidence that this was the time when Africa was divided by an arbitrary grid into anglophone, francophone, and lusophone conquest states, though the increase in missionary numbers was partly due to a new willingness to accept women.

No one became a missionary in order to spread colonialism, and Protestant missionaries, in particular, were often at loggerheads with local officials, whom they accused of favoring Islam and alienated by their hostility to drink, horse races, and dancing. Nevertheless, it was easy to identify with one's country of origin: "We shall endeavour to hold high the banner of the Sacred Heart and the flag of France," wrote a White Father from the Sahara.[26] It was largely pressure from Scottish Presbyterians that prevented Nyasaland (later Malawi) from becoming part of Mozambique. They cared about it greatly because of its two famous missions, Livingstonia and Blantyre.

Many missionaries believed that colonial rule was preferable, from both a humanitarian and a religious viewpoint, to that of white settlers or traditional kings. They felt more secure in a colonial situation, and travel was safer and easier. Often, they rejoiced in the fall of rulers whom they believed had hindered their work, though Colenso defended the Zulu king, as did his daughter after him.

CONTINUITIES: WARRI AND KONGO

In 1840, a visitor to Warri found that "the Church or Catholic Chapel had disappeared and the streets were covered with grass."[27] In the Congo, however, "Some old people about the country call themselves minkwikizi, 'believers,' in some of whom there seems to have lingered some faint glimmerings of such light as had been brought in former times." When the Baptists established a mission there in 1879, one of their first converts was Nlemvo, who was destined to play a vital role in the translation of the New Testament. His uncle "had a small brass crucifix—his Christo—to which he prayed every day."[28] Later, Nlemvo lost his sight, but his faith was unshaken. In a sense, the new churches founded in the Congo in the late nineteenth century were a continuation of a much older Christian tradition. In a few weeks in 1921, a Kongo Baptist, whose educational attainments were too humble for him to become a pastor, would transform the position of Christianity in west central Africa.

CONTINUITIES: ETHIOPIA

The king of Ethiopia retained the title Negus Negast (king of kings, or emperor), but his power did not extend much beyond his capital; this was also true of his Kongo counterpart. Ethiopians remember the time as the Era of Princes or the Era of Judges, a reference to the period in the history of Israel when "everyone did as he saw fit" (Judges 21:25).

The church was divided by Christological controversies. Ethiopia was dominated by three powerful and virtually independent states: Tigre in the north, Shoa in the south, and an Oromo kingdom near Lake Tana.

The Oromo (formally called Galla) originally lived near what is now the Kenya-Ethiopia boundary. In the sixteenth and seventeenth centuries, they suddenly embarked on a great expansion and migrated onto the Ethiopian plateau. They were pastoralists and religous "traditionalists," and some remained so. Some individuals became Christians, but many turned to Islam. More than one missionary saw them as the key to the conversion of Africa: "To my mind, Ormania is the Germany of Africa."[29]

The first Protestant missionaries, Germans working for the Church Missionary Society, arrived in 1830. Ethiopians and Germans recognized in each other a deep religious devotion. Shortly before he was killed in battle, the ruler of Tigre told a missionary, "I love you, not because you are a great man, not because you are a white man, but because you love the Lord whom I wish to love with all my heart. I pray you to be my brother and to consider me as your brother."[30]

Ethiopia's rulers had hoped for various forms of technical assistance from the missionaries. "He [the ruler of Shoa] wishes to make use of us as physicians, architects, artists, etc." but "does not seem to feel the necessity of a reformation of their Church, and endeavours to preserve all things in their old state."[31] The missionaries hoped for what would in effect have been a Protestant reformation, eliminating monasticism, fasting, veneration of the Cross, and, above all, devotion to Mary and the saints. Soon the missionaries were expelled. The Ethiopians explained that they had put up with them in the hope of persuading them of their errors: "We had been tolerated only, they had expected us to repent of our heresies and practices."[32]

In 1855, the Era of Princes came to an end when a soldier of fortune and minor nobleman seized power in Ethiopia, and was crowned Negus Negast. He took the name Tewodros (Theodore), on which so many prophecies had focused. Tewodros (1818–1868) was deeply religious, and often called himself the slave of Christ. He was monogamous, although his marriage was childless. He came to the throne with high ideals, but spent much of his reign fighting rebellions. Adversity darkened his character; he was capable of great cruelty, and some doubted his sanity. His life ended in suicide.[33]

Tewodros's successors were Yohannes IV (r. 1872–1889), king of Tigre, and Menelik (r. 1889–1913), king of Shoa. Yohannes adjudicated the Christological controversies that were tearing the church apart, deciding that the Tewadeho (Union) Party was correct. He attempted to convert "heretical" Christians, as well as Muslims and traditionalists, by force. Menelik united north and south Ethiopia and established the boundaries of the modern state—in a very real sense, he was a participant in the scramble for Africa. At the battle of Adwa, in 1896, a victory over an invading Italian army preserved Ethiopia from colonial rule.

The Ethiopian church did not develop a missionary organization until 1963, and it did not, traditionally, feel a calling to preach the Gospel in distant lands. Christianity spread within Ethiopia largely through the conquests and policies of kings. Inevitably, it was linked with Amharic domination and cultural ascendancy.

CONTINUITIES: THE COPTS

In 1855, the patriarch of Alexandria estimated that there were 217,000 Copts in a population of 5 million. Coptic identity, like Jewish identity, is ethnic and cultural as well as religious, and some who identify as Copts have no strong religious beliefs or affiliation. In the nineteenth century, as before, the Copts were a flourishing and prosperous body with a special expertise in financial management. Boutros Ghali, assassinated in 1910, was Egypt's first and last Coptic prime minister.

In the mid-nineteenth century, there were only nine monasteries with 300 monks, and five convents with 100 nuns. It was a symptom of weakness, because monasticism had been so central to Coptic tradition and because it was monks who became bishops. The ancient tradition of radical holiness never died out entirely. Anba Abraham, the long-lived bishop of Fayum (1829–1914), is remembered as a saint who gave everything he had to the poor, making no distinction between Muslims and Christians.

The first Protestant missionaries arrived in 1829. Like their counterparts in Ethiopia, they saw their role as one of revival and reform. To the Copts, their presence was damaging and divisive, though a small minority joined them. A Coptic bishop said to an American Presbyterian, "We have been living with Christ for more than 1,800 years, how long have you been living with Him?"[34]

Chapter 12

African Christian Initiatives: Two Case Studies

I do not know who is a Christian in this country. It was only Christ who was a Christian.

—the Zulu King Dinuzulu, at his trial[1]

SOUTH AFRICA

In this chapter, we turn from a continentwide survey to two case studies, regions that were mentioned briefly in the preceding chapter. In the first, in present-day South Africa, Botswana, and Lesotho, African Christians were profoundly disconcerted by the discrepancy between the teachings of Christ expounded by white missionaries and the often very different conduct of the settlers. They were asking, in essence, the question that haunts the work of Lesslie Newbigin: "Can the West be saved?" A Tembu chief asked, "Why do not the missionaries first go to their own countrymen and convert them?"[2]

In 1854, a Tswana prince complained:

Do you not see that we have been, without a fault on our part, shot down like game . . . by the Boers? Is it because we have not white skins that we are to be destroyed like *libatana* [beasts of prey]? . . . Are we only to obey the word of God because we are black? Are white people not to obey the word of God, because they are white?[3]

In 1911, it was said that except for the Pacific islands, South Africa was the most densely occupied mission field in the world. Yet the white settler churches maintained varying degrees of segregation from their black co-religionists. It was a separation partly due to and justified by geography and language difference, but this was not the fundamental cause.

In South Africa, Christianity began as the faith of a white settler community. By 1710, there were about 2,000 Dutch settlers, the forebears of the far more numerous Afrikaners. The Cape of Good Hope became a British colony in 1795, and more permanently in 1806. Extensive British settlement began in 1820. In 1836, some Afrikaners embarked on a migration inland, a journey that would become part of folk mythology as the Great Trek, motivated partly by the abolition of slavery. They came to see themselves as a Chosen People in exodus, fleeing from the British Pharaoh. Conflicts with powerful African states led to a hardening of racial attitudes:

> In their own estimation, they are the chosen people of God, and all the coloured race are "black property" or "creatures"—heathen given to them for an inheritance.[4]

Until the end of apartheid, this link with white racism was Christianity's enduring dilemma.

The indigenous people of the Cape were the hunter-gatherer San (Bushmen) and the pastoralist Khoikhoi, once called Hottentots because of the distinctive click sounds in their languages. The Cape San were soon dead or displaced to the desert. In time, the Khoi lost their separate identity—their language had died out by the late nineteenth century. Together with the enslaved (often from Asia or Madagascar) and the Dutch, they were the ancestors of the "Cape Coloured" population. For a time they became important cultural intermediaries, the often forgotten individuals who carried Christianity far beyond the Cape, to places where Khoi/mixed-race frontier bands acquired a new identity, as Griqua. Christianity became a core dimension of their identity. When the Griqua state issued its own coinage, it bore the image of the dove, the symbol of the LMS.

Afrikaner Jager, who died in 1823, was a Khoi shepherd who became the leader of one of the frontier bands—regarded by the settlers as bandits—as a result of bitter experiences of white injustice. He became a Christian and a devoted friend of the missionaries. Like so many African Christians, he was converted through a dream in which he found himself near a fiery furnace, but was able to climb to safety on a green mountain, where a shining figure awaited him. Like many others, he was distressed by the gulf between the Gospel and the conduct of supposedly Christian settlers, whose God "must be one of a very different character from that God of love to whom the missionaries directed the attention of the Namaqua."[5]

Despite these contradictions, Christianity took deep and lasting root in many African hearts. One can distinguish three patterns of response among those who assumed leadership roles: the prophet, the improver, and the king who is either a Christian or a friend of missionaries.

Xhosa Prophets and Improvers

On the well-watered eastern seaboard, two groups of pastoralists were advancing simultaneously from the south and from the north, a process that would inevitably lead to conflict—the so-called Hundred Years' War between the Xhosa and the Afrikaners. After a defeat in 1811, the Xhosa realized that the settlers could, and would, advance farther. As so often happens in this kind of unprecedented situation, new prophets arose.

Nxele had grown up on an Afrikaner farm and began as an orthodox Christian, then gradually adopted the lifestyle of a traditional diviner. He came to see the world in terms of a cosmic conflict between the God of the whites and the God of the blacks. Africans should worship God in dancing, enjoyment of life, and love, rather than "pray with their faces to the ground and their backs to the Almighty." He led his people to a disastrous war in 1819 and drowned while trying to escape from Robben Island.[6]

Ntsikana (d. 1820) is remembered as a prophet who was brought to Christianity by an independent revelation, but it is possible he was influenced by van der Kemp when he worked for a time among the Xhosa. He moved in the opposite direction from Nxele, from diviner to Christian. In 1815, he had a mystical experience in which he saw a rainbow-colored light next to his favorite ox. He washed off the traditional red ocher in a local river. (Believing himself baptized, he sought no further baptism.) He urged the Xhosa to pray and held daily services that focused on the singing of four hymns he had composed, which are still sung to this day. They include the Great Hymn:

He is the Great God, Who is in heaven;
Thou art Thou, Shield of truth.
Thou art Thou, Stronghold of truth.
Thou art Thou, Thicket of truth.[7]

Feeling called to monogamy, Ntsikane asked his second wife to leave, and he opposed the war of 1819. When he was dying, he asked his people to bury him in the Christian fashion. When they hesitated, he began to dig his own grave.

In 1824, the Glasgow Missionary Society founded Lovedale. In time it would grow into a massive educational complex with programs that included technical training, and with its own press. It was open to everyone, but nine-tenths of its students were black. It was closed in the 1950s, as a result of the Bantu Education Act, but for over a hundred years it had a transforming impact on its graduates and, through them, on the lives of countless others.

One of these graduates, Tiyo Soga (1829–1871), was a Xhosa, the son of a follower of Ntsikana. He studied in Scotland for ten years, then returned in 1857 with a Scottish wife. A Presbyterian, he was South Africa's first ordained African minister. He returned to a Xhosaland in a state of chaos and despair. The previous year, a young girl, Nongqawuse, had transmitted a message from two ancestors whom she met in the fields. If the cattle were slaughtered, the dead would return to life and the Europeans would be swept away. This was less irrational than it seems. The Xhosa herds had been decimated by lung sickness, and the idea of the returning dead was an echo of missionary teaching.

Not all Xhosa accepted this message, but the results were catastrophic: with vast herds destroyed and thousands dead from starvation, their homeland opened up to white settlement. More than a hundred years later, people sang:

> Sir George Grey took our country.
> He entered in though Nongqawuse,
> The cattle died, the sheep died,
> The power of the Black people was finished off.[8]

Soga urged his people to embrace Western education and earn money with which to purchase their lost lands. He was a man of great intelligence and religious devotion who translated the first part of *The Pilgrim's Progress* into Xhosa and revised the Xhosa New Testament. He died young, of tuberculosis, putting down his pen part of the way though Acts, when he could do no more. He called Scotland "home" but advised his sons to make their way as Xhosa, not as Britons.

The Xhosa distinguished between Red People (that is, traditionalists, decorated with ocher) and School or Book People, but the distinction was an artificial one. As these examples show, every African Christian needed to make a personal synthesis of inherited culture and missionary precepts. There was no single pattern to follow.

The Pilgrim's Progress was often the first book to be translated after the Bible. Christian leaves his family behind in his pursuit of eternal life. This was the experience of many African Christians. Later, his family decides to follow him. This was often the case, too.

We have seen that it was the poor and disinherited who tended to be the first Christians. In South Africa, Christianity was welcomed not only by the Khoi, who had been stripped of their lands, and the mixed-race communities of the frontier, but also by the Fingo or Mfengu of Natal, Zulu-related Nguni who were fleeing from Shaka's wars. (Shaka died in 1828; his praise name was The Ferocious One.) Marginalized by the Xhosa as refugees, the Mfengu welcomed Christianity, Western education, and the plow. A new black Christian middle class emerged, known in Natal as *kholwa*.

For a generation or so, Mfengu and Xhosa formed a prosperous, innovative peasantry, but it was unable to survive a rising tide of white settlement and racist legislation.[9]

Tswana and Sotho Kings

The peoples now differentiated as Tswana and Sotho are closely related in language and culture. Most but not all Tswana live in Botswana. Tswana and Sotho were divided by the period of war and social dislocation that they remember as the Difaqane, and by the Afrikaner settlements founded after the Great Trek. Moffat was their first resident European missionary.

The Tswana kingdoms, like Buganda, are exceptions to the rule that the first Christians were the poor and marginal, or missionary dependents. The first Tswana Christians were largely, though not exclusively, drawn from a male elite. In the late nineteenth century, some Christian masters "did not like the [cattle herders] to become Christians. . . . They [herders] were minor people and . . . the masters said it would only waste their time." Later, "the Ngwato Church [came] to be populated overwhelmingly by women." By 1922, women outnumbered men two to one: "Women had practically taken over the Church."[10]

Sechele (1808–1891), the only African baptized by Livingstone, was ruler of the Kwena Tswana. He learned to read with great enthusiasm, dismissed all wives but one, and was baptized in 1848. He fell out with the missionaries when he resumed marital relations with a former spouse, and was barred from communion for forty years. Nevertheless, he continued a vigorous Christian life and was a regular preacher. This pattern of excluding committed Christians from formal church membership was to be a surprisingly widespread and enduring one.

Khama, who ruled the Ngwato from 1875 until his death in 1923, is the most famous of the Tswana Christian kings. He came to the throne after a civil war with his traditionalist father, who had accepted missionaries but not their teachings. The point of conflict was the communal male circumcision ceremony, an important agency of education and socialization, which died out under his government—or, rather, was replaced by schools. Khama enforced Sabbath (Sunday) observance, always wore Western dress, was monogamous, and tried, unsuccessfully, to prohibit the preparation and consumption of local beer. He made good use of his Christian image and missionary contacts. In 1895, he visited London and succeeded in having Bechuanaland, the future Botswana, placed under direct British rule rather than becoming part of the future Union of South Africa.

By the early twentieth century, all the major Tswana states had Christian rulers. But the 1946 census showed that fewer than half the Tswana were Christian, and under 20 percent of the Ngwato. Khama was a Christian king, but not the king of a Christian people.

Moshoeshoe (1786–1870) was the architect of Lesotho, the founder of a new state in an age of such brutality and disorder that it was remembered as the Time of Cannibals. He was not a hereditary ruler, and created a new state without the autocracy and fear that characterized the Zulu and Ndebele kingdoms.

As a young man, Moshoeshoe was influenced by a diviner named Mohlomi (d. 1816). Mohlomi, a figure not unlike his Xhosa contemporary, Ntsikana, had a vision in which God told him, "Go, rule by love, and look on thy people as men and brothers." Mohlomi told the young Moshoeshoe that God knows no one as a poor man.[11]

Moshoeshoe was, above all, magnanimous. There is a famous story—probably a "true fiction"— of how he met the cannibals who had eaten his grandfather, and honored them at the grandfather's grave. The first missionaries, from the Paris Evangelical Missionary Society, arrived in 1833. One of them, Eugene Casalis, became the king's close friend. When he finally returned to Paris, in 1855, the king said, "O, Casalis, you are my teacher, my father, my mother. . . . *You are a true MoSotho.*" (Close personal friendships between southern African rulers and white missionaries thread their way through the history of the period.)

Moshoeshoe sympathized with mission teachings, and sought baptism (without success) on his deathbed. When several of his wives became Christians, he gave them their freedom and continued to support them, but felt unable to give up polygamy: "[W]ho will prepare food for me and for the strangers who come to visit me?" A teetotaler, he adopted Christian burial rites, abandoned the traditional communal circumcision rituals, and took a public stand against witchcraft accusations. He told a British general, "Peace is like the rain which makes the grass grow, while war is like the wind which dries it up."

African Missionaries

In southern Africa, as elsewhere, Christianity was very largely disseminated by African Christians. Sometimes they were catechists, employed by the mission for a pittance, and sometimes unpaid volunteers. Most, naturally, worked in their home area. Labor migrants often carried their faith with them. Some settled in regions far from their home in order to preach the Christian message. The missionary Coillard went to Bulozi with Sotho Christians, who had the precious qualification of speaking a closely related language. Tensions developed when African Christians were perceived as rivals rather than assistants. Other white missionaries came to feel uncomfortable with the Sotho role: "I do not subscribe to the evangelisation of Zambezia by Basutos. I would really be *frightened* to see them arrive in great numbers."[12] One of the Sotho, William Mokalapa, left the mission, joined an African-American church, and attempted to establish an independent school at the Lozi court.[13]

William Koyi was a Xhosa who had studied at Lovedale. With three other South Africans, he volunteered to work at Livingstonia, on the shores of Lake Malawi. His language was related to that of the Ngoni, who were northern Nguni migrants, like the Ndebele, and he exercised great influence among them.

SIERRA LEONE AND THE CREOLE MISSIONARIES

The second case study is set in West Africa and focuses on the Creole community of Freetown and the all-African Niger Mission that its members staffed.

By 1800, there were fewer than 2,000 free black setters in the Freetown area: the survivors from the first settlement in 1787, the Nova Scotians, and a small group from Jamaica. The company that had founded the settlement as a Province of Freedom continued to suffer major financial losses, and in 1808 this small enclave became a British colony.

The previous year, the British Parliament had passed a law prohibiting the trade in slaves. This applied, of course, only to British subjects, but by making anti-slave-trade treaties with other nations, the government attempted to make the ban more widespread. In time, others passed anti-slave-trade legislation. The British government placed a naval squadron off the coast of West Africa to intercept illegal slavers. Many got through, however, and the slave trade survived until the 1850s.

When slave ships were captured, their human cargoes were released at Freetown, since it was impracticable to return them to their homes. In the eighteenth century, a large proportion of the enslaved were Igbo. In the nineteenth, as a result of protracted internal wars, very many were Yoruba. It is because they were enslaved so late that much of their culture survived in the New World.

Cut off from their homes and culture, the Liberated Africans—or Recaptives, as they were called—were highly receptive to mission teaching. They were settled in missionary-controlled villages with names like Waterloo and Wilberforce. Soon the Recaptives greatly outnumbered the earlier settlers. Those who had been Muslims remained so, but the others welcomed Christianity and Western education.

In some cases, the Recaptives' earlier life histories have been recorded. They had been suddenly snatched away from parents, spouses, children, community. They emerged from terror, trauma, and despair to form a new middle class. They created a new cultural mix that was symbolized in their language, Krio. Yoruba masquerades are still performed in Freetown, but the emerging Freetown elite were proud to be black Englishmen.

The Creoles, as they were called, made money in trade and invested it in education. Fourah Bay College was founded in 1827 and, beginning in 1876, awarded degrees from the University of Durham. Africanus Horton, the son of poor Igbo parents, won a scholarship to the University of London and became an army doctor. He wrote books on a number of subjects, including draft constitutions for future West African nations. J.F. Easmon, another Creole doctor, was the first to isolate blackwater fever. Sir Samuel Lewis, who qualified as a lawyer in 1872, became the first mayor of Freetown and the first West African knight. Muslim Creoles contributed to church construction, and Christian Creoles to the building of a mosque.

In the mid-nineteenth century, because of the health problems faced by Europeans in West Africa, the British were happy to utilize the talents of men like Horton. As health conditions improved and the scramble for Africa began, white colonial officials came to see the Creoles as rivals. As one of the latter wrote sadly in 1916, "The upset of the Sierra Leonian began with the upset of the thought of his white rulers concerning him. . . . Segregation was the first blast of the trumpet; then other things and other things."[14]

Like the American Liberians, most Creoles felt no sense of identity with local peoples, whose language they did not share. P.P. Hazeley was called the Apostle of the Limba, but he was exceptional. Some Creole Christians became remarkable missionaries, but their chosen mission fields lay elsewhere.

African Missionaries in Nigeria

In 1839, three Creoles of Yoruba descent began to run a passenger service to their homeland. Many of their compatriots chose to return home, where they were collectively known as Saro. Like the Nova Scotians in Freetown at an earlier time, they provided role models: black Christians with Western skills. Some of them were missionaries, the most famous of them being Samuel Ajayi Crowther.

Born in 1806, in the Yoruba town of Osogun, Crowther had been kidnapped as a boy, freed on the high seas, and released in Sierra Leone. He became an Evangelical Anglican and soon displayed a remarkable scholastic aptitude. He was the first student at Fourah Bay College. He became a celebrity when he went on the 1841 Niger expedition and subsequently published his journal. In 1843 he was ordained, and three years later, with an English fellow missionary, he founded a CMS post at Abeokuta, not far from the ruins of his former home. It was acclaimed by English missionary supporters as a "sunrise within the tropics."[15] Soon he met his mother, who later became a Christian.

In 1857, Crowther became head of the newly founded all-African Niger Mission, and in 1864, he was consecrated bishop. His diocese, however, was not in his native Yorubaland because of the objections of white missionaries. Initially defined in general terms, the diocese proved to be the lower Niger and Niger Delta. All its staff were Africans from Sierra Leone, and the mission's symbolic significance was immense. Most of its members were men of little education who endured years of isolation and poverty. Several were of Igbo descent, but born in Sierra Leone.

Crowther, a Yoruba, did not speak any Niger language, though he studied Nupe. He did not live on the Niger, but visited it twice a year. He spent the rest of the time in Lagos, where he devoted himself to scholarly pursuits, appointing two able clergymen as archdeacons to run the Niger mission.

The mission's greatest success was in the Niger Delta. The first station there was founded in 1865, in the island state of Bonny. It had a great appeal to the enslaved, who were often Igbo; they paddled the great trade canoes along inland waterways to buy palm oil, the new export commodity, for their masters. They built small chapels along these routes, though the chiefs complained: "They never sent their boys to be 'Bishops' in Ibo, but to 'Trade.'" Some of these Anglicans died a martyr's death; among them was Joshua Hart, who in 1874 was killed for refusing to eat food offered in sacrifice. Later, Bonny Christians prayed, "Give us the firmness of Joshua."[16] Traditional religion declined, and by the 1880s, the shrine of skulls dedicated to the Bonny war god was in ruins.

Brass was a trading state farther west. Like Bonny, it was situated in mangrove swamps, and dependent on trade for its existence. At first, Christianity had a spectacular success; it was adopted by the whole community, including the king, who in 1879, shortly before his death, was baptized as Josiah Constantine. But the Royal Niger Company soon used its powers to exclude the people of Brass from their sphere of trade on the lower Niger, and in 1889, a later king renounced Christianity at his coronation. The Brass chiefs explained:

> . . . many Chiefs who were brought up as Christians have now gone back to fetishism, among these King Koko, the reason for this being that they had lost faith in the white man's god, which had allowed them to be oppressed.[17]

All missions are by their very nature transitory, intended to become self-governing churches. Henry Venn, secretary of the CMS from 1841 to 1872, realized this clearly, and often spoke of the euthanasia of missions as an ideal. The Niger Mission was a fulfillment of this dream. It was not, however, a dream necessarily shared by white missionaries in the field. Like the young men who joined the Colonial Service in the early 1950s, convinced that the system would last their lifetime, foreign missionaries tended to think that this transition would happen in the distant future. There were exceptions, of course: Livingstone was an impassioned advocate of mission euthanasia, and wrote in 1851, "No European ought to go where a native Church is already formed. . . . The true missionary field [in southern Africa] begins at the Kuruman."[18]

The golden age of the Creoles gave way to an era of white domination, and this was also true of the Niger mission. The process began in 1879, when a European was placed in charge of the mission's "temporalities," and was complete by the time the old bishop died, in 1891, and was replaced by an Englishman. By 1883, Crowther was lamenting "nearly a total clearance of its members . . . by disconnection, dismissal and resignation."[19] The Europeans soon died or left the mission. The Niger Delta became a self-supporting pastorate, still part of the Anglican Church and still run by Sierra Leonian clergy.

By 1896, only one of the Europeans was left. Too late, he realized that a great injustice had been perpetrated:

> I greatly long to see an African Diocese formed. . . . May God forgive us the bitter, slanderous and lying thoughts we had against [Archdeacon Henry Johnson] and others in those dark days of 1890. We have suffered, no one knows how much, by those rash and hasty actions. We condemned others and we ourselves have done less than they did.[20]

The Niger Mission had undoubtedly had its weaknesses and the occasional scandal. This was also true of other mission fields. But some who had served the CMS faithfully also fell victims to this clearance. Charles Paul, an ordained minister, had worked for the CMS for thirty-one years, twenty-five of them on the Niger. He was dismissed with no source of income but the help of his friends. He worked in the Niger Delta until his death. During his last illness, he thought of little but the way the CMS had treated him.

INDEPENDENT CHURCHES

In both South Africa and Lagos, a number of independent churches were founded in the late nineteenth and early twentieth centuries, and were known collectively as "Ethiopian" in South Africa and "African" in Lagos.

In South Africa, the first "Ethiopian" church was established in 1872, and others soon followed. In 1892, a Methodist minister, Mangane Mokone, founded the Ethiopian Church. He listed fourteen grievances, including his inadequate salary and poor housing, but the essential problem was the failure of Europeans to treat Africans as equals: "No African pastor is respected by the white brethren. . . . The White pastors always build their own houses one or two miles away from their parish. The separation shows that we cannot be brothers."[21]

The name "Ethiopian" symbolizes the symbolic significance of its ancient tradition of Christianity and its continuing independence, and reclaims the promise of the Psalmist: "Ethiopia shall stretch out her hands to God."

In 1898, a Lovedale graduate, an ordained minister named Pambani Mzimba, founded the African Presbyterian Church. He was an Mfengu, and so were his supporters. One of them wrote the great hymn "God Bless Africa" ("Nkosi Sikeli Africa"), first sung in 1899, which is now the South African national anthem.

The Ethiopian churches were churches of the urban and the educated, founded as a protest of perpetual white domination of church life and the segregationist racism of many congregations. They grappled with a shortage of funds, a lack of educational facilities, and a shortfall of trained personnel. Because of these problems, the Ethiopian church affiliated itself with the (American) African Methodist Episcopal Church, though this eventually led to similar conflicts over leadership.

In 1904, two leaders of a newly formed independent church described their experiences. Asked why he left the Anglican Church, one replied:

> When we found that we could not get ahead, Makone and myself came together to raise the Church of Ethiopia, and later on we joined the A.M.E. Church of America, because we found at that time that it would go better if we joined the American Church as they had education and other things better than we had—so that they could help us, being coloured people themselves.

In due course, they left the AME Church:

> . . . we thought that, as they were our own colour, they would help us up, but we found they helped us down, and they took all the best positions, without telling us a word, sending men from America.[22]

In the first years of the twentieth century, migrants carried the A.M.E. Church to what is now Zambia, where it became the third largest denomination. But by the 1970s, it was described as "a slowly dying church."[23] The churches that would win a remarkable and enduring success were those which were rooted not in the grievances of black clergy or the shortcomings of settler congregations, but in a vision of a kingdom not of this world, whose name is Zion.

The Ethiopian churches are only one manifestation of a much broader phenomenon. Charles Domingo, from the Mozambique coast, was a protégé of William Koyi. For a time he, too, worked for Livingstonia, and then established an independent church, the Seventh Day Baptists, which foundered for lack of funds. After years of grinding poverty, he became a clerk in government service. In 1911, he wrote one of the best-known denunciations of the European and missionary role. The imperfections of his English are eloquent in themselves:

> There is too much failure among all Europeans in Nyassaland.
>
> The Three Combined Bodies: Missionaries—Government—and Companies or Gainers of money do form the same rule to look on a Native with mockery eyes. It sometimes startles us to see that the Three Combined Bodies are from Europe, and along with them there is a title "CHRISTNDOM." And to compare or make a comparison between the MASTER of the title and His Servants it pushes any African away from believing the Master of the title. If we had power enough to communicate ourselves to Europe, we would have advised them not to call themselfs [sic] "CHRISTNDOM" but "Europeandom." We see that the title "CHRISTNDOM" does not belong to Europe, but to future BRIDE. Therefore the life of The Three Combined Bodies is altogether too cheaty, too thefty, too mockery.[24]

Between 1891 and 1921, a number of similar churches were founded in Lagos through secessions from the Baptists, Methodists, and the CMS. In their heyday, a third of all Christian Yoruba were members. Significantly, it was the laity who took the leading part in these movements. The secession from the CMS reflected the deep feelings of injustice when Crowther was replaced by a white successor, although a number of outstanding African clergy were available.

In only one of these secessions—the Methodist, in 1917—was polygamy the key issue, and here it was less plural marriage as such than the hypocrisy that turned a blind eye to the realities of many church members' lives. A Yoruba cocoa planter had a vision in 1900: "Coker, I want you to go and preach that polygamists become full members of my church."[25]

Some African Church members conducted successful missionary work in the Yoruba interior. They donated generously to their churches; Bethel cathedral, when it was completed, was the tallest building in Lagos.[26] As the clergy had foreseen, independent churches cut themselves off from the financial resources of the missions and from their schools. They often found themselves embroiled in litigation with the missionary societies over property. They were founded over issues of leadership, and in other ways remained very similar to the churches they had left: "They call themselves 'African,' but their services, the robes and titles of their ministers, their surpliced choirs, are all borrowed from England."[27] Their members longed for respectability and for the acceptance of the mission churches. This was their weakness. By 1920, they were in decline, surviving largely out of a sense of family tradition, and it was the prophetic churches, called Aladura among the Yoruba, that attracted a mass membership. Respectability was the least of their concerns. As one of their members put it in 1974:

We Aladuras in Nigeria are a peculiar church. We want to remain peculiar. We want to remain indigenous . . . many people who do not understand us ridicule us. They say that we are not sophisticated, that we are not educated. We know these things, but we are happy that we are an indigenous church, practising Christianity in the indigenous way. . . . God does hear us in this indigenous way and has been doing marvelous work through our hands. Halleluiah.[28]

Chapter 13

Christianity in the Twentieth Century: The Older Churches

The chiefs, the chiefs, to whom do they pray?
To the shades! To the shades! . . .
The Europeans, the Europeans, to whom do they pray?
To money! To money!. . . .
The baptised, the baptised, to whom do they pray?
To Jesus, to Jesus.
    —Hymn sung by Nyakusa Christians in Tanganyika, in the 1930s[1]

In the course of the twentieth century, Christianity's position in Africa, and Africa's in world Christianity, was transformed. Such figures are little more than well-informed guesses, but it is thought that there were some 10 million Christians in Africa in 1910, and that there are at least 300 million now; some estimates are much higher, though there is a demographic factor in figures of this kind that is often overlooked. As early as the 1970s, it was becoming apparent that

> perhaps one of the two or three most important events in the whole of Church history has occurred . . . a complete change in the centre of gravity of Christianity, so that the heartlands of the Church are no longer in Europe, decreasingly in North America, but in Latin America, in certain parts of Asia, and . . . in Africa.[2]

In 1893, over 80 percent of the world's Christians lived in Europe or North America. A century later, some 60 percent lived in the Two-Thirds World—Africa, Asia, Latin America, and the Pacific: "Africa has quietly slipped into the place once occupied by Europe."[3] A Ghanaian theologian has written of "the renewal of a non-western religion."[4] It is often suggested that every day 16,400,[5] and perhaps more, Africans become Christians, while in the Western world about 7,500 cease to be Christians. In 2001, it was said that "the average Anglican [in the world] is a 24-year-old African woman."[6]

Africa's role in world Christianity was illustrated in 2003, when the ordination of openly gay Anglican bishops became an issue and the (anti-gay) views of Nigeria's Anglican archbishop were quoted all over the world.

In about 1900, a slogan immensely popular in mission-minded circles was "The evangelization of the world in this generation." Ten years later, a great (Protestant) missionary conference was held in Edinburgh. Those attending—over 1,200 in number—were mainly American, British, or others of European descent. There was a small contingent of Asian Christians, and one anonymous Liberian.[7] It was the apogee of the nineteenth-century missionary movement, and optimistic plans were laid for future expansion and cooperation.

Four years later, the First World War broke out, vast numbers of young men were slaughtered, and many missionaries joined their national armies or were interned as enemy aliens. A huge crack appeared in Europe's cultural self-confidence, and it would have a profound impact on Christian theology. Later, the Great Depression reduced mission funding dramatically. In 1939, the Second World War broke out.

In mainstream churches, Christian exclusivism waned, and missionaries and others became more aware of the value and religious insights of other cultures. If the heathen were not in danger of perishing, it seemed less urgent to convert them. As early as 1910, Protestant missionary recruitment was falling. The London Missionary Society ceased to exist in the late 1970s. From the 1960s on, the Catholic missionary congregations struggled with declining recruitment, part of a major international downturn in religious and priestly vocations.

Since the beginning of the twentieth century, there has been a dramatic decline in religious conviction and church attendance in the Western world that has had an obvious impact not only on missionary personnel but also on finances. The rise of Evangelism and Pentecostalism in America is the most obvious exception. Apart from this, post-Christian secularity has tended to prevail, interspersed with pockets of intense religious conviction.

So much has been written on Africa's independent churches that it is easy to lose sight of the vast numbers of men and women who lived and died in the mission churches. By 1990, almost half of South Africa's black Christians were members of Zionist churches. We know far more about them than we do, for instance, about black Anglicans or Methodists. As we shall see below, they had more in common than is often recognized.

Many Christians, however, have felt at home in quite traditional church structures. Michael Iwene Tansi, an Igbo Catholic priest who died in 1964, and was beatified in 1998, is a good example. His father was a traditionalist who named him Iwene ("let malice not kill me," a reference to the sacking of their town by the Royal Niger Company). He sent Iwene to school so that he would be better able to protect himself and his family from white oppression. Michael, as he became, was devout from childhood. He became a village schoolmaster and then a diocesan priest, following a life of Franciscan poverty and charity. He inspired vast parishes; Francis Arinze, now a cardinal, was a schoolboy in one of them. In 1950, seeking a still more perfect way, Tansi joined a Cistercian abbey in England, where he died. Tansi was extremely close to his Nigerian parishioners but had no interest in acculturation. He made war on mask societies and was totally obedient to his white bishop.

One reason for the intense religious devotion of many first-generation Christians was the fact that they knew Christianity only from missionary teachings and the Bible. Like Saint Antony in the Egyptian desert, they took it for granted that the Gospels were a map to live by. In the highly secularized and largely post-Christian Western world, this insight is almost invisible. The words of an Asian Christian thread their way through the writings of Newbigin, who was a missionary for forty years in India: "Can the West be converted?"[8]

There was often a sense of new beginnings that were communal as well as individual ("Behold, I make all things new"):

> The Gospel began to form a new nation from that of old Kikuyu. . . . We are at the beginning of a great building up of new customs and the forming of Christianity.[9]

Missionary sources and histories tend to concentrate on entrances rather than exits, but a considerable number of Christians were under some form of ban, depending on the church (excluded from communion, in the Catholic case). Polygamy was a frequent reason, though not the only one. Such was the value placed on children that monogamy required heroic faith if a marriage was childless, though an aristocratic couple from Buganda, Isabella Birabwa and Alexis Sebbowa, chief of Buddu, followed this path, as did many other obscure—and not so obscure—couples. A situation where large numbers of fervent Christians were excluded from full church membership reflects the rigidity of missionary practice.

Some became Christians because they were disappointed with the failure of traditional gods to meet their needs. Some left Christianity for the same reason:

> I had believed that, being a Christian, one would no longer fall sick; but I now see that the worship of God and idolatry is one and the same thing, for wherever one is, one falls sick and dies. Therefore I have gone back.[10]

During the years of civil war and famine that followed the Sudan's independence, many Dinka turned to Christianity because the gods seemed unable to protect them. They came to appear greedy, demanding cattle in sacrifice but giving nothing in return. They are called Satan (in Arabic, *shetani*). The Christian God is identified with the traditional supreme God, Nhialic.[11]

MISSIONARIES TO YOURSELVES

The line between mission and independent churches was in many ways an artificial one. Both had self-supporting African congregations and relied heavily on African staff. The difference lay in whether leadership was foreign or local, in international affiliations (and consequent access to external resources), and, to varying degrees, in worship styles.

In 1969, Pope Paul VI visited Uganda and said, in words that have often been echoed since, "You Africans must be missionaries to yourselves." Africans had always been missionaries to themselves, both in the missions and in the African Initiated Churches that are the subject of the next chapter. Between 1925 and 1954, two remarkable blind Methodists, Pa Mbovai and Matthew Moamie, made a major contribution to the spread of Christianity among the Mende of Sierra Leone: "[T]hey memorised and repeated whole sections of the Bible, making their way alone along the difficult paths between villages. Both men were prolific in the composition of Christian songs in Mende mode, which are still sung and loved in mission churches."[12]

One of the really remarkable aspects of twentieth-century mission history is the way in which churches often expanded when the missionaries departed. Perhaps the most dramatic example, internationally, is China. In Africa, there were striking examples during the First World War. The Bremen mission began work among the Ewe of southeastern Gold Coast in 1847. When the war broke out, its German missionaries were interned. The Ewe church became the independent Evangelical Presbyterian Church in 1922.[13] The Sudan Interior Mission began work in Ethiopia in 1927; they had forty-eight baptized members ten years later, when they were forced to leave after Mussolini's invasion. When they returned in 1942, they had 10,000 adherents.

Churches flourished in the absence of missionaries; they also relied heavily on African agency when missionaries were present. Each mission became the headquarters of a network of outstations where foreign faces were seldom seen. The European missionary became more of a manager than a pastor, and the local congregation was led by a teacher-catechist:

> These indigenous auxiliaries, catechists and teachers, are, so to say, the extensions of the Fathers. They teach the catechism, the life of our Lord and of the Blessed Virgin, and church history in school (five times a week), and instruct those preparing for baptism. They sow the good seed profusely, the Father can only provide the organisation and supervision.[14]

In 1949, the Methodist Church in Ivory Coast had 3 pastors, 160 cat-echists, and 50,000 members. But by this time, the roles of teacher and cat-echist were becoming separated, and the catechist system was declining, largely because the poor rates of pay made it unattractive to the educated. Most catechists, often men of transparent devotion and dedication, lived and died in obscurity. They were paid so little that they were essentially volun-teers. J.W. Abruquah's lightly fictionalized memoir of his father, a Fante Methodist catechist who repeatedly applied unsuccessfully for training as a minister, reflects his poverty and frustration. His large family survived on his meager salary only because his wife baked and sold bread. He was initially a teacher-catechist, but during his career, the roles were separated: "I hated the name [catechist], I hated the profession, but [I] was too old to try to get out."[15] After fifty years of service, he retired without a pension.

The first catechist in Upper Volta (now Burkina Faso), who was one of its first Christians, has become more famous than most of Africa's mission-ary bishops. Alfred Diban Ki-Zerbo (ca. 1875–1980) was rescued from slave traders by the White Fathers and was baptized in Segu in 1900. Like many other early evangelists, he spent some time as a domestic servant, working as a cook and mason for the priests. In 1910, he became a catechist and worked for sixty years in his hometown of Toma. Before he died, he had an audience with the pope in Rome, and is now a candidate for beatification. His fame is due to the fact that his son, Joseph, an internationally famous historian, wrote his biography.[16]

Some early catechists volunteered to work far from their homes. David Kaunda (d. 1932) was a Tonga Presbyterian from Livingstonia who left his home in 1904 to work among the Bemba in northern Rhodesia. He was fi-nally ordained in 1930. His wife, Helen, was one of the country's first African women teachers. Their youngest son, Kenneth (b. 1924), was the first presi-dent of independent Zambia.

Bernard Mizeki, from Inhambane Bay in Mozambique, became a Chris-tian in Cape Town. He was one of five catechists chosen to accompany an Anglican bishop to the Shona area of Rhodesia in 1891. He was much loved, but lost his life in the rising of 1896. He is revered as a martyr, and his grave is a place of pilgrimage.

There was a serious, ongoing shortage of black clergy, due largely to a reluctance to ordain them. Those who wished to become Catholic priests had to master Latin and to commit both to long years of study and to celi-bacy. They were rejected for the slightest shortcoming. Two hundred semi-narians came and went in Gabon before the first priest, Rapunda Walker, was ordained in 1919. Exemplary teacher-catechists waited for many years for ordination. David Kaunda is an example. "Let us be ordained before we die," cried an Ngoni Presbyterian.[17] Even when they reached their goal, they were not treated as the equals of their European counterparts. In Tanzania, in the

1920s, African CMS priests were paid less than one-fifteenth of the salaries of European ones.[18]

MISSIONS AND EDUCATION

By the early twentieth century, it had become apparent that the Christian village was a marginal ghetto; whole societies would not be converted in this way. Some missionaries, such as the Irish Holy Ghost Father, Bishop Joseph Shanahan (1871–1943), realized with great clarity that their best strategy was to concentrate on education.

All colonial governments were anxious to cut expenditures to the minimum. In the sphere of local government, they did this by relying heavily on African agency: the "traditional" ruler, who was often far from traditional, and in any case now filled nontraditional roles. The British and the Belgians in the Congo relied on the missions to run schools, except in Muslim areas. (The situation was different in French colonies, because of the separation of church and state.) The Holy Ghost Fathers began to send Irishmen, not Frenchmen, to southeastern Nigeria. Their schools received government subsidies, which solved their chronic financial problems and gave them the chance to form the minds of a generation (and through them, of generations to come). By 1945, over 94 percent of all the students in British African colonies were at mission schools. As we have seen, the close links between Christianity and Western education meant that at independence, Muslims were disadvantaged.

In the nineteenth century, there was only a handful of Igbo Catholics. By the late 1920s, the Holy Ghost Fathers were overwhelmed by the demand for baptism. There were 47,000 catechumens in one village group alone, some of whom had waited for seven years:

> They are not baptised because there is no one to conduct the examinations, and because one could not cope with such a large number of Christians. . . . It is a deplorable situation. . . . Confessions have been deliberately limited. These sacraments are not necessary every time that the Christians would like to receive them.[19]

Children and/or their parents gradually became aware that school paved the way to a salary. Kikuyu schoolchildren sang:

> Father, mother,
> Provide me with pen and slate,
> I want to learn.
> Land is gone,
> Cattle and sheep are not there,
> Not there anymore.
> What's left?
> Learning, learning.[20]

In southern Nigeria, a man from the Yoruba-Edo borderland, who had become a Christian when enslaved, ultimately returned home:

> He told us of heaven where the angels paraded with their gracious and merciful wings. . . . He told us also of the benefits that would accrue to us in the form of salary. We wondered what salary was. It was later on that we started to understand everything.[21]

On the other side of Africa, a Chagga from Kilimanjaro remembered:

> The first advantage was the joy and hope of going to heaven. The second was to know the craft of carpentry.[22]

They are not, of course, as the life of Jesus reminds us, mutually exclusive!

School was attractive because of its novelty, and because of the prospect of economic betterment, but those who encountered Christianity in this way often became fervent and dedicated Christians. Filipo Njau, another Chagga, went to school because as a younger son, he would inherit little. He became a notable Lutheran teacher and preacher, one of those who sustained the local church when the German missionaries were interned. He wrote in his (German) autobiography:

> Many boys came to instruction to learn to read and write, things to their advantage. Then behold! In the midst of their craving to read and write, the Word of God in their reading books overwhelmed them. . . . They became Christians, saved by Jesus, children of God. So it was with me.[23]

At first, the missions concentrated on primary school education, which was initially sufficient for employment. Later, boarding schools were established so that a tiny fraction of the primary school graduates could go on to secondary studies, though this was an artificial and harsh environment, which cut them off from village life. The elite of independent Africa came largely from these schools. Often, they were the children of catechists, village schoolmasters, or Protestant clergy.

Not all converts sought education or were the product of mission schools. In the early 1980s, I got to know an old man who lived near Jos, in central Nigeria, in an area dominated by a faith mission. Nyampi was the first Anaguta Christian, converted by a Berom villager who taught him to read, but not to write. When I knew him, his eyesight was failing, but he slept with his beloved Hausa Bible under his pillow. In his younger days, he had built a small church near his house, its pulpit and pews shaped from clay. He told me that one thing alone had attracted him to Christianity: the prospect of eternal life.

STRIKE A BLOW AND DIE

Christians on the whole took little part in anticolonial uprisings, which tended to be led by Muslims or neotraditional prophets. When such uprisings occurred in areas where Christianity was well established, the Christian community was divided. Some Christian Zulu took part in the Bambata uprising of 1906, but the majority realized that success was unlikely, and preferred to follow the path of improvement.

Namibia was German South West Africa at the beginning of the twentieth century. The population of this barren and sparsely inhabited land included two groups of pastoralists: 80,000 Bantu-speaking Herero in the north and 20,000 Khoi-speaking Nama in the south. As with the Griqua farther east, mixed-race Dutch-speaking Christians called Oorlam (a Malay word for "rascals") had introduced both Christianity and a measure of Afrikaner culture. In 1904, the Herero rose against colonial rule, under the leadership of a Christian, Samuel Maherero: ". . . it is my wish that we weak nations should rise up against the Germans. Either we destroy them or they all will live in our country. There is nothing else for it." Missionaries, women, children, and non-German nationals were to be spared.[24] In 1905, the Nama joined them, and fought on until 1907. At the end of the uprising, 80 percent of the Herero and half the Nama were dead.

An extremely small uprising in what is now Malawi, in 1915, has been studied in detail by scholars and has become famous. John Chilembwe (d.1915), a Yao, was the archetypal improver. Most Yao were Muslims, but Chilembwe went to work for a missionary as a boy. He embraced Christianity and Western education, and five years later he was able to study in America. His benefactor was Joseph Booth (1851–1932), who moved restlessly from one denomination to the next and in the process exercised an incalculable influence. Booth was unusual for his time in his radical identification with African causes—in 1897 he published a book titled *Africa for the Africans.* He founded the independent Zambezi Industrial Mission in what is now Malawi, which is where he employed Chilembwe. Booth went on to join the Watch Tower Bible and Tract Society (now called Jehovah's Witnesses). Chilembwe returned home and founded the Providence Industrial Mission, initially with African-American Baptist backing. It educated hundreds of children, but he struggled with lack of funds and with the fact that most of the local land was in white hands—ironically, it belonged to Livingstone's son-in-law, and later his grandson.

When the First World War broke out, Chilembwe wrote in the local newspaper, "In time of peace, everything for Europeans only. . . . But in time of war it has been found that we are needed to share hardships and shed our blood in equality."[25] Soon afterward he led a small band in a foredoomed attack on local plantation owners; several lost their lives, among them William Livingstone. Chilembwe was killed soon afterward.

By far the best-educated Malawian of his time, Chilembwe, a partially sighted asthmatic, was an unlikely revolutionary. He seems to have intended to make a symbolic gesture: "John said this case stands the same as that of Mr. John Brown. Let us then 'strike a blow and die,' for our blood will surely mean something at last."[26]

PATTERNS OF CHANGE

The growth of Western education and Christianity created new divisions in village society. Older men, who in the past regulated local affairs and were respected for their knowledge, were suddenly marginalized as illiterate "pagans." In what is now northern Zambia, in 1908, complaints were made that "The school-teachers have been trying too much to take chiefship on themselves of late."[27] Some African Christians embarked on confrontations with masking societies. Others destroyed traditional shrines, sometimes plundering their offerings. They were, from the point of view of the district officer, disturbers of the peace, and were treated accordingly.

"Traditional" rulers' relationship with Christianity varied considerably. In some areas, even where Christianity was well established, it was thought that the role of these rulers was incompatible with it. It was said of Akuapem, in southeastern Ghana, in 1993, "Most kings since the beginning of this century have been brought up as Christian, but even in this almost totally Christian kingdom it is still not possible for the ruling king himself to be one."[28]

In other places, such as Buganda and Rwanda, Christianity became virtually a state ideology. The young king of Buganda, Daudi Cwa, had an Anglican coronation in 1914. In 1931, a Catholic catechumen succeeded to the throne of Rwanda as Mutare IV, after the deposition of his traditionalist father. By 1936, 54 out of 69 chiefs and 756 out of 900 subchiefs in Rwanda were Catholic.[29]

TRANSPORT AND LAND

Both missionaries and African Christians could now travel much more easily and safely, a fact that made the outstation system possible. In the late nineteenth century, missionaries walked from the coast to Uganda. After 1901, they caught a train. They started to ride bicycles down the bush paths. Some African Christians embarked on long journeys, on foot or bicycle, in order to spread their message. Hancock Phiri, a Chewa from Nyasaland who had studied at Livingstonia, joined the African Methodist Episcopal Church in 1924, in Bulawayo, Rhodesia, and devoted himself to spreading its teachings in his homeland. He walked 500 miles to attend an annual conference. John Membe, another Livingstonia graduate, who had been refused baptism for no apparent reason, joined the A.M.E. Church as a young clerk, in 1928, and in time became a minister. He was appointed as a pastor at Abercorn:

"I suffered and troubled a lot before I reached Abercorn . . . there is many miles from Railway Line say about 574 miles away from Railway Line [Broken Hill] and is very hard and important thing for a person to walk from there to Broken Hill or to Ndola by walking only."[30]

Much greater numbers of Christians traveled as labor migrants, taking their religion with them. In 1925, soon after the Zambian copper mines were opened, African Christians working in the area—initially educated clerks from Nyasaland, rather than miners—established an interdenominational school and church, the Union Church of the Copper Belt, and preached in the local villages. In 1936, the missions followed in their footsteps. The miners were active Christians, too—"passing through a compound after dark on almost any night you could find little groups of people gathered around the light of an underground worker's acetylene lamp, singing Christian hymns."[31]

In the nineteenth century, as we have noted in relation to Natal, missions in eastern and southern Africa often acquired vast tracts of land, a pattern that continued in the twentieth century. Sometimes mission land passed into private hands—including those of missionaries or their children—or missionaries acquired additional land for themselves. At the other extreme, we have the saintly High Church Anglican priest Arthur Shearly Cripps, another remarkably long-lived servant of God (b. 1869). He reached Zimbabwe (then Rhodesia) in 1901, and stayed there, except for a short interval abroad, until he died in 1952. (He went blind at sixty.) He acquired 7,000 acres at Chivhu, but lived and died in a traditional thatched house next to his small Church of the Five Wounds. Transparently, his aim was to protect the Africans living there from the encroachment of white settlers.

Missionaries often sought to use the land they controlled to generate income. This was, in a sense, a legitimate aim, but it meant establishing plantation agriculture, rather than leaving the land available for African farmers. "There is no difference between a missionary and a settler," said the Kikuyu grimly.

CHANGING PERSPECTIVES

The idea that the heathen are perishing is not entirely dead. A Nigerian Evangelical defended the viewpoint that Africans who never heard the Christian message are in Hell.[32] But in general, succeeding generations of missionaries came to believe that there are many different paths to God and that, for instance, the traditional religion of the Yoruba is a Yoruba Old Testament. Some missionaries became outstanding ethnographers. Henri Junod was a Swiss missionary working among the Tsonga (Shangaan) of Mozambique. His *The Life of a South African Tribe,* a two-volume work published in 1912, is a classic, and still a precious resource.[33] Not all missionaries at the time believed that ethnographic research was a good thing. John Roscoe's *The Baganda,* another classic, was condemned as searching "in the dustbin and rubbish heaps of Uganda for the foolish and unclean customs of the people long thrown away."[34] Since then, many missionaries have contributed in profound ways to our understanding of Africa, and they have produced some notable ethnographies.

African theologians such as John Mbiti and Bolaji Idowu, who emerged at about the time when African nations were regaining their independence, naturally concentrated on affirming the elements in their own culture that were most compatible with Christianity. This was not, as we have seen, the optimum way of studying "traditional" religion, but they were attempting to reach some kind of satisfactory synthesis between the religion of the past and their own faith, a matter of paramount importance to African Christians. But there were many ways of achieving a synthesis, and far more lives were touched by the Aladura churches than by books of theology.

Over the years, African Christians in mainstream churches and elsewhere have formed their own syntheses with the past. Wole Soyinka's delightful memoir of his childhood in a Christian teacher's family in the Yoruba city of Abeokuta reflects a time when aspects of tradition were still part of everyone's cognitive map. Uncle Sanya, with the aid of forest spirits, manages to eat fifty bean cakes. Abruquah's father, a Fante catechist constantly transferred from one place to another, had a number of encounters with mysterious spirits: "I do believe in ghosts and particularly in the ghost of Sekondi."[35]

Some lamented the absence of a synthesis. Kenneth Kaunda paid tribute to his parents' unquestioning faith, but said, "I feel within myself the tension created by the collision of two worlds which I have never completely reconciled."[36]

Colonial missionaries typically experienced an unresolved contradiction, too. They were hostile to many aspects of traditional life, including some that now seem neutral from a religious point of view. But many missionaries, like many colonial administrators, were also strongly opposed to "detribalization" and urbanization. In practice this sometimes meant a refusal to provide the literacy in English that African students craved. Some thought that education would disqualify girls for marriage. There was a profound symbolism in the fact that missionaries opposed the construction of a bridge between the Christian village of Freretown and the city of Mombasa.[37]

Some aspects of some traditional religions—human sacrifice, the twin taboo—were clearly incompatible with Christianity. Some selection and synthesis was necessary. The question was whether this should be created by foreign missionaries or by local Christians. Where their syntheses were incompatible, confrontation sometimes resulted—the bitter conflict between Kikuyu Christians and missionaries over female circumcision in 1929 is an example. To missionaries, it was cruel, and surrounded by sexually explicit (hence undesirable) rituals. To Kikuyu women, it was an essential prelude to adult life and marriage. In 1982, the government of Kenya banned the practice, but it still survives and is much debated in a number of African ethnic groups.

MOVEMENTS WITHIN THE CHURCHES

The East African Revival, Balokole (Saved Ones), anticipated in many ways the neo-Pentecostal movement that became a major feature of the African Christian landscape from the 1980s on. It began in Rwanda and Uganda in the 1930s, with the interaction between a foreign missionary, a CMS doctor named Joe Church who was working in Rwanda, and a member of the Ganda educated elite, Simeon Nsibambi (1897–1978). They met in 1929, when Church introduced Nsibambi to the ideas of the Holiness movement,[38] a particular culture within Evangelism. The basic concept is that after conversion, one should go through a second religious experience which will empower the believer for holy living.

Nsibambi, a public health officer, gave up his work and became a full-time evangelist. His younger brother, Blasio Kigozi, went to Rwanda in 1931 to work with Church. The brothers held several revivals that had the watchword "Zukaka" (Awaken). Blasio died in 1936 while on an evangelistic journey. The word "Zukaka" is on his tombstone. Nsibambi was afflicted with a mysterious illness in 1941 and was a housebound invalid until his death in 1978.

Church and his associates broke away from the CMS. Their outlook was very similar to that of the white missionaries who destroyed the Niger Mission in the 1880s, though the results turned out to be much more constructive. Like the earlier missionaries, they condemned the "dead" spiritual state of their fellow Christians. Holiness was often defined in terms of prohibitions: the Rwanda missionaries would not baptize a baby unless both parents were teetotalers.

The Saved Ones radically rejected traditional religion, often symbolizing this rejection by eating taboo foods. Like the members of the Oxford Movement, they stressed the public confession of sins, and felt that, in the words of a Tanganyikan Christian, "the church had become worldly and the world churchly."[39] All this was, of course, bitterly distressing to the African Christians they called Laodiceans. In the words of a pioneer Tanganyikan pastor:

> They hopped and danced and despised those who had not yet been revived. They refused to eat coffee-beans or groundnuts or to use ornaments and spears. They soon started to have their own services and despised their former friends, saying, "You have not yet been saved."[40]

With the exception of a few splinter groups, the Saved Ones stayed in the church, and in time became its leaders.

The Mau Mau war broke out in Kenya in 1954, soon after the Revival had reached the area. It was essentially a Kikuyu struggle for settler-occupied land, its ideology rooted in neotraditional religion, but it also became a civil war, since many Kikuyu opposed it. The Saved Ones refused to take the oaths that the Mau Mau required, and many lost their lives.

A later and less well-known movement, the Legion of Christ's Witnesses, was founded in 1948 by two Zulu Anglican priests: the future bishop, Alphaeus Zulu (1905–1988), and the future canon, Philip Mbatha. It is still flourishing among Zulu Anglicans, although initially some Europeans thought the emphasis on healing was "un-Anglican." It is a charismatic movement in the Holiness tradition, with a strong emphasis on the confession of sins: "The power of the Holy Spirit is seen to manifest itself in tongues, visions, prophecy, healing and exorcism."[41] Clearly, it has much in common with the Zionist churches.

Emmanuel Milingo (b. 1933) became the Catholic archbishop of Lusaka in 1969—for many Africans, both inside the churches and outside them, it was a decade of golden opportunity. In 1973, he began a public ministry of healing and exorcism that won the hearts of local people but alarmed expatriate missionaries. (Again, there was an interaction with foreigners, in this case American charismatic Catholics.) Milingo made no secret of his belief in the reality both of witchcraft and of the possessing spirits that had become generically known as *mashave*. In 1983 he was removed from his office after complaints from other bishops, and was summoned to Rome, where he was given a minor post. He continued to practice healing and exorcism among Italian charismatics. In 2000 he caused a sensation when he was married in one of the Unification Church's mass weddings. Apparently he saw the Unification Church as an interdenominational body that would give him the openings for healing and evangelism that his own church denied him. He soon renounced the marriage and returned to Catholicism. Milingo still lives in Italy, a controversial figure with strong supporters and detractors. The former believe that Zambian Catholics were deprived of a charismatic leader with remarkable gifts of healing. Yet even they tend to feel uneasy about his emphasis on exorcism and the identification of the spirits of neotraditional religion with Satan. Milingo has much in common with the Balokole, the Legion of Christ's Witnesses, and the neo-Pentecostals, whose remarkable expansion is the subject of chapter 15.

CHURCH LEADERSHIP

A situation in which black churches were led by white bishops or the equivalent lasted well into the nationalist era. It was, understandably, hard for white missionaries to relinquish control of the churches to which they had devoted their lives: "Lord, make our church self-governing, but not yet." The first black Catholic African bishop since the consecration of Don

Henriques in 1518 was a Ugandan named Joseph Kiwanuka, who was consecrated in 1939, at the same ceremony as a bishop from Madagascar. He was the only such bishop until 1951, the year in which the first African Anglican bishops since Crowther were appointed, both in Nigeria. (There had been assistant bishops earlier, a position described by one of them as "half bishops.")

As African nations became self-governing, African churches inevitably did the same. By 1990, 95 percent of Africa's Catholic bishops were Africans. They still depended heavily on funds from abroad and, in some areas, on expatriate personnel.

In South Africa, the first black Catholic bishop was appointed in 1954; the first black Anglican one in 1960; and the first black president of the Methodist Church in 1964. African church leaders in apartheid South Africa led difficult lives. When Alphaeus Zulu became bishop of Zululand in 1968, some Europeans left the church, and the government did not permit him to move into his official residence. The Anglican archbishop of Uganda, an Acholi named Janani Luwum, who had been converted by the Balokole, was put to death by Idi Amin in 1977 for publicly protesting the brutalities of his regime. His last words, to a fellow bishop, were "They are going to kill me. I am not afraid." His statue stands in Westminster Abbey.

Luwum was a martyr, but churches, like all human societies, embrace both saints and sinners, and as Saint Augustine knew well, we will know which is which only in eternity. African priests and nuns had varying degrees of complicity in the frightful events in Rwanda in 1994, which led to the creation of a new word, *genocidaire*. (There were courageous exceptions, several of whom lost their lives.)

African churches aspired to economic independence as well as self-government. In 1974, a meeting of the All-African Council of (Protestant) Churches in Lusaka called for a temporary moratorium on "external assistance in money and personnel," though it proved impossible to implement. The Catholics were still dependent on foreign clergy; a Kenyan bishop said, "For some time the missionaries are still a necessary evil."[42] All this contrasts with the increasing need for foreign aid in the 1980s and later, a direct result of Africa's deepening financial crisis that would produce another neologism, Afro-pessimism.

GENDER

Hastings has suggested that African churches began as, and have returned to being, "'feminine alternative societies to the male dominated secular world'; that when the church was marginal to society, women were central to it, and that they have become so again. In the colonial period, the church became less marginal and women more so.[43] This is not entirely convincing; as we have seen, the opposite pattern has been documented among the Ngwato Tswana.

In the nineteenth and early twentieth centuries, many of the first Christians were women. Not all were marginal in traditional society—one thinks of the Ganda aristocrats—but many of them were accused of witchcraft or in some other way belonged to the world of the disinherited, where Christianity so often first took root.

There is no simple answer to the question of the impact of Christianity on women's lives. Some believe that the unmarried Protestant women missionaries, who came to play such an important role, provided models of autonomous behavior (though in practice, their independence was limited). In the Zionist-Aladura type of churches, there are many instances of women founders and leaders, but often women played a subordinate role. The Celestial Church of Christ excludes menstruating women from church services. Some individuals were empowered by Christianity, such as Bribina, an Ijo woman from the Niger Delta, who became a Christian in 1905. She gave birth to twins, refused to abandon one of them as local custom dictated, and was forced to leave her home with her infants. She was rescued by a passing trader, settled elsewhere, and went on to become a notable Christian evangelist.[44] On the other hand, we have the comment of an Igbo fourth wife in the 1920s: "Why fourth wife no fit be good like fourth wife? Suppose God make that law, God no do good fashion."[45]

In traditional cultures, women were often empowered by acting collectively. By the 1940s, powerful women's organizations had developed, called Manyano in South Africa. In Rhodesia, the equivalent, Rukwadzano, was founded in 1939 by the wives of Methodist ministers. They have many counterparts elsewhere and still flourish, dominated by the middle-aged and hostile to drink and polygamy. Like their Zionist counterparts, they wear distinctive clothing that symbolizes their solidarity and separation from the world, and hold regular meetings for prayer and healing.

Both individually and collectively, women tend to bear more than their share of the churches' financial burdens. It was said of Methodists in the Gold Coast, "The women were wonderful. They paid their class and ticket money at all costs and I saw that they were buried with their latest ticket in their hand."[46] One of Africa's largest neo-Pentecostal churches, the Zimbabwe Churches of God, Africa, was initially financed by the "penny capitalism" of its women members.[47] When the South African Pentecostal leader Nicholas Bhengu was advised in a vision to stop seeking overseas funds, he was told to obtain them "from the women of your church," and he did so.[48]

Despite the emphasis on motherhood, many African Catholic women chose to become religious—again, the appeal of collectivity. In 1984, a Kongo woman who had been a sister since the early 1940s said, "The fact that I have chosen to live as a celibate woman religious costs me greatly even now in my later years. . . . I will leave no children of my own in this world.

And yet to give myself to God and to his people is what I do want to do with my life. I am so happy."[49]

Again, the Ganda were the pioneers. Maria Matilda Munaku was the sister of one of the martyrs and had asked, in vain, to share his fate. Baptized in 1886, she made a commitment to celibacy and formed a group of single women to care for the seminarians of Buddu, long before the first European sisters arrived in 1899. In 1908, the new African congregation was formally established, the Bannabikira (Daughters of the Virgin). In 1924, their first African mother superior, Mother Ursula Nalube, was appointed. By 1957, they had over 500 members, devoted mainly to primary school teaching, who were working both in Buganda and far beyond it. This is the most famous example, but there are many other African congregations and many African women in international ones. They greatly outnumber priests, and it is often said that the future of the Catholic Church in Africa lies largely in their hands.

RELIGION, STATE, AND SOCIETY

Today's missionaries lament the ethnocentricity of their predecessors. There is a profound irony in their advocacy of an enculturation that has long since arrived, and there is, as Milingo pointed out, often an unsconscious paternalism in its presentation:

> ... we have been surprised that those who have specialised in African liturgical adaptations have been the Westerners. . . . What they approve, we Africans must approve.[50]

There is a real sense in which both African Christian theologians and foreign missionaries have, for a long time, been fighting yesterday's battles, opposing long-dead stereotypes and looking backward to a romanticized past, rather than forward. Outside South Africa during the apartheid era, liberation theology has had little impact in Africa. (In Latin America, where it first developed, it has not stemmed the tide of neo-Pentecostalism.)

African and white neo-Pentecostals enthusiastically seek converts. This has long since ceased to be the core activity of mainstream missions, which are now more concerned with providing social services than with direct evangelism.

> In Africa the Christian involvement in development is enormous, not just in traditional areas of schools and hospitals, but in digging wells, housing projects, farming, or weaving cooperatives.[51]

The Catholic agency Caritas is the third largest nongovernmental organization in the overwhelmingly Muslim Gambia. All this reflects a change in attitudes, a transition from a privatised, pietistic, supernaturalised Christianity. . . . Salvation is understood as liberation not just from sin and hell, but from fear, from want, from hunger, from ignorance, from anything that diminishes the image of God in a human being.[52]

It becomes a paramount duty to struggle for social justice, both by development strategies and by the critique, where appropriate, of oppressive and corrupt governments. After Luwum's death, Desmond Tutu declared:

Political leaders have often been let down by a sycophantic Church leadership . . . who are content to be time servers. The Church in Africa is faced with this challenge of injustice, corruption, oppression and exploitation at home, and it has no option but to fulfil its prophetic vocation or seriously call in question its claim to be the Church of Jesus Christ.[53]

As the murder of Luwum illustrates, this kind of critique could lead to exile, prison, or death. It often did so in South Africa.

Political histories, however, were shaped not by theologians but by politicians. Julius Nyerere (1922–1999), a former teacher in a Catholic school, was the first president of Tanzania, from its independence in 1961 until 1985, when he retired voluntarily. In his last years he devoted himself to the quest for peace in Burundi. He was called Mwalimu (the teacher). He rigidly excluded religion from political life and was succeeded by a Muslim. He advocated *ujamaa* (from the root *jamaa*, family), African socialism, a blend of an idealized African past and Christian principles. Its implementation, by measures such as the creation of *ujamaa* villages, ran into problems that were hugely exacerbated by the economic crisis which gripped the country from the 1970s on, and by the nation's intrinsic poverty. It was abandoned by his successor. Nyerere's African critics said you cannot have socialism with only one socialist. There was more than one when I worked in Tanzania.

Ujamaa is now of essentially historical interest. Nyerere came to regret his mistakes, such as the adoption of one-party rule. But in an age when the word "kleptocracy" was coined to describe African politics, Nyerere, the incorruptible if fallible idealist, will not be forgotten.

Kenneth Kaunda (b. 1924) was president of Zambia from independence in 1964 until 1991, when he lost an election—few African rulers have relinquished power in this way. He always emphasized his own Christian background and beliefs, and adopted a philosophy similar to *ujamaa*, which he called "humanism"—an unfortunate choice, because of the word's agnostic overtones. This, together with an interest he developed in Eastern gurus, alienated the Born Again. A researcher has recorded a critique of a different kind, from a Zambian mine worker in the 1880s:

[A]ll these books have not brought anything [for] a Zambian to enjoy. So personally, how dare we toil over a book which has brought hunger on my body— imagine I got two boys, not knowing what was to come. I am unable to meet their needs, then to hell with humanism or socialism.[54]

The cause of this poverty and suffering was a catastrophic fall in copper prices.

CHURCH AND STATE IN SOUTH AFRICA

It was in South Africa that the interactions between Christianity, state, and society became particularly tragic and traumatic. In 1948, the National Party came to power, committed to a policy of apartheid that in many respects was the culmination of earlier legislation. The Land Act of 1913 restricted the black 70 percent of the population to 7 percent (later 13 percent) of the land. The age of the prosperous entrepreneurial peasant was replaced by one in which men worked as labor migrants in the mines or cities while their families struggled to wrest a living from overcrowded and degenerating land. Tiya Soga, like countless other Africans, had seen education as the key to a better life for his people, but the education of a black child cost a tenth or less of that of a white child. In the 1930s, half of all African children did not go to school, and of those who did, only 0.6 percent went past primary school.

Apartheid, the Dutch Reformed Church, and a sense of identity as the chosen people of God were closely associated in a complex of ideas rooted in Afrikaner history. The sense of a special destiny was shaped by folk memories of the Great Trek and of the South African War, and by the tendency of English speakers to marginalize their language and culture, implicit in the word Boer (farmer).

D. F. Malan, the Dutch Reformed minister who led the National Party to victory, said, "Our history is the greatest masterpiece of the centuries . . . the history of the Afrikaner reveals a will and a determination which makes one feel that Afrikanerdom is not the work of men but the creation of God."[55] This kind of identification is a sort of civil religion. The Afrikaners saw themselves as opposing "godless communism," and found the growing body of Christian criticism painful.

Interracial marriage became illegal. Older "pass laws" were systematized, so that only Africans employed by whites could live in towns. The rest were virtual prisoners in the reserves, which came to be called Homelands. The Bantu Education Act removed education from missionary control and organized it in a way designed to keep the black majority in perpetual subordination. The Suppression of Communism Act of 1950 gave the government extreme powers to crush dissent, whether "Communist" or not. Thousands chose exile or were imprisoned (many died mysteriously) or were placed under house arrest. Ten Bantustans were created, beginning in 1976. Their sovereignty was an illusion, and since they had no international recognition, their passports were useless and their citizens effectively stateless.

The architects of apartheid claimed that they were maintaining the uniqueness of each ethnic group, giving each the chance to shape its own destiny. The fatal flaw was that political power and economic resources were monopolized by the white minority. While the rest of the continent moved toward independence, black South Africans lacked both political freedom and economic and educational opportunities. The Lutheran Bishop Manas Buthelezi pointed out that a just society would free Africans from oppression, and white South Africans from fear.

The dreams and aspirations of educated black Christians took a long time to die. The much-loved Dr. A.B. Xuma, president of the African National Congress (ANC) from 1940 to 1949, said that the ANC was "working for the good of all South Africans, working to promote the ideals of Christianity, human decency and democracy."[56]

Chief Albert Luthuli (1898–1967) looked back to his days as a young teacher and remembered:

> . . . the world seemed to be opening out for Africans. It seemed mainly a matter of proving our ability and worth as citizens, and that did not seem impossible. We were, of course, aware of the existence of colour prejudice, but we did not dream that it would endure and intensify as it has.[57]

Luthuli's frame of reference remained specifically Christian: "The road to freedom is via the Cross." He was awarded the Nobel Peace Prize, as Desmond Tutu was, years later. He came to believe that "thirty years of my life have been spent knocking in vain, patiently, moderately and modestly at a closed and barred door."[58]

A younger generation of black activists, though often Christians, did not adopt this framework of public discourse, partly because they were disillusioned with the role of the churches—which rioters often burned down— and partly because of the extent to which they mirrored the values of white society. They knew that equality must be demanded as a right, not be earned by education.

The Dutch Reformed Church had three separate ethnically based "daughter" churches: African, "Coloured," and Indian. (It also had a missionary outreach that extended as far as the Tiv of central Nigeria, and maintained a large network of orphanages, schools for the deaf and blind, hospitals, homes for the incurably ill, and so on.[59]) In 1978, it rejected an invitation from the "daughter" churches to unite.

In the 1950s, the dissident Christian voice was predominantly that of Africans such as Luthuli, or of white liberals like Michael Scott and Trevor Huddleston, whom Steve Biko, the architect of Black Consciousness, later condemned for articulating the problems of one world while enjoying the privileges of another.

Trevor Huddleston (1913–1998) was an Anglican priest in the Community of the Resurrection. He had a notable ministry in Sophiatown, a slum in Johannesburg, until his bishop sent him back to England in 1956, fearing that he would be deported. He then wrote a book, *Naught for Your Comfort*, which had an electrifying impact, and went on to work in Tanzania and elsewhere. Michael Scott (1907–1983), another Anglican priest, devoted himself to political activism. Imprisoned and then deported, he went on to represent Namibia at the United Nations, where year after year he protested South Africa's illegal rule there.

In 1960, at Sharpeville, police fired on a crowd protesting the pass laws, killing 69 and injuring 186. It was a defining moment. An Afrikaans poet wrote:

> The child has become a giant and travels through all the world
> Without a pass.

Thousands were arrested, and the ANC was outlawed. In 1961, representatives of the World Council of Churches met representatives of the South African member churches at Cottesloe. Those present, including the Dutch Reformed Church delegates, signed a declaration condemning apartheid. The synods of the Dutch Reformed Church not only refused to ratify it, but withdrew from the World Council of Churches. One of the Dutch Reformed signatories, Dr. Beyers Naudé, resigned from his ministry and founded the interracial and interdenominational Christian Institute, which was declared illegal in 1977. Naudé was first imprisoned, and then subjected to a banning order that restricted his freedom of speech and ability to travel. He became a minister in the African branch of the Dutch Reformed Church.

In 1976, hundreds of schoolchildren were killed during riots that protested the use of Afrikaans in schools. All over the world, Soweto suddenly became familiar to those who had never heard of it and thought it was an African word. The following year, Steve Biko was beaten to death in prison.

The South African government was isolated internationally and unable to stem the tide of black urban protest, despite repression. Between 1985 and 1989, at least 50,000 persons were detained without trial, and over 5,000 were killed:

> Hundreds of clergy and church workers were detained; many were tortured. Others were banned and severely restricted. . . . Death squads assassinated Christian activists.[60]

Michael Lapsley, a New Zealander, is an Anglican priest and member of a religious order, as Huddleston was. He moved to South Africa in 1973 and was expelled in 1976 because he had become the chaplain of the outlawed African National Congress. In 1990, while working in Harare, Zimbabwe, he was sent a letter bomb wrapped in religious magazines. In the explosion he lost both hands and an eye, and suffered other injuries. In 1992 he moved back to South Africa, and the following year, he helped found the Institute for Healing of Memories in Cape Town.

Frank Chikane (b. 1951) is a Pentecostal who was ordained in 1980 as a minister in the Apostolic Faith Mission, a conglomerate of four separate, ethnically defined churches. He was imprisoned and tortured for his political activism. His church suspended him from his ministry from 1981 to 1990. He refused to leave South Africa or join a different church. In 1988, he became, like Tutu and Naudé before him, general secretary of the South African Council of Churches. When the African, Indian, and "Coloured"— but not the white—Apostolic Faith Mission churches amalgamated, Chikane was chosen as president. He is now a key adviser to President Mbeki.

The ebullient Anglican, Desmond Tutu (b. 1931), has been an international figure since the 1980s. His career has been a series of firsts. He became the first black Anglican dean in Johannesburg in 1975 and chose to live in Soweto. In 1986, he became archbishop of Cape Town, the first black head of the Anglican Church in South Africa. He had studied and worked abroad, and his international reputation and contacts did much to protect him. Together with Nelson Mandela, revered for his forgiveness of those who imprisoned him, Tutu became the international face of the new South Africa. Later, he headed the Truth and Reconciliation Commission, which documented, but did not punish, politically motivated crimes committed by both sides during the apartheid era.

Many of those who died in the struggle, both black and white, had no religious affiliation. Mandela has been called "Christ-like." He has exemplified Christian virtues more than most Christians. But in the words of his official biographer, "He was not a formal believer like Oliver Tambo, he did not quote the Bible or discuss theology." It was said that "character, not religion, was his strength."[61]

The fall of apartheid was the end of a repressive experiment in social engineering. Social and economic problems, including widespread poverty and the spread of AIDS, still abound.

CONTINUITIES

In 1850, even in 1880, it was possible to survey all the forms of Christian activity in Africa. In the twentieth century, this had become impossible. In 1500, the ancient churches of Egypt and Ethiopia were the dominant Christian presences in Africa. Now it is easy to lose sight of them in the vastness and complexity of Christian life there. But these churches, with their unbroken continuity with the days of the early church, have a special role not only in African but in world Christianity.

In Ethiopia, by the 1920s the Western-educated had become critical of many aspects of the church, especially the schools, where children (mainly boys) were taught to read, but not to write, a long-dead language. In 1959, Basileos, the first Ethiopian *abuna*, was appointed. He promptly appointed twenty-two Ethiopian bishops. In 1974, the ancient links of church and state were shattered with the overthrow of the last of the Solomonic kings, Haile Selassie, and the accession to power of a Marxist military regime.

In Egypt, as we have seen, the Copts have been increasingly involved in conflict with Muslims. There have been many other developments in Coptic life, including, earlier in the twentieth century, unsuccessful attempts to revive the Coptic language for daily use. The Copts have continued to produce professionals of great distinction, such as the heart surgeon Magdi Jacoub and Boutros Boutros Ghali, who served as secretary-general of the United Nations from 1992 to 1996.

There has been a remarkable monastic revival, led by Matthew the Poor (Matta el-Meskeen; b. 1929), a pharmacist who at the age of twenty-nine followed in the steps of Saint Antony; he sold his possessions, gave the money to the poor, and moved to the desert, where others followed. Later, they obeyed a church directive to move to the ancient, ruined monastery of Saint Macarius the Great, in the Wadi Natrun, which was inhabited by six aging monks. They turned it into a flourishing community with over a hundred monks. (They run a huge mechanized farm, which to some represents a departure from the tradition of the desert solitaries.) Matta has said that the only qualification for admission is "that the aspirant should have felt his heart stirred by love for God, even if but for a single time." When he first embarked on the desert life, Matta sought guidance from Abd al-Masih, the Ethiopian who has been called "the most extraordinary Christian hermit of the Egyptian Desert in the twentieth century."[62]

Abba Justus (1910–1976) was originally a tailor named Naguib. He became a monk in the monastery located on the site where Saint Antony lived as a hermit. He was never ordained and never left the monastery. His life has been called an unwritten parable of "seclusion, simplicity, poverty, fasting, silence and humility."[63] He practiced total silence, and when he was young, he would sleep in the branches of trees as a penance.

In 1968, the Virgin Mary was thought to have appeared to thousands in a series of apparitions in a Cairo church. She was silent. There have been many such apparitions throughout the world, usually in Catholic countries and usually with a message. The phenomenon is not easy to understand.

It is sometimes said that Orthodoxy attracts outsiders rather than seeking to convert them. It has had an interesting history in sub-Saharan Africa. In South Africa, Daniel Alexander, a member of the Ethiopian Church (founded in 1892), joined the American African Orthodox Church in 1920.

He became a bishop, established the church in South Africa, and made a number of missionary journeys to East Africa. There were questions about the validity of the orders of those who had ordained him, so in Coptic eyes, this was not a true Orthodox church. In 1993, some of its members joined the patriarchate of Alexandria.

Reuben Spartas, a Ganda who was originally an Anglican, was drawn to Orthodoxy by the written word.[64] He was ordained by Alexander in 1932, but joined the patriarchate of Alexandria in 1946. He is famous for translating Coptic liturgies into his own language. Whereas many other East Africans joined the Revival, he—and others—were drawn to the ancient church of Athanasius and Cyril. By 1998, there were about 100,000 African Orthodox Christians in East Africa, with 113 indigenous priests, who for the most part earned their living as peasant farmers. In 1994, a Ugandan named Theodore Nagiama became the first black diocesan bishop in the Orthodox Church.

CONCLUSION

Western missionaries, it is now generally recognized, found it difficult to distinguish Christianity from their own culture, but no religion exists outside culture. From its inception, Christianity has come in diverse cultural and linguistic packages. Paul believed that on the road to Damascus, Jesus spoke to him in Hebrew (Acts 26:14). He preached to the Gentiles in Greek.

The prophetic churches, in many respects, stay close to African culture and have sometimes been accused of syncretism. Peel, an ethnographer, commented that everyone is a syncretist; no one derives all his or her ideas from religion.[65] Newbigin's theology was exclusivist, emphasizing what he believed to be the unique truth of Christianity,[66] but he was insistent on the need to separate it from Western cultural packaging.[67] It was, he believed, the West that most needed missions, its rampant consumerism being a form of paganism.

When civil war broke out in Algeria in 1991, there were 200 Catholic missionaries in the country, some of whom were foreign nationals who had taken Algerian citizenship. Some provided social services, such as running a science library. A few were contemplatives devoted to prayer. Among the latter was an isolated community of Trappists, who referred to the combatants as the "brothers of the mountain" and the "brothers of the plain." Eight of them were killed in mysterious circumstances, either by the GIA (Armed Islamic Group) or by agents provocateurs. Shortly before he died, the abbot wrote to his family, saying that he hoped that if he was killed, he and his assassin would meet, like happy thieves, in Paradise.[68]

Chapter 14

African Initiated Churches: The Prophetic Model

> We are . . . a group of small churches under the bridges of our country,
> under the trees of our country, in the dining rooms, in the sitting rooms.
> —A member of the [South African] Council of African Instituted
> Churches, to the Truth and Reconciliation Commission[1]

Expansion and indigenization were the essential characteristics of Christianity in twentieth-century Africa. It has become conventional to write of AICs, usually, but not always, interpreted as African Initiated Churches.[2] The term, however, is too wide to be useful. AICs fall into three major categories. First, there are the African/Ethiopian churches, founded over leadership issues in the late nineteenth and early twentieth centuries, and discussed in chapter 12. Here we focus on the churches called Zionist in South Africa, Spirit or Spiritist in Ghana, and Aladura in Nigeria. They are grouped as prophetic, not in the sense of denouncing injustice but because their history is dominated by individuals who are usually referred to as prophets. The third category, indigenous expressions of neo-Pentecostalism, is the subject of chapter 15.

These are not watertight compartments. In 1996, a black South African scholar noted:

> I have felt for a long time . . . that too large and too artificial a wall often built between AICs and other Black churches. The reality is that growing sections (e.g., worship) of traditional Black churches—the so-called mission churches—are becoming "AIC" and "Pentecostal" in both theology and praxis.[3]

Prophetic churches flourish in some parts of Africa, but not others. They are important in Kenya and Congo/Zaire, as well as in the countries listed

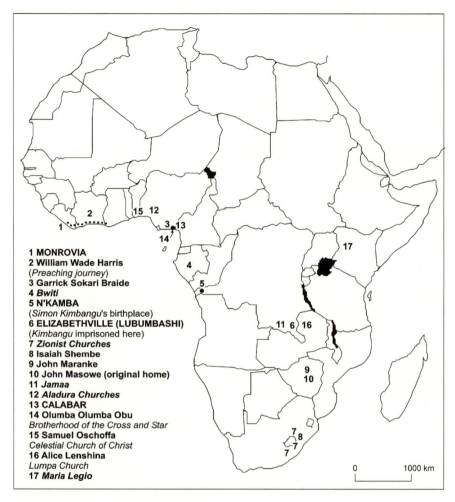

1 MONROVIA
2 William Wade Harris
(*Preaching journey*)
3 Garrick Sokari Braide
4 *Bwiti*
5 N'KAMBA
(*Simon Kimbangu*'s birthplace)
6 ELIZABETHVILLE (LUBUMBASHI)
(*Kimbangu* imprisoned here)
7 *Zionist Churches*
8 Isaiah Shembe
9 John Maranke
10 John Masowe (original home)
11 *Jamaa*
12 *Aladura Churches*
13 CALABAR
14 Olumba Olumba Obu
Brotherhood of the Cross and Star
15 Samuel Oschoffa
Celestial Church of Christ
16 Alice Lenshina
Lumpa Church
17 *Maria Legio*

African Initiated Churches and Leaders.

above. In Swaziland, Zionism has become "almost the national religion."[4] They are not a major feature in Tanzania, Uganda, and Rwanda.

The prophetic churches differed from each other in many respects—they had, for instance, different views on whether polygamy was permissible and whether the Sabbath should be observed on Saturday or Sunday. Some churches take the identification with the Old Testament far beyond Sabbath observance and pork taboos. But in general, the similarities are overwhelming.

In twentieth-century Africa, religious landscapes were transformed by the teachings of a number of charismatic African Christians, usually men but sometimes women. Each prophet's ministry began with a vision, a direct supernatural call. Some were primarily healers; some, preachers. Some prophets founded churches; others did not, though in these cases, the founding was often done by their followers. Some, like William Wade Harris and Joseph Babalola, preached primarily to non-Christians, while others drew their members mainly from the older churches. Many of these churches emerged in the 1920s and 1930s. In some cases, their founders did not know that there were similar churches elsewhere.

How do we explain this remarkable flowering of religious energy and creativity? The churches' members would attribute it to the Holy Spirit. Some religious movements can be linked to external catastrophes, such as the influenza epidemic or the outbreak of bubonic plague in Nigeria, when the Aladura churches were founded. It was the heyday of colonialism, a time of rapid change and increasing economic and social polarization. One can scarcely better this account of the Zulu prophet Shembe:

> . . . many Zulu in Shembe's early years, a century ago, were clearly conscious of powerlessness, deserted by god and king alike. The visionary Shembe reconstructed for them a sense of power, of agency, of steadiness and organisation that he radiated, preached, and then regimented—in writing—in a growing church following whose miraculous history proceeded to re-map Zululand into paths and shrines of sacred communication, healing, praise and worship.[5]

Although there are exceptions, it is sometimes claimed that the typical prophet is marginal in both the traditional and the modern world. He internalizes the conflicts and tensions of his society, and from the deep wells of the subconscious draws on both African and biblical imagery to create a way in which to make all things new.

These churches are an original and creative mix of traditional and biblical cultures, which so often reinforce one another. (A CMS archdeacon in Kenya opposed the translation of the Hebrew Bible into Luo, lest it should encourage polygamy!)[6] Most of them have detailed prohibitions—that of pork is virtually universal—which echo both the taboos of the past and the detailed prohibitions of Leviticus. In many churches—the Kimbanguists, the Nazirites, and the Celestial Church of Christ among them—worshipers remove their shoes. They lay much importance on dreams, visions, and faith healing, all of which are aspects of biblical religion that receive little emphasis in mainstream orthodoxy in the West.

The Bible is often used as a ritual object, in much the same way as the prophet's staff or healing water. There is a fascination with literacy, which finds expression in many different ways. An illiterate Seraphim prophet in Nigeria was told in a vision, "Print it in books, effect complete circulation, and I will make you a holy Apostle for the whole world." Some churches, including the Maranke Apostles in Zimbabwe and the Deima Church in Ivory Coast, have their own sacred texts. The belief that language has an efficacy of its own is reflected in the names of churches, such as the Star Nazaretha Church in Zion of Sabbath and the Holy Spirit Jerusalem Church in Zion. One of the great attractions of these churches was that, unlike most foreign missionaries, they tended to accept the ontological reality of witchcraft, and offered protection from it.

Within a period of less than ten years, three prophets emerged, in Liberia, the Niger Delta, and western Congo/Zaire, each of whom would have, in the course of a brief preaching ministry, a remarkable impact on the history of Christianity in Africa. In every case, this ministry was ended by a colonial government, through either deportation or imprisonment.

WILLIAM WADE HARRIS (1865–1929)

William Wade Harris was a middle-age, middle-class Liberian when he embarked on a remarkable preaching tour. Liberia, one of two African states to retain its independence in the colonial era, was founded by free black settlers from the United States. Only 17,000 African-Americans ever took this step. (There were about 200,000 free African-Americans in the early nineteenth century.) It was intended to call the capital Christopolis, but in the end it was named after the president of the day. Liberia's independence was recognized in 1847, but the indigenous people were invisible in the motto on its crest: "The love of liberty brought us here." In a sense, the settlers provided a role model of black, Western-educated Christians, but they monopolized political and economic power. The Americo-Liberian True Whig Party held power from 1870 until it was overthrown by a coup in 1980. Christianity, which had empowered the enslaved, came to define the perimeters of a ruling class, as did Western dress, European names, and the English language.

Harris, an indigenous Grebo, was brought up by his uncle, a Methodist pastor. He worked for the Episcopalian Church and as a government interpreter, becoming a political prisoner when he symbolically raised the Union Jack. (The idea was that the Grebo would fare better under a British protectorate.) In 1910, while in jail, Harris had a vision of the Angel Gabriel that changed his life. He was told to abandon Western dress—he had previously imported his shoes from America! He adopted a white gown with black bands, wore a turban, and carried a Bible and a staff. In mid-1913 Harris traveled to the French colony of Ivory Coast and embarked on a remarkable preaching tour in the coastal villages. There were Catholic missionaries there already, but they had had little impact. He did not speak the local languages, so he preached in pidgin English. In each village, Harris left behind an organization of "Twelve Apostles," often young men from Sierra Leone or the Gold Coast who were working locally as clerks or storemen. He reached western Ghana (then the Gold Coast) and began to retrace his steps. Meanwhile, the First World War had broken out, and at the end of 1914, the French authorities deported him. Harris made eight attempts to return to Ivory Coast but was not allowed to cross the border. He later preached in Liberia and Sierra Leone, but never with the same success.

Harris condemned all forms of traditional religion and urged people to burn their charms and "idols." Like virtually all African prophets, he condemned alcohol. He baptized converts immediately, whereas the mission churches demanded a long period of probation and instruction. Harris is thought to have baptized between 100,000 and 120,000 people in eighteen months. He did not condemn polygamy, and came to practice it himself. With this exception, his teaching was much the same as that of the missionaries. He died in poverty.

Harris urged his followers to await Christian missionaries with Bibles. Some joined the Catholics, but when a Methodist missionary arrived some years later, he was amazed to find a network of ready-made congregations. The Methodist Church in Ivory Coast dates its beginning not from 1924, when the first Methodists arrived, but from 1913, when Harris did.

In time, differences developed over polygamy and compulsory church dues. Both missionaries and Harris Christians visited Harris in Liberia; he said that polygamy is permissible, though not ideal, and that Christianity must be free.

A number of Harrist churches grew up in Ivory Coast and western Ghana; one study lists nine. Several were founded by women, such as the Church of the Twelve Apostles in western Ghana, established by Grace Tani (d. 1958), a former diviner who had been baptized by Harris. The Deima Church, founded by Marie Lalou (d. 1951), is the second largest Harrist church in Ivory Coast. Lalou taught that the God worshiped by the missionaries lacked the power to expel witches. Harris had been able to do this, but they had returned, and Lalou could drive them out again. The church has a striking body of sacred texts, one of which tells of a cosmic rebel against God, a European called Abidise, whose name may be a rearrangement of the first four letters of the alphabet.[7]

GARRICK SOKARI BRAIDE (d. 1918)

Garrick Sokari Braide, a poor fisherman in the Niger Delta, was an adult convert to Anglicanism. He had a vision in 1912, developed a healing ministry, and in 1916 began to call himself Prophet Elijah II. He condemned alcohol to such good effect that government revenues from a tax on imported liquor dropped dramatically. Braide's prophetic claims were profoundly unacceptable to the Sierra Leonian clergy in the area. When his followers began to pillage traditional shrines, the colonial authorities imprisoned him. He died soon after his release. Some of his followers founded the Christ Army

Church, but his teachings spread far beyond this and contributed to the spread of mission Christianity in south eastern Nigeria.

SIMON KIMBANGU (1889–1951)

Simon Kimbangu was a Kongo Baptist who grew up in N'kamba, a village near the lower Zaire River, in what was then the Belgian Congo. He had hoped to become a pastor but did not pass the required examination. He began to have visions calling him to heal the sick; he initially resisted them, fleeing to Léopoldville (now Kinshasa). Later, he returned home, and in April 1921 he performed his first public healing. Crowds flocked to N'kamba, new prophets emerged, and colonial authorities, fearing an uprising, attempted to arrest him. Kimbangu escaped, but gave himself up in September. He was initially condemned to death by 120 lashes; the sentence was commuted, but he spent the last thirty years of his life in jail in Elizabethville (now Lubumbashi), 1,500 miles from his home. His followers compare this with the thirty years of hidden life that preceded the public ministry of Jesus. Kimbangu never saw his wife and children again. Many of his followers were flogged, imprisoned, and exiled.

In 1923, a group of former Baptist deacons wrote to a white missionary:

> As for what you say that we are following a "new teaching"—this is not so, our Teacher. . . . As for the sentences given us, some are for 10 years, some 20, others for life: this is the sentence of imprisonment. When these sentences are finished, we cannot go back to our own country, we must die here. But as for us, these tribulations and these sentences "cannot separate us from the love of Christ and of God, nor can any other tribulation." . . . We assure you we have not broken a single State law, nor been disrespectful to our rulers. . . . Two deacons died at Thysville in 1921. . . . They died through being much beaten. Others also died, but there is no time to give their names. . . . We get beaten with canes and have other troubles, but Jehovah is our shepherd.[8]

Until 1959, when they were finally recognized, the Kimbanguists led a hidden and persecuted existence. Kimbangu's wife, Muilu Marie (1885–1959), provided effective leadership to this underground movement. The rapid and successful transition to a major church, under the leadership of Kimbangu's youngest son, Joseph Diangienda (1918–1992), who was a toddler when his father was imprisoned, is in its way as remarkable as Simon's initial ministry. In 1969, the Kimbanguist Church joined the World Council of Churches. Its official name is, in French, the Church of Jesus Christ on Earth through Simon Kimbangu.

N'kamba, now called N'kamba New Jerusalem, has become a place of pilgimage and a source of healing waters. In 1968, a European Christian came to study the Kimbanguists and stayed to join them: "If you live with the Kimbanguists, you find yourself transferred to the time of the earliest

New Testament witnesses."[9] The church went through something of a crisis when the statesmanlike Diangienda was succeeded by a controversial and eccentric older brother.[10] He died in 2001 and was succeeded by his son, Kiangani Simon Kimbangu.

Both during the years of persecution and later, there have been a great number of other prophets in the Congo who claim to speak in Kimbangu's name, a phenomenon often generically called "ngunzism" (after the Kongo word for "prophet"). Their relationship to the Kimbanguist tradition is disputed. They have emphasized ecstatic religious experience, faith healing, and protection from witchcraft, and often have told stories about the secret teachings of Jesus. In one version, Diangienda travels to Jerusalem, where he opens a set of seven boxes that nest inside each other. The innermost box contains the true Bible, which the missionaries had hidden from Africans.

The Kimbanguist Church is thought to be the largest of Africa's prophetic churches. It has spread throughout the continent and beyond, and may have up to 10 million members.

THE ZIONIST CHURCHES

The Zionist churches of South Africa call themselves amaZiyoni or Churches of the Spirit or Churches of the People, as distinct from the (older Protestant) Churches of the Law, or "Institutional Churches of the Whites."[11] By 1991, they had over 9 million adherents, almost half of the nations' black Christians. There were at least 6,000 AICs.

A study conducted in and around the town of Mafeking in 1969 revealed the existence of fifty-six distinct religious movements (thirty-three of which were distinct Zionist churches and nine Ethiopian) and several hundred congregations, in a population of 45,000.[12] Zionists were described by their neighbors as "people who baptized," "practiced healing," "observed taboos," or "followed the drum."[13]

Zionists tend to be critical of the older churches for the cold formality of their worship and for the racism that has often divided them. Their ideal is biblical Christianity, reflected in names such as the Apostolic Nazareth Jerusalem Corinthians Church in Zion.

The Zionist churches have been profoundly indigenized for nearly a century, but the initial spark came from a Dutch Reformed Church missionary working among the Zulu, an Afrikaner named Pieter Le Roux. He was drawn both to the concept of Zion and to faith healing, and in 1902, at great personal cost, joined a small Pentecostal church based in Zion City, near Chicago, the Christian Catholic Apostolic Church in Zion. It was marginal in American religious life, and soon fragmented, but Zion would take new roots in southern Africa. Le Roux soon left it, uncomfortable with the direction it was taking in Africa: "He did not want people to have contact with their ancestors or to wear white garments or to carry staffs."[14] He became the leader of the Apostolic Faith Mission, which grew into one of South Africa's leading Pentecostal churches. Between 1911 and 1925, a large number of African Zionist churches were founded, a process that continues to this day. Their great period of expansion took place after 1960.

A Sotho named Edward Motaung (Lion) established "Zion City" in 1917. In 1925, one of his followers, Engenas Lekganyane (1885–1948), founded the largest of the Zionist churches, Zion Christian Church (ZCC). Estimates of its present membership range from 2 million to 6 million. It is the most rapidly growing prophetic church in South Africa,[15] with its own Zion City, Morija,[16] in the northern Transvaal, which attracts a million pilgrims at Easter. The Lekganyane family is known for its wealth, but at the grassroots level, Zionist churches were, and are, communities of the poor and disinherited. As a group of Zionist church leaders said in 1985:

> The members of our Churches are the poorest of the poor, the people with the lowest jobs or with no jobs at all. . . . Our people, therefore, know what it means to be oppressed, exploited and crushed.[17]

There is a sense in which their elaborate organization, with archbishops and bishops, represents an alternative source of esteem and authority. Edward Motaung called himself "General Overseer of the World."[18]

The Zionist churches vary greatly in size—some consist of a single congregation. ZCC was founded nearly eighty years ago, but others have been ephemeral. George Khambule (1884–1949), a Zulu, was one of those whose church did not survive. He "died" and recovered during the 1919 influenza pandemic. He was fascinated by the precious stones of Revelations, and collected pebbles in Natal streams, placing them in his own Ark of the Covenant. Khambule took a new name, Saint Nazar, and his Zulu diary reflects the intoxication of writing for the newly literate: ". . . the Lord Jesus Christ revealed to me the Scripture of truth . . . H.G. Latin RIO EST M.B. % MGU."[19]

The appearance of Halley's comet and the influenza pandemic of 1919 contributed to the formation of some new churches. Timothy Cekwane (d. 1949) was a Presbyterian who founded the Church of the Light in 1910, after he saw the comet from a mountain in the Drakensburgs, which remained his church's sacred place.

Zionists have a tendency to revere their founders—this is, indeed, one of the criticisms made of them. The founder of ZCC is remembered simply as Immanuel. After the founder's death, his leadership role is usually inherited by one of his sons, and in some ways his descendants come to resemble traditional royals. The transition from the leadership of a prophet with a direct mandate from God is a difficult one, and there are often succession disputes and schisms. There is a dramatic rise in educational levels from generation to generation. In Nigeria, the present head of the Church of the Lord

(Aladura), Rufus Ositelu, has doctorates in computer science and the philosophy of religion.

When a woman prophet founded a church, she tended to concentrate on healing and prayer while a husband or son ran the organization. Christina Nku (Ma Nku), a noted healer, was the founder of Saint John's Apostolic Church, named after her eldest son. She built a large church with twelve doors in a suburb of Johannesburg, its design revealed to her in a vision, and had about 50,000 followers. Her husband, Lazarus, ran the church, and after his death, her son Johannes attempted to succeed him. By 1970, much to Ma Nku's distress, Petrus Masango had gained control of both the church and its finances. It is one of the episodes deemed worthy of mention in the pamphlet written by Zionist leaders, *Speaking for Ourselves.*

The Zionists wear distinctive robes, a symbol of their separation from an unjust and oppressive world. White, blue, and green are favorite colors. In Kenya, Legio Maria members wear gowns of white, yellow, pink, or blue. The Kimbanguists of Zaire wear green (for hope) and white (for purity), and decorate their churches in these colors.

Water symbolism is important to Zionists and other prophetic church members, especially in areas where drought is endemic, and there is a special reverence for John the Baptist. Among the Tswana, Zionist churches are called wells. Zionists practice adult baptism by immersion in rivers, and healing through use of holy water. The rivers of South Africa become the Jordan.

Members of the Church of the Light, atypically, wear red robes; for them, blood symbolism is all important. Their founder and some of his followers were stigmatics, like Francis of Assisi. (They also give a distinctive ritual importance to brooms.) Men in ZCC wear quasi-military uniforms, easily understood as a critique and parody of structures of power and authority. But in general, Zionist churches were not involved in political activism, and ZCC was criticized, in the past, for its cozy relationship with the apartheid regime. A vast gathering assembled at Morija in 1985 to hear an address from President Botha on submission to the powers that be (Romans 13).[20] In a world of white domination, official acknowledgment seemed of great value, but it has not always been recognized that ZCC emphasized nonviolence— its members greet one another with "Peace." The ZCC's present head remained silent before the Truth and Reconciliation Commission.[21] His silence was more eloquent than many words.

Members of the prophetic churches embraced the new South Africa. In due course, Nelson Mandela and F.W. de Klerk spoke at Morija, as did the Inkatha leader, Mangosuthu Buthelezi.

A sacred place is typical, though not universal, in Zionist churches. The numinous quality of natural features such as lakes, rivers, and hills is also a core insight of "traditional" religions. In 1921, the quest for an earthly Zion led to disaster when Enoch Mgijima (another prophet converted by the sight of Halley's comet) led his Israelites in an attempt to found one on government land near Bulhoek. They were fired on, and 187 lost their lives. (This is another episode singled out in *Speaking for Ourselves.*) The Israelites thought that they were the true Jews, kept the Sabbath, celebrated the Passover, and believed that Jehovah would rescue them from white bondage.

The fundamental emphasis of the amaZiyoni is on healing through spiritual means. "This is not a church, it is a hospital," said a Swazi Zionist. Church founders were often healers rather than preachers. Engenas Lekganyane became a Zionist when an intractable eye disease was cured by baptism by immersion. It has been estimated that 80 percent of ZCC members joined the church after an experience of healing.[22]

The church of the Nazirites (amaNazaretha) was founded by Isaiah Shembe (d. 1935) in 1910, after a series of visions. He had once been a laborer on the Durban docks. Its membership is thought to be over a million. Its meetings, too, have been addressed by Mandela and other leading South African figures. Shembe is often called the Path-Beginner.

AmaNazaretha is a specifically Zulu church with two sacred places, both on mountaintops, one not far from Durban and the other eighty miles away. Each is the site of a great annual festival that includes dancing in neotraditional Zulu dress. There is a great reverence for Shembe; his followers often wear his image around their necks, and he is sometimes thought of almost as a Black Christ, though he made no such claim for himself.[23] He was the author of 218 hymns, revealed in visions, that are still sung by vast congregations. Fifty of them celebrate the holy mountain Ekuphakameni, the Exalted Place:

> Ye all who thirst
> come to Ekuphakameni,
> there freely to drink
> from springs of water.[24]

Shembe emphasized God the Father and the Holy Spirit, rather than Jesus, though one of his most beautiful hymns is addressed to Him ("O Wondrous Hen, Thou Dost Not Love Jerusalem Alone").

> I believe in the Father
> and in the Holy Spirit
> and the communion of saints
> of the amaNazaretha.[25]

Shembe was succeeded by his son, Johannes Galilee Shembe, who in 1958 described his father's death: "As he was about to die, he told us, 'Throughout my life I have worked for God alone. I came with nothing, I leave with nothing.'"[26] It was Johannes who organized the massive archive of Nazirite written sources, part of which has now been published.[27] They were hand-written in notebooks, often with hen feathers and gall.

Johannes, a graduate teacher, healed the sick and wrote more hymns. After his death there was a schism, with the larger branch headed by his brother Amos (d. 1996) and a smaller one by his son, Londa (d. 1989). The Nazirites are now headed by Amos's son, Vimbeni Shembe, another noted healer.

Women are a majority in the Zionist churches. The first Swazi Zionist, Johanna Nxumalo, was a woman. In the 1970s, it was estimated that women made up two-thirds of Zionist membership.[28] In 1990, "The ratio of women to men is roughly three to one. Not only that, but the women of various groups meet together every week at an all-female gathering. This means that women are a formidable force within Zionism, in both weight of numbers and unity of purpose."[29]

John Dube, a member of the African Methodist Episcopal Church, was an archetypal improver. In 1901 he founded Ohlange School, with no financial help from the missions. There is a certain symbolism in the fact that it shared a common boundary with Ekuphakameni, and that after the prophet's death, Dube wrote his biography.

ALADURA

Aladura (Owners of Prayer, in Yoruba) is the name given to a complex of churches that grew up among the Yoruba after the First World War and later. Until the 1980s, the movement was dominated by three churches founded between 1922 and 1930: Christ Apostolic Church, Cherubim and Seraphim, and Church of the Lord (Aladura).

Christ Apostolic Church was not founded by a prophet—though some of its early members had visions—and did not initially appeal to the masses or the very poor. It grew out of an Anglican prayer group that met when the churches were closed during the influenza pandemic of 1918. It was called Precious Stone Society—one of its founders was a goldsmith—a name that echoes the gems of Revelations. It had nineteen members in 1922, and perhaps a thousand by 1930. They were literate—clerks, traders, and so on.

In 1922, the Precious Stone Society broke with the CMS because its members had come to reject infant baptism and all medicine, whether traditional or Western. For a time it was attached to Faith Tabernacle, a small church in Philadelphia the members had discovered through the study of pamphlet literature. Later, from 1932 to 1939, it was affiliated with the (British) Apostolic Church, but broke with its missionaries over leadership issues and their use of quinine. Its key emphasis was not on visions or glossolalia, but on faith healing.

It turned into a mass movement as a result of a revival preached from 1930 to 1932 by another Yoruba, Joseph Babalola (1906–1959). He was a grader driver (roads, in twentieth-century Africa, had powerful symbolic links with modernity) and, like Kimbangu, initially resisted this call to preach. He was another prophet with a brief ministry but a remarkable and lasting impact. Babalola rapidly acquired a great reputation as a healer. Under the impact of his teaching, there were great bonfires of traditional religious images. After he served a prison term for witchcraft accusations, he never again had the same degree of success.

Of all the Aladura churches, it is Christ Apostolic Church that is most similar to the mission churches. It has always emphasized education and insisted on monogamy, and is the only Aladura church accepted by the Born-Again in contemporary Nigeria. It is thought to have several hundred thousand members.

None of the other Aladura churches founded in the 1920s had overseas affiliations. One of them became known as the Cherubim and Seraphim, a name revealed in a vision. In 1925, during a Corpus Christi procession, a girl from the Lagos elite, who became known as Captain Abiodun, went into a trance state, from which a prophet named Moses Orimolade was able to rescue her. Initially, the organization was founded as an Anglican prayer group, like the Precious Stone Society. It left the CMS in 1928, the year in which the founders separated. There was a strong emphasis on protection from witchcraft and on dreams and visions: "He challenged witches openly. In previous years we were very afraid of them. There were thousands in Lagos."[30] The members felt a strong sense of identification with the angels in Heaven, and the Archangel Michael was their captain. The Cherubim and Seraphim were known for long missionary journeys and distinctive white robes. Both polygamy and Western medicine were permitted.

Orimolade, who had been acknowledged as Baba Aladura, died in 1933. Captain Abiodun tried unsuccessfully to succeed him as head, citing the precedents of the women prophets in the Bible and Queen Victoria. The movement fragmented into many branches, most of which later reunited.

The Church of the Lord (Aladura) was founded by Josiah Ositelu, who died in 1966. A first-generation Christian, he became a CMS catechist. In 1925 he began to have visions in which he was called to be a prophet. The following year, he was dismissed from the CMS. He joined the group that later became the Christ Apostolic Church, but left it in 1930 because its leaders were dubious about his emphasis on witch-finding, his use of revealed holy names, seals, and a secret script, and his attraction to magical texts such as the Sixth and Seventh Books of Moses: "Knowledge that somebody is a witch can bring no benefit to anybody." "These names can bring no forgiveness, salvation, or benefit of any kind to anybody."[31] Unlike the Christ Apostolic Church, Ositelu accepted polygamy and had seven wives. Since the Church of the Lord's foundation, more than twenty-five new churches have broken away. Despite this, it has spread internationally and claims over a million members.[32] In 1975, it became one of the few AICs to join the World Council of Churches.

In 1947, a new church was founded that was destined to overtake the three older ones which had dominated the Aladura movement. The Celestial Church of Christ, popularly called Cele, was founded by Samuel Oschoffa (1909–1985), a poor fisherman from Porto Novo, on the coast of the Republic of Benin (then Dahomey). In 1947, he had a visionary experience while paddling his canoe in the coastal lagoons: "I constantly heard a voice which said, 'Grace to God.'" Later, "I saw a very brilliant light like that of a car's headlights, and further in the light I saw an angel with two bright shining crystal eyes."[33] This angel instructed him to preach and empowered him to perform miracles. Oschoffa spent a period lost in the wilderness, and then began his ministry. His first followers were poor Gun fishermen. In 1952, they carried Cele to Lagos, and it acquired a following among the Yoruba middle class. A new church marked by miraculous healings seemed more attractive than its older Aladura counterparts. It has 2,000 branches in Nigeria and more worldwide, with a total membership of several million.

Oschoffa died at the age of seventy-six, as the result of a car accident. He consoled his grieving followers by pointing out that he had lived much longer than Jesus.

THE VAPOSTORI

One of the most remarkable synchronicities in this extraordinary story lies in the foundation of two churches in what was then Rhodesia, in 1932. Two men, both Shona, both called John or adopting this name, had visions that led them to found a church of Apostles, Vapostori. There are similarities with the amaZiyoni, but also differences. The Apostles did not attempt to found a holy city and had a much more extensive missionary outreach.

A man named Peter Shoniwa adopted the name John Masowe (John of the Wilderness, i.e., John the Baptist) after a visionary experience. He led some of his followers on a migration to Port Elizabeth in South Africa, where they lived as a community and became known as the Korsten Basket Makers. Women wore white; men had beards and shaven heads. They practiced polygamy and emphasized Sabbath observance and Old Testament food taboos. They did not farm or work for others, but supported themelves by making baskets, pots and pans, and so on. Masowe himself lived secretly and anonymously in this community. Deported from South Africa to Lusaka, Zambia, in 1963, the group soon moved on to Nairobi, which they believed to be the heart of Africa referred to in Isaiah 19:19 (Egypt representing Africa). Their ultimate destination was Jerusalem. A group of celibate women formed a living Ark of the Covenant. Masowe's Apostles worshiped in the open air, barefoot, having no abiding city. Masowe died in 1973, at the age of sixty-three, to the distress of his followers; he was the only baptizer and was not expected to die. He was buried in a glass-topped coffin to give him a good view of the Second Coming.

Whereas Masowe chose the name of John of the Wilderness, John Maranke (1912–1963) was named after the district where he grew up as a Methodist. His first converts and officials were his relatives, but the church spread far beyond its ethnic origins, through Shona migrant workers and evangelists. An important sacred text written in Shona, *The New Revelations of the Apostles*, contains the messages in his visions plus the contents of two books in foreign languages that he was able to understand through the Holy Spirit. It is full of biblical echoes. An American who came to do research on the movement joined it.

Maranke's Apostles keep the Sabbath on Saturday, permit polygamy, practice faith healing, and avoid Western and traditional medicine. The movement divided when the founder died, and the two sections remain hostile to one another.

ALICE LENSHINA AND THE LUMPA CHURCH

Alice Lenshina (1919–1978), a Bemba from the village of Kasomo in northern Zambia, was a Presbyterian who attended the same primary school as President Kaunda. In 1953, she had a near-death experience: "Send her back. Her time has not yet come." Within two years, her millennial and anti-witchcraft emphasis led to a break with the mission church. She founded a new church called Lumpa, which means both "to excel" and "to go far." Kasomo became Zioni, and a large church was built there. Lenshina composed 380 Bemba hymns, which she attributed, like Shembe, to divine inspiration. Her teachings were close to those of the mission churches—she opposed "paganism," beer drinking, and polygamy. She was concerned with protection from witchcraft, but stated that this was to be won by prayer and a holy life. Unlike some prophets who emphasized Jehovah, her spirituality centered on Jesus and the faithful love of the married couple.

The Lumpa believed the End was at hand, and tried to withdraw from the world in their own villages. This led to conflict over land with local chiefs. The government of newly independent Zambia intervened, and in 1964, some 700 Lumpa were killed and others went into exile. Alice died in detention in 1978, as had her husband, Petros Mulenga, six years earlier.

THE RELIGIOUS COMMUNITY

Many Lumpa attempted to live in separate villages. Some of his Vapostori lived with Masowe in community. The Holy Apostles of Aiyetoro was a splinter group that broke off from the Cherubim and Seraphim in 1947 and founded a village on stilts in the western Niger Delta; about a thousand members were attracted there by the promise that they would not die. They lived in poverty; their labor, under a remarkable leader, made it possible to build up a major economic complex with refrigerated deep-sea trawlers. Inevitably, the members became dissatisfied, and the movement declined in the 1960s.

Sadly, the life of a very different small community at Kanungu, in southwest Uganda, ended in the equivalent of Jonestown[34] in 2000. It was called the Movement for the Restoration of the Ten Commandments. Its leaders, originally Catholics who included a highly educated priest, had repeatedly foretold the date of the End.[35] When it did not occur, members became restive and asked for the return of the money and land they had contributed. About 900 members were burned alive in a church, the doors of which were nailed shut.

MOVEMENTS OF CATHOLIC ORIGIN

Prophetic churches tend to flourish in areas once dominated by Protestant missions. Protestant history is full of examples of the foundation of new churches and divisions within existing ones For instance, I have referred to "Presbyterians" for clarity, but there were many Presbyterian divisions and reunions, both in Scotland and in North America, that lie beyond the scope of a study such as this. This does not mean that Presbyterians were quarrelsome or litigious, though some were—they divided over profound issues of principle.

Catholicism, with a strong tradition of obedience to central authority, had far fewer breakaway churches,[36] but one of the largest AICs in Kenya is Maria Legio (sic), founded among the Luo in 1963 by a bereaved young mother, Gaudentia Aoko, and by a former catechist, Simeon Ondeto. The name comes from a Catholic lay organization, the Legion of Mary, which originated in Ireland and played a major role in some parts of colonial Africa. Maria Legio, however, was a new church that combined aspects of Catholicism, including "Latin," rosaries, and (polygamist) bishops, with other elements such as healing and protection from witchcraft through holy water. It is ironic that it attempted to preserve Latin just at the time the Catholic Church was turning to the vernacular. By the 1980s, the Legio was multiethnic, with considerable middle-class support and perhaps a quarter of a million members. Ondeto, who died in 1991, has become Baba Messias (the "Virgin Mary" is his stepmother), and Aoko seems to have dropped out of the picture. Since a local Catholic church is a contradiction in terms, the Legio is conceptualized as a reformed Catholic church, potentially part of an international network of such churches. It is the Catholic Church, with its adoption of vernacular liturgies, that is thought to have become local.[37]

Jamaa (Swahili for "family") was the name of a movement for renewal within the Catholic Church in Shaba, in eastern Congo/Zaire. It is another example of interaction between foreign missionaries and local Christians. In this case, the missionary was a Flemish Franciscan, Placide Tempels (1906–1977). He was famous in quite a different connection, as the author of *La Philosophie bantou* (Bantu Philosophy), published in 1945. Seldom read today, except by specialists in African philosophy, it had a great influence on a generation of francophone African priests. They included Alexis Kagame, a Rwandan aristocrat, whose extensive publications included *The Rwandan Bantu Philosophy of Being* (written in French).

Jamaa members were African (Luba) married couples, often copper miners' families, and Flemish Franciscan missionaries. The couple, the Baba and Mama, are central. The Baba sought a spiritual encounter with Mary; the Mama, with Jesus. They advanced from level to level, a progression authenticated by dreams.

In 1963, Tempels was summoned to Rome; he subsequently lived in Belgium, under censure, until he died. In 1974, the movement was banned by both the church and the government. A form of it was permitted to continue in the church, under regular supervision and control; another branch survived unofficially and independently. Jamaa was banned in the first place because it was thought that the intense relationships of Jamaa sometimes found illicit sexual expression. This fringe movement was called Katete. Whether this still exists—or, indeed, ever existed—is uncertain.[38]

Most of those who study them, including the present writer, regard the prophetic churches as profoundly acculturated expressions of Christian faith. Both black and white Evangelicals were often critical of them, accusing them of "occultism" and "Messianism"—that is, giving to a prophet the worship that belongs to Christ. In the words of a Nigerian Evangelical, Ogbu Kalu: "There has been a tendency to glorify the Independent Churches. Most of them are neo-pagan, engaged in non-Christian rituals."[39]

These critics feel that at least some of these churches elevate their founder to something like a Christ for Africa. This is perhaps best understood as saying that a Shembe or Ondeto is Christ's special messenger to Africa. It should also be understood in terms of traditions of praise singing. In 1895, a White Father, Bishop Dupont, came to work among the Bemba of northern Zambia, who still sing

"A Hymn to Mgr. Dupont, Our Redeemer":
He gives life to our children,
And nurtures them with food.
He hurls down the lions
And heals our ailments[40]

Having praised Dupont, the song goes on to wax still more lyrical about his mother! Some observers believe, however, that the leaders of these movements deliberately downplay the messianic element in their interactions with Western scholars.

In the rest of this chapter, I discuss two movements of a different kind. The Jehovah's Witnesses are neither a church nor African initiated. Witnesses prefer to be referred to as an organization; the movement was founded by a white American from Pennsylvania who owned a chain of clothing stores. However, it was deeply indigenized in Africa, and its preachers had more in common with their prophetic counterparts than is often realized. Members of the Brotherhood of the Cross and Star also reject the name "church," considering their movement more wide-reaching. Both the older and the prophetic churches are hostile to the Brotherhood because of the claims made by and for its founder. However, members are adamant that they are Christians.

THE JEHOVAH'S WITNESSES

Founded by Charles Taze Russell (1852–1916) in the late nineteenth century, this movement was originally called the Watch Tower Bible and Tract Society, and adopted its present name in 1931. The details of its belief and practice differed considerably from those of the mission churches—for instance, it members reject the doctrine of the Trinity, and do not celebrate Christmas or Easter—but African Witnesses presented it in a way that had much in common with their prophetic counterparts. Sometimes African branches became so deeply indigenized that the parent organization disowned them.

The heart of the Watch Tower message was a form of millennarianism. Russell and later leaders of the movement believed that the end of the world was very near. The date has been revised repeatedly (1874, 1878, 1914, 1925, 1975 . . .), but it is still held to be close at hand. There will be a great battle, Armageddon, after which Witnesses will be saved. A few of them will reign with God in Heaven, and the rest will live in health and happiness in God's Kingdom on Earth. All other people will be annihilated (a much less alarming alternative than Hell!). The world's present governments and churches are under the sway of Satan—hence the refusal to salute the flag, take part in politics, and so on.

Today, Nigeria has the fourth largest number of Witnesses in the world, but it was in Malawi and Zambia that the movement first took root. Like Zionism, it was introduced to South Africa by a European, in this case the ubiquitous Joseph Booth, the patron of Chilembwe. Migrant workers from Malawi took these teachings with them when they returned home. One of them, Elliot Kenani Kamwana, had studied at Livingstonia but been denied baptism, for no apparent reason. He returned to Malawi in 1908, and had baptized over 9,000 people within a year. Like so many religious leaders in the colonial period, he spent much of his life in exile.

Witnesses, like the prophetic churches, practice baptism by immersion. The offer of immediate baptism, without a long period of probation and study, was an immense attraction. Witnesses were expected to live godly lives, shunning idolatry, witchcraft, and violence.

The outbreak of the First World War seemed to confirm that the End was near. Ten years later, an anxious Zambian asked a local magistrate:

> Please am asking you shall this year 1924 the whole world finish? Shadrack . . . is baptizing people. . . . He is judging you Boma [local administration headquarters] people and other missions. Free Church all of you there is a rock on your heads and you will be smashed up.[41]

The Witnesses' emphasis on Bible study has always been attractive in Africa. The words of a Zambian Anglican who became a Seventh-Day Adventist reflect the fascination of the Bible's prophetic books:

> I was very much puzzled about Daniel and Revelation. But they [Anglican missionaries] said, "These are only dreams. You need not read these books. They are very hard and nobody can understand these books. It is better to read the Gospel." But there was a great demand in my mind to understand these.[42]

Both Watch Tower preachers and members of prophetic churches practiced faith healing and speaking in tongues. To their hearers, the similarities must have been much more obvious than the differences.

Witnesses' missionary zeal springs from the belief that Armageddon is at hand. The idea that a world of perfect happiness is available in one's own generation led Africans to reflect on the injustices of the world in which they lived. As a group of Watch Tower copper miners said in the 1930s, "It stands out clearly from this book that all men are equal. It is not just that the black man who does the work should remain in poverty and misery."[43] Some Witnesses proclaimed that black and white would exchange color (and with it socioeconomic status). Colonial authorities saw the Witnesses as a danger, fearing a millennial rising, but they never embarked on anything of the kind.

Many Watch Tower proclamations—such as "God is great," "Those who are baptized are saved," "Thy Kingdom come," and "Leave adultery and witchcraft"—could equally well have been voiced by any missionary. But missionaries, like colonial governments, saw the Witnesses as a threat. A White Father met a solitary man in the wilderness who was proclaiming, "Take care, God is great. Pray to God alone." He flogged him.[44]

Because of their refusal to salute the flag, Jehovah's Witnesses were cruelly persecuted in Banda's Malawi, and the movement was outlawed. Some became refugees in Mozambique, where, in the 1980s, they offered strikingly effective passive resistance to Renamo's brutal regime.[45]

THE BROTHERHOOD OF THE CROSS AND STAR

Calabar, in southeastern Nigeria, is the center of a very successful but highly controversial movement, founded in 1956 by Olumba Olumba Obu (b. 1918). By 1992, it claimed 2 million members, with many branches outside Africa. Both the older churches and the Aladura are highly critical of it. A survey by a Nigerian Christian academic calls it "neopagan."[46] However, an English Unitarian minister and his wife who joined it, together with their sons, are dedicated advocates.

Obu grew up in Calabar but was born in an inland village, Biakpan, which is now Bethlehem or Jerusalem. The Biakpan stream is thought to have healing powers. Obu has little formal education, but enjoys displaying his detailed knowledge of the Bible. He initially traded in cloth, but gave away his stock when he turned to full-time ministry. He attracted ever greater numbers of followers through his gifts of healing. He dresses very simply, goes barefoot, and never enters a car or leaves Calabar. He follows a fruitarian diet and urges his followers to be vegetarians. He advocates celibacy and believes in reincarnation. Now very old, he has designated his son, Roland, as his successor, a move that has led to divisions within the movement.

Obu's followers refer to him as Triple O, and use his initials as a protective talisman. He is the Sole Spiritual Head, and the only exponent of Brotherhood of the Cross and Star (BCS) doctrine. He holds three services daily, preaching at one of them. His sermons are recorded, transcribed, translated, and printed. He foretold that the world would end in 2001, in a prophecy that appeared, perhaps oddly, in a Nigerian government-owned daily in 1985, when the country was ruled by a military regime:

> After the year 1999 there will be no Army, Navy, Air Force, Police, Law courts, Judges, Magistrates and Lawyers will no longer exist . . . only "love one another" will reign supreme.[47]

Obu teaches that God appears under different names in different generations. He has manifested himself as Adam, Enoch, Noah, Melchizedek, Moses, Elijah, and Jesus, and now does so as Olumba Olumba Obu.[48]

The most controversial aspect of BCS teachings is the claim of the founder's divinity. In a survey, 85 percent of his followers considered him divine because of his miraculous deeds and his supposed ability, which Obu himself emphasizes, to appear simultaneously in many different places. Of those who left the movement, 90 percent did so because of these claims.[49]

Obu himself is ambivalent on the issue. He has published a pamphlet titled *I Am Not God but Olumba Olumba Obu.* But the official BCS hymnal, first produced in 1977 and in constant use, makes many references to his divinity:

> Let glory be to our most high God—
> Olumba Obu. . . .
> Thou wilt never leave us helpless
> Save us, O Lord.[50]

> Olumba Obu is the King
> Great Saviour and a helper
> King of kings, Lord redeemer is on
> Earth among men to dwell.[51]

Obu and BCS members are adamant that theirs is a Christian body, and Obu preaches from the New Testament and quotes it constantly. Members of other churches consider the claims made for him blasphemous.

In many ways, Obu's life and teachings are similar to those of some Hindu gurus: a vegan or fruitarian diet, an ascetic lifestyle, the claim to be an avatar of divinity, a belief in reincarnation, the miraculous powers—but apart from Biakpan, which he has not visited for many years, he has never left Calabar. What is not disputed is that his daily life is one of transparent kindness, joy, and peace, and that love is the core of his message.

Chapter 15

The Global and the Local: Neo-Pentecostalism

> . . . pentecostalism speaks a language which renders understandable the absurd and anarchic realities of contemporary urban life, enabling action and mastery.
>
> —a researcher, referring to Nigeria, in 1991[1]

From the 1980s on, Christianity in Africa has been radically changed by the spread of what is variously called the charismatic movement[2] or neo-Pentecostalism—its African adherents call themselves the Born Again. It is part of a global picture, and the movement has spread like wildfire in Latin American countries such as Brazil. The world's largest single church is the neo-Pentecostal one founded by Paul Yonggi Cho in Seoul. Pentecostalism (fragmented, of course, into countless churches) has been called the largest Christian community in the world after Catholicism and, with 372 million members in 1990, the fastest-growing.[3] The majority of the world's neo-Pentecostals are in the Two-Thirds World.

All Pentecostals have certain things in common They agree with Evangelicals on the need for a conversion experience and on the divine inspiration of Scripture, but their core teaching is the baptism by the Holy Spirit, which will lead to glossolalia (speaking in tongues) and the "signs and wonders" that characterized the early Christians after Pentecost, which include faith healing. Since illness is often attributed to evil spirits, there tends to be an emphasis on exorcism. (This was equally true of Archbishop Milingo.)

However, even within a single African country, there are, as we shall see, many differences among the various Pentecostal churches, and we do better to write of Pentecostalisms. Clearly, the worldwide neo-Pentecostal movement has been much influenced by American revivalists and televangelists, and their books, pamphlets, and study courses. Some African churches seek links with their American counterparts, primarily in a quest for financial aid—the need for this reflects the economic collapse that is so widespread in Africa. These churches are, however, indigenous and for the most part self-supporting. One of the best-known, Nigeria's Deeper Life Ministry, refuses external financial aid or overseas links, and finances a major network of Nigerian missionaries working in other African countries. The whole phenomenon of Two-Thirds-World missionaries working in other Two-Thirds-World countries has been called "the great new [mission] fact of our time."[4]

In the United States, Pentecostals are part of a wider grouping often called fundamentalist, or the New Religious Right. In the 1970s, they moved from marginal to mainstream, largely through the preaching of revivalists, including televangelists, some of whom were Pentecostals. The movement reached its high point in the early 1980s. In 1988, Pat Robertson was a serious candidate for the Republican presidential nomination, but much of neo-Pentecostalism's confidence and public image was shattered by a series of financial failures and scandals. The Bakkers, whose *PTL* program had played regularly on Nigerian television, became a byword for the luxury and ostentation of their lifestyle, and Jim Bakker served a jail term for financial irregularities. One book on the televangelists is titled *Ministry of Greed*.[5] The mistakes of individuals, however, do not undermine a whole movement.

The starting point of modern Pentecostalism is usually taken as 1906, though it has older roots in the nineteenth-century Holiness movement. In that year, an African-American, William Seymour (1870–1922), preached in the Asuza Street revival in Los Angeles. This was followed by a dramatic dispersal of Pentecostal missionaries to fifty countries in two years. They thought, optimistically but wrongly, that the gift of tongues solved the language problem in foreign missions, and that they could really speak Cantonese, Tamil, and so on. In the years that followed, a large number of Pentecostal churches were founded on both sides of the Atlantic; they initially called themselves Apostolic. Some of the larger and better-known ones include the Assemblies of God, founded by an Arkansas pastor in 1914; the (British) Apostolic Church, founded in Wales in 1911; and Elim, founded in Ireland by a Welsh revivalist in 1915.

Some scholars regard the Aladura/Zionist churches, Churches of the Spirit, as an integral part of a wider Pentecostal history in Africa.[6] The linkages are evident. Africa's Zionist churches owe their initial inspiration to a small and obscure Pentecostal church in Illinois. Nigeria's Christ Apostolic Church, in its early years, affiliated with an equally small and obscure Pentecostal church in Philadelphia, and later with the (British) Apostolic Church. In Africa and elsewhere, many Pentecostals remain in mainstream churches, as charismatic Catholics, Anglicans, or Methodists. They are obviously in the same tradition as the Balokole, the Legion of Christ's Witnesses, and Arch-

bishop Milingo and his supporters. Neo-Pentecostals and members of prophetic churches, however, do not regard themselves as one movement, and
there are, as we shall see, significant differences between them.

A dimension that has sometimes been overlooked in studies of the Born
Again is the much earlier establishment of mission branches of Pentecostal
churches such as the Assemblies of God, which have typically been spread
by Africans. Many founders of neo-Pentecostal churches have come from this
background, and some of the best-known churches were established well
before the Born Again became a dominant feature of the African Christian
landscape in the 1980s (or, arguably, the 1970s). A famous and influential
Pentecostal of an older generation, a Zulu named Nicholas Bhengu (1909–
1985), founded an African branch of the Assemblies of God in South Africa, in 1938. Later, he studied at a Bible institute in Alberta. A gift he was
given there financed his Back to God Crusade, begun in 1950.

All of the three church founders whose careers are outlined below came
from older Pentecostal churches. Idahosa was converted by the pastor of an
Igbo Assemblies of God church in the Nigerian city of Benin; Kumuyi had
been a member of the Apostolic Faith Church, and also of an Aladura church;
and Guti was originally a member first of the Apostolic Faith Mission, and
then of Bhengu's branch of the Assemblies of God.

The history of these churches illustrates the diversity of Pentecostalisms.
In South Africa, Pentecostalism also flourished among Afrikaners, many of
whom, in the early twentieth century, were recently urbanized and poor. One
of the most famous figures in Pentecostal history, David du Plessis (1905–
1987), was an Afrikaner. Pieter Le Roux, as we have seen, founded the Apostolic Faith Mission, which remains one of the largest Pentecostal churches
in South Africa, the others being the Assemblies of God and the Full Gospel Church of God. Like other churches in South Africa, in the apartheid
era these churches were affected by the racism of the wider society, with separate churches for different ethnic groups and a white monopoly of power.
White neo-Pentecostal churches, such as Ray McCaulay's Rhema Bible
Church in Johannesburg, flourished in the late apartheid era. Their critics
accused them of endorsing the status quo.[7]

Pentecostalism also had a remarkable success among some of the Indians
of Natal, who originally came to South Africa as indentured laborers. In
1931, J.F. Rowlands established Bethesda in Durban. Cut off from their
original culture, some Indians, often Hindu Tamils, embraced it, and by 1970
there were 30,000 Indian Pentecostals.

African neo-Pentecostal evangelists differ in some respects from their
American counterparts. The New Religious Right had a strong political
agenda on issues such as the teaching of evolution in schools, much of which
is not relevant to Africa. Pentecostals, like fundamentalists, accept the ver-
bal inspiration of the Bible; at its worst, this can lead to an unscientific and

uncritical literalism. (Gordon Lindsay, the teacher and patron of Guti and Idahosa, suggested that the Bible foretells both television and the internal combustion engine.[8])

It has, however, been suggested that "almost all African Christianity is fundamentalist."[9] In the words of the Zionist authors of *Speaking for Ourselves:*

> We take every word in the Bible seriously. . . . When we are asked about Jordan baptism [by immersion in a river] . . . again we can only reply that that this is what we read in the Bible. . . . Some people will say that we are . . . "fundamentalists." We do not know whether that word applies to us or not. . . . We do not have the same problems about the Bible as White people have with their Western scientific mentality.[10]

Fundamentalists and neo-Pentecostals in the United States generally believe that the End is close at hand. They tend to believe in dispensationalism, an eschatology developed by the founder of the Plymouth Brethren in the nineteenth century. Dispensationalists are convinced that we are living near the end of the sixth of seven ages. Soon Christ will return, and true Christians will be "raptured" into Heaven. Those left on Earth will endure seven years of tribulation, followed by Armageddon, after which Christ will reign on Earth for a thousand years. A book popularizing this scenario, Hal Lindsay's *The Late Great Planet Earth*, is said to have sold 20 million copies. In Africa, there is much less emphasis on eschatology than on healing and exorcism.

American fundamentalists often advocate a Christian Zionism, which has nothing to do with the faith of the amaZiyoni, but applies various biblical prophecies to the modern state of Israel. This has often reinforced anti-Islamic attitudes, both in the United States and in Africa. A book published in Ibadan in 1990 actually equated Allah with Satan.[11]

In African neo-Pentecostal churches, the key emphasis is on healing and protection, "signs and wonders." Both traditional religions and the prophetic churches also emphasize this-worldly blessings, especially healing and protection from evil. Some of America's and Africa's Pentecostal preachers stress what adherents call the Faith Gospel (and its critics call the Gospel of Prosperity). No aspect of neo-Pentecostalism has been more widely condemned. The basic idea is that giving (by which is meant donations to the revivalist and his mission) will generate a much greater material return from God. The Bakkers were exponents of this theory, as was Archbishop Benson Idahosa. At a crusade in Douala, in 1993, he is reported to have said that "his faith had brought him so many clothes he did not know he had them, a car that even Nigeria's President Babangida could not match."[12] McCaulay's Rhema church is named after Kenneth Hagin's church in Oklahoma. (*Rhema* is one of several New Testament expressions for "word.") Hagin is one of the foremost exponents of the Gospel of Prosperity. A church in Calabar is named after Robert Schuller's Crystal Cathedral.

The Born Again have often had good relations with bad leaders—Kenya's Daniel Moi, Liberia's Doe, and so on—though this is not peculiar to neo-Pentecostals. Paul Gifford, who has published extensively on these churches, believes that their views are an obstacle to development. Faith, rather than action, becomes the solution to society's problems. For instance, at a Liberian prayer breakfast a lack of rice, the staple food, was ascribed to a demon of shortages.[13] In 1983, as Nigeria was engulfed in economic ruin, the graduate woman founder of the Shallom Christian Mission declared, "This year the Lord told me, 'The greatest problem in Nigeria today is how to curb the activities of water spirits in her midst.'"[14]

The struggle to overcome poverty and injustice becomes less urgent if the End is at hand. Disasters such as famines and epidemics can be understood as signs of its approach. Gifford points out that the Faith Gospel simply could not work in, for instance, the state of civil war and chaos which followed Doe's regime in Liberia. Faith Gospel advocates seek not the transformation of society, but the prosperity of individuals. The problem is that their panacea is open only to the Born Again.

Not all African—or American—neo-Pentecostals support the Faith Gospel. Although it is based on biblical texts, many regard it as a travesty of the teachings of Jesus. What has happened to "Blessed are the poor"? Clearly, many neo-Pentecostal preachers make a good deal of money from their ministry: "It's the biggest growth industry in the country [Nigeria]." There is a growing awareness of this, and a tendency to move away from the emphasis on enrichment.[15] In the words of a Lagos neo-Pentecostal publication, "The problem of the church begins with its leaders. Their insatiable appetite for wealth and position."[16]

The appeal of the Faith Gospel is obvious. Africa has been engulfed in an ever deepening economic crisis in which even the well-educated struggle to survive. The promise of a magical escape from poverty seems overwhelmingly attractive. Some commentators believe that the Faith Gospel helps believers make moral sense of the harsh and difficult world in which they live, and gives them community, confidence, and hope.

Mission and Ethiopian churches laid much emphasis on bricks and mortar. Neo-Pentecostals, in Africa and elsewhere, tend to meet for worship in schools, warehouses, or cinemas, and to hold crusades in tents or the open air. For financial reasons, they register not as churches but as nongovernmental organizations, but do not provide the range of social services that tends to characterize the mainstream churches: clinics, hospitals, primary and secondary schools. They do run a vast network of Bible colleges and training establishments for pastors, and often administer relief donated abroad.[17]

A number of people in high places have joined the Born Again, such as the Nigerian head of state, President Olusegun Obasanjo, who took this step when he was a political prisoner. Frederick Chiluba (b. 1943), who replaced Kenneth Kaunda as president of Zambia in 1991 and held office until 2002, made much of his Born Again credentials. He refused to move into his official residence "until its buildings had been cleansed from witchcraft and demonic influence by a team of pastors."[18] Despite the opposition of the churches, Chiluba declared Zambia officially Christian and enshrined this in the constitution. His regime became notorious for its corruption, and the initials of his party, the Movement for Multiparty Democracy, were reinterpreted as Make Money and Depart.[19]

Clearly, Pentecostalism and the prophetic churches had much in common: an emphasis on the Holy Spirit, faith healing, prayer for this-worldly benefits, and the expulsion of evil spirits. The relationship between them is complex. Neo-Pentecostals have worked to influence Aladura pastors, filling a gap in their education of which they are only too aware. But they tend to condemn the Aladura churches, calling them contemptuously, in Yoruba, "White garment churches."[20] "Only the Christ Apostolic Church is accepted by neo-Pentecostals: "It is believed by many born-agains that the other Aladuras, such as the Celestial Church of Christ and the Cherubim and Seraphim Church, are satanically inspired."[21] Neo-Pentecostals recruit their members from existing churches, including the Aladura. There is a widespread perception that the latter are declining, with an aging membership.

The differences between the neo-Pentecostal and prophetic churches are very considerable. The prophetic churches use African languages, have a deeply acculturated liturgy, and, often, follow a leadership model similar to that of an African kingdom. Neo-Pentecostal services are held in English or French, and their members wear Western dress. Prophetic churches are opposed to elements in traditional religion they perceive as evil: witchcraft and "idols." Neo-Pentecostals tend to turn their back more radically on their own inherited cultures, in favor of one that is global and American-influenced.

The neo-Pentecostals have a polarized view of the world: the Born Again, and everyone else. We should not use foreign sources to illustrate African ideas, but a correspondence course emanating from Georgia, which is widely used in Africa, states:

> Satan's world system includes commerce, politics, religion, education, entertainment, world kingdoms, world organizations and many other things. The Lord Jesus has delivered us from Satan's world system.[22]

One of the most troubling aspects of both American and African neo-Pentecostalism is an obsessive interest in demons and demonology.[23]

Whereas many Zionist or Aladura prophets were illiterate, neo-Pentecostal leaders are well-educated, often graduates. The leading historian of neo-Pentecostalism in Nigeria[24] believes that it originated in nondenominational study groups at universities in the 1970s. The students graduated and scattered, spreading these ideas widely and sometimes founding new churches. They make an intensive use of printed materials, often from America, and produce a good many themselves. The prophetic church leaders, with rare exceptions, do not write books. (Neither, of course, did Jesus.) Often, they do not read books, either.

The Born Again use the revivalist and fund-raising techniques and music of their counterparts in America. They make a sophisticated use of sound equipment and the media, and often run television programs. These churches have a strong appeal to women, and also to the young, who here, as elsewhere in the world, are attracted by Gospel pop. In some ways, they are part of an Americanized global culture, just like Coca-Cola and Nike sports gear. But the most influential revivalist in Africa is a German named Reinhard Bonnke (b. 1940), who lived in South Africa from 1967 to 1986. He began his crusades in 1975, and now holds about twelve a year in sub-Saharan Africa. They attract enormous audiences; half a million were present at the last session of his 1990 revival in Kaduna, Nigeria. In the year ending in September 1991, he is said to have preached to 8 million people, a quarter of whom declared their faith in Christ.[25]

In Rhodesia, Ezekiel Guti and his associates separated from the South African Apostolic Faith Mission in 1959. This had been brought to Rhodesia by a black South African in 1915. Its African members in Zimbabwe had much in common with the Vapostori: they shaved their heads, grew beards, wore white, followed Hebraic dietary laws, and practiced faith healing and witch-cleansing. The head pastor commissioned Masowe and baptized Guti. The latter, like so many prophetic leaders, went through a time of visions and tribulation in the wilderness.

Guti and his companions joined Bhengu's branch of the Assemblies of God. In 1969, they founded their own church, the Zimbabwe Assemblies of God, Africa. Guti, like Idahosa, studied at Gordon Lindsay's Christ for the Nations Institute in Dallas, Texas. Both adopted the title of archbishop. Both have their critics—in Guti's case, from within his own church.

> The critics take offense at the vast amount of tribute Guti exacts from the membership to finance his chauffeur-driven Mercedes and his travel abroad, while so many of his pastors and members remain as poor as church mice. They are worried about a leadership cult in which members pray to the God of Ezekiel.[26]

The contrasting careers of two celebrated Nigerian Born Again leaders illustrate the diversity of Pentecostalisms. Archbishop Benson Idahosa (1939–1998) was the founder of the Church of God Mission.[27] A Nigerian from Benin, he was, as a young man, an enthusiastic member of the Assemblies of God, which he left in 1968 to found his own church. A meeting with Gordon Lindsay led to a study opportunity at Lindsay's Christ for the Nations Institute. Later, Idahosa became closely linked with Jim Bakker and Oral Roberts. He converted to the Prosperity Gospel in 1973. He was a role model for countless aspiring Nigerian and Ghanaian church leaders, and the first of them to establish a regular television program. He also founded a large and flourishing Bible school. Idahosa was often criticized for his whole-hearted adoption of the Gospel of Prosperity, which clearly reflected both American influences and the financial strains involved in sustaining his ambitious enterprises.

Far from making a career of evangelism, a Yoruba named William Kumuyi (b. 1941) sacrificed a brilliant one—he has first-class honors in mathematics and was once a university lecturer, a position he gave up in 1983 to concentrate on full-time Christian work. Originally an Anglican, he joined first an Aladura church and then an older Pentecostal one, the Apostolic Faith Church. In 1973, Kumuyi began a Bible study group that attracted many university students and others. In 1975 he was expelled from his church on the grounds that only ministers should teach religion. This was the origin of the Deeper Life Christian Ministry (generally known as Deeper Life). In the 1970s, large numbers attended its retreats, with their expenses paid. Vast numbers of pamphlets and cassettes of Kumuyi's teachings were sold cheaply. In the economic collapse of the 1980s, the free retreats were no longer possible, and his ministry came to emphasize healing and miracles. There was nothing new about his message: the absolute necessity of conversion, restitution, and holiness. Far from advocating the Gospel of Prosperity, Kumuyi insisted on an ascetic lifestyle, which until the mid-1980s prohibited television sets, soft drinks, and personal jewelry. He is called General Superintendent (GS). Such is his role in the movement that it will probably face a crisis when the time comes for someone to succeed him. By 1993, Deeper Life had 350,000 members and missions in forty-two countries.[28] It is widely thought to be the largest neo-Pentecostal church in Nigeria.[29]

African church statistics are not particularly reliable, though they are cited in this study to give some idea of order of magnitude. There is much that they do not reveal. For instance, are new recruits mainly "traditionalists," like the Harris converts, or Christians already, like most of those who join the neo-Pentecostal churches? How long do people stay in a given church? (We have seen that Kumuyi was a member of three before founding his own.) Do those who remain poor lose confidence in the Faith Gospel? Do they move from church to church? Does repeated disappointment lead to a loss of faith in Christianity in general? Clearly, these are directions for future research.

One of the reasons for Bonnke's success is the enthusiastic participation of local churches, including mainstream ones. The unsatisfied hunger for education and study materials means that people from a wide variety of church backgrounds study neo-Pentecostal/fundamentalist courses emanating from the United States, which has led to a very extensive dissemination of ideas of this kind.

Scholars are deeply divided in their assessment of neo-Pentecostalism. Paul Gifford, the first scholar to publish extensively on the Born Again, is highly critical of them, especially of the Gospel of Prosperity and of the way in which they have been influenced by American televangelists, some of whom are now discredited. Others, including the present writer, have come to realize that neo-Pentecostalism grew largely out of older mission churches at a time when they had become essentially African ones, and that African neo-Pentecostals themselves have become increasingly critical of the Gospel of Prosperity and pastors with high-flying lifestyles. To Gifford, neo-Pentecostalism is a form of false consciousness. To others, it is patronizing to assume that those who attend such churches are foolish or misguided. Marshall calls the Born Again "the most dynamic group of Christians in Nigeria today." Neo-Pentecostal churches undoubtedly give their members hope and community in an age where independence has brought little but suffering and disappointment to most ordinary people. It is certainly more productive than Afro-pessimism. However, one remembers the words of the Christians of tenth-century Nubia, who also led difficult lives:

The Cross is the sister-friend of the poor . . .
The Cross is the watering of the parched . . .
The Cross is the rescue of those who are being drowned . . .
The Cross is the alleviator of those who have been oppressed.[30]

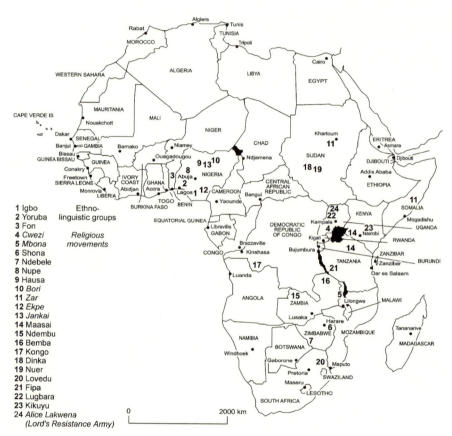

Case Studies: Neotraditional Religion.

PART IV

The Changing Face of "Traditional" Religion

Chapter 16

Divinities

The baby-sash of safety . . . which you tie me to your back with, don't undo it.

—a prayer to Shango[1]

RELIGIONS IN DECLINE

The most obvious change in "traditional" religion in sub-Saharan Africa since the beginning of the twentieth century has been its demographic decline. In 1900, "traditional" religion was almost universal outside Muslim Africa. Christianity, as we have seen, was highly localized, restricted to parts of South Africa, the coastal regions of Liberia and Sierra Leone, southern Uganda, and a few other enclaves. Even where missions were long established, Christianity tended to be the faith of a small though often fervent minority. In 1997, after almost half a century of Catholic and Anglican mission work, a CMS representative wrote of the Igbo towns on the Niger:

> In a small district we perhaps touch one percent of the people, the remainder are indifferent or hostile to our work. . . . Progress is slow & the great mass of heathenism around is still untouched.[2]

Now the churches there are packed to overflowing, and one very rarely meets an Igbo who does not identify as Christian.

By 2000, very few Africans indeed considered themselves traditionalists, and those who did so were often old and generally lacked Western education. By the late 1980s, in a community in northwestern Tanzania, 90 percent were Christian and 6 percent were Muslim.[3] In the small Yoruba town of Okuku, 60 percent of the people were "nominally Christians,"

30 percent were Muslim, and 10 percent were traditionalist.[4] In the Yoruba culture sphere, in the 1970s, it was estimated that 90 percent of the people were Muslim or Christian, rising to 98 percent in the south.[5]

In the past, a Yoruba devotee would worship only one divinity, partly because of the expense involved. Because it is generally felt that these cults should not die out, when a worshipper dies, he or she is now replaced by an infant or by a sometimes reluctant adherent of a different *orisa*.[6] These changes were mirrored in the "true fictions" of mythology. In an eastern Yoruba town, there was "a gentle oracular spirit who lived in the forest . . . where she looked after the wild creatures and answered people's queries." In 1927 she told the local ruler that "her pot of indigo dye had been broken by the new road, and that she was leaving, Efon to return no more."[7] An Igbo prophet of the nineteenth century foretold a time when the gods would starve to death, and those who survived would have hot oil thrown in their eyes.[8]

The ways in which "traditional" religions are practiced and understood have been modified by encounters with other religious traditions—especially but not exclusively with Christianity—and by an ongoing experience of modernity and Western technology. We have noted Horton's theory that the shift from the microcosm of village life to a wider society encouraged the growth of Christianity and Islam. But Christianity, in particular, also modified older understandings of divinity, some of which are studied here.

The "stamp collecting" approach to neotraditional religions—the compilation of apparently similar religious phenomena, out of context—has long been unacceptable. To avoid it, each chapter in this volume that deals with neotraditional religion focuses on a small number of case studies. In this chapter, they are drawn from the Yoruba and Igbo culture zones in southern Nigeria,[9] with some reference to their immediate neighbors, followed by two examples of enlargement of scale: the syncretistic cult of the mermaid, Mami Wata, and the ongoing life of Yoruba and Fon "traditional" religion in the New World.

The Igbo of southeastern Nigeria and the Yoruba of southwestern Nigeria and the Republic of Benin live in much the same natural environment. At the village level their lives are similar: both have traditionally relied on agriculture, especially yam cultivation. Both today have populations of perhaps 20 million.[10] In the past, their political systems were totally different. The Igbo lived in small village democracies; there were well over 2,000 of these. Most Yoruba lived in centralized kingdoms. This difference is mirrored in their religious institutions.

Yoruba religion, like Igbo religion, had many regional variants. In a sense "traditional" religion is ethnic religion, but not all the great divinities of Yorubaland were found throughout the Yoruba culture area, and in many cases they were also worshiped by neighboring peoples: the Fon to the west,

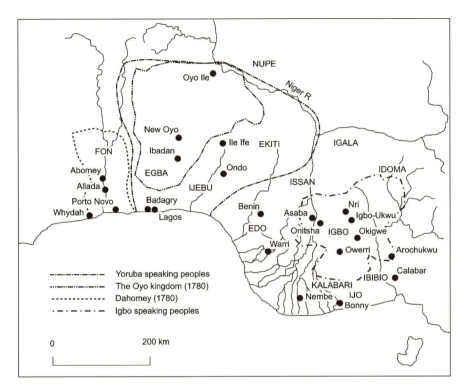

Igbo and Yoruba Speakers and Their Neighbors.

and the Bini or Edo to the east. Statements about "Igbo religion" or "Yoruba religion" are inevitable, but traditional religion was at once more local and more widespread. "The Yoruba" and "the Igbo" first acquired a sense of common identity in the colonial period, or when forcibly exiled from their homelands. These expressions are a kind of shorthand, referring in each case to speakers not of a single language but of a language cluster, whose culture varied considerably from one region to the next.

If the use of ethnic shorthand is problematic, so is the act of outlining a cosmogony. Vansina, writing of the Tio of Congo/Zaire, observes, "One should not consider that the Tio had a set of beliefs in the supernatural. There was no system. Beliefs were linked to ritual and symbols, and ritual was tied to specific situations. . . . The Tio had no . . . compulsion to believe the same things as long as they participated fully in the same rituals."[11]

Brenner suggests that the difficulty with cosmogonies lies in the question of who constructs them. If they come from a single individual, like the Dogon elder Ogotomeli, they may represent nothing more than his own

thoughts. If they claim to reflect the religious worldview of a particular society, this suggests difficulties:

> Since they are the products of abstraction and systematisation, one cannot know
> to what extent their constituent elements are shared in a given area nor how
> they relate to actual behaviour.[12]

This caveat is true of generalizations about any religious group, including Anglicans in Manchester, and would make their study impossible. The
basic point, however, needs to be kept in mind.

PERCEPTIONS OF DIVINITY: THE SUPREME GOD AMONG THE IGBO

In widely different African contexts, ethnographers and other observers
have described a cosmology with striking apparent similarities. There is a
remote High God, sometimes symbolically identified with the sun or sky,
who is not represented in art or offered sacrifices or embodied in spirit possession cults. It is the lesser divinities, often identified with local natural land-
marks or forces of nature, who are much more involved in daily life, as are
the ancestors.

Among the Igbo, the High God Chukwu (*chi ukwu*, "great spirit") or
Chineke (etymology unknown), often symbolically identified with the sun,
sky, or lightning, was far from remote. In 1841, a visitor to Aboh, an Igbo
town at the apex of the Niger Delta, documented a shrine to Chukwu and
noted, "The word Tshuku, God, is continually heard."[13] Farther east, there
was a famous oracle at Arochukwu, where God spoke from a cave, that attracted clients from a wide area. The Aro were long-distance traders, and
this may be an instance of an enlargement of religious scale as one leaves
the microcosm of village life. In the 1960s, an aged and illiterate traditionalist living far from Arochukwu pondered the oracle's claims, in a text where
"government" is a synonym for modernity:

> Government is teaching now, saying that Chukwu is not fixed to a spot; that
> where we go to consult Chukwu is a fake. That is what they are teaching and
> we cannot tell whether they are telling the truth or deceiving us.

Clearly, Chukwu was not particularly remote in Igboland, though it was
the local nature divinity, typically a river goddess, who inspired greater fear
and active propitiation.

Somewhat speculative theories have been advanced to the effect that
Chukwu was originally a local god of Arochukwu or, alternatively, that
Chineke was originally Chi Eke, contrasting principles of creation and de-
struction, but there is no real evidence of this.

In Igboland and elsewhere, an originally ungendered concept has been modified by missionary translations, and all Igbo now take for granted that Chukwu is God the Father. The same pattern has been described elsewhere in Africa; the changing understanding of Modimo in Botswana is an example.[14]

THE SUPREME GOD AMONG THE YORUBA

The Yoruba supreme divinity was Olorun (Owner of the Sky) or Oludumare (etymology unknown). His remoteness is reflected in creation mythology. Interestingly, Oludumare has declined in importance in recent decades, while the god of iron, Ogun, now patron of truck and taxi drivers, is still a living force.

Peel has suggested that "Muslims first pressed the idea of a single creator God upon the Yoruba," and were followed by Christian missionaries who translated "God" as Olorun. He points out that in the parts of Yorubaland farthest from Muslim influence, both the High God and lesser divinities belong to the same category, *orisa*. The latter include Obatala, who creates the world.

When a Pan-Yoruba cultural organization was created in 1948, it was called Egbe Omo Oduduwa, the Society of the Children of Oduduwa. In some legends, Oduduwa is an immigrant king who founded a state in Ife and whose sons then went on to found their own kingdoms. Their rulers are distinguished by their beaded crowns, and their number, in various sources, ranges from six to sixteen. Some scholars regard Oduduwa as a historic figure; to others, he has always belonged to the world of myth. In the southwest, Oduduwa was seen as female and was closely linked with Obatala. In some versions, she is his wife.[15]

Farther west, among the Yoruba's neighbors, the Fon, Mawu is a female creator god closely linked with Lisa (cognate with *orisa*), who is either her husband or her son. In some versions, they are fused in a single individual. The world is created with the aid of a cosmic serpent, on which the Earth rests. Still farther west, the Ewe of Ghana, who speak the same language as the Fon, believe in an ungendered High God called Mawu.

Mawu-Lisa is undoubtedly a cosmic male-female duality, and something similar may once have existed among the Fons' closest Yoruba neighbors. But in general, the remote High God is so widespread in Africa that we do not need to find an explanation in Muslim or Christian influences. Indeed, among the Fon there is also such a figure, Nana-Buluku, the parent of Mawu-Lisa.[16] As Peel points out, divinity can be ungendered only when it is remote; personal interaction requires conceptualization in personal terms, which must be either male or female.[17]

It is difficult for a Westerner not to think of God, divinities, and ancestors as a hierarchy, but one comes closer to the realities of what is described if this hierarchy is inverted: "It is curious how often in looking for a 'system of ideas' ethnographers assume that it would take the form of a hierarchy of spirits fitted into a chain of command leading up to god. This is of course the model of a centralised religion, appropriate to a centralised state. . . . It could well be that in the study of a particular religion, the concept of a high god, though present, might be inessential or residual, the least important concept upon which to focus."[18]

THE SACRED EARTH AMONG THE IGBO

In some African cultures, the Earth Mother is a divinity. The Earth differs from other nature spirits, being a chthonic force rather than an anthropomorphic figure. Ala or Ana is of central importance in much of Igboland. Many crimes are seen as abominations because they offend her. The whole body of inherited custom is Omenala, and ritual prohibitions are *nso* Ala. Those who died forbidden deaths, such as suicides or lepers, could not be buried in the earth, and their corpses were cast into the Evil Forest. Missionaries were sometimes given such areas for their churches, as a trial. The Igbo priest Michael Tansi cleared such a plot single-handed, until others came to join him. Nri, dedicated to the Earth, was one of Igboland's great ritual centers. Ritual specialists from Nri, their faces marked by distinctive scars, traveled from village to village, purifying the earth from abominations. Instead of weapons, they carried a staff of peace.

In the Owerri area, people honored the Earth in a different way, by creating *mbari* houses, shrines of clay sculpture that were allowed to disintegrate. It was the act of creation itself that honored the Earth. One of Igboland's great oracles was called Igwekala (Heaven Is Greater Than Earth). But in 1966, when village elders debated whether the Earth or Chukwu was supreme, opinion was divided.[19]

The cult of Ala, apparently so universal, illustrates the impossibility of making valid generalizations about the whole Igbo culture area. In the Okigwe area, Ajala (the local form of Ala) was less dominant; in one community, she was recently introduced, and she was often less important than the yam god.[20] In a village group south of Owerri, Ala is thought of as male.[21] Ala is clearly linked with the Nri ritual sphere, though her cult is found well beyond it. Legend suggests that yams were first cultivated at Nri. A Nri elder explained in 1967:

> The earth produces the food that man eats. The earth becomes the greatest supernatural force. Eri controlled yam and other food and the earth that grows them. No person should defile the earth by spilling human blood in violence on it. This is the covenant. It must be kept. We Nri keep it. We told other Igbo to whom we gave yam to keep it.[22]

THE SACRED EARTH AMONG THE YORUBA

In some Yoruba kingdoms, a powerful male secret society, Ogboni[23] (Elders), was dedicated to Ile, the sacred Earth. In Oyo, there was a strong link between the Ogboni and kingship. Ogboni officials played an essential role at the burials and installations of kings, and all the members of the royal council were senior Ogboni members. A woman attended their deliberations in order to report back to the king. Here, too, the Earth abhorred bloodshed. Each Ogboni lodge had ritual objects, a male and a female figure linked by a chain and made of bronze, symbol of changelessness. They were placed on the ground where blood had been spilled, and were used in ritual ways to punish offenders.

The *orisa* are linked with the sky, and the ancestors with the earth. Ile has both a nurturing and a dangerous aspect; she is the foremother of witches (*aje*). "Mother's breast milk is sweet," say the Ogboni, but she is also

Earth . . . who combs her hair with a hoe,
The owner of a bag full of evil,
She has a stomach big enough to swallow human beings.[24]

There are two forms of Ogboni, and some men belong to both. The Reformed Ogboni Fraternity was founded in 1914 by a Yoruba Anglican clergyman who was a former Freemason, specifically for Yoruba (especially Egba) Christians. Many eminent Nigerian Christians have been members; some of them compare it with membership in AMORC (the Rosicrucians, an organization to which many of the African elite belong). Other Christians condemn it.[25] Muslims do not join either form of Ogboni, and the Muslim who came to the throne of Oyo in 1948 banned it.

DIVINITIES: THE IGBO EXAMPLE

Apparently similar spiritual beings, such as river goddesses, were in fact quite different in various cultural settings. Most rivers and lakes in Igboland are associated with a goddess (or, very rarely, a god). The goddesses are stern authority figures, swift to punish infringements of their decrees but ready to protect the local community. Unlike their Yoruba counterparts, they do not marry, or have lovers or a life history. The goddess of Oguta Lake is an important figure in the fiction of Flora Nwapa.[26] In the Niger town of Asaba, the goddess Onishe is the town's tutelary divinity. She is thought of as a tall woman dressed in white, with flowing hair. Christianity is virtually universal, but people still speak of these goddesses as living presences. For instance, during the Nigerian civil war, a naval vessel sank in Oguta Lake; this was thought to be the work of the goddess. After a large number of men were massacred in Asaba, during the same war, Onishe is said to have appeared and said, "You are killing all my children."

Farther south, the Ijo people of the Niger Delta, living in a world of mangrove swamps and intricate waterways, have a quite different perception of water beings, a parallel world of male and female spirits, attractive and finely dressed, living in towns under the creeks. Sometimes a water spirit has a human partner, typically a wife.

Water goddesses were typically the dominant (though not the only) local divinities in Igboland. There were a number of boisterous spirits, such as Ekwensu, who had no shrines or sacrifices. Missionaries chose Ekwensu as the equivalent of Satan, and as early as the 1920s, he was described as God's arch enemy. This passed into general usage. There was an annual Ekwensu festival in Asaba, a time to celebrate, in the words of an Asaba elder who died in 1973, wealth, the enjoyment of life, and military prowess (which often led to fights). By the 1960s, there were moves afoot to change the festival's name. Agwu, another troublesome spirit, was linked with divination. There is a new proverb to the effect that "baptism . . . is no antidote against possession by Agwu."[27] In several Igbo communities, a new "traditional" divinity has been introduced as a protection from the real or imagined dangers of ritual murder.[28]

DIVINITIES: THE YORUBA EXAMPLE

The number of divinities worshiped varies greatly from one society to the next. There was a vast number of them in the Yoruba culture sphere—the Yoruba sometimes speak of 201, 401, or 1,700 divinities: symbolic totals, like seventy times seven. It is highly likely that this complex cosmology reflects the elaborate political structure of the Yoruba kingdom. Yoruba myths explain this multiplicity. Obatala, also known as Orisanla (Great God), owned a slave. Although he was kindly treated, he resented his servitude and rolled a boulder down a hill, shattering the god into fragments. Some were reassembled by his friend Orunmila, god of divination, and the others turned into new divinities.[29] Each divinity has a number of distinct manifestations. Again, myth explains the phenomenon: Ogun and his wife, the Niger goddess Oya, fought with magic staffs and broke one another into pieces.[30] In the small town of Okuku, there are seventeen forms of the smallpox god, Soponnan. (These manifestations can be compared with the many images of Mary, ranging from Our Lady of Guadalupe to Our Lady of the Snows.)

One's choice of divinity could be shaped by family tradition, one's occupation, or simple attraction. Often a diviner would tell a client that her problems were caused by the fact that a particular divinity was calling her to its service. If her prayers were unanswered, she could turn elsewhere, but it was not a step to be taken lightly, since the abandoned god might seek vengeance. However, the relationship between divinity and worshiper was reciprocal:

Sàngó, if you don't bless me, I will go and make an Òsun image
Sàngó, if you don't bless me, I'll go and turn Christian.[31]

This focus on one particular cult helps explain the inconsistencies between various accounts of the relationships between divinities—the others enter the story only as a supporting cast. Idowu represented the rich world of Yoruba divinities as "diffused monotheism." This has long been regarded as a classic instance of the distortion of traditional religion in the name of Christian apologetic.[32] But in a sense, the devotee of Shango was a monotheist, with little interest in other spiritual beings.

Some gods possessed certain of their devotees on ritual occasions; to open oneself to possession, medicines were applied to the head, and were removed at death.

There is much nineteenth-century evidence that women dominated the worship of the *orisa,* whereas men were particularly drawn to Ifa divination.[33] It was women who composed and performed the gods' praise songs, unless the cult was a specifically male one. "Calm" gods were sometimes praised for their cruel behavior, a symbol of their unbridled power, and violent ones could have a maternal, nurturing aspect, as is evident in the epigraph to this chapter. Barber points out that a knowledge of myths is dying out, and that the rich, ongoing corpus of *oriki* (praise songs to a particular god) is a better contemporary source. Orisa Oko is the god of farming, and farm work was done by men. Most devotees were women, however, because of Orisa Oko's famous witchcraft purification shrine.[34]

Olokun, the sea, was the most important divinity in the Edo kingdom of Benin, and was also worshiped in coastal, but not northern, Yorubaland. Olokun is sometimes thought of as male, and sometimes as female. Obatala, to whom Oludumare delegates the work of creation, was closely associated with Ife, and in some versions of tradition, was an early Ife king. Shango was closely associated with the empire of Oyo, which began as a small polity on the northern edge of the Yoruba culture area, and expanded into an empire in the seventeenth century. (A nineteenth-century king, faced with Muslim invasions, moved the capital hundreds of miles to the south, where the present city of Oyo is located.) In some versions, both Shango and the ancestral *egungun* cult came from the northern state of Nupe. Oyo kings were crowned at Shango's shrine.

A legend which is often retold suggests that Shango was an early king of Oyo who experimented with magic and inadvertently drew lightning down on his court and family; in despair, he committed suicide. The story is a favorite one in contemporary Yoruba popular theater. Scholars disagree as to whether Shango is a god of lightning who became a king, or a king who became a god, but the former is the more likely. Shango's symbol is a double-headed axe; he is a possessing god, and his priests wear eyeliner and women's hairstyles, which are shaved off when they die.[35] When a house has been struck by lightning, they extract the thunderbolt, for a fee. The thunderbolt is a Stone Age axe.

Ogun, the god of iron, carries two cutlasses, one for farming and one for war. The center of his cult is at Ire, in Ekiti. As we have seen, he has become the patron of motor transport, so his worship flourishes. He is honored with sacrifices of dogs. Myths describe how the land was initially cleared for human habitation. Obatala attempted this unsuccessfully with a cutlass of lead; then Ogun tackled the task triumphantly, with a cutlass of iron. The people of Ire invited him to be their king, but there was a misunderstanding and he killed many of his subjects in a fit of rage, then departed. Ogun is worshiped as Gu among the neighboring Fon, to whom he is the greatest divinity after Mawu-Lisa.[36] Presumably, his cult began with the origins of ironworking in Nigeria, in the first millennium B.C.E., though language evidence suggests that it evolved out of still more ancient roots. ("Ogun" is apparently cognate with, for instance, *ogbu*, the Igbo word for "killer," a component in Igbo ceremonial titles.[37]) The sacrifice of dogs, peculiar to Ogun, is first mentioned in 1603.[38]

Eshu[39] is another divinity who crosses ethnic boundaries—he is Legba among the Fon, and a good example of a divinity modified by missionary translations. In the Yoruba Bible, Satan becomes Eshu, and this equation has passed into general usage. But, in fact, he is a complex and paradoxical figure, closely linked with cowries (the shell money of the slave-trade era) and the market. Frobenius, who visited Ife in 1910, wrote:

> Wherever a missionary has set his foot, the folks today talk of the Devil, Edju. Yet go into the compounds . . . and they well tell you, "Ah, yes! Edju played many tricks. . . . But Edju is not evil . . . he gave us the Ifa oracle. . . . But for Edju, the fields would be barren.[40]

Eshu's shrine is in the market or at the crossroads. He has many of the characteristics of a Trickster and is far from wholly evil. It is said that he became a Trickster, and introduced divination, to save the gods from hunger. He causes the misfortunes that lead people to consult diviners, who, in their turn, recommend the offering of sacrifices. Among the Fon, Eshu is the only channel of communication between Mawu and the lesser gods who are her children.

Oshun, divinity of the river of that name and one of a number of Yoruba river goddesses, is a beautiful woman, wife of the creator god Obatala or, in a different story, of the lightning god Shango, and the lover of Ogun.

The herbalist/healer god, Osanyin, adorned with bright beads and associated with the forest, is the paradigm of the wounded healer: he has one eye, one arm, and one leg. One cannot choose one's ancestors, but in Yorubaland one could choose which divinity to serve. Polytheistic re-

ligions, whether in ancient Greece, India, or Yorubaland, offer a real freedom of choice.

ANCESTORS

In many ways, the supernatural beings closest to the living were their own,
not too remote, forebears. The Nykyusa hymn (quoted on p. 171) implies
that the cult of ancestors is the essence of traditional religion. In Igboland,
those who die a good death at an appropriate age, and have the correct burial
rites (a ceremony conducted some time after the actual funeral) become ancestors. They defend the lineage, expect regular offerings, and punish evil-
doers. Those denied these burial rites, perhaps because they died a "bad
death," become homeless, malicious ghosts. Igbo buried their dead near the
family home, and often still do so. Yoruba buried them under the clay floor
of the house as a symbol of their enduring links with the family, a practice
that missionaries denounced. Elderly men lived close to the ancestors, whom
they would soon join. But the world to come was shadowy and uncertain,
and ancestor cults centered not on the welfare of the dead, but on their impact on the well-being or otherwise of the living.

In the past, both Yoruba and Igbo believed that the dead can re-enter
the world of the living through specific masking cults. Both Yoruba and Igbo
have the concept of the Returner—Abiku among the Yoruba, Ogbanje
among the Igbo—a child who dies and is reborn repeatedly in the same family, a concept that probably reflects the realities of sickle-cell disease. Several
well-known Nigerian authors have written Abiku poems. To the Born Again,
Returners are real demons, like water spirits.

Both Yoruba and Igbo believed in a personalized destiny, which the former
called *ori* (head), and the latter, *chi* (spirit). One selected one's *ori* before
birth and could make some improvements to it by divination and sacrifice,
but could not radically change it. The Yoruba divination god was present
when this choice was made. Those who made good choices had practiced
Ifa divination even before birth.[41] Some profound Yoruba proverbs make the
point that destiny and character are the same thing:

> There is no destiny [*ori*] to be called unhappy in Ife city.
> Character is all that is requisite.[42]

In Asaba, it was thought that one's *chi* was a particular ancestor; a diviner
would ascertain which one, and the infant would inherit the same taboos.
Every year, separate festivals were held to honor everyone's paternal and
maternal forebears.

Clearly, aspects of Yoruba and Igbo cosmogonies are quite different. The
Yoruba nocturnal forest spirits (*iwin*) and personalised misfortunes (Ajogun)

have no Igbo counterparts. The Ajogun are Death, Disease, Loss, Paralysis, and Wickedness.[43]

There is no Yoruba equivalent of Ikenga, the male cult of the right hand, or of *osu* (hereditary ritual slavery), which was found in a small number of Igbo communities.[44]

ENLARGEMENT OF SCALE: MAMI WATA

The mermaid known as Mami Wata[45] is a remarkable example of enlargement of scale. She is a generalized form of a multitude of local water spirits, who are also often called Mami Wata as well. The first image of a single-tailed mermaid in African art is an African-Portuguese ivory salt cellar made by local craftsmen in Sierra Leone for a foreign patron, probably before 1520. The carved figure of a mermaid was often placed on the prow of a sailing ship; it seemed to confirm that water spirits really existed. The most common image of Mami Wata in West Africa is that of a woman shown from the waist up, wreathed in two snakes, one around her waist and one around her shoulders. This originated from a chromolithograph of a snake charmer brought to the Niger Delta by a British district officer in the late nineteenth century. He commissioned a local carver to copy it, and the image became enormously popular. It is now found, for instance, far from the sea in southern Mali. The first written reference to Mami Wata I know of dates from 1914 (in southern Nigeria); in French, she appeared as Mami Ouata, in a story from Togo, in 1927. By the 1930s, Igbo *mbari* houses included images of a woman wreathed in snakes who was equated with the European mermaid and called Mami Wata.

In central African countries, such as the Democratic Republic of Congo, Mami Wata is one of the most popular motifs in an urban art created by and for the poor, in which she is depicted in mermaid form. In West Africa, however, she is the subject of a cult of affliction. Mamisi, as Mami Wata devotees are called in Togo, are mainly women; they tend to turn to her for help with problems such as ill health, mental illness, or infertility. Mami Wata shrines are an African Invention of the West, adorned with icons of Western consumerism, such as Fanta orange soda or talcum powder, and sometimes books or paper.

Mami Wata is sometimes thought of as a Christian—a clay sculpture of her in an *mbari* house, in 1966, shows her with a cross around her neck. But to the Born Again, she is a demon. Though devotees often seek children from Mami Wata, the general image of her that prevails in the wider society is of a spirit who offers material wealth at the cost of children: "Instead of children there is a golden tree. Instead of a womb there are golden scallop shells."[46]

Mami Wata is a product of what has been called interculture, the complex and changing interface between African societies and the Western world.

There is an interesting link between her and highlife, another dimension of interculture. The Nigerian musician Victor Uwaifo attributed his success to Mami Wata:

If you see Mami Wata O!
Never never run away.

ENLARGEMENT OF SCALE: THE NEW WORLD

The transference of African religions to the New World is one of the most dramatic examples of change in traditional religion and of an enlargement of scale. Yoruba and Fon religions, in particular, evolved into Voudoun in Haiti, Santería in Cuba, Shango in Trinidad, Candomblé and Umbanda in Brazil, and Winti in Surinam. Voudoun is especially interesting, since the importation of slaves to Haiti ended in the eighteenth century. Eshu is Legba in Haiti, Elegba in Cuba and Eshu in Brazil. Papa Legba controls the entrance connecting the human and the spiritual realms, and every ritual begins with his invocation. Ogun is Ogum in Brazil and Ogou in Haiti. The divinities have evolved in a dialectic with Catholicism, and have become identified with various saints. Ogun is Saint George in Brazil and San Juan in Cuba. In Haiti, he is Sin Jak Majè (Saint Jacques Majeur).

It is in a sense surprising that Oshun, so closely identified with a particular African river, is worshiped in Brazil and Cuba. She has different, and apparently mutually incompatible, manifestations, or *caminos* (paths): sixteen in Brazil, fourteen in Cuba. In Cuba she is both the Virgin Mary, as Our Lady of Charity, and a strongly sexual being who is sometimes called "the whore saint":

I bow to Oshun
Iyalode so very great, splitting the sands . . .
Elegant woman who has jewels of cast copper
There is no place where it is not known that
Oshun is as powerful as a king.[47]

In all cultures, people feel a need for protection and guidance. Many contemporary Africans are involved in several different religious traditions at once, without any sense of incongruity. In times of crisis, individuals may seek out a Christian healer, a marabout, and/or a diviner. While the Born Again, like the foreign missionaries of an earlier day, remain hostile to every aspect of the religions of the past, others have moved toward an inclusiveness that was always inherent in these traditions. Nigerians attend traditional religious ceremonies out of ethnic loyalty or simply to enjoy the costumes, music, and dance. Masked figures leave their original realm of the secret-sacred to perform in cultural festivals. Some individuals make a conscious effort to ensure that the old religions do not die out. In 1977, despite the hostility of many Christians and Muslims, a "traditional" shrine was erected on the campus of the University of Ife, in western Nigeria.

ARTIFICIAL SYNCRETISMS

In a small number of cases, educated men have tried to found new religious movements based on traditional religion. This is very much a post-Christian phenomenon, quite different from popular reinventions of traditional religion, which usually, though not invariably, have an ethnic base. In Ghana, Afrikania Mission was founded in 1982 by a former Catholic priest, Vincent Damuah (b. 1930). Perhaps surprisingly, it has considerable prominence in Bediako's *Christianity in Africa*,[48] but has little popular support and recently merged with a similar small movement, Godianism. The latter owes its survival to the dedication and persistence of its Igbo founder, K.O.K. Onioha. He set out to establish a movement based on the concepts and values shared by all religious traditions, especially African ones. (His African critics pointed out that it had a foreign name!) In practice, it has always been strongly identified with Igbo culture—it has an Igbo name as well—and there is a tension between its ethnic and international aspirations. Both Afrikania Mission and Godianism are artificial constructs, like Esperanto, and have never had a mass following. The Yoruba Church of Orunmila, though considerably older, is comparable. Since it is based on Ifa divination, it is discussed in that context.

The presence of Christianity could weaken old beliefs without replacing them: "We no longer believe in the old rituals because we see that the Christians do not do these things and nothing happens to them," said a young Nyakyusa in southern Tanzania, in the 1930s.[49] A study of a Tonga community in Zambia twenty years later, several decades after an American fundamentalist mission was established there, suggested much the same thing: schoolboys, though not committed Christians, had lost their faith in traditional religious teachings because teachers and missionaries disregarded them and suffered no harm.[50] In the 1960s and 1970s, as they acquired families, livestock, and crops, they became more involved in the old ways: ancestral cults, local shrines, and divination. They now had something to protect or to lose.[51]

Chapter 17

Ancestors as Divinities

I had come to destroy all that he wished to preserve.
   —an early Christian catechist, on an *mbandwa* medium[1]

In large areas of eastern and southern Africa, the heart of ritual is the worship of the divinized dead—often, but not always, royal ancestors. Some Yoruba divinities are referred to as if they once were living people, but they do not form part of a quasi-historical narrative. It is impossible to construct a consistent picture of their kin and life histories from myth or from the references in the Ifa divination corpus. Shango is often described as an early king of Oyo, but his wife was the spirit of the Niger.

Scholars are divided as to whether the personalities discussed in this chapter are historical or mythical figures. The research done on the remote origins of these cults dates mainly from the 1960s and 1970s. Contemporary researchers are more likely to focus on change taking place today, rather than on a distant past in which evidence is scant and knowledge is largely speculative.

Spirit possession, in which the identity of the living person is temporarily overcome by a divinity or spirit, is more common in Africa than elsewhere in the world. It takes many forms, including that of the Shango devotee who becomes known as Iya (Mother) Shango in ordinary life, and the Mami Wata initiate. In the cults of the Cwezi, dead kings of the interlacustrine area of East Africa, and of *mhondoro* (royal ancestors among the Shona of Zimbabwe), mediums play, or once played, a major institutional role. That of the Cwezi medium is now defunct or individualized and privatized. *Mhondoro* mediums are still a major force to be reckoned with. They are almost always men, as were the mediums of Ryangombe, in Rwanda. Many of the Cwezi mediums were women. Mediums of the Cwezi and of Ryangombe are collectively known by a form of *kubandwa* (possessed).

The Interlacustrine Kingdoms, ca. 1700.

THE CWEZI

Traditions collected in southern Uganda and northwestern Tanzania tell of a short-lived dynasty of mysterious kings, called the Cwezi, who were followed by the historic Bito rulers of Bunyoro. Some historians have thought that these were real kings in a dynasty that came to an end about 1480. To others, they belong, and have always belonged, to the world of myth.[2] The Cwezi stories were recorded and elaborated during the colonial period—not surprisingly, colonial officials took a lively interest in stories of white rulers from the north. There was also a supreme God, Ruhanga, with associated creation narratives.

The Cwezi ruled for only two generations, and the Cwezi kings, Ndahura and Wamara, have become the gods of smallpox and death, respectively. (In some versions, they are separated by a third ruler.) When the end of their power was foretold by dire portents, they descended beneath the waters of a lake after sending for a Cwezi illegitimate son, Rukidi, who became the first Bito king of Bunyoro.

In Bunyoro, Ankole, Rwanda, and Burundi, and the smaller kingdoms of Buhaya, a minority of pastoralist aristocrats ruled over a much larger agricultural population. The values of a pastoral people thread their way through the Cwezi legends. The last pre-Cwezi king goes to the underworld in search of lost cattle. A Cwezi royal commits suicide when his favorite cow dies.

It is possible that ancient women's rituals became marginalized by the growing cult of dead kings; in Bukiga, where there was no kingdom, the term used is *emandwa zabakazi* (spirits of the women).[3] In Bunyoro, the hereditary priest of Ndahura was a woman. The hilltop shrine was a place of pilgrimage, her advice was sought by kings, and she played an essential role in coronations. Wamara's priest was a man; again, there was a shrine on a hill.

The priests of great divinities were different from the bands of mediums (*mbandwa*), who were members of a cult of affliction. The mediums often joined a cult because of sickness or infertility, and were subjected to terrifying initiation rituals that constituted a symbolic death and rebirth. They then enjoyed high status. The first European visitors to Bunyoro, in the nineteenth century, described the strikingly dressed women who were prominent at court and as itinerants, and who, in a trance state, spoke in the voices of dead royals. It is likely that these roles grew out of the widespread practice of appointing spirit wives to divinities.[4] In the twentieth century, *mbandwa* came to play individual roles as diviners and no longer acted as a group.

By the mid-twentieth century, there were said to be nineteen Cwezi spirits in Bunyoro, many identified with forces of nature, such as Mukasa, the spirit of Lake Victoria/Nyanza. The spirits were divided between "white" Cwezi spirits, nearly all of whom were male, and the "black" spirits of wild animals or foreigners. During the first half of the twentieth century, the latter came to include the spirits of tanks, airplanes, "Europeanness," and "Swahiliness."[5]

An early Christian catechist in Buhaya called the *mbandwa* mediums "clubs of malcontents and reactionaries, just as my house was the meeting-place of the young, of eager and simple hopes for a better future."[6] Cwezi rituals there lasted into the 1950s, though Christian youths had attacked their shrines, in the name of the king, in the 1920s. The fact that the king encouraged the destruction of the shrines of royal ancestors reflects the way in which Christianity had become an official religion (as it would soon be in Rwanda). The main shrine was dedicated to Wamara, "ruler of the universe, supreme among all other *bachwezi* deities and judge of the dead." According to one estimate, there were 350 *mbandwa* in Buhaya in the 1940s and fewer than a hundred by the late 1960s. In 1967, the government of Tanzania abolished the positions of traditional rulers, which further undermined the cult of dead royals. In 1990, a few individuals still offered private sacrifices to Wamara.

RYANGOMBE

Farther south, in Rwanda and Burundi, the pastoralist aristocrats were the Tutsi; their peasant subjects, the Hutu. Here there was a cult of Ryangombe, known as Kiranga in Burundi, a hunter slain by a woman disguised as a buffalo, after he had ignored the warnings of his mother. He was not a dead king, but had been the leader of the *imandwa*. In the late nineteenth century, the Tutsi were still offering Hutu girls as spirit wives to Ryangombe; these "wives" led celibate lives at his hilltop shrines. In Burundi, the spirit wife of Kiranga was of great ritual importance:

> She and the king are equals and hold Burundi in common. The king is the visible chief of it. Kiranga incarnates himself in his wife.[7]

By this time, the *imandwa* mediums in Rwanda were all men. It seems that the older women's cults had been replaced in a pattern of rapid and total religious change, one that would recur when the Rwanda king and chiefs adopted Christianity. In Bunyoro, the spirit pantheon changed, providing a mirror of changing worlds, and thus survived.[8]

The cult of Ryangombe, or Lyangombe, was more extensive. In Buhaya, he was part of the Cwezi pantheon, as Wamara's herdsman. His cult was introduced to the Nyamwezi by visiting Tutsi, and is documented there in the mid-nineteenth century. Here he became a savior figure, promising salvation to his followers: "Whoever will adore and pray to me, I shall come to his aid in all his needs."[9] Here and elsewhere his initiates believed that they would live with him after death in a place of abundance, while others would burn in volcanoes. It is an eschatology strikingly unlike that usually associated with "traditional" religions, and may well reflect Muslim or Christian influences.

The Kiga lived in small-scale polities north of the powerful kingdom of Rwanda. In the late eighteenth century, they developed a cult of the divinity Nyabingi, who was thought of as a murdered queen. In the colonial period, this cult became a focus for opposition to colonial rule.[10]

RELIGIOUS CHANGE IN MALAWI

In vast expanses of eastern and southern Africa, there is an ancient substratum of hilltop shrines and spirit wives visited by a great divinity that sometimes takes the form of a serpent. At a later stage, cults of long-dead royals, apical ancestors, and a murdered rainmaker developed. The cults described in the pages that follow conceptualized spirit beings in different ways. What

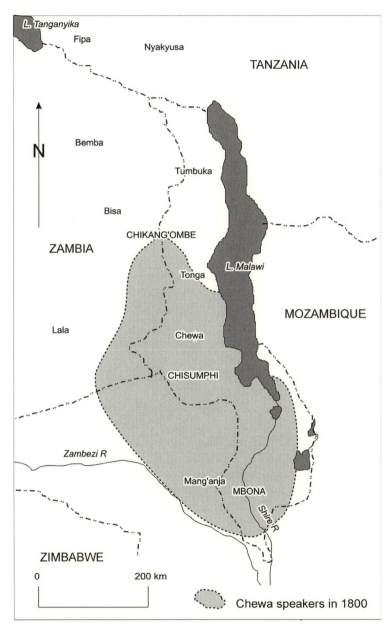

Ritual Spheres: Chewa Speakers and Their Neighbors.

they had in common was an association with the land and the quest for rain and for human and agricultural fertility, all of which depended on a state of ritual order. The black or dark blue garments worn by Shona spirit mediums symbolize rain clouds.

Like so many ethnolinguistic groups, chiChewa speakers were divided by colonial frontiers, and today live in Malawi, Zambia, and Mozambique. Their linguistic and cultural continuity is often obscured by different ethnic labels. They are part of a great continuum of matrilineal peoples to which the Ndembu and Bemba also belong. The chiChewa-speaking Mang'anja live in the Shire valley in southern Malawi, where they are now very much outnumbered by Yao and Sena/Tonga immigrants.[11]

In the remote past, in central and southern Malawi, there was a divinity called Tunga who had spirit wives on hilltop shrines that he visited in serpent form. He is associated with storms and rain—his destructive and creative aspects—and with a great rain god called Chisumphi. Tunga is now largely forgotten, but survives as a figure in the Nyau mask society.[12]

Tumbuka speakers, who live farther north, are thought to have originally worshiped Chikang'ombe, a manifestation of the supreme god, also in serpent form, who similarly visited spirit wives on hilltop shrines. Clearly, all this grew out of the same ancient roots.[13] The remote High God, who lacked propitiatory rituals or shrines, was called Chiuta (Great Bow, often interpreted as Rainbow) or Leza (Lightning). The celestial serpent, sometimes linked with the rainbow, is a very common image in central Africa. Often, the rainbow serpent is a harmful force associated with drought. Lightning, in a tropical environment, is often deadly. But it is also true that both rainbows and lightning link Heaven and Earth.

By the late sixteenth century, there were three kingdoms to the west or south of Lake Malawi, each known by the title of its king (in the case of the Shire valley, the Lundu). Oral traditions are unanimous that at the time there were only two Chewa/Mang'anja clans. The ruling class belonged to the Phiri (Hills) clan. The Banda clan consisted of the original inhabitants, who had a special ritual role as owners of the land. The name means "those who tread the grass under their feet" (that is, lived in the valleys[14]). Tunga's spirit wives were supposed to be Banda. Interestingly, there are now far more Phiri than Banda in the Shire valley.

These three kingdoms were together known as Maravi (hence, Malawi). The word means "flames," and their kings tended sacred fires, fueled by the mats used in girls' initiation rituals, that were extinguished when they died. They worshiped divinized royal ancestors (comparable with the Cwezi) whose ritual centers were located at their graves. The kings were rain callers, an essential function of sacred royalty in areas where rain is uncertain and lethal droughts are always a possibility. They had no traditions of spirit wives, or of sacred pools and serpents. After the kings' deaths, their spirits possessed both human mediums and lions, as was true of their Shona counterparts. They introduced blood sacrifice, which some cult centers rejected.[15]

MBONA

Whereas the Cwezi are real or imaginary dead kings, Mbona (Seer) was a real or imaginary rain caller and diviner who was killed by a king. His cult flourished in the southern Shire valley, the kingdom of the Lundu. The late sixteenth century was a time of unrest and disorder. This has been variously interpreted, but seems to have been caused partly by the presence of the Portuguese in the Zambezi valley.

There are a number of different versions of the Mbona story.[16] In one of them, "M'bona" is the spirit wife of Tunga, the mythic serpent.[17] (Some have thought that this is the original form of the myth, but, as with so much else, there is no real evidence.)

Usually, Mbona is a male diviner. In a well-known version, he succeeded in bringing rain where the Lundu had failed, and was accused of thwarting the latter's attempts by witchcraft, but refused to prove his innocence by taking the poison ordeal. He fled, but was captured and beheaded. His spirit spoke through a villager, demanding that a shrine be built for his head and that a spirit wife live there. This seems to be a narrative that critiques the autocracy of kings and, perhaps, witchcraft accusations. His blood formed a sacred pool whose waters were red in the past. Sacred pools are a widespread symbol in southern Africa—Mwari's most popular praise name is Great Pool.[18] Mbona fed the hungry with miraculous rice or pumpkins.

Mbona's shrine, not far from the confluence with the Zambezi, is in an area of sacred forest where animals, including snakes, and people were thought to live together peacefully. The ritual importance of fire and an age of primal harmony are also reflected in the local version of Paradise Lost. Originally the supreme God, Chiuta, lived with people and animals. But man discovered fire; it spread to the grasslands, and both animals and God fled. Chiuta took refuge in the sky, and humanity was punished with mortality.

Originally Mbona's spirit wife, the Salima, was appointed for life. Since about 1900, the position has been filled only during the chief Mbona ritual, the rebuilding of his shrine when it falls into disrepair. The cult is in decline, though there was a revival during the famine of 1949. The last Mbona medium died in 1976, and the shrine buildings are in ruins, but Mbona is still a living presence in local consciousness, often described as a black Jesus, an African counterpart to the white one.[19] There is an interesting contrast with the way in which the Born Again or Archbishop Milingo regarded possessing spirits as demons.

To Schoffeleers, who devoted many years to the study of the subject, Mbona is a historic figure. To Wrigley, he is not a long-dead diviner but the spirit of the Zambezi River. As he points out, the Mbona/Lundu contest is set in Kaphiri Ntiwa, where the story of creation is set. In the history of religion, whether the Cwezi or Mbona ever existed is less important than the changing role they played in religious beliefs and institutions.

ANCESTORS AS LIONS AMONG THE SHONA

The chiShona speakers of Zimbabwe and Mozambique, like "the Yoruba" or "the Igbo," acquired a corporate identity only in the context of colonial invasion and rule. They originally saw themselves as Zezuru, Korekore, Karanga, Kalanga, Ndau, Manyika, and so on. "Shona" was an Ndebele word adopted by the people themselves in the 1890s. (In the same way, the Shona called the immigrants maTebele, a name that they adopted.)

They had their own history of the rise and fall of kingdoms. The famous stone ruins of Great Zimbabwe, a royal capital of the past, were abandoned in the late fifteenth century. Oral tradition suggests that the move was due to ecological factors. A son of the last Zimbabwe king traveled north, seeking salt for the royal herds, and founded Mutapa, north of modern Harare. The northern Shona did not build in stone. Their king was called Mwene (Conqueror, which is probably cognate with the titles of the Rwanda king [Mwami] and his Kongo counterpart [Mane], though some have questioned this). Mutapa survived into the nineteenth century, but in a weakened and divided state. In the late seventeenth century, a Shona general founded a new kingdom, the state of the Rozwi (Destroyers), which was in decline after 1750. Older books tended to telescope Great Zimbabwe, the Mutapa state, and the Rozwi, and to see the cult of the High God, Mwari, as the unifying ideology of empire. The careful research of Beach separated these stages, stressed the predatory nature of the Rozwi state, and suggested that its association with Mwari was invented after the Ndebele conquest. One response to defeat was to stress the glories and divine blessing of the past.[20]

In the Shona culture sphere, there are three categories of possessing spirits: *shave,* the spirits of animals and strangers, who never speak; *midzimu,* family ancestors; and *mhondoro,* royal ancestors.[21] Each *mhondoro* has a precise territory, often called a spirit province. They are called *mhondoro,* "lions," because this is the form they take when not speaking through a human medium. Most *mhondoro* mediums are male; in 1980, three out of sixty were women. They are possessed rarely, in particular ritual settings.

In 1883, the medium's role was described as follows:

> He sends sunshine and rain when it pleases him. He foretells the future of the Natives, he forecasts the disaster that will fall upon them, he gives judgement on all the matters submitted to him. . . . He is submitted to the most scrutinising tests which consist of naming all the Muanamotapuas from Mutato to the present ruler.[22]

A medium embodies only one spirit, and each spirit has only one medium at a time, except in rare cases where there are parallel cults in different places. A given spirit may not have a medium at all for periods of time. A medium is initially called by sickness. To be accepted, he must pass tests by senior mediums, showing, in trance state, a detailed knowledge of his spirit's life and selecting, from a bundle of ritual staffs, the one used by his predecessor. A medium must be a "stranger," belonging to a different clan from that of the spirit. It is a vocation accepted reluctantly, for it imposes many restrictions. He holds office for life, unless he loses his powers.

In present day Zimbabwe, virtually everyone opts for Western dress, even in remote rural areas, but mediums wear a distinctive garment of black cloth. If they see blood or the color red, they will die. They are endangered if they encounter any aspect of modernity, even a soda bottle: "They may not use Western medicines. They may not ride in cars or buses." Even asphalt roads are dangerous.[23] Money, however, can be handled without risk. Mediums are not expected to become rich, and redistribute the gifts they receive. In the nineteenth century, *mhondoro* mediums in the Zambezi valley mixed freely with Europeans. A hundred years later, such meetings were felt to endanger the medium. What the ancestors objected to was a history of white land alienation and political dominance.

Mutota, the apical ancestor of the Korekore of the Zambezi valley, is an example of a *mhondoro* spirit. He is thought of as an invading king who migrated to the Zambezi valley, but died before entering it because of ritual dangers. Lesser spirits in the area are his children; they have smaller territories and their own mediums. Mwari is not mentioned in Mutota's rituals, which refer to him as a creator spirit. Nehanda, who has a woman medium, is his daughter. (There is another medium of Nehanda near Harare.) A Nehanda medium was put to death by the British after the 1896–1897 uprising.[24]

Spirit mediums played an important role during the Zimbabwe war of independence (1972–1979), among them the very old woman who was Nehanda's medium at the time:

> She hated all European things. We told her ". . . we want to liberate Zimbabwe." She was very much interested.

She died in 1973, in political exile, and was buried near the Zimbabwe border; guerrillas entering the country would visit her grave. On Independence Day, an official choir sang on national radio:

> Grandmother Nehanda,
> You prophesied,
> Nehanda's bones resurrected,
> ZANU's spear caught their fire.[25]

In settler-ruled Rhodesia, as elsewhere in colonial Africa, "traditional" rulers became salaried employees of the state, and both their power and their ritual importance declined. Paradoxically, it was the mediums, embodying the rulers of the past, who assumed a leadership role and a central place in ritual. Unlike neighboring peoples who retain male, and sometimes female, initiation, the Shona have no other major rituals: "Only the rituals of possession remained as the moment in the peasants' lives when they felt themselves to be most profoundly themselves."[26]

MWARI

In most African cultures, the High God lacks shrines, sacrifices, and mediums. There are, however, exceptions. The cult of Chisumphi in central Malawi is fragmented and very much in decline, but that of Mwari still survives in southern Zimbabwe.

The main oracles of Mwari/Mwali are in the Matopo Hills near Bulawayo, not far from the Zimbabwe/Botswana border. Members of a number of different ethnolinguistic groups are involved, including Shona and Venda and the eastern edge of the Tswana culture sphere, as well as the Ndebele, whose nineteenth-century history is an interesting example of religious change.

The Ndebele were originally the Khumalo, kin to the Zulu, by whom they were defeated in 1821. Their king, Mzilikazi, led about 300 warriors to the interior, where they and their descendants became a ruling caste. They spent a period in the Transvaal, where their numbers were swollen by many captives of Sotho/Tswana origin who became the second stratum of society. Later, the Ndebele migrated farther north to avoid Afrikaner settlers and Zulu attacks. In 1838, they reached western Zimbabwe. Those local people whom they incorporated became a third caste. The Ndebele founded a new state, forming tributary relations with some Shona polities while others remained independent. The Matopo Hills were now in Matabeleland.

In Khumalo/Ndebele religion, there was a remote High God, Nkulunkulu, who is also the first ancestor; he emerged with his wife "out of a marshy place where there were reeds." Having raised their children, they descended under the ground, where they live in snake form.[27] Nkulunkulu had no shrines or cult, and religious activity centered on ancestors, both at the family level and at the state level, where the focus was royal ancestors. The most important state festival was Inxwala, during which the king offered them massive sacrifices. The kings were rain callers, addressing prayers to royal ancestors at their graves.

When they began their migration, the Ndebele left the royal graves behind. In 1829, Mzilikazi told a missionary that their god was Molimo (the Sotho/Tswana High God, Modimo). In Matabeleland, they encountered the cult of Mwari, whom they called Mlimi. At one point the Ndebele king persecuted Mwari's devotees, but in time this cult spread among the Ndebele,

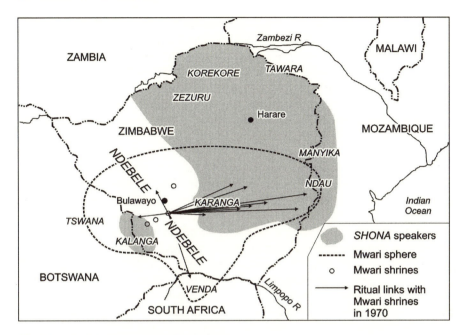

The Mwari Cult in Southern Zimbabwe.

an addition to their existing beliefs rather than a replacement. Lobengula was a famous rain caller, but in times of drought, they turned to Mwari as well.

In 1893, the Ndebele state was conquered by Rhodes's British South Africa Company, and much of the land and cattle were seized. In 1896, the Ndebele rose in revolt, and were followed soon afterward by some Shona polities. Ranger believed that this was coordinated and blessed by Mwari spirit mediums who were trying to restore the Rozwi state, but further research has cast new light on these issues. As we have seen, there seems to have been no connection between the Rozwi and the Mwari cult, and the priests of the major shrines were Venda from the south. The Ndebele had defeated the Rozwi in 1866, and the uprising was headed by Ndebele royals. Only 30 percent of Shona were in favor of war: those who had been most exposed to European pressure (or, alternatively, those who were in a tributary relation to the Ndebele). Their uprisings were not coordinated.[28] The main concern of Mwari mediums, then as at other times, seems to have been ecological: the distribution of anti-locust medicine.

Scholars have different views about people who may or may not have lived in the remote past. They disagree equally vigorously about extremely well-documented events at the end of the nineteenth century. These uprisings, however, became part of the folk history of a new nation. In 1962, in Southern Rhodesia, an old man who had fought in the 1896–1897 uprising gave Joshua Nkomo a ritual axe.[29]

Mwari has three aspects. One is the Mistress of Tribes, who has a single eye, ear, breast, arm and leg, and lives in the sky to the east. The implication may be that one divine breast is enough to sustain the world. There are interesting parallels in distant and totally unrelated cultures. Her husband, the Great Head, lives in the sky to the south. Her son, the Awl, lives in the sky to the west. They communicate through shooting stars.[30]

Mwari is not worshiped in family rituals. Local oracles have "priests," called minstrels or leaders, as well as messengers, who bring seeds to bless and other requests, and return with the consecrated seeds and messages from God. They also have initiates, who sing and dance in praise of Mwari and, in a trance state, writhe on the ground, overpowered by his love.[31] It is likely that the cult has, over the centuries, been influenced by *mhondoro* spirit possession.

In a séance at one of the great oracles of the Matopo Hills, Mwari spoke through a woman medium, in a high-pitched voice, in antique Rozwi dialect. Those attending must turn their backs to the cave, lest they be blinded.[32]

Mwari is opposed to bloodshed: "Mwali is a conservative God. He does not like change. He wants the old ways." Oracles urge people to resist the cash economy, to store or share grain rather than sell it: "Mwali objects to sales, for the country is not sold. It is given to its owners."[33]

An often-quoted Mwari song, collected in 1960, is a cry for divine intervention:

Ay, this world fails one,
Ay, this world fails one,
Ay, the unburnt pot has entered here,
Ay the unburnt pot [the white man] has spoiled the world . . .
Yelele the god who is in heaven has given us his back.[34]

Inevitably, the missionaries translated God as Mwari. There seems to have been an amicable relationship between the cult and local Ethiopian churches. The head of a well-established local Zionist church, however, attacked it as Satanic.[35] The cults of Mbona, Mwari, and Mutota had much in common. Their purpose was to sustain the health and fertility of the land and its people, as well as an associated state of ritual health and harmony.

Chapter 18

Powers Embodied: The Medium and the Mask

God made things double: masquerading for men and witchcraft for women.

—the Ebirra of central Nigeria[1]

In some cults of affliction, initiates, who are often women, are possessed not by divinities but by spirits that have no existence outside this particular ritual context. The two examples that follow—Bori, among the Hausa of Nigeria and Niger, and Zar, in the Republic of Sudan (and Somalia)—flourish in societies that have long been Muslim, so that possessing spirits are conceptualized as djinns. This is followed by a case study of an area where spirit possession dates only from about 1960. The second part of this chapter deals with male masking cults, which have, as we shall see, many points of resemblance with spirit possession. In both, a spiritual power is temporarily embodied in a human person.

BORI

The Kano Chronicle, a traditional history of the Hausa city of that name, describes an ancient cult on the top of Dala hill. When Islam reached Kano, there was a struggle between the supporters of the new religion and the old. Islam was victorious, here and elsewhere in Hausaland. The transition is remembered in a "true fiction"—the story of Bayajida, a prince from Baghdad who comes to the Hausa city of Daura, slays a snake that lives in its well, and marries the queen; their sons become the founders of seven Hausa kingdoms.

But in the countryside, the ancient spirits of an earlier day survived in Bori: a cult dominated by women that induces possession through ritual drumming and dancing. Its spirits are called *iskoki* (winds). (It is noteworthy that the English word "wind" is the origin of the name of the African-Surinam religion, Winti.)

Most initiates are brought to Bori by sickness; a few inherit the allegiance of their parents. There are obvious links with the subordinate state of many Hausa women.[2] Bori is also practiced among secluded women in purdah, where it is called the Bori of the home. Women speaking as spirits are sometimes empowered to make requests or demands that would otherwise be impossible. Bori meetings also provide an element of conviviality and sociability in their lives.

Bori initiates acknowledge the existence of a supreme God, Ubangiji. He has, however, no cult, sacrifices, or shrine, and does not possess initiates. Bori spirits are thought of as djinns that existed before Adam and were visible until the time of Solomon. There are two categories. The white Bori spirits of the town, who are Muslims, pray five times a day, keep Ramadan, and so on. The dark spirits of the bush are much more dangerous. They include the spirits of wild animals, such as lions, hyenas, and some snakes, as well as the boisterous spirits of past warriors and hunters.

Like many masking cults, Bori depicts both the animal and the human worlds. The latter is a parallel social universe. An early twentieth-century account listed sixty-five spirits. They included Mallam Alhaji, a scholar and pilgrim "who pretends to be old and shaky and to be counting beads with his right hand while reading a book with his left."[3] There is a strong satirical element—the *mallam* is bent double, with a cough; the Prince of Cavalry dances boldly but finally falls over, and wears a woman's clothing. There is also much compassion—Bebe, the deaf mute, sits alone and weeps, his lips moving soundlessly. The leper begs with distorted hands and drives flies away from imaginary sores.

Like other spirit pantheons, Bori expanded to mirror a changing world. In 1914, its spirits included Fulbe searching for their cattle and a "pagan" called Gwari.[4] Now they represent Nigerians from the south, such as the Yoruba woman spirit Iyawo, and European Christians who speak English, wear Western clothes, and smoke cigarettes. Spectators can ask possessed initiates questions, so that the possession becomes a form of divination, and give them gifts. Bori has its roots in Hausaland, but an early book on the subject was based on research in North Africa, among the enslaved, who had taken it with them.[5]

ZAR

Zar is not dissimilar: it is a cult that is very widespread in the Muslim societies of northeast Africa, including the Sudan and Somalia. An excellent study of it was made in the 1980s, in a village near Khartoum, where it had been present only since the 1920s.[6] It was dominated by women, who were drawn to it by particular kinds of sickness. Forty-seven percent of married women were members. Like their Bori counterparts, they created a parallel universe by enacting spirit roles that depicted, parodied, and critiqued the changing world in which they found themselves. The visiting ethnographer represented their lives in her writings. Zar initiates do the same, not by creating texts but through performance. Zar spirits include famous Sufis, but the most popular are Europeans, who demand items such as canned food and white bread, and Christian Ethiopians. The former include an archaeologist dressed in khaki and wearing a pith helmet, and Dona Bey, a heavy-drinking American big-game hunter who is a doctor by profession. With his elephant gun he destroys the miniature antelope that locals kept as pets, a symbolic indictment of the wastefulness and inappropriateness of much Western technology.

Zar spirits have much in common with Mami Wata. They "love cleanliness, beauty, expensive human finery. . . . [I]f thwarted they can be vindictive. . . . Zayran are essentially amoral, capricious, hedonistic."[7] Zar has also been studied in Somalia, where it includes spirits of soccer.

An enlargement of scale, so evident in Mami Wata, is also apparent elsewhere. *Mashave*, the plural form of the name of the Shona spirits of animals and strangers, has become a general name for possessing spirits in Zambia. Spirit possession is expanding and has been adopted in a number of areas where it was once unknown. The Maasai culture sphere is an example.

SPIRIT POSSESSION AMONG MAASAI WOMEN

Until about 1960, the Maasai (Masai) had no spirit possession cults: "The Maasai conceptual system does not include any category of extra-human spirits except the Supreme Being. . . . Possession, then, would seem an anomaly."[8] These cults reached them from the Muslim and Swahili coast, where they are common and are called *shetani*. Only Maasai women become possessed—as many as 50 percent of them in some areas. Some act out human roles: Maasai, other African peoples, or Europeans who request books, soap, and Western clothes. Some play animal roles as lions, snakes, or leopards, while others are djinns from the coast. Possession is regarded as a sickness, not as a call to a cult of affliction. Since it is not a traditional Maasai condition, there are no traditional Maasai remedies. Those who are possessed sometimes have recourse to Swahili diviners, but the surest cure for possession is Christian baptism. Possession is variously interpreted as women's response to their subordination or as a way of obtaining the consent of male relatives to their becoming Christians, which is often given reluctantly.

There are many different ways of interpreting women's participation in spirit possession cults. The spirits often demand new clothes, jewelry, or meat. Possession provides an acceptable way of extracting resources or making complaints. This is not the whole story, but it is part of it. Bori enables women to play out roles, such as the scholar or the prince, that are otherwise unattainable. Their role-playing presents a mirror to society that is often satirical. The cults are flexible enough to accommodate new spirits, and enable participants to locate social change in their own intellectual world. There is also a recreational element; Zar or Bori women get together and have a good time.

The medium is always considered passive. In Hausaland, the medium is the horse, and the spirit, the rider. The Shona call the medium an empty bag and believe that anyone who fakes possession will die.

MASKING CULTS

In chapter 1, we mentioned the way in which the antiquity of masking is reflected in Saharan rock art and perhaps also in traditions about the early history of Ife. Masking and spirit possession cults have a great deal in common. In both, a human being is overpowered by a supernatural force that acts or speaks through him or her. In spirit possession, the devotee is sometimes costumed, or carries or wears an item that symbolizes a particular spirit. In masking, the whole body is covered by a costume that is usually made from cloth or raffia. Often there is a carved headpiece; these have frequently found their way into museums or private collections without the full costume. In masking, as in spirit possession cults, the spirit may belong to the natural world: a leopard or a generalized forest spirit. It may represent a specific ancestor or ancestors as a collectivity, or embody a spirit peculiar to the world of masking, the equivalent of Zar or Bori spirits. It may speak in a secret language that requires an interpreter. The identity of the man wearing the costume is always a secret. Some spirits take the form not of maskers but of disembodied voices.

There are, however, major differences. Spirit possession cults are responses to affliction, and their members are individually called to them by illness or other misfortunes. They are dominated by women. Masking societies are secret male organizations. (Often an older woman will be associated with a masking society, as the "mother" of the mask.) In many cultures, initiation into the mask society is an essential part of the adolescent boys' rite of passage, so that all male adults are members, at least in theory. In other cultures, mask societies are joined voluntarily. Some have a number of levels; members move from one to the next, acquiring a deeper knowledge of its secrets. The major emphasis of spirit possession cults is therapeutic, but masking's many functions do not include healing. They do include the exercise of male power and various forms of social control, whether over the youthful initiates or those the maskers perceive as deviant.

Women know that the mask is worn by a male dancer, but preserve the fiction that it is a supernatural being. A woman sang at a Yoruba mask festival:

Women can do nothing about it, they are not allowed to know the secret cult
Women cannot know the sacred grove
If women were allowed to know the secret cult
I would wear one masquerader's costume on top of another.[9]

As her words make clear, she does know the secret. In the early twentieth century, some Christian women risked their lives by challenging masquerades.

The examples that follow are drawn from three of the regions which were selected for case studies in earlier chapters: the chiChewa speakers of southern Malawi, the Yoruba and Igbo culture spheres, and two adjacent areas. The first of the adjacent areas is the Nupe kingdom in central Nigeria, which has a history of cultural interaction with the old Oyo capital. The second is the Ekpe/Mgbe tradition of southeastern Nigeria and southwestern Cameroon, a good example of the way in which masking cults spread across ethnic groups.

Masking cults, which are not, of course, peculiar to Africa, are almost invisible in some surveys of African "traditional" religion. But they are at the very heart of the cultures of the past, an area where religion, art, and power relations intermingle in an infinite variety of complex forms. There is an Igbo proverb that to appreciate a masquerade (to use the term for masked figures current in Nigeria), one must observe him (*sic*) from all sides at once. This is, of course, impossible.

NYAU IN MALAWI

Nyau is an ancient mask society that flourishes among the Chewa and Mang'anja, but is absent among the Tumbuka.[10]

Masking cults often preserve narratives about their origins, which clearly belong to the world of myth, not history, but may also include clues about real events. One legend attributes Nyau's origins to a time of hunger, when a Phiri dancer was given food in return for his performances, and others followed his example.[11] Another tradition links it with girls' initiation: "Initiation of girls is a very old custom observed far earlier than Nyau from earliest times." The older women are said to have called on Nyau to frighten and intimidate the neophytes.[12]

Traditions suggest ancient linkages between Nyau and the shrines of Chisumphi, both in rain rituals and in girls' initiation ceremonies, but for centuries the Nyau have been forbidden to go near these shrines, and shrine officials cannot watch Nyau performances. Several myths explain this. In one, girls drowned while washing in a pool during the initiation rites—in some versions, they were drowned by Nyau—and Chisumphi's spirit wife banned these ceremonies from the vicinity of her shrine. Alternatively, when they

were being initiated by Nyau, a rock came down and crushed them. Paradoxically, Tunga survives as a figure in Nyau performances.

The Nyau call themselves "wild beasts." The beasts of the day are dead
people; the beasts of the night are wild animals or caricatures of human
outsiders. Animals are represented in large grass or wicker structures worn
by several men at once.[13] In some interpretations, the conjunction of human and animal masks mirrors the primal harmony of man and beast.

The dancers, as wild beasts, stand outside Chewa society and reverse its
norms. They are often violent, and their songs obscene. In the past, they
would abuse women and steal food from them. Nyau is a law unto itself,
and cases involving its members can be tried only by Nyau officials. Nyau
meet in forests or wooded graveyards to prepare masks and initiate boys as
new members. They have a secret language and tend to be led by Banda.

Masks express adult male solidarity, and both mirror and enforce male
power. This may be particularly welcome to Chewa men, who live in a society that is both matrilineal and uxorilocal, so that husbands live in their wives'
villages, but it is equally true of masking cults in those African cultures—
the vast majority—which are patrilineal and virilocal.

From the 1920s on, Nyau was locked in conflict with missionaries and
African Christians, which sometimes led to violence. The missionaries were
opposed to obscene songs and the near nudity of some Nyau dancers. But
more fundamentally, traditionalists, foreign missionaries, and African Christians agreed that masking cults were a central representation and symbol of
the spiritual powers of the past. Nyau members were excluded from baptism
and from mission schools. In their turn, Nyau, who originally recruited
young men, now accepted much younger boys, to keep them away from
these schools, which they saw as agents of unwelcome change. Its members
saw Nyau as an essential element in their inherited culture. It was said in
1929, "We Achewa cannot allow our customs to disappear. They are the
precious legacy of our ancestors. We hold to them as sacred things."[14]

As the cash economy expanded, Nyau members charged increasing fees
for their performances. And as initiations and traditional burials declined with
the spread of Christianity, there was less demand for their services, which
impoverished villagers naturally resented. Nyau appeals to the poor, who have
not managed to enter the privileged world of the educated and salaried. A
survey made in the 1960s found that 516 out of 597 Nyau members were
illiterate, and the rest were semi-literate.[15] One recalls the early Haya Christian who saw spirit mediums as "malcontents and reactionaries" and Christianity as the faith of those with "hopes for a better future." Today, Nyau is
closely linked with the village headman, whose role is undermined by modern institutions of government.

Masking cults, like spirit possession cults, often represent and critique
aspects of their changing world. Nyau masks make fun of unpopular colonial officials in the past and of American Peace Corps workers. Saint Peter,

Saint Joseph, and the Virgin Mary are ridiculed in their comic Nyau forms.[16] Nyau structures represent cars as well as wild animals. In 1985, a new Nyau character appeared, a predatory white man who attacked people and demanded money. His name was Kamazu (The Warrior). Who was Kamazu? The president of Malawi at the time was Hastings Kamazu Banda.[17]

MASKING IN NIGERIA: YORUBA TRADITIONS

Gender hostility, often in the form of an ideological polarity between Mask and Witch, is a recurrent feature of mask cults in Nigeria. This takes different forms in the three major Yoruba mask traditions introduced here: Egungun, Oro, and Gelede (there are, of course, many others).

Egungun incarnates dead male ancestors. These masks appear at funerals and at great annual festivals for the dead. They take three forms. The Good Egungun wears a plain costume and represents the dead as a collectivity. Two other forms represent specific dead "big men" and often behave in a dangerous and aggressive fashion.[18] In the past, if the swirling cloth panels of an Egungun touched a spectator, both dancer and onlooker were put to death.

In some versions, Egungun is the son of Oya and Shango, who, as we have seen, were closely linked with Oyo royals. In the Oyo kingdom, the head of Egungun, the *alapini,* was one of the seven members of the king's council. A royal mask in modern Oyo appears as a funnel of red cloth that rises to twelve feet and is called "I devour in the forest."[19] In the past, it executed witches.

The authority of the collective ancestors both upheld male power and law and order, and suppressed potential threats, especially the dangers posed by witches: "The original three cloths of Egungun were of the colour red. They terrorised the witches. . . . Afterwards, whenever important elders died, these powerful cloths were added to their corpse and the body rose up as Egungun."[20]

The corpus of Ifa divination poetry, memorized by generations of diviners, is a precious source of information on the religious insights of the past. It has remained unchanged at least since the 1890s, and probably much longer. Obatala and his wife were swallowed by witches when she defiled their wells. Egungun and Oro tried to save him, but were swallowed up as well. Ifa, the god of divination, rescued them.[21] Another Ifa poem runs:

Whenever the Human Being gave birth to children,
The Witch would kill them . . .
The Human Being went back to his Ifa priest
And performed the sacrifice which he previously neglected. . . .
He put on the robes of his Egungun
And started to use proverbial language against the witch.[22]

Oro, another ancestral spirit, was closely linked with Ogboni and was particularly powerful in Abeokuta. It may not have existed in Oyo Ile. It manifested as a terrifying sound created by a bullroarer, or rhomb, and, like Egungun, executed criminals, including witches. When Oro was abroad in masked form, on occasions such as the funerals of titled men, women had to stay indoors on pain of death.[23] Like many other secret male cults, both Oro and Egungun admitted several token women members, not as active participants but as "mothers."

While Egungun and Oro executed witches, Gelede, a mask tradition of the southwestern Yoruba, placated them, calling them, euphemistically, "the Mothers." Gelede rituals have been very fully published and are justly famous for their beauty and creativity. They begin in the evening, when a masked satirist called Efe appears—he is able to criticize the world around him with impunity. The next day, male and female Gelede dance, both roles being played by men. Women devotees also dance, balancing wood carvings on their heads and wearing iron anklets (thought to protect from witches) and the sash that secures the infant on its mother's back (symbol of babies to come). In some myths, this dance with statues is described as the original form of Gelede. Women and men often join Gelede because of sexual or reproductive difficulties.

At the heart of Gelede is Yemoja (Mother of All Waters), also called Iya Nla (Great Mother). In a myth recorded in the late nineteenth century, her body swelled up with water and exploded after an incestuous rape. From that rape, many divinities were born, among them Ogun, Shango and Olokun, and the river goddesses Oya, Oshun, Oba, and Olosa (the spirit of Lagos lagoon).[24] Yemoja is both Great Witch and the goddess of a local river, closely linked with others. Her cult survives in the New World.

Ifa poetry describes Gelede as a protection against witchcraft:

> Thus declared the Ifa oracle to Orunmila, who was going to visit the haven of
>   the-wielders-of-bird-power [witches]
> He was advised to sacrifice a wooden image, a baby sash and metal anklets
> He performed the sacrifice.
> He visited the haven of the-wielders-of-bird-power and returned safely.[25]

Gelede celebrates the power and creativity of women while giving eloquent expression to the terror of the witch: "The one who has water in her house yet washes her face with blood."[26] Expressions of this kind are also applied to various *orisa:* the same combination of a creative and nurturing aspect, on the one hand, and a cruel and violent one, on the other.

In the 1950s, a researcher among the southwest Yoruba, the home of Gelede, wrote that Egungun, Oro, and Gelede were declining, Gelede most of all.[27] Like many other comparable institutions, they have survived largely, it would seem, as celebrations of indigenous culture.

Both traditionalists and Christians tend to see masks as loci of spiritual power, the symbol par excellence of the old religions. But according to Abimbola, "Interviews show that a good number of those who celebrate festivals such as *Egungun* and *Oro* in most parts of Yorubaland are either Muslims or Christians,"[28] though probably as onlookers rather than performers. Gelede is more of a cultural spectacle, and some dancers make no attempt to hide their identity. One Efe masker combined verses of the Quran with other prayers.[29]

Peel quotes a study of mask societies among the Ijebu Yoruba that stresses their popularity, "especially if one regards them more as a social and artistic institution." He asks, with typical insight:

> What is in the mind of active Christian obas like the Timi of Ede or the Owa of Ilesha as they celebrate their Ogun festivals? If they are continued for socio-cultural reasons, like much European folklore . . . they stop being "religion." But I would hesitate to believe that this is the case yet. They retain importance . . . not merely because of some continued belief in the power of the old gods, nor yet because of potential tourist value, but because no other religion or sect can claim for itself a monopoly in expressing community feelings.[30]

MASKING IN NIGERIA: NUPE

The kingdom of Nupe was adjacent to Oyo Ile, and their histories are interwoven at many points. According to a mid-nineteenth-century source, Yoruba and Nupe informants agreed that both the cult of Shango and masks incarnating the dead were borrowed by the Yoruba from the Nupe.[31] The people of Nupe, like many others, including the Yoruba and the Igbo, thought that witchcraft is largely the preserve of women. A researcher in the 1930s found that the living head of the women's market guild was thought to be the head of a coven of witches.

There were a number of masking cults in Nupe. One was a royal mask, in the form of a tall tube of cloth, that specialized in discerning and killing witches, very much like its counterpart in Oyo. Gender and generational hostility are evident in the myths that explain Nupe's origin. In one, it was invented by a diviner to assist a king engaged in a power struggle with his mother, and duly swallowed her up. Alternatively, it was introduced in a time of general lawlessness: "The older women, especially, caused much trouble." The only woman to resist the mask was an older woman, who was put to death not by the mask but by the older men.

In the early nineteenth century, a Muslim scholar founded a new dynasty in Nupe. A king of this line, Masaba, took control of this mask in the 1840s, assuming the title Magajin Dodo (Master of the Mask). It was actively involved in finding and executing witches, for a fee. It was banned by the colonial government, and Nupe people lamented that witchcraft had consequently become rampant.

In 1934, despite the mask's illegality, a researcher was able to observe a performance of it, and recorded a women's song on the subject:

> One does not call him friend
> When he comes to stay in the bush:
> A friend [he] is when he leaves.[32]

Kohnert notes, "Whether this prohibition has ever been really effective is open to question," and that it had reemerged by 1960.[33]

THE TALL GHOSTS

There are thousands of named masks in Igboland. A lifetime would be insufficient to study them, and a book of this length devoted to them could not do them justice. They include terrible and dangerous figures, graceful performances where men wearing maiden masks dance as girls, and also comedians. In the dry season, in the past, so many young men would appear as maskers that they were called "locusts." Their dance was a competitive display of youthful athleticism. Older men would wear the dangerous horned masks called *mgbedike* (time of heroes). Ijele, a gigantic celebration of wealth and craftsmanship, may well be the largest mask worn by a single dancer in Africa.

Some masks are understood as the collective dead, like Egungun, but never incarnate specific ancestors. Here I have space only to outline one of these many mask complexes, which has much in common with those found among northern neighbors.

The Niger Igbo have a dangerous ancestral mask most fully studied in Onitsha, where there were in theory nine such figures but in practice more. Variously called Terrible, Tall Ghost, or Hooded Cobra, it was a conical cloth figure, with the apex formed by a raised hand, sometimes holding a stick. It was banned by the colonial government, and by the early 1960s was already in a state of "decay," so that a researcher depended on accounts of the past.[34] In the past, youths were initiated into the secret of the mask and all adult males were members, except the enslaved and the king. The latter was forbidden to meet the Tall Ghost, for this would be an encounter of rival loci of spiritual power. Its counterpart in Asaba is forbidden to cross the main road, symbol of modernity. Women, children, and, in the past, the enslaved stayed indoors when such masks were abroad. Onitsha traditions insist that the Tall Ghosts were introduced from Igala, where there is a similar cloth-draped figure, controlled by one of the nine Igala Mela (titled Kingmakers), that can reach a height of fifteen feet. Its function was not to persecute witches but to create "a ritual condition which witches in general cannot tolerate."[35]

The Idoma ancestral mask, Alekwu, was also a conical figure; it would strike at onlookers with its cobra head, and its blows were believed to be mortal. Unlike its counterparts, it performed long chants that outlined, among other themes, the story of a migration from an ancestral home.[36]

THE SPREAD OF MASK TRADITIONS:
JANKAI AND EKPE

Masking societies, like spirit possession cults, have often expanded widely, covering a number of ethnolinguistic groups. Poro, which is a secret society rather than a masking cult, and which has a women's counterpart, is found in no less than sixteeen ethnic groups in Liberia and Sierra Leone.

Jankai is a mask that is found over a large area of central Nigeria. I studied it among the Anaguta, who live near Jos; they agree that the original form of supernatural presence was that of disembodied voices. Jankai was a later import. Its name is Hausa for Red Head—it wears a helmet mask made of red seeds, and Hausa dress. Jankai is a dangerous and powerful spirit that seems to be linked with the perceived power of the Hausa-Fulbe emirates to the north. It was introduced before the colonial era; the trees that produce the red seeds still grow near the hilltop settlements which were abandoned in the early twentieth century.[37]

The Ekpe/Mgbe mask tradition is much better known and more fully studied. It is best documented in Calabar, originally a coastal cluster of settlements dating from the early seventeenth century, and now a modern city. Its people, the Efik, speak the same language as the Ibibio of the hinterland, their original home. They have a strong sense of separate ethnic identity— yet another example of the way in which people who consider themselves distinct often speak the same language.

Ekpe was adopted in Calabar in the mid-seventeenth century, though it did not originate there, and developed into a major institution of government. An early colonial officer described the way in which its powers still endured: "Before the coming of the 'white man' this institution ruled the land, and even now it has more influence in many ways than government itself."[38] Like other mask traditions, it kept women and the enslaved in a subordinate role. In the words of a mid-nineteenth-century source, "The sound of 'Egbo Bells' and the name of 'Egbo Day' are enough to terrify all the slave population of Duketown."[39]

Ekpe/Mgbe means "leopard"; it is a forest spirit that sometimes manifests as a roaring noise and sometimes as a masker. The latter wears a black knitted body suit with colored attachments and carries a leafy branch in one hand, symbol of its origins. In the nineteenth century, the masker would hold a whip in the other hand and flog every slave he met.

New lodges were founded, for a fee, when delegates acquired the secrets of an existing one. Some Europeans joined because it provided an effective way of recovering debts. There were nine ranks—at first, slaves could not join; later, they were allowed to enter the lower levels. Members communicated in a secret language, and Ekpe may have been linked with *nsibidi*, a locally invented form of writing that was recorded by a number of observers in the early colonial period.[40] The name has been translated as "cruel writing." Both Mgbe and *nsibidi* were taken to Cuba in the early nineteenth century by enslaved Ejagham.[41]

What has happened to Ekpe today? An account of Calabar published in 1989 states that it is hard to know whether it is flourishing or declining, but that the leading members of Efik society are members. Some Efik Christians refuse to have anything to do with it. Others believe that there is no contradiction between Ekpe and Christianity, pointing out that the former fosters brotherhood. Ekpe masquerades appear on the streets, not only for chiefs' funerals or installations but also on public holidays.[42] I watched and photographed Ekpe in Jos at the time of a university graduation ceremony. (The Obong of Calabar was the university's Chancellor, and a number of "traditional" figures, including Mami Wata dancers, came with him.) But at the heart of Ekpe is a body of secret-sacred lore that is closely guarded.

CONCLUSION

A legend from a northern Igbo community tells of a woman who revealed the mask's secret and was ostracized by other women. She refused to pay the punitive fine.[43] Rebels, whether real or mythical, were rare indeed, and the wise words of First Australian woman shed light on this: ". . . it was not blind terror which kept our heads bowed at initiation, it was respect for the Law which restricted both men and women."[44]

Mask societies are always secret societies, but not all secret societies are primarily or at all involved in masking. Some women's societies revolved round secret ritual knowledge. Some myths suggest that various mask traditions were founded by women—this has been recorded among the Dogon and in traditions about the origins of Ekpe. Clearly, this belongs to the genre of myths that define by inversion.

Masking has innumerable functions and forms: it may be terrifying or satirical or humorous or an art form like ballet. But of course it is impossible to observe the masker from every direction at once.

Chapter 19

Ritual and Divination

The traditions have been lost because those who practised them have all died, and the people who are still around don't do a thing except bring in European customs.

—an Ndembu elder, in 1985[1]

Rituals are not created in order to make statements about the nature of reality. They do so obliquely, partly through symbolism, and also in the selection of their occasions. Rituals create a web of contested meanings, but their goal is to heal an illness or mark the transformations of adolescence. In Bantu languages, ritual is often called "drum," reflecting the all-important role of percussion in song and dance.

Divination, which is a form of ritual, is a quest for patterns of meaning underlying human existence. It presupposes that such patterns exist and that they can be accessed by the appropriate technology for the help and guidance of individuals.

Ethnographers make a distinction between what ritual "says" and what it "does." In the Niger Igbo town of Asaba, there was an annual ritual in which cooking fires were extinguished except for one flaming branch, which was thrown into the river, with the words "suffering go away," "sickness go away," and so on, followed by a meal as specific as the Thanksgiving turkey. The explicit intention of the ritual was to throw away the troubles of the past year and make a new start. At a psychological level, it did just that, but it also affirmed the unity of the community and its attachment to the ways of the ancestors. Functionalist interpretations stress the way in which ritual legitimizes the existing order and preserves older values. Like Mwari, ritual has often been conservative. But rituals survive when they meet a felt need, and in a rapidly changing Africa, they are often abandoned or modified.

A CHANGING WORLD OF RITUAL

In contemporary Africa, the main forms of neotraditional religious ritual are the private consultation with the healer/diviner (roles that now tend to merge) and the public celebration of festivals. Funerary rites, as well as weddings, are frequently composites of Christianity and the neotraditional.

School attendance has often replaced initiation as a rite of passage; where the latter survives, it tends to be drastically shortened because of educational requirements. Sometimes colonial or independent governments prohibited initiation rituals because of the sufferings so frequently inflicted.

The spread of Christianity and the growth of urbanization and labor migration have, in some cases, led to the abandonment of "traditional" rituals or to their modification. In Lusaka, a marriage ritual from a particular area has been adopted by people from elsewhere. An old Bemba woman commented, "In the past there were ethnic groups. Now we are mixed up. We adapt from others."[2]

Some rituals died out for reasons that had nothing to do with external forces. When I did fieldwork among the Anaguta of central Nigeria in 1983–1985, I found that they had abandoned their male initiation ritual in 1929. This had been an essential part of their social structure, defining the membership of age grades. Initially, I assumed that it had been banned by the colonial government. Later I discovered that it had lapsed because several of the elders whose duty it was to organize it had died in rapid succession, and others became afraid to take on the task.[3] A recent ethnographic film documented a similar pattern in a contemporary Dogon village in Mali—the Dama ritual was postponed because a diviner foretold that it would cause a local elder's death.[4]

Male (and less often, female) rites that mark entry into adult life are very widespread in Africa. They belong to a wider genre of individual and communal rites of passage that include, or may include, marriages, funerals, infant-naming ceremonies, and installations to office, such as kings' coronations. Typically, they involve a period of liminality, a time of suffering and helplessness before the subject moves on to a new phase of life. This is true of initiates, of newly bereaved widows, and of those about to become kings.

THE INITIATION OF BEMBA GIRLS: CHISUNGU

Bemba speakers, belong to a vast matrilineal belt that also includes the Chewa and Ndembu. It crosses southern Africa and covers parts of the Democratic Republic of Congo and much of Malawi and Zambia. In a matrilineal society, goods and political office are inherited by a man's sister's son. In some areas, the couple lives near the wife's kin; elsewhere, near the husband's. Matrilineality declined in twentieth-century Africa, through a

complex process one cannot explore here. In my account of Nyau among
Chewa speakers, I mentioned its association with girls' initiation rituals. Now
I return to these rituals among Bemba and Ndembu speakers, whose cultures have much in common with them.

The Bemba kingdom grew up in the seventeenth century in northern
Zambia. Its people acquired a warlike reputation; perhaps they became raiders
because of the poverty of their homeland. Bemba men, it was said, preferred
the spear to the hoe.

In 1956, Audrey Richards published an account of a Bemba female initiation ritual, Chisungu.[5] She had seen it only once, in 1931. It is one of a
widespread complex of similar girls' initation rituals called Chisungu,
Chinamwali, or Nkanga in different parts of Zambia. All involve a period of
seclusion and instructional songs and dances. Some peoples with such rituals, including Ndembu, Luvale, and Chokwe speakers, also have boys' initiation, where circumcision and an encounter with a masked spirit play a
central role. (This is an extremely common pattern elsewhere in Africa.)

Chisungu's distinctive feature was the use of pottery emblems, wall paintings, and symbolic objects, with associated songs as instructional aids. Like
other such rites, it imparted sexual skills—the emphasis on pleasing the husband may not have been part of the original ritual.[6]

In 1956, Richards noted, "Such ceremonies are rapidly dying out in Central Africa . . . it may even be quite extinct."[7] In the 1990s, a researcher in
Zambia found that it was very much alive, both at the village level and in
Lusaka, where it was perpetuated in Catholic women's groups. There were
several versions, a Christianized and a more traditional one, complete with
pottery models and sexually suggestive songs. The overt function was to
prepare girls for marriage, but they were also an affirmation of women's
solidarity and attachment to their inherited culture. (Alice Lenshina was a
Bemba, and some older Bemba symbolism, such as the bored stone,[8] is evident in her hymns.)

Originally there were two rituals, one for first menstruation and one for
marriage, both called Chisungu. Now only the first survives, and marriage
instruction has become part of the wedding ceremony.[9] A different ritual,
which protects a baby by ritual intercourse and the lighting of a new fire, is
now considered "pagan" but is still performed.[10]

THREE NDEMBU RITUALS

Between 1950 and 1954, Victor and Edith Turner did fieldwork in the
Ndembu culture area, near the Zambian border. They originally had a different research agenda, but came to concentrate on a rich and complex network of rituals and its associated symbolism. Victor Turner's accounts of this
became internationally famous, though his work was criticized for its lack
of a historical dimension and for its failure to integrate his microstudies with

the regional complexes of which they were part. After his death in 1983, Edith published her own memoirs of fieldwork; she also revisited the area in 1985 and did a follow-up study.

Her books[11] make an interesting contrast with Victor's writings from the 1960s, reflecting changing patterns of ethnographic writing. Edith is more open about her own role, involvement, and responses—this is called reflexivity—and also about her use of interpreters. Her style is much more lively and immediate.

The Ndembu word for a symbol is the blaze or slash with which one marks one's way in the bush. The milk tree and the blood tree, and associated color symbolism, thread their way through many rituals. The former exudes a white latex, and the latter a red gum. White is linked not only with maternal milk but also with semen, the staple foods maize and cassava, and the honored white hair of old age. It represents purity, goodness, health, life, and similar qualities. Red is ambiguous, representing the blood of menstruation and childbirth, animal blood shed in hunting, human blood shed in violence, and witchcraft, so often understood as astral cannibalism. Black—mud, charcoal, vegetable dye, or black fruit—is linked with evil, suffering, and death. But after the wedding night, the doors, not only of the newlyweds but also of other villagers, are anointed with river mud, which in this case is a symbol of fertility. Red, white, and black symbolism has been very widely described in Africa.[12]

In the first chapter of this book, I introduced the problems inherent in interpreting ritual and symbol. Victor Turner extracted these meanings partly by discussions with informants, but these symbols often operate at the subconscious level. He also studied the different roles a given symbol played in diverse ritual settings and in a particular one. But the interpretation of ritual, especially by outsiders, is rather like the interpretation of poetry written in a foreign language.

Girls' initiation, Nkanga, a prelude to marriage, marked not the first menstruation, as is common in these ceremonies, but the development of the breasts. In the 1950s, it began in the forest. The initiate lay motionless under a blanket beneath a young milk tree, which she dared not look at under pain of insanity. This symbolic return to the womb is common in both male and female initiation rituals elsewhere in Africa. In the tree hung an arrow, a male symbol, and the beads of white latex that symbolized her future children, beads that she would wear later, when she danced. The adult women sang bawdy songs, and the mother made a symbolic attempt to regain her daughter. (At the heart of many such rituals is the need to leave the family into which one is born in order to create a new one.) The women, but not the initiate, drank and feasted.

The second phase took place in a specially built hut made of milk tree branches, constructed by the girl's future in-laws on the edge of the bush, the boundary between wild and inhabited space. Here the girl spent three months in seclusion. She did not cook, but collected wild food. She could not name anything directly. The women beautified the initiate and taught her sexual skills. In the third phase, she danced bare-breasted in the village and received gifts, before spending her wedding night with her husband. In the morning, the couple ate a boiled chicken together, carefully preserving the unbroken bones, which symbolized perfect children.

The bare-breasted dance and the symbolic beads were abandoned in the 1970s. By 1985, there was little forest left—an expanding population desperately needed new farmland. The rite survived in a truncated form—the girl was left in a makeshift bedroom until money was available for beer. She then put on new Western clothes and sat in the village meeting place to receive gifts. The focus was now on the adult women, their "generalized carnival spirit": "A defiance of the missions among traditionalists began to surface in an even greater scurrility and violence expressed in the songs' words."[13] When Edith asked an older woman to perform the bare-breasted dance, she felt she had to do it in the seclusion of a house—and even so, Edith landed in trouble.

The male initiation ritual, *mukanda,* was primarily a test of courage in which boys were circumcised under a milk tree. Again, they were separated from their mothers:

Mother, keep out and wail,
Your child is taken from you . . .
In the lodge beyond the world
The prince and the slave are one.[14]

Later, the boys sat on a fallen log from a blood tree that symbolized the life of the hunter and warrior. While their wounds healed, they went through a period of liminality and were fed like babies (from the circumcision knife). They learned alternative names for things, and encountered the dreadful mask and the bullroarer (made from the wood of the blood tree). After three months of seclusion, they returned to the village triumphantly, as adults.

The Ihamba ritual belongs to a wider genre of cults of affliction, to which many of the movements discussed earlier in this study also belong: Lemba, Mami Wata, Zar, and Bori, among them. It is intended to cure a sharp pain thought to be caused by the tooth of a dead hunter in the patient's body. Kept in a jar and nourished with animal blood, the tooth brings good fortune. Neglected, it is impelled, by the meat hunger that drove the hunter in life, to escape and find a home in a human host. Those who have been cured, by the extraction of the tooth, become the healers and perform the same ritual for others. Victor Turner, in Edith's words, saw this as "a mixture of moving poetry and undoubted hocus-pocus." Edith, however, believed that she actually saw a mysterious substance leaving the patient's back.[15] This raises issues to which we shall return.

Central to the ritual, both in the 1950s and in the 1980s, were the "words" by which both patient and participants voiced the grudges they felt:

> I was angry with my friend;
> I told my wrath, my wrath did end.[16]

Ihamba had changed in some respects over the intervening thirty-odd years.[17] More important, the climate of village opinion had changed. In the early 1950s, only 5 percent of the villagers were Christian. By 1985, Christianity was strongly established. Some Ndembu disapproved strongly of "pagan" rituals or thought, wrongly, that Ihamba was no longer practiced.

Although she was a Christian, Edith deplored the way in which Christianity had undermined traditional rituals. She returned to the Ndembu armed with Victor's publications as a guide to how these rituals "should" be performed. The ethnographer as observer of ritual had become not only a participant but also a (foreign and long absent) teacher. There are many ironies in all this.

SACRIFICE

In what sense are these rituals "religious"? Rites of passage are concerned not with communication with spiritual beings, but with the recognition of life's major transitions. Much more has been written on these rituals and on cults of affliction than on prayer. A notable exception is Barber's work on *oriki* (praise songs to Yoruba divinities).

Sacrifice is often an intrinsic part of prayer and ritual. For people whose lives revolve around their cattle, an ox is the supreme sacrifice. The Nuer and Dinka never killed their beasts for food, though they gladly ate an animal that had been sacrificed. If none was available, the Dinka made a symbolic temporary substitution of a bitter blue cucumber.[18] The meat of a sacrificed beast was shared among participants and kin. Some cultures—and divinities—have no blood sacrifice. In the Yoruba culture sphere, Obatala is honored with sacrifices of snails.

The belief that cattle should be killed only in sacrifice was reflected in the Nuer saying "Cattle are not killed for nothing." By the 1980s, Christianity had spread widely in the southern Sudan, and Nuer Christians cited the identical proverb with the opposite meaning: cattle should be killed for meat, not sacrifice. The growth of the cash economy, and the sale of cattle or their meat, had become increasingly common.[19] A similar transition was described among Dinka speakers. As Christianity spread, and the region was engulfed in civil war and afflicted by famine, the old divinities (*jok*, "powers") seemed powerless to protect. They were seen as greedy, demanding cattle and giving nothing in return. As a sign of faith, Dinka Christians would slaughter an ox for meat and have a feast.[20]

The offering of human beings was, in precolonial times, the most valuable sacrifice of all. Among the Niger Igbo in the late nineteenth century, two slaves were sacrificed at the installation of a titled man, and two at his funeral. In centralized kingdoms, the numbers were much greater, though some, such as royal wives, did not always die unwillingly. In some polities, one person was put to death each year to expiate the sins of the community. At the international port of Whydah, this was done to placate the ocean. There is evidence that the practice of human sacrifice expanded in the era of the Atlantic slave trade; it was a way of disposing of unsalable slaves: "[S]everal poor wretched Men, who through Age or Inability are become incapable of Labour, are sold on purpose to be made Victims in these accursed offerings."[21] At the the brine springs in northeastern Igboland, weak or disabled slaves were purchased specially for ritual sacrifice. But Nri ritual specialists opposed all bloodshed, whether in war or ritual sacrifice, because it pollutes the sacred Earth.

DIVINATION

Divination is intended to elucidate meanings, especially moral meanings, in daily life, and to find remedies for affliction. Many traditions of a people's origin emphasize that crucial choices were made in obedience to the advice of a diviner. Sometimes divination is linked with a particular divinity or spirit. There is often an explicit affirmation that the underlying order which is accessed by ritual is the work of the supreme God. In the words of a Fon diviner, "Fa is Mawu and Mawu is Fa."[22] A Nupe diviner, having cast his divining strings, would say, "Good, God is there."[23]

Divination was a skilled—typically male—profession, a form of technology. The forms it took were enormously varied. In the Dogon culture sphere in southern Mali, there is a distinctive form of divination that involves interpreting the footprints of a desert fox on patterns traced in the sand by a diviner. He scatters peanuts there, in order to attract a fox during the night. It is thought that the fox could once speak, but now can communicate only in this way. There are far fewer foxes than in the past, but sometimes one responds to the lure of peanuts. As we saw in chapter 1, there has been a great deal of controversy and reinterpretation in the sphere of Dogon religion. In the writings of French ethnographers of the past, the fox was the cosmic rebel, Ogo, but this and related myths are now in doubt.

The questions to which clients sought answers varied, to some extent, from one society to the next. Zande asked the Benge oracle, "If I go hunting, will I return safely?" Ndembu sought an explanation for misfortunes that had already occurred. The Ifa client asked, "Which sacrifices will bring me the desired outcome?" In Yoruba mythology, the friendship of Eshu and Ifa/Orunmila is symbolic. Eshu stands for the unpredictable aspects of life; Orunmila, for the orderly and predictable.

DIVINATION: IFA

Ifa is the dominant, but not the only, divining tradition in the Yoruba culture sphere. The Ifa divination corpus is a collection of oral poetry memorized over years by apprentice diviners, virtually all of whom are male. The poems are arranged in 256 sections, or *odu*. An apprentice must learn at least four poems for each *odu*—a total of 1,024 poems, of from five to fifty lines each. A master will know eight for each *odu*. An Ifa diviner, who is also a priest of Orunmila, is called *babalawo* (father of secrets). When he is consulted by a client, he will ascertain the *odu* appropriate to his or her needs by mechanical means—it is a perceived strength of Ifa that the choice of *odu* is uninfluenced by human volition.

Each *odu* has a signature with eight components, each of which consists of one or two lines.

Here are two of the 256 possible signatures:

I II
II II
II I
II II

I I
I II
I I
I II

The signs are ascertained by throwing a chain of eight objects (where the concave side represents one line, and the reverse, two) or by snatching palm nuts from the left hand and seeing how many remain. The diviner then recites the poetry from the relevant *odu*. In each story, someone—who may be Orunmila, the divination god himself—has divination performed, and the consequences are shaped by how well the diviner's advice is followed and whether the suggested sacrifices are made correctly. It is noteworthy that Orunmila can be weak and fallible, needing to be rescued by his friends.

One of the poems tells how Squirrel was warned in divination not to talk too much. When his wife had twins, Squirrel neglected this advice and invited everyone to come and see them, with the result that the babies became somebody's dinner:

And they travelled down the gullet with the soup.[24]

The moral is obvious.

Farther west, among the Fon, there is a related but distinct form of divination called Fa, which was introduced in the early eighteenth century, when the king of Dahomey brought Ifa diviners to his court. Later, it spread in society as a whole. Parallel mythic and quasi-historical narratives account for its origins. In the first, Fa is the child of Mawu; she has sixteen eyes and lives on top of a palm tree, observing all that takes place in the world. At night she sleeps; at dawn she needs the help of her brother Legba (Eshu) to open her eyes. She speaks to him through palm nuts.

The historical narrative describes the borrowing of Ifa from the Yoruba culture zone. It largely replaced an earlier form of divination, which the king disliked, in which an ancestral voice spoke in a calabash (though the latter did not disappear). Fa became popular when *babalawo* succeeded in ending a drought.[25] Fa priests are called by either the Yoruba term, *babalawo*, or *bokono* (repellers [of danger]). Interestingly, the Fon poems are quite different from the Yoruba ones. Among the Fon, Fa became a universal, two-tier male cult.[26]

This form of divination was also well established among the Ewe of Togo (as we have seen, they spoke the same language as the Fon, but lived in small communities, not a centralized kingdom). Again, it was attributed to Yoruba origins.

Whereas other forms of Yoruba religious life focus on intense and exclusive devotion to one divinity, Ifa offers a broad spectrum of all the diverse supernatural forces that may impinge on a client's life and fortunes. Its texts are preserved unchanged; a version recorded in the 1890s is much the same as those recorded by three different researchers in the 1960s and 1970s.[27] In a situation of cultural encounter, many Yoruba Christians and diviners came to see Ifa as the template of Yoruba culture, a sacred text comparable with the Bible and the Quran. A small but interesting movement, originally called Orunmilaism and now known as the African Church of Orunmila, reflects this. It dates from the 1930s, and is an attempt by diviners to adapt the cult to a modern world. It holds church-style services, and has published a new sacred corpus of *odu*, written in the 1940s, that is divided into chapters and verses, as the Bible is. In this new version, Oludumare, the supreme God, is all-important, and Orunmila is the first being created by God. A senior member claimed that Ifa worshipers were the original Muslims and Christians, and that the Yoruba knew how to write before foreigners destroyed this inheritance.[28]

AFA DIVINATION

There are less well-known forms of divination that appear to be related to Ifa, such as Afa among the Igbo.[29] Because Igbo neotraditional religion has so often been viewed through Christian spectacles, there has been a plethora of studies of the supreme God, and a strange neglect of this little-known and perhaps dying genre of ancient knowledge.

There are two main schools of Afa divination. In the northern one, the diviner casts four chains, each with four seed pods that may fall in a concave or convex position. They are cast repeatedly, and the position in which they fall is interpreted in a secret language, which is later translated. In the southern version, the diviner has some twenty small symbolic objects that are cast on the ground; he reads the meaning of the positions in which they fall. Each item has one or two meanings: blood, visitor, money, and so on. Every Igbo "traditional" diviner has a collection of small sculptures, each with a symbolic meaning, and keeps his ritual apparatus in a tortoise shell. Sometimes the markings on the shell are used in divination, and myth explains the relationship between tortoise and Agwu, the god of divination. Consultations usually take place in Agwu's shrine.

Similar divining systems have been recorded to the north of Igboland, in the Idoma and Igala culture spheres, with no traditions of Yoruba origins, as well as among the people of Benin. In each of them, there are sixteen configurations, and they have cognate names. Armstrong believed that the similarity in names meant that the whole Ifa/Afa/Ebi system had spread fairly recently,[30] but in the Igbo culture sphere there is no tradition of Afa's Yoruba origins, as there is among Ewe/Fon speakers, and Igboland and Yorubaland were separated by the Benin kingdom. Afa is regarded as indigenous and ancient. Perhaps the system moved gradually from west to east, diffusing in the way that is well documented for masking cults. Supernatural mysteries from a distance always have a special attraction. Or do the similar names, and other parallels, in these divination systems mean that they all sprang from the same ancient substratum of culture?

Since the nineteenth century, it has been widely suggested that the Ifa-related divination complex was an adaptation of Muslim geomancy. In 1864, Burton visited Dahomey and described Fa, which he attributed to a form of divination called sand writing (*khatt a-raml*).[31] Muslim scholars disagreed about its legitimacy, and Uthman dan Fodio condemned it. The classic text on the subject was written in the twelfth century by al-Zanati, who may have been one of the Zanata Berbers of North Africa. It was popular not only in the Arab world, but also in Europe, from the late Middle Ages on, and was called *Punctation* or *Punktierkunst*.[32]

In *khatt a-raml*, sixteen signs are marked in sand on a tray. Each is a tetragram; its four components consist of either one or two dots. These are distributed randomly among sixteen "houses." Both signs and houses have names and a range of meanings, including male and female, good and bad, the points of the compass, the four elements (earth, air, fire, and water), and the signs of the zodiac.[33] When Nadel did research in Nupe in the 1930s, he found that sand writing and *ebi* divination (which had much in common with Ifa, but lacked a corpus of divination poetry) existed side by side. The links between Nupe and the Oyo kingdom are ancient and well documented. Perhaps this gives us an insight into the complex and now obscure linkages between the Ifa-related complex and geomancy.[34]

FOUR TABLET DIVINATION

Four Tablet divination (*hakata*) originated among Shona speakers in Zimbabwe, where it is first recorded in the early seventeenth century. The system was the same then as it is now. Each tablet has a distinguishing pattern, and front and back are differentiated: a total of sixteen possible combinations. They are categorized as male and female, senior and junior. In the late nineteenth century, *hakata* was starting to spread among the Shangaan. There was a simpler oracle, also called *hakata* and consisting of six nutshell halves that could fall in a convex or concave position, a total of seven possible configurations.

Four Tablet divination is now widespread in southern Africa. The Ndebele acquired it from the Shona, and it is also well established among the Sotho, Tswana, Zulu, and others. In Zambia it is replacing the "basket divination of the Lunda and Luvale, whose practitioners tend to be older, to specialise in the identification of witches, and whose status as accomplished professionals is alleged to be sealed by human sacrifice."[35] Among the Venda, Four Tablet divination is replacing the divining bowl. The original Shona symbols, which include a pool, a crocodile, and abstract snakeskin patterns, have been replaced, in Botswana, by images of a house and an ax.[36]

There were many Muslim traders in Zimbabwe in the sixteenth century, including those at the Mutapa court. It is possible that Four Tablet divination grew out of nutshell divination, in response to the stimulus of sand writing.[37] There is also a well-known and much-studied form of divination in Madagascar, called *sikidy*, that is a response to Muslim stimuli.

BASKET DIVINATION

Basket divination is an ancient and widespread complex found in vast areas of central and southern Africa. The equipment is a basket—often a winnowing basket, to sift truth from falsehood—and a collection of symbolic objects. In different cultures, there may be twenty of these, or a hundred, or even more—205 were counted among the Chokwe.[38] The use of symbolic objects with specific meanings, here or in rituals such as Chisungu, can be seen as a form of writing, and learning their interpretations and the many possible configurations is a complex and demanding task.

Victor Turner studied divination among Ndembu speakers, and a diviner called Muchona (the Hornet) was one of his chief informants. Muchona became a diviner after falling ill at the age of thirty-five. His symptoms, such as asthma, showed that he was being called by the divining spirit. Clients would come to him in a family group, with a problem such as "Why is X ill?" He would ask them a series of questions to which a unanimous yes or no answer was required. He would then, in a mild trance state, shake a basket that contained about twenty symbolic objects, and see which configuration came to the top. This was repeated several times. The aim was not to predict the future but to make moral sense of the present, and in particular to see if misfortune was due to an angry ancestor or to witchcraft. In the past, a witch was expelled or killed, and a diviner was sometimes attacked by angry kin. Because of this, the colonial government outlawed basket divination, and some consultations took place on the border, where escape was easy.

Edith Turner's evocative account of a divining consultation on the Angolan border lists some of the symbols:

> The winnowing basket was ready before him, filled with the Pieces of Perception. There were the Family (mother, child and father), the Hypocrite, the Tale Bearer, the Knotted Hide (representing the twisted mind), the Phallus, the Mirror, the Mountain (representing a weighty matter), Frozen Tears, the Funeral Fires (a stick burnt in notches), the Hyena, the Coin, the Sea of Calabashes (three shards of a string, representing marriage), and the Ancient Nut of Time.[39]

Divination resolved conflicts in the family or village, and made sense of suffering, which was thought always to have a moral cause.

Junod described basket divination among the Tsonga in the late nineteenth century:

> . . . all the elements of Native life are represented by the objects contained in the basket of the divinatory bones. It is a résumé of all their social order, of all their institutions and the bones, when they fall, provide them with instantaneous photographs of all that can happen to them.[40]

THE ZANDE *BENGE* ORACLE

Divination is not always performed by a professional specialist. *Benge* divination, practiced among the Zande of central Africa, is especially well known because of E. Evans-Pritchard's account of it. *Benge* is a poison, imported from a distance, that is fed to a young chicken. When questioned, it answers through the chicken's death or survival. The procedure was carried out by men, who needed to be prosperous enough to buy *benge* and to devote chickens to this purpose. It is now dying out, but when Evans-Pritchard conducted his research, Zande regularly sought guidance from *benge*—for instance, before going hunting or embarking on a journey. Evans-Pritchard used it himself: "I found this as satisfactory a way of running my home and affairs as any other I know of."[41]

There were also much cheaper forms of Zande divination available. One could place two sticks in a termite mound and see which one they nibbled. (If neither, they were refusing to cooperate.) A wooden rubbing board was also used; the answer depended on whether it stuck or not. Most African societies had do-it-yourself divination methods of this kind. Victor Turner listed ten among the Ndembu. Among the Fon they included casting kola nuts and studying the entrails of a fowl offered in sacrifice, and by the 1930s, the use of European playing cards.[42]

BELIEVERS AND SKEPTICS

Edith Turner is not the only person who believes she has experienced "real" but inexplicable psychic phenomena in Africa. Colonial officials sometimes described experiences of this kind. Paul Stoller apprenticed himself to Songhay sorcerers in Niger. In 1980, he experienced a frightening night visitation that left him briefly paralyzed, but at first he did not mention this experience in his academic writing. Later, it led him to reflect on the nature of fieldwork and the way in which the researcher tends to edit out what, from his or her own cultural perspective, is "impossible": "'Gaze' is the act of seeing; it is an act of selective perception. Much of what we see is shaped by our experience, and our 'gaze' has a direct bearing upon what we think."[43] Evans-Pritchard observed healers who extracted harmful substances from Zande patients. He described it as trickery because it was "impossible." But he also admitted that he was unable to detect the sleight of hand, and that patients often recovered.[44]

We have noted cases of researchers who studied African Initiated Churches and ended up joining them. Charles Smith, an authority on Hausa history, became a Muslim, changing his name to Abdullahi. Some Westerners have joined neotraditional religions—perhaps the best-known example is the Austrian artist Suzanne Wenger, who devoted herself to restoring Oshogbo's ruined shrines.

The Turners went to the field as agnostics and later became Catholics. Their studies of religious practice, in Africa and elsewhere, seem to have convinced them of the reality of spiritual presences. Evans-Pritchard, an Anglican by upbringing, also became a Catholic. He called his year among the Nuer "an experience which has greatly influenced my life."[45]

While Westerners reflected on the reality of unseen worlds, African participants in rituals sometimes expressed a sad skepticism about their efficacy. We noted a LoDagaa example in chapter 1.

Shambaa villagers in northern Tanzania were often skeptics, too:

> "If someone starts talking about a jini (jinn) I know he has a nail pushed aside [that is, a screw loose]."
> "I don't consult diviners. Divination is mutual self-deception."[46]

The Shambaa do not have an exceptional number of freethinkers. They were visited by a researcher attuned to and sympathetic to the varieties of thought and interpretation in village life.

NEW STYLES OF DIVINERS

African politicians and military rulers, in their efforts to gain and keep power, have often turned to diviners, gurus, Christian prophets, and/or marabouts. Kenneth Kaunda alienated many Christian Zambians when, in his last years in power, he relied heavily on the guidance of an Indian guru. In Ivory Coast, President Houphouet-Boigny had a strong public commitment to Catholicism and spent his last years building a vast, hugely expensive, and highly controversial basilica, but in his long years in power, he also had regular recourse to neotraditional rituals.[47] The acknowledged tendency of some politicians to seek supernatural assistance often led to dark rumors and attributions of witchcraft, to which we turn in a later chapter. African rulers were also drawn to foreign forms of the secret-sacred. Some heads of state in francophone Africa are Rosicrucians, while others are Freemasons. A president of Madagascar built a Rosicrucian temple in his official palace.[48]

In general, the roles of diviner and healer now tend to be combined. Those who practice as diviners, often with no background in "traditional" divination, incorporate new rituals and shrine objects. In Calabar, a certain Okon Okopedi studied "astroscience" in India. There is a thriving trade in religious paraphernalia: "Okopedi Enterprises (Mystic Division) . . . Merchants, Mystic Adepts and Master Occultists" retails "Indian amulets," "lucky jewellery," "love-potions," lodge accessories, and books on Kabbalah, astrology, Egyptian religion, yoga, and "secret" biblical texts.[49] Ritual items often originate in India, but in this case, they apparently came from Chicago. In the Igbo culture sphere, diviner/healers often work in the name of Mami Wata.

The demonization of ancestral spirits means that in Zambia (and elsewhere), diviner/healers now often work in the name of the supreme God. People are keenly interested in the movie stereotype of the medicine man." In the 1950s, Ndembu diviners wore Western dress or a waistcloth. Now one will wear a headdress of fur, a grass skirt, and a tortoise medallion, and carry a black doctor's bag. In Zambia and elsewhere, they have formed professional associations with membership cards—another example, perhaps, of enlargement of scale. Modern bureaucratic forms and a new exoticism are part of a reinvention of tradition.[50]

Chapter 20

Royals, Priests, and Prophets

> . . . the holiness for quite a long
> had performed the most
> wonderful interests, but
> all these were not fulfilled.
>
> —a soldier of Alice Lakwena, in 1987[1]

One of the ways in which the history of neotraditional religion differs from that of Christianity and Islam lies in the way in which the latter, but not the former, are full of named historical individuals. Sacred roles thread their way through the history of "traditional" religion—the diviners, the spirit mediums—but they are usually anonymous and generic. Ironically, it is often the ethnographer, the outside observer, who is named. In this chapter, with its historic prophets and queens, we return to the specificity of known actors and particular events.

NAMING ROLES

The labels that Western scholars, writing in English or French, use for African realities are perennially unsatisfactory, whether we are writing of witchcraft or of specialists in the sacred. Because there is such a poor fit between foreign terms and African concepts, MacGaffey has suggested that we use local categories, citing Kongo examples:

	Public sphere	Private sphere
Death	chief (*mfumu*)	witch (*ndoki*)
Life	prophet (*ngunza*)	magician (*nganga*)[2]

There are two difficulties here. First, this is peculiar to the Kongo; when writing of a specific ethnic group, it makes a good deal of sense to use their own terminology, but it is impracticable when covering a much wider area. Second, three of these categories refer to real people; witches, most ethnographers are agreed, exist only in the mind. But the problem is a very real one.

Earlier in this book, I referred to a pioneer Igbo Christian as a "diviner." He was, in fact, a *dibia*, a class of ritual specialists with a number of subcategories. *Dibia afa* was a diviner; *dibia aja* offered sacrifices, often those which the *dibia afa* prescribed. *Dibia ogwu* (medicine) was a healer and an herbalist, and often a bonesetter. There was also a category of rain callers. The tutelary priests of divinities were sometimes, but not always, *dibia*. *Dibia afa*, in particular, were famed for their supernatural feats, such as astral travel. They might well be termed "magicians."

In the Ibibio and Efik culture sphere, the naming of such specialists is very much like the Igbo pattern. A diviner is *abia idiong* and an herbalist, *abia ibok*; both roles are now usually combined. In the city of Calabar, rain callers, *abia edim*, now stop rain for social functions![3] This is, however, a dying occupation. In a modern city, there is more need for healing than for rain or its absence.

In general accounts of "specialists in the sacred," the women who ran girls' initiation rituals are invisible. There is no adequate foreign word to describe their many functions—they tend to be called "midwives" or "mentors." Rasing, making this point, uses the Bemba term *nacimbusa* (sing.). The Bemba *nacimbusa* was indeed a midwife, teacher, and mentor, and often an herbalist and a traditional healer. She practiced divination during a baby's naming ceremony.[4] She was always drawn from the royal clan, and had the status of a chief.[5] These women are "the transformers in rites" who commune with the "blood spirit."[6] They were and are diviners, healers, and priests.

SACRED QUEENS AND KINGS: PATTERNS OF CHANGE

The position of Africa's "traditional rulers" was fossilized at the imposition of colonial rule. In some cases, such as Benin, in Nigeria, the kingdom was hundreds of years old, but in many instances, the "traditional" state and ruler dated only from the first half of the nineteenth century—the Zulu, Swazi, Ndebele, and Sotho kingdoms are examples. In the colonial period, the role of the king was eroded—a change symbolized by the adoption of the terminology "chief"—and he became answerable primarily to colonial overlords. In some cases, the ruler adopted Christianity, which inevitably eroded the mystique of sacred kingship. In others, it remained essential for "traditional" rulers to adhere to "traditional" religion. Independent nations sometimes abolished these positions altogether—we noted the examples of Tanzania and Guinea in earlier chapters.

There was no correlation between institutions of sacred kingship and the size of the state or its antiquity. The Swazi kingdom dates from the early nineteenth century but is a much-studied example of the sacred king (and queen mother). The Igbo polity of Onitsha was, in precolonial times, a small town, but its ruler had all the characteristics of a sacred king. Even where kingdoms were ancient, colonial conquest fossilized them at a particular point in their changing history.

The Benin kingdom seems to have been founded in the thirteenth century. Ewuare, in the fifteenth century, was a magician and warrior who did much to build up royal authority and established primogeniture. In sixteenth-century Benin, the king, or *oba*, was a warrior who led his troops on expeditions. But in 1606, the last of the warrior *obas* drowned in the Lagos lagoon, and for a century his successors lived in seclusion in their palace, while the affairs of state were controlled by others. At the end of the century, after a civil war, a powerful *oba* emerged triumphant. In the contemporary world, the people of Benin remain profoundly attached to their king.

The state of Oyo had also been through great changes. Like Benin, it expanded from a mini-state to a great one; its period of imperial expansion lasted only from the early seventeenth century until the late eighteenth. Until the 1730s, the king (*alafin*, "owner of the palace") was succeeded by his eldest son. To prevent the heir from conspiring against him, a king then ruled that the son must die with his father, a fate shared by a number of great officials. In the mid-nineteenth century an eldest son not only abolished the custom and succeeded to the throne, but moved his capital hundreds of miles to the south.

"Traditional" kingdoms varied in many respects, including the system of succession. In Benin, the oldest son succeeded; this did not prevent brothers from fighting for the throne, and the death of every nineteenth-century *oba* was followed by war. In the central Nigerian state of Igala, the large royal clan was divided into four segments, each of which in turn provided not only the king but his officials as well. When a king died, the courtiers who had served him went into retirement.[7]

In kingdoms as distant and different as Onitsha and Swaziland, the king lived in seclusion, emerging once a year to dance before his people, demonstrating his undiminished health and vitality. The king was sacred, and the *alafin* was called the Companion of the Gods. Yoruba kings lived secluded in their palaces. The face of a great Yoruba ruler was concealed by a veil that was part of his beaded crown. There was a widespread fiction that the king did not eat.

In some states, the health of the king and his people and their crops were so intimately entwined that he could not die a natural death. In central Nigeria, the Jukun king was strangled after a seven-year reign. The Shilluk kingdom on the upper Nile, with its capital at Fashoda, is another much-studied and much-debated example.

Dinka speakers had no kings; their priestly clan provided Masters of the Fishing Spear. Lienhardt, who did his fieldwork in the late 1940s, described a practice that was prohibited by the colonial government but had existed until recently and perhaps still survived in secret at the time. When a Master of the Fishing Spear fell ill, he would ask his people to bury him alive:

> They then lift up the master of the fishing-spear, and put him into the earth while he yet lives. And he will not be afraid of death; he will be put into the earth while singing his songs. Nobody among his people will wail or cry because their man has died. They will be joyful because their master of the fishing-spear will give them life, so that they shall live untroubled by any evil.[8]

THE LOVEDU RAIN QUEEN

In 2001, the Lovedu rain queen, Modjadi V (sometimes written Mujaji) died; she was born in 1937 and had succeeded to the throne in 1981. Her predecessor, Modjadi IV, was queen from 1960 to 1980. Because Modjadi V's daughter and designated heir died almost at the same time, she was succeeded by her twenty-five-year-old granddaughter, who became Modjadi VI in 2003, the first Western-educated holder of the title. The Lovedu queens are a notable example of religious change and of the sacred ruler.

The Lovedu live at the foot of the Drakensburgs in the Transvaal. Their numbers were estimated at 50,000 in the 1930s,[9] and they were greatly outnumbered by their neighbors: the Tsonga/Shangaan to the east, the Venda to the north, the Pedi to the south. KiLovedu is a Sotho language with a considerable Venda admixture. Tradition claims that the royal dynasty was founded by seventeenth-century Karanga immigrants from the Shona culture sphere.

About 1800, after a period of bloody conflict between princes, the last king instituted a dramatic change to a sacred queen and mother-daughter succession. The reigns of the first two Modjadis spanned almost the entire nineteenth century, though neither died a natural death. The queen was a ritual figure, not a ruler. She lived in seclusion, and her paramount duty was rain calling; she is the Transformer of the Clouds. Great kings, including the Zulu ruler, sent delegations to seek her assistance in time of drought. The Zulu saw her as "the greatest magician of the north. Queen of Locusts and Drought, a four-breasted marvel."[10]

The queen had no consort, but conceived children with a secret genitor. Her "wives" bore children to men of the royal family; these "marriages," which have parallels elsewhere in Africa, cemented alliances. Her "wives" cultivated her fields, brewed beer, or cooked. The Lovedu queens are now sometimes cited as examples of single motherhood and same-sex marriage, but their social reality was a different one.

The first Modjadi was queen from 1800 to 1850. Her successor, who was childless, reigned until 1894; her suicide was followed by drought, rinderpest, locusts, and consequent famine. Modjadi II chose the daughter of her "Great Wife" as her successor.[11] Modjadi III also had a remarkably long reign.

These queens were thought to be immune to sickness, but in the nineteenth century, each was expected to poison herself during the fourth male initiation school of her reign. It was part of her sacred character that she could die only by her own act, not through human weakness.[12] Rain medicine made from the skin and exudations of the dead woman's corpse was used by her successor.

Modjadi II inspired Rider Haggard's famous 1887 novel *She*, in which Ayesha is a queen who preserved her youth and beauty by magical means. She is, however, 2,000 years old, and white!

The Lovedu queens were at one end of a spectrum. Studies of Ganda kingship emphasize the fact that it was dead kings, rather than living ones, who were sacred there. When he became king, the nineteenth *kabaka* is said to have insisted that he should not become the medium of the divinity Mukasa. The power of rulers varied, and many, including the *alafin* of Oyo, were surrounded by an elaborate system of checks and balances, but this belongs less to religious than to political history. In the study of sacred royals, as elsewhere in "traditional" culture, it is impossible to separate religion from other dimensions of society.

THE DECLINING ROLE OF ROYAL WOMEN

The Lovedu mother-daughter succession was unique, but other precolonial societies had important roles for royal women, notably the queen mother in Swaziland. In the Lozi kingdom in the Zambezi flood plain, the king's sister was the virtual ruler of the southern province: Queen of the South. In Ghana, where Akan societies are matrilineal, queen mothers played a key role that was eroded in the colonial period because, like their counterparts elsewhere, they received no official recognition. Even colonial officials who came to Africa near the end of the long reign of Queen Victoria took it for granted that all states were ruled by kings. An official who devoted himself to the study of indigenous cultures discovered that he had unaccountably overlooked the role of the Asante queen mother:

I found it difficult to believe what is here described is still in some measure alive today. I have asked the old men and women why I did not know all this—I had spent very many years in Ashanti. The answer is always the same: "The white man never asked us this; you have dealings with and recognize only the men; we supposed the European considered women of no account, and we know you do not recognize them as we have always done."[13]

"PROPHETS" AND "PRIESTS": THE NUER EXAMPLE

"Priest" and "prophet" are words employed with very diverse meanings in the different sections of this book. "Prophet" was first used in the context of neotraditional religion by Evans-Pritchard, to replace "witch doctor," a long-obsolete term that fossilizes the attitudes of the past. A "witch doctor" was originally a diviner whose functions included discerning witchcraft and suggesting forms of protection. In colonial parlance, it acquired the resonances of "witch."

"The Nuer" and "the Dinka" are good examples of the artificiality both of ethnic labels and of the colonial concept of the "bounded tribe"—these peoples call themselves Jieng and Naath, and in the past, like the other peoples in this study, identified primarily with a smaller local unit, such as Jikany rather than Naath. The Nuer and Dinka languages, religions, and cultures are very similar.

According to the 1955–1956 census, there were then just over a million Dinka and just under half a million Nuer. The Nuer are almost entirely surrounded by Dinka, and in the nineteenth century were expanding at their expense. But there was a great deal of mutual assimilation and interaction, and the pattern was less one of invasion than of a complex pattern of advances, sometimes followed by retreat and Dinka reoccupation of particular ecological niches. In one interpretation, the Nuer were Dinka who acquired a separate identity. But paradoxically, many Dinka became Nuer; 75 percent of the Lou Nuer were of Dinka descent.

In his famous and influential studies of "the Nuer," Evans-Pritchard distinguished between the prophet (called Possessor of Spirit) and the two main forms of priesthood—the earth master and the cattle master. The earth master was able to remove pollution resulting from murder or other offenses, and acted as a peacemaker. He avoided potters, lest his presence crack their wares. Cattle masters, as their name suggests, were concerned with the health and welfare of the herds so central to Nuer life. Despite the apparent significance of these roles, Evans-Pritchard laid little emphasis on them.[14] Both earth master and cattle master were members of a family of hereditary ritual experts, not all of whom would follow this vocation. The prophet is a self-selected ecstatic and wonder worker (or, more correctly, chosen by Spirit, though the famous Ngungdeng came from a family of earth masters).

Ngungdeng Bong (ca. 1838–1906) is remembered as the first Nuer prophet.[15] His name means "Gift of Deng," the great Dinka rain divinity. He went through several periods of insanity, during which he wandered in the bush, refused milk and other food, and ate human excrement, then emerged to declare himself the voice of Deng. He rose to fame through the role he played in winning a victory in 1878—in some versions, he did nothing more than sacrifice an ox and raise his baton. After this defensive battle, he sanctioned no further wars.

From there they decided to capture the Dinka cattle. He refused. He said, "This war was not brought by me. No people who are called children of one man, who are born of Divinity, should fight. I am defending myself."[16]

Ngungdeng seems to have been influenced by the story of the mythical Dinka culture hero Aiwel, and his biography, as now told, stresses these parallels. Aiwel is remembered as a source of both life and death. Ngungdeng killed his enemies by supernatural means, but also restored the fertility of many childless women. He responded to the terrible crises of the 1890s—smallpox and rinderpest pandemics—by ordering the construction of a vast mound of earth and ashes, where these plagues were buried. Later, the British destroyed the mound with the utmost difficulty.[17] When British forces, with Dinka allies, attacked a village near the mound in 1902, people expected Ngungdeng to repeat his feats at Pading. "Ngungdeng raised the baton, declared that Divinity was absent, and disbanded his force."[18]

Some time after Ngungdeng's death, his mantle descended on his son Gwek, whose possession states were closely linked with the mound. He shouted his prophecies from its summit. In 1929, when the British were planning an attack, members of his age grade urged him to slay them with his baton, as Ngungdeng had done at Pading. At first he refused: "Divinity did not show me this." Finally, he tried to sacrifice an ox, but was shot before he could do so. The British then hung his body on the Tree of Bad Things.[19]

Nuer prophets lived in a way contrary to the norms of their society—they had long, disheveled hair and beards, which among other Nuer men was a sign that they were in a state of mourning or ritual pollution.

> Prophets may speak in tongues, go into trances, fast, balance on their heads, wear feathers in their hair, be active by night rather than by day, and may perch on rooftops.[20]

Some, including Gwek, sat impaled on cattle pegs. It was their ability to heal, to stem plagues, or to win battles that showed they were prophets, rather than insane.

By the late twentieth century, despite the spread of Christianity, the prophetic tradition was far from dead. Both Christians and traditionalists quoted Ngungdeng's prophecies, which were thought to predict the ultimate success of the south in Sudan's long civil war: "We know that all these deaths are not meaningless because they were foreseen by Ngungdeng and will ultimately result in our freedom."[21] A southern military leader brought an offering of ivory to the mound, a symbolic statement of unity with the past. New prophets were still appearing on the scene. One was a young man who cooperated with Christian pastors and advocated local unity and economic independence. He urged his hearers to shun reliance on aid and to work to produce enough food to help others as well as themselves.[22]

There are parallels between the lives of African Christian prophets and "traditional" ones, including the initial mystical experience, the sojourn in the wilderness, and mysterious gifts of healing.

PRIEST/PROPHET/KING: IGBO EXAMPLES

The writings of Evans-Pritchard were so influential that it was sometimes assumed that the Nuer distinction between prophet and priest had some kind of general validity, but in some cultures, the priest behaves much like a Nuer prophet.

In the Igbo town of Asaba, the *orhene* was the "priest" of the river goddess Onishe. He was chosen when he manifested supernatural capacities in a specific ritual setting. He was an uncouth figure whose accurate predictions are still remembered. The position has been vacant since the early 1950s. Other water divinities in the area have their own priests, who describe their mystical experiences beneath the surface of lake or stream.[23] Like the Nuer prophet, the *orhene* combined a disheveled appearance, ecstatic states, and a gift of prediction. Also like the Nuer prophet, he was a perennial outsider, but extremely influential.

Historians and ethnographers have always applied the word "king" to a wide range of dignitaries located at different points along a range from priestlike ritual figures to powerful rulers.

There is a proverb to the effect that the Igbo have no kings (*eze*). In some polities, including Asaba in the late nineteenth century, *eze* was a title held by many men. In Asaba, traditions suggest that the title was multiplied deliberately, as a safeguard against oppressive rule. (It is now dying because of its ritual restrictions, though Christians take the lesser title, *alo*, freely.) Despite the proverb, some Niger and western Igbo communities had a sacred king.

The Eze Nri is "king" of the ancient Igbo ritual center dedicated to the sacred Earth. Bronzes and other treasures, radiocarbon-dated to the ninth century, were excavated in the area; they are thought to have belonged to an Eze Nri. He was, however, closer to being a priest/prophet than a territorial ruler.[24] His position was not hereditary, and there was often a long interregnum. The new *eze* was revealed by his supernatural powers; the ritual of his installation included going to the Anambra River, an ancient cradle of Igbo civilization, where he made a mystical journey beneath its waters and recovered sacred stones.

HEREDITARY PROPHETS: THE MAASAI EXAMPLE

The original Maasai (Masai) heartland was in the Rift Valley of central Kenya, though by the nineteenth century they had fought their way as far south as central Tanzania. They were divided into twelve territorial sections that, on occasion, formed wider alliances. Pastoralism was central to their culture and livelihood, and at the core of their social organization was a system of named male age sets.

After undergoing initiation, which included circumcision, a young man became a *murran* (a warrior, cattle herder and raider), a way of life that would become very difficult to follow in the colonial or postcolonial situation. After ten years as a *murran*, the youth became an elder. It was the elders who shaped policy and controlled cattle and wives.

Hereditary families of prophets (*laibon*) played a leadership role, and with one exception each Maasai section followed a particular prophetic family.[25] The most famous, the Inkidongi, lived near Mount Meru. At any given time, such a family would produce a single major prophetic leader, though some of his brothers and sons might work privately as diviners. Prophets are remembered by name; other Maasai, including great warriors, only by age set.

Prophets' social behavior and appearance were very different from the Maasai norm. Like their Nuer counterparts, they stood outside the conventions of their society in a perpetual liminality that was symbolized by traditions that prophetic families originated outside Maasailand. The first prophet was said to have been found as a child, wandering in the hills near Nairobi.

They live apart from ordinary people . . . conduct their affairs secretly and are unashamedly competitive. [T]heir clients regard them with a mixture of fear, resentment and contempt. These traits . . . are magnified by the deliberate cultivation of the ambiguous and abnormal in dress and behaviour of some laibon.[26]

They prophesied through dreams or in a trance state and also divined, using a gourd of stones. Their words were obscure and elliptical, easily reinterpreted in the light of later events. The prophet was consulted before the initiation of an age set and before embarking on a cattle raid.

Supeet, of the 1810 age set, is credited with masterminding Maasai expansion to the south. His successor, Mbatiany, played a crucial role in a Maasai civil war. He is said to have foretold the advent of Europeans and the rinderpest pandemic. He died in 1890, just before it swept through Maasailand. His death was followed by a struggle between his sons, Olonana and Senteu, each of whom hoped to inherit his position. Olonana, who died in 1911, lived in Kenya, where he formed an alliance with the British, who recognized him as paramount chief—a strange transformation. Senteu, who settled in Tanganyika, lived until 1933.

Although they were famous warriors, the Maasai waged no wars against colonial invaders. They found it more profitable to fight as their allies and conduct cattle raids with impunity. Having restocked their herds, they retreated to their earlier way of life. In time, they would be stripped of much of the land on which this lifestyle depended.

The role of the *laibon* declined; there were bitter conflicts between rival candidates, but more fundamentally, the establishment of the colonial state made cattle raiding, the favorite occupation of the *murran*, illegal. Divining before such raids had been one of the prophet's chief functions. In a sense, *laibon* and *murran* had been allies in this pursuit. Now the elders opposed cattle raids, fearing government reprisals and stock confiscations.

THE PROPHET AS AGENT AND OBSERVER OF CHANGE

The "prophet," who is often a spirit medium, has played a wide variety of major roles in Africa since the mid-nineteenth century, sometimes as a social commentator or as a leader in anticolonial resistance. Neotraditional religion and various ritual specialists have also played a major role in postcolonial African wars.

The Prophet as Social Commentator

In many parts of Africa, stories are told of prophets of the past who predicted the shape of things to come with remarkable insight. In an Igbo village group, the prophet was a man who became insane when his only son was killed in a local war. Like the Fool in *King Lear*, his madness was prophetic. He predicted an unprecedented escalation in land values and the decline of "traditional" religion: He foretold foreign rule. 'Those quarrelling over political powers are merely fighting over another's property.'"[27] He foresaw the European invaders who would "usurp the children of the clan," viewing them as "white and reflecting in the wilderness." Such predictions, linked with named prophets, have been very widely recorded elsewhere in Africa.[28] We have noted the ongoing significance of Ngungdeng's prophetic songs.

Kaswa was a Fipa prophet from southern Tanzania who likewise foretold colonial invasion:

He said, "There are monstrous strangers coming,
Bringing war, striking you unawares, relentlessly,
O you people, you're going to be robbed of our country."

He predicted that the young would move to the towns, leaving the old to struggle with the tasks of farming:

And he said, "The grasshoppers are your children,
And they are flying away, all of them!
You remain behind, old and dying, and to the very end they are not there."
"Everything will have its price."[29]

How are we to understand these seers? It seems most probable that they were historical figures whose predictions have been expanded and revised by later generations. They located overwhelming and unprecedented changes in the sphere of African foreknowledge. This is also true of AIDS.[30]

THE PROPHET AND RESISTANCE TO COLONIAL CONQUEST

During the protracted and complex process of colonial conquest, some "traditional" rulers sought an accommodation with the new order, while others adopted a policy of armed resistance. The disparity in resources meant that in the end, these wars failed. Many aspects of the early colonial state, such as forced labor, compulsory cotton cultivation, and taxation, were often sufficiently unacceptable to encourage people to embark on war after a colonial regime had been in place for some time. Frequently, a new leadership arose that we can loosely term "prophetic." Naturally, such men looked for an ideology in traditional religion; they could find a source for their ideas only in the world they already knew. Typically, they introduced new rituals, often involving sacred water, that promised protection from the overwhelmingly superior arms of the invader. These new rituals contributed to a new unity between ethnic groups that in some cases had previously been hostile to each other.

Anticolonial Wars: Maji Maji

One of the best-known of these risings was the war against the German government of Tanganyika in 1905 to 1907, which united twenty different ethnic groups and is remembered as Maji Maji. It began, symbolically, with the uprooting of cotton plants. Oral traditions relate how the people hated German rule, but hesitated to embark on an uprising. "They waited for a long time because they were afraid. . . . Who would start? . . . While there were no superior weapons should people not fear?"[31]

In 1904, in southern Tanganyika, a man named Kinjikitile was possessed by a spirit called Hongo, which was subordinate to Bokero, a divinity linked with a rock in the Rufiji River. (Emissaries of the movement, and those who accepted the *maji*, were later called *hongo*.)

> Then he disappeared into the pool of water. . . . The following morning he emerged with his clothes dry. . . . He said, "All dead ancestors will come back. . . . Be it Pogoro, Kichi or Matumbi, we all are the Sayyid Said's" [that is, free, equal, and united].[32]

Kinjikitile began to distribute sacred *maji* (Swahili for water) that would protect fighters from European bullets. Some grew impatient, and in late July 1905 began the uprising. Kinjikitile was hanged in early August, the

movement's first victim. His role had been that of a catalyst. The uprising became widespread, and lasted long after it had become only too clear that *maji*
could not protect anyone. Many were mowed down by machine guns or died
of famine, a total, according to one estimate, of 250,000–300,000 dead. Fifteen Europeans, and 389 of their African soldiers and allies, were killed.[33]

The immediate consequences of Maji Maji were catastrophic. In the
1950s, many hesitated to support the nationalist movement, fearing a repeat of this disaster.[34] But speaking to the United Nations, in 1956, the future president, Julius Nyerere, cited Maji Maji as a precedent. They rose "in
response to a natural call, a call of the spirit, . . . to rebel against foreign
domination." He went on to say that the goal of modern nationalism was
"not to create the spirit of rebellion but to articulate it and show it a new
technique."[35]

In 1973 a student poet, disillusioned with the fruits of independence,
pointed out that "ideology"—development, African socialism, the Arusha
Declaration—could be just as magical as *maji:*

Once before
In 1904
We believed
And believed it was enough to believe
Believed in the water. . . .
And we died
And we failed.
Now again we believe
And again believe
That it is enough
To believe
Now we believe in Azimio [ideology]
Believe again that it is weapon enough . . .

Not so, not so
Do not die
Do not fail.[36]

The Yakan Water Cult

Neotraditional religion and prophetic leaders played a major role in other
anticolonial movements. We have noted the debate over the role spirit mediums played in the Shona/Ndebele uprising of 1896–1897, and their involvement in the guerrilla warfare of the 1970s in Rhodesia/Zimbabwe.

Another cult that involved magical water was first recorded among the
Dinka in 1883, and spread rapidly to the south. In 1890, a man called
Rembe[37] acquired a supply and began to distribute it among Lugbara speakers in what later became northwest Uganda. The movement was variously

called Yakan or the Allah water cult. The water was thought to give protection not only from bullets but also from meningitis. When Belgian officials established a short-lived regime there in 1900, initiates were appointed government chiefs—they seemed to their fellow Lugbara to have a foothold in the world of modernity already.

In 1914, the area became part of Uganda. Rembe resumed distributing magic water, and set up a pole in each village called *dini* (religion). Men drilled with imitation rifles in anticipation of a day when they would be armed with real ones.

In some areas, Maji Maji had acquired strong millennial overtones. This was also true of the Yakan cult—it was thought that the water would protect initiates from death, that ancestors and cattle would return to life, and that people could avoid paying taxes with impunity, since no bullet could harm them. There were clashes with government forces in 1919 and 1920, after which the movement declined among Lugbara speakers, though it survived elsewhere.

Rembe was both a diviner and a prophet; he had a snake oracle in a pool on the borders of the Kakwa and Lugbara culture spheres. The snake was called *dede* and was thought to be the source of Yakan messages. Rembe himself called the movement by a form of its name. Rembe is remembered as "a man of God," and his career may have been inspired by that of the Mahdi in the Sudan. When Middleton did fieldwork between 1949 and 1952, he was told:

> Rembe was a little man. But he was like a king . . . his words were great and many. . . . Is Rembe dead? Where is his grave? We have never heard how or where he died . . . We still look for him. Where did he go?[38]

Yakan still exists among the Lugbara in a different form, as a healing cult.

Mau Mau (1952–1956)

Anticolonial uprisings in which neotraditional religion was a central factor were not always led by a single prophetic figure. Mau Mau was a Kikuyu uprising that became, as we have seen, a Kikuyu civil war. "Mau Mau" was a term used by the movement's opponents, and was not a Kikuyu word. An apparently meaningless name was part of its demonization in European eyes.[39] The insurgents spoke of "the community," of the Kikuyu ancestors, Gikuyu and Mumbi, and of "land and freedom."[40]

Mau Mau was strongly linked with Kikuyu neotraditional religion, which made it difficult to include other major ethnic groups, though some members of neighboring peoples, the Embu and Meru, did take part. The insurgents were bound by draconian oaths that were unacceptable to many Kikuyu Christians, especially because they included a clause about missionary influence, but were a reinvention of older elements in Kikuyu culture.[41] Conflict broke out only after a state of emergency was declared (the government had previously outlawed oaths).

Land was the central issue. Many of the guerrillas were squatters on land that had belonged to their ancestors but was now held by white settlers. Others were unemployed youths from Nairobi. As one of them remembered later, "For my part I was only hoping to be given a small piece of land somewhere and to be treated a little more decently by the Kenya government and by the white settlers."[42] The insurgents were typically young, poor, and landless. Only five of the forest fighters had a secondary education. "Loyalists" tended to be Christians, "chiefs," and the more prosperous—often the same people.

The guerrillas based themselves in the forest, on the slopes of Mount Kenya, or in the Aberdare Range, where many died of hunger and cold. Soon, the forest fighters were divided into two mutually hostile groups. One, the literate, was led by Dedan Kimathi, who called himself "Field Marshal of the British Empire, Prime Minister of the Southern Hemisphere,"[43] and was hanged in 1957. Its modernizing aims were reflected in its name, the Kenya Parliament.

One of its members reconstructed, in a later memoir, a speech he made at the time:

> I would like to elect the best twelve persons we have in this forest so that we could have the best government possible. . . . We are not fighting for regions or clans or tribes. We are fighting for the whole Kenya, including our enemies. . . . Some of us may seek privileges, but by the time we achieve our freedom you will have learned to share a grain of maize or a bean among several people, feeling selfishness as an evil. . . . You will not like to become another class of "Black" Europeans ready to oppress and exploit others.[44]

The other wing, led by Stanley Mathenge, was called Kenya Rigii (doors). When captured fighters were placed in large dentention centers, the relatively educated often held literacy classes, dissolving the original barrier between them. The government introduced Kikuyu ritual specialists to carry out de-oathing; they were soon referred to, ironically, as "H.M. Witchdoctors."

During the conflict, 80,000 Kikuyu were imprisoned in detention camps; 10,000 insurgents were killed and 1,300 were executed. Fifty-eight Europeans died in the conflict—as in Maji Maji, this disparity is significant and symbolic.

In a sense, the forest fighters failed because they lacked resources and arms. But it was the Mau Mau war which convinced the British government that majority rule was inevitable; one white settler called it a Kikuyu victory. Kenya became independent in 1963, led by Jomo Kenyatta. A Kikuyu who had lived abroad for a long period, he had condemned Mau Mau, but his popularity had been greatly enhanced by his detention during the state of emergency. A small number of Mau Mau, who felt that the land reforms they fought for had not been realized, fought on into 1965, when they were defeated by the government of independent Kenya.

The guerrillas who survived were marginal in the new Kenya, which was dominated by the well-educated. A class of "big men" emerged, and the poor often remained landless. The novelist and political dissident Ngugi idealized Mau Mau, which he saw as part of a tradition of opposition to oppressive governments. Nineteen years after independence, he wrote:

Great love I found there
Among women and children
A bean fell to the ground—
We split it among ourselves.[45]

Generally speaking, historians are supportive of anticolonial uprisings, emphasizing the courage of the fighters and the reality of their grievances. Neotraditional religion has also played a major role in the postindependence wars, and here scholars are much less sympathetic. The atrocities committed by Renamo and the Lord's Resistance Army are well documented. Whereas anticolonial struggles are universally regarded as a good thing, wars of regional separatism, such as these two movements, tend to be condemned.

WAR AND PEACE IN MOZAMBIQUE

Mozambique became independent after an armed struggle against Portugal in 1975. It was ruled by Frelimo, the party that had spearheaded the independence struggle. Its first leader had been assassinated; Samora Machel, first head of state of independent Mozambique, died in a much- debated plane crash. Frelimo was committed to secularism and socialism. Idealistically, it closed the railway linking the white minority regimes of Rhodesia and South Africa. Rhodesian security forces retaliated by training and arming Frelimo's opponents. When Zimbabwe adopted majority rule in 1980, South African forces continued to support this group, which became known as Renamo; by the time this support evaporated, Renamo was well established. A catastrophic civil war came to an end in 1992.

Foreign interference created a guerrilla army only because there was a considerable body of opposition to Frelimo. This was partly ethnic—Frelimo was seen as Shangaan-dominated—but some of its policies, such as the introduction of state farms, were unsuccessful and unpopular.[46] Renamo commanders made much use of neotraditional religion, claiming to be invulnerable due to their use of charms. Their forces often operated with extreme cruelty, frequently of a ritual nature—an example of the political use of terror.[47] But neotraditional rituals were also used to create peace zones.

In Mungoi, an area of fifteen square miles in southern Mozambique, the spirit of a dead chief spoke through a woman descendant in 1987, demanding peace. Frelimo and Renamo soldiers could enter the area only if they were unarmed.

The movement usually referred to as Naprama, in northern Mozambique, began in late 1989 and declined when its leader, Manuel Antonio, was shot in 1991. Antonio was a prophetic figure who claimed that he had been raised from the dead to end the war. Shortly before his death he said, "What is Barama [Naprama]? Barama is the suffering of the people and God said it was necessary to empower somebody to respond." (*Barama* means "vaccinated"—a magical substance was thought to protect initiates from bullets.) Naprama's rituals had a considerable admixture of Catholicism. Although the aim of the movement was to end the war, members took part in fighting, though at first they used spears, not guns. A Naprama commander explained, 'We have a merely defensive mission. We are defending the people because they are tired of war."[48]

ALICE LAKWENA AND THE LORD'S RESISTANCE ARMY

The *mhondoro* mediums who supported the Zimbabwe gurrerillas spoke in the name of long-dead kings. The women who joined spirit possession cults such as Bori enacted roles that they could never fill in reality. A long war in northern Uganda was led by mediums possessed by spirits that, like Mami Wata or some Zar spirits, were constructions of modernity.

Alice Auma (generally known as Alice Lakwena) was a young Catholic Acholi woman from Gulu in northern Uganda. She was first possessed in 1985, and claimed to have begun her prophetic career with a forty days' sojourn in the wilderness and an equal period of immersion in the Nile. She called herself *nebi* (the word for "prophet" in the Swahili Bible), and was hostile to (other) spirit mediums (*ajwaka*). She called her possessing spirits by the names missionaries used for the Holy Spirit or angels. They included a North Korean (Invisible Chairman) and the feared Wrong Element. Her chief spirit, the Lakwena (Messenger), was originally conceptualized as a ninety-five-year-old Italian physician who spoke seventy-four languages and had drowned in the Nile. It was not uncommon for women who, like Alice, were childless to become diviners and healers, but Alice's voices, like Joan of Arc's, came to call her to war.

Alice's vision was a millennial one. She urged her followers to attack the central government, which she identified with witchcraft, and believed that aspects of the world of nature, including bees, snakes, and rivers, also supported this struggle. Her followers were anointed with oil that was thought to protect them from bullets. If they died, it was attributed to lack of faith or to ritual infringements. Her "technicians" employed magical instruments such as miniature tanks; stones, after a special ritual, were thought to explode like grenades. Her army got within fifty miles of Kampala, but at the end of 1987, after a major defeat, Alice fled to Kenya. She has lived there ever since, and no longer prophesies.

After a brief period when Alice's father claimed authority, Joseph Kony became, and remains, the acknowledged leader of the Lord's Resistance Army. He was possessed by new spirits, headed by that of Juma Oris, who had been a minister in Idi Amin's regime. His (female) war commander was Sili Silindi (Saint Cecilia) from the Sudan. Ing Chu, Chinese or Korean, was in charge of spirit jeeps, and Major Bianca, an American, of intelligence. King Bruce (Bruce Lee?), another American, controlled magical grenades.[49] Soldiers called themselves by names such as James Bond or Karate.

The initial support for Alice's millennial message came from a people demoralized and impoverished by years of oppressive government, human rights abuses, and civil war. The Acholi are kin and neighbors to Obote's ethnic group, the Langi, and many Acholi soldiers were massacred at the beginning of the Amin era. The dark years that Ugandans remember as Obote II ended with an Acholi coup in 1985, which soon ended in defeat. Since they had not been through the traditional cleansing ceremony required of those who had shed blood, returning soldiers were thought to bring with them the angry spirits of those they had killed. This and other factors—the years of war, the spread of AIDS—encouraged the belief that witchcraft was running rampant.

In 1987, an anonymous soldier poet in the Lord's Resistance Army gave voice to their grievances, including a long-standing sense of regional neglect, for which Alice provided a focus. He also sketched the dream for which he fought:

> The focal point of economy
> Is freedom, Dignity material welfare and happiness
> This Uganda should have. . . . [50]

In 1985, the southern-based National Resistance Army came to power in Uganda. Its leader, Yoweri Museveni, has been head of state ever since, a far more satisfactory one than his predecesors. But his government has so far been unable to defeat the Lord's Resistance Army.

Nineteen years after Alice's initial visions, the main victims of a civil war that still continues have been the Acholi people. The Lord's Resistance Army consists of kidnapped, brutalized children, led by commanders who were originally recruited in this way. Many of its soldiers were born into the movement. It has created a regime of terror in the civilian population, and there have been countless casualties. There is a profound and tragic irony in the fact that a movement which was started to eradicate evil, conceptualized as witchcraft, has caused so much human suffering.

THE RITUAL REJECTION OF COLONIALISM: MUMBO

Northern Uganda was historically underdeveloped, neglected by colonial and postcolonial governments. Mumbo was a movement that flourished in a remote and undeveloped area of Kenya, among the Gusii of the southwest and their Luo neighbors, on the shore of Lake Victoria/Nyanza. (The Gusii, who speak a Bantu language while surrounded by Nilotic speakers, are a well-known example of the "invention of ethnicity."[51])

Mumbo, like the Xhosa cattle-killing in nineteenth-century South Africa, was an attempt to expel an unpopular European presence by ritual means. Like the Xhosa, the Gusii turned to ritual opposition after successive defeats in war. In 1913, a giant snake appeared to a Luo prophet, who was swallowed and regurgitated, an echo of Jonah and the whale. The snake's words echoed those of Jahweh in the Hebrew Bible:

> I am the God Mumbo whose two homes are in the Sun and the Lake. . . . Go and tell all Africans . . . that from henceforth I am their God. Those whom I personally choose and also those who acknowledge me will live forever in plenty . . . there will be no more need to work. . . . I will cause cattle, sheep and goats to come up out of the lake in great numbers. . . . The Christian religion is rotten and so is its practice of making its believers wear [Western] clothes.[52]

Adherents wore goatskin hats and capes. Fortunately, they did not, like the Xhosa, embark on large-scale cattle-killing, though they slaughtered the odd beast for a communal feast. Apart from this, they did not form an organization—each individual awaited Mumbo. The apocalyptic element may have been influenced by the teachings of local Seventh-Day Adventist missionaries. In a sense, Mumbo, like Mami Wata, is a case of enlargement of scale, a gigantic form of Africa's innumerable sacred serpents with a universal message. Mumbo's followers were hostile to chiefs, the allies of the colonial order; one chief who, exceptionally, supported them, wore his goatskin costume under Western clothes, a singularly uncomfortable compromise! An official, recognizing the ritual nature of the movement, made a bonfire of goatskin hats and capes.

The movement flourished until about 1920. Mumbo had declared, "All Europeans are your enemies, but the time is shortly coming when they will all disappear from your country."[53] There were various accounts of what would happen; in one, the water would turn to blood (there would be a special water supply for Mumbo followers). In another, people in Western clothes would have their arms cut off.

The movement stagnated in the 1920s, had a brief revival in the early 1930s, then virtually disappeared. Education, closely linked with the missions, came to appear a more promising path to the future, if not for Mumbo's followers, then at least for their children. In the early 1990s, one adherent survived, still waiting for Mumbo. Grievances continue to loom large in Gusii sensibility.[54]

Chapter 21

Mythology and Proverbial Wisdom

There are imaginations, not "the Imagination," and they must be studied in detail.

—William James, *Psychology*[1]

Much African mythology is an attempt to make moral sense of lived experience, and especially to account for suffering. Not all myths do this—an Igbo myth, which is part of a worldwide genre, explains the origins of agriculture: when Nri, the founder of the ritual community that bears his name, sacrificed his son and buried him, yams then grew from his body.[2] The Nuer have a myth that attributes their political fragmentation to disputes over cattle.[3] Yam cultivation was central to Igbo life, as cattle were to the Nuer.

Scholars have come to realize that in their concrete nature, myths are closer to the specificity of life than abstract statements about reality:

Myth is a reality immeasurably greater than concept. It is high time that we stopped identifying myth with invention, with the illusions of primitive mentality, and with anything, in fact, which is essentially opposed to reality. . . . Myth is always concrete and expresses life better than abstract thought can do; its nature is bound up with that of symbol.[4]

Fernandez writes of "the actual images in which African thought is expressed and embedded" and of "the coding of thought in images and symbolic forms . . . thought embedded in images, symbols and actions is complex thought." He contrasts this with "imageless ideas."[5] Myths can be called "true fictions."

Myth, like ritual, is in a process of constant change. New myths evolve in novel situations. Thus, some are a response to the vast disparity in wealth and power between colonial Europeans and Africans. Myths draw on new sources of ideas, such as biblical episodes, which are often transformed in the narration. Not all African peoples have a rich store of mythology; in some cultures, religious meanings are expressed in the symbolism embedded in ritual or in proverbs.

There is an intricate and varying relationship between myth, ritual, and sacred roles. In the previous chapter, mention was made of the Dinka culture hero Aiwel. There are many regional variants of the story.[6] In one well-known one, he was born to a widow impregnated by a river spirit. When he grew up, his ox, Longar, was the color of rain clouds. When the people were dying of drought, Aiwel offered to lead them to a place of grass and water, but they refused. He set off alone, and they decided to follow him. They came to a river, but Aiwel speared them as they tried to cross. In the end, one man succeeded in doing so, fending off the spear with the sacrum of an ox. Those who crossed the river received fishing spears, and became the founders of priestly spear-master clans, with Flesh as their totem. Those who crossed later founded warrior clans. In another version, Aiwel quarreled with the Sun and hid in his cow barn, coming out only at night. In some accounts, the cow barn was constructed from living people. At the Sun's request, the Moon speared Aiwel. He was buried, still alive, in a vast mound.

These myths not only provided a founding charter for spear-master clans, but clearly inspired much of the Ngungdeng story. (Like Aiwel, he is said to have been born with all his teeth to a woman past childbearing age, and so on.) Like prophets, Aiwel "had long hair, like a ghost."

CREATION MYTHS

Not all African peoples speculated on the origins of the visible world. Traditions recorded as far apart as Nigeria and Mozambique sometimes mention in passing "when the world was still a swamp. . . ." Where creation myths exist, they often include an explanation of the origin of death and suffering.

Perhaps the best-known example, recorded among the Yoruba,[7] also sheds light on the remoteness of Olorun/Oludumare. Matter is not created out of nothing. As in many of the world's creation stories, order is established in primeval chaos. This myth explains the origins of physical defects, including albinism (which led to many health problems in tropical Africa). Olorun delegates the task of separating the dry land from the waters to Obatala, who sends down a five-toed cock, which scratches away and casts up the land. Obatala goes on to create humanity. He becomes drunk on palm wine and creates people with deformities—hence his abhorrence of alcohol. His sacred color is white (his name means King of Whiteness), his sacred metal is lead, he is honored with bloodless sacrifices of snails, and he does not possess his followers.

In the kingdom of Bunyoro, in Uganda, a complex myth explains the creation of the world, the origins of suffering and death, and the establishment of the ancient and mythical dynasty that preceded the Cwezi. The first written English version dates from 1914. Is it in some sense a response to Christian teachings? It was published by a missionary, but she insisted that it was obtained "from old heathen men who have had no opportunity whatever of coming into contact with Christian teaching."[8] The account that follows is a summary of a much more detailed narrative.

Ruhanga gradually created everything in the world at the request of his brother, Nkya. Nkya had four sons; one was called Kantu, "Little Thing,"[9] but the other three had no names. After various tests, Ruhanga called the youngest Ruler; the second, Herdsman; and the eldest, Servant. Kantu, angry at his exclusion, resolved to make war on the world God had created, introducing sin, strife, and hatred. Ruhanga and Nkya left the Earth for Heaven, shattering the iron bar that connected the two. Angry at human prosperity, Kantu asked God to take away the desire for food, with the result that people and animals became weak. Kantu told Ruhanga that the king was cursing him in his heart, and Ruhanga responded by releasing hunger and disease into the world. The king's little son died, and he lamented, "Now that my son is dead, let the grass and trees perish, and let man and beast die." The king disappeared and was succeeded by a different son, who founded the Batembuzi dynasty.

In Buganda, Kintu (Man) is both first man and first king, and different narratives locate him in both roles. As first man—and probably also as first king—he clearly belongs to the world of myth. In 1902, the Ganda statesman Apolo Kaggwa published the story in his own language—he "tried very hard to ask older Baganda who knew the story very well." Initially, Kintu lived alone with one cow. He was so ignorant that he did not know how to milk her, and survived on her excreta. He met Nnambi, daughter of Ggulu, king of Heaven, and they decided to marry. Kintu successfully passed a series of difficult tests, and set off for Earth with his new wife. They were told not to turn back, lest they encounter her brother Walumbe (Death). Nnambi had forgotten the millet for her chickens; she turned back to get it and, as warned, met Death, who followed them. Death began to kill the couple's children. Ggulu sent another brother to capture Walumbe and bring him back to the sky. The people were told to hide in their houses while he laid in wait for him. But children went out to pasture their goats—again the theme of disobedience—and Death was warned, and escaped. Then followed Kintu's famous cry of defiance: "If Walumbe wants to kill my children, let him. But he will not be able to finish all of them because I, Kintu, will always continue to beget more." It is an affirmation of humanity's power to survive adversity.

According to an earlier version of the story, it was Kintu, not his wife, who returned for the millet. It is possible that even this early text reflects Christian influences, in particular the story of Eve, a comparison that Kaggwa himself made. Later texts were even closer to the Genesis story, but a version collected in the late nineteenth century stated that Kintu was a favorite of the sky god and often feasted at his court, returning with a gift for his people. He was forbidden to return for anything he had forgotten. In a drunken state, he forgot some corn he had been given, and returned for it. He was sent back to Earth with a servant, Death, to remind mankind of the results of disobedience.[10] Again it is the man, not the woman, who disobeys God's (arbitrary) law.

The Ruhanga story is clearly always and only myth, whereas the Kintu legend is formulated as early dynastic history. Both have an overriding preoccupation: to explain suffering and misfortune, and especially death, thus making life morally intelligible. Kintu has sometimes been listed as the first in a series of thirty-one kings of Buganda that came to an end with the deposition of the last of them in 1966. His story has many dimensions of meaning, one of which belongs to a vast genre about the origins of kingdoms.

The founding myth of the Bemba kingdom tells of an immigrant Luba prince, from eastern Congo, who married a woman with elephants' ears, a member of the Crocodile clan. Their children attempted to build a tower to heaven, but it collapsed, causing many casualties. The king sought to kill them in a concealed game pit. After migrations, a capital was built called Crocodile, the name a symbolic indictment of the rapacity and cruelty of kings.[11]

EXPLAINING SUFFERING: PARADISE LOST

Stories of Paradise Lost, which imply that our natural state is a happy one and that death was not always inevitable, often follow one of two patterns: the distancing of the sky (and God) and the cosmic race.

The Distancing of the Sky

A widespread genre of myths suggests that God was once close to humanity but withdrew to the sky, and that this departure caused suffering, sickness, and death. The unwitting cause of this disaster is very often a woman. God's proximity is a source of blessing; our sufferings come from his present remoteness, caused by a human mistake. In one of a number of Dinka versions, people had been told to limit themselves to a single grain of millet, but an old woman either cultivated or ground more. The handle of her hoe or pestle disturbed God, who sent a bluebird to cut the rope that joined Heaven and Earth.[12] A strikingly similar version was collected in Asante (now in Ghana) early in the twentieth century:

> Long, long ago, [God] lived on Earth or at least was very near to us. Now there
> was a certain old woman who used to pound her *fufu* [mashed yams, etc.], and
> the pestle used to constantly knock up against [God]. So [God] said to the
> old woman, "Why do you always do so to me? Because of what you are doing,
> I am going to take myself away up into the sky." And of a truth he did so.

The people then attempted to follow God, and built a tower of mortars, which collapsed, causing many deaths.[13]

The Kantana live in central Nigeria, on the Jos Plateau's steep southern escarpment. In 1976, an old man related a story he heard from his father, about a time when the sky, the home of God, was close to the ground: "When the sky was close to the ground, there was fertile land, peace, enough food, and you could travel anywhere and come back safely, even during the night." There was no fire on Earth, and food was cooked by utilizing the heat of the sun. God's daughter would visit a friend on Earth and bring fire to cook with, taking it with her when she left. But the earthly woman stole some fire; God retreated in anger; and war, poverty, disease, and suffering entered the world.[14]

These and similar stories, one of which is outlined below, imply that nearness to God is our natural state. They are clearly independent inventions—the peoples concerned are separated by vast distances. In each, a woman is the scapegoat and is punished for carrying out what were regarded as her duties, such as cooking.

The Dinka have more than one myth about the origins of death and suffering. Some are clearly retellings of the Garden of Eden story, complete with snake and forbidden fruit. In one text, the bird cuts the rope joining Heaven and Earth out of anger at his wife's death. She was hungry after childbirth, but forbidden to eat the available grain—perhaps an echo of Genesis's forbidden fruit. In yet another version, people originally grew old and blind, and then were made young again. A blind old woman asked river fishermen for a share of their catch. They deceived her by throwing down the same fish in front of her again and again. She threw a potsherd in the river and cursed them: "A person will die and never return."[15]

This sheds some light on the problem posed by the existence of similar myths in widely separated cultures. A given ethnolinguistic group may well have a number of myths on the same general theme; if we select only the one that has parallels elsewhere, we exaggerate the element of convergence. Four different Dinka myths about the origins of death are cited in this chapter—five, if we include the Garden of Eden—and several more have been published.

As we noted in the case of myths about Aiwel, there are many regional variants. Deng collected myths among his own Gwok Dinka in the 1970s that were not known to Lienhardt, who had worked with a different Dinka group in the late 1940s. This reflects differences in place and time, but it

would be possible for an elder to make up a story or retell one that originated far away (such as the Genesis story), which the researcher would then
solemnly record as part of "traditional" Dinka mythology.

The Cosmic Race

One genre of myths suggests that God has always been so far away that
he can be contacted only by intermediaries, which always belong to the animal kingdom. Like stories about the distancing of the sky, they explain the
existence of death, and also like them, they imply that death is unnatural,
the result of an unfortunate mistake or mischance.

The Swiss missionary H.A. Junod, who worked for many years in
Mozambique, recorded a version among the Shangaan in the late nineteenth
and early twentieth centuries: "When the first human beings emerged from
the marsh of reeds, the chief of this marsh" sent them two emissaries. The
chameleon carried the message that men would die and rise again; the blue-
headed lizard, that they would die and rot. The lizard arrived first; when the
chameleon arrived with his message, he was told he was too late: "That is why
men are subject to death."[16] Shangaan shepherds would feed chameleons tobacco, so that they died in agony, to punish them for their tardiness.

A similar myth was collected among the Berom of central Nigeria and was
published in 1970. People sent a common frog and a tree frog to God, to
ask that they might be reborn after death. The tree frog arrived first, with a
garbled message: "It would be better if men died and remained where they
are." The common frog came later, with the correct version, but too late.[17]
There is absolutely no connection between the Shangaan and the Berom,
and they live thousands of miles apart.

ECOLOGY

Some myths about the origins of death embody an awareness of ecology,
a consciousness that people must die in order to make room for their successors. A moving version of Dinka myth describes the creation of the first
man and woman, Garang and Abuk, from clay. They were small, half the
length of a human arm, but fully mature:

> And they married. And they bore children. And the creator said, "Your child
> will die but after only fifteen days he will return." Garang disagreed and said,
> "If people return again they will be too numerous. Where will they build their
> homes? There will not be enough land."[18]

A myth collected among the Nupe of central Nigeria, at the beginning
of the twentieth century, shows the same ecological awareness. God created
people, stones, and tortoises. Tortoises and people had sexual identities but

no children; they did not die, but regained their youth when they grew old. The tortoises asked God for progeny and were told that this would mean death. They accepted this condition, as did people. The stones preferred immortality and childlessness.[19]

CHANGING MYTHOLOGY: SYMBOLIC CHOICES[20]

Mythology, like ritual and cosmogony, changes over time. Stories about Ogun, or other narratives that mention iron, are clearly more recent than the introduction of ironworking (about 600 B.C.E. in Central Nigeria), though the evidence of language suggests that Ogun's cult grew out of older rituals.[21]

Over hundreds of years, myths have been recorded in many different parts of Africa that attempt to explain the relative power and wealth of Europeans vis-à-vis Africans. Like stories of Paradise Lost, they are an attempt to make moral sense of the known world. Typically, they involve two men, an African and a European. The African chooses one of two symbolic objects—often a book and hoe—in a situation where the consequences are immense but unknown. He has first choice because he is the senior or is especially loved by God.

In the era of the slave trade, such stories sought to explain why whites were slavers and Africans were captives. In the colonial era and later, they are a reflection on why Europeans are rich while Africans remain poor.

Often they are adaptations of other stories of symbolic choices. Bockie tells several different myths about the origin of death that were current in his own Kongo community. In one, the first human being annoyed God by telling his secrets to the animals. God withdrew, but introduced death as an act of mercy, to save mankind from the infirmities of old age. In a different story, God sent the first man into the world bearing a green leaf, symbol of life, and the second man bearing a dry leaf, symbol of death. Humanity chose the second, fearing eternal life in advanced old age. In yet another variant, God offered humans two parcels—one containing death and one containing eternal life. Again, fearing prolonged old age, they chose death, and God withdrew in anger.[22] The stories about the book and the hoe developed from earlier myths of choices of this kind.

In the earliest version known to me, recorded in the Gold Coast about 1700, Africans chose gold, leaving literacy for Europeans: "God granted their Request, but being incensed at their Avarice, resolved that the Whites should for ever be their Masters, and they obliged to wait on them as their slaves."[23]

A story collected among the Luba of the eastern Democratic Republic of Congo in the mid-twentieth century reflects, like many others, the perceived significance of literacy. God offered the black man and the white man a choice between a large, heavy box and a small, light one. The black man was God's favorite and could choose first. He picked the large box, which turned out to contain hoes, axes, water pots, and poles on which loads are carried: "And since then the black man has usually had the work of chopping wood, drawing water, and carrying loads." The white man's box contained a pencil and paper; this meant that when he died, his knowledge did not die with him, but was passed on to the next generation.[24]

Sometimes the difference in the fortunes of Europeans and Africans is explained by retelling biblical stories. There are two particular favorites: the stories of how Jacob, by a trick, won his elder brother's birthright (Genesis 27) and of how Noah's son Ham was punished for looking on his father's nakedness when he lay drunken in his tent (Genesis 9: 20–28). A version of the first, recorded among the Limba of Sierra Leone in the 1960s, tells of two brothers, a white one, who was the mother's favorite, and a black one, preferred by the father. The father had a book in which "He wrote everything, how to make a ship, aeroplane, money . . ." He prepared a hoe and cutlass for the less favored brother. Each was asked to go hunting and bring back game. The white brother, Trickster-style, killed a domestic sheep, and obtained the book: "The unfairness of our birth makes us remain in suffering."[25]

TRICKSTER NARRATIVES

Myths, of course, are only one form of oral literature. There is a rich body of stories told to entertain and to reinforce moral values, especially among children; often these follow the adventures of a Trickster—the spider Anansi among Akan speakers in Ghana, the tortoise in Yorubaland and Igboland, the hare among the Shangaan of Mozambique and other peoples in eastern Africa. The Br'er Rabbit stories told by enslaved Africans in America belong to this genre. Trickster narratives have an underlying seriousness—they are stories of the victories of the weak over the strong. The Trickster represents humanity, with its weaknesses and imperfections. Tortoise is punished, like Br'er Rabbit, for his greed, but survives.[26]

Trickster imagery was sometimes used in an implicit indictment of the colonial presence: "Eshu brought the British to Nigeria." In Zambia, in the 1940s, someone explained:

> The hare caused the death of the lion. It need never have happened if the lion had heeded the warning of the bird. . . . You Europeans are few, but you are very clever, like the hare. You know how to make aeroplanes. But we Africans are many and we are strong, like the lion. . . . [T]hey are weak but they always win over us, just like the hare tricked the lion in the legend. The little bird warned the lion but he would not listen.
>   Who is the bird?
>   Our forefathers.[27]

PROVERBS

Proverbs encapsulate and fossilize folk wisdom, and often express insights of enduring significance. These Igbo examples were recorded in the 1850s:

> He who embezzles the public funds will have to refund it.
> Like the sprouting of the yam is the birth of the firstborn.
> The wealthy has no enemy, but all esteem him for his wealth's sake.
> The rain beats upon the slave dealer as well as the slave.
> When two persons talk in secret, God says, "I make a third."[28]

A 1914 compilation of Igbo proverbs had 1,022 entries.

CONCLUSION

One of the most striking and mysterious aspects of mythology, both in Africa and internationally, lies in its similarities and parallels. One explanatory model suggests that mythic complexes have spread from common origins—perhaps from small Stone Age populations—continuities and relationships also reflected in Africa's language families. The second is that of independent invention—in Wrigley's words, "the operations of the laws of chance on the limited creative capacities of the human mind."[29] One scholar has suggested that "the material culture is meagre, so that relatively few objects and things are available to sustain the ideological and affectual freight of the culture. Each of these . . . sustains enormous and complex symbolic weight."[30] But any given African environment is full of an extremely rich known and named natural world—its plants, birds, fish, reptiles, animals, fungi—to which are now added the varied icons of modernity, such as cars and television. Convergences and parallels are not due to a lack of objects that are good to think with.

Chapter 22

Suffering and Its Interpreters

> I have read of many episodes of witchcraft, and am certain that most of
> the writers have never met a witch. They quote so many essays from re-
> search scholars who have never actually met a witch. . . . I can dare to
> write with authority and certitude. I have talked with the witches, and
> I have dealt with the dead.
> —Emmanuel Milingo, former Catholic archbishop of Lusaka[1]

Myth interprets suffering at a universal level; divination, at the individual
level. The problem of evil, often but not always identified with witchcraft,
threads its way through this book. It was one of the great strengths of Africa's
Christian prophets that they offered protection from an embodiment of absolute evil that liberal foreign missionaries tended to see as an illusion. In
1969, Parrinder observed, "In modern times these magical and witchcraft
beliefs ought to disappear with the growth of education."[2] Instead, witchcraft beliefs have proliferated and taken new forms.

"Witch" or "sorcerer" translates a wide number of African words and
concepts: *mbatsav* in Tiv, *aje* in Yoruba, *amosu* in Igbo, *aboro mangu* among
the Zande, *nfiti* in chiChewa, and so on. The witch is often thought of as
an older woman. Essentially, he or she is an astral cannibal who feeds on the
life force of the living. Sometimes his or her powers are inherited, sometimes
acquired, or she becomes a witch because she is tricked into incurring a flesh
debt. In some cultures, witches form an astral coven, incurring flesh debts
that are repaid by astral offerings of members of their family circle. The witch
is sometimes a shape-shifter or closely linked with an animal familiar. Whereas
people eat animals and seek companionship from their own kind, witches eat
people and prefer the companionship of a familiar. Sometimes—the Tiv and
Zande are examples—witchcraft is thought to be a physical organ in the body.

In some cultures, the witch is—or has become—a supernatural capitalist profiting from the labor of zombie slaves. This has been documented in Tanzania and South Africa, and has been extensively studied in Cameroon, where the concept seems to have developed in the colonial period.

Evans-Pritchard distinguished between witchcraft—an inherent quality— and sorcery, which is a form of technology that relies on magical preparations and often requires a period of apprenticeship.[3] In French, both are called *la sorcellerie*, and in Swahili, *uchawi*. Contemporary studies lay little emphasis on the distinction.

In the case studies that follow, I return to some of the ethnolinguistic groups introduced in earlier chapters.

IMAGES OF THE WITCH IN THE IGBO CULTURE SPHERE

The witch (*amosu*) was typically an older woman. Witchcraft accusations sometimes grew out of the tensions in polygynous households, or were linked with anxieties and resentments sparked by the independence of women traders. A well-educated western Igbo, a male secondary school teacher, told me in 1975:

> We believe in witchcraft everywhere. . . . It is believed that witchcraft causes infant mortality, premature death, and misfortune. The majority of women are witches. It is believed that witches "eat" human beings. It is the victim's soul which is stolen and "eaten," and not the physical body itself. They have a gathering, or meeting. However, it is only the witch's soul which attends. . . . In some cases they confess to their crimes. They will admit that they were responsible for killing members of their own family.

He went on to add further information that a named (male) friend, who believed himself a witch, had supplied in 1960:

> Witches can travel from here to Lagos in the night. . . . He told me that they could turn into flies or into owls or goats or any bird or snake, as the case may be. . . . He said that they could carry a baby from a mother's womb and turn it into another thing, or eat it . . . it was compulsory for all the members in the society to partake of human meat. . . . the meetings could be held in the marketplace or on an iroko tree [or] along the bank of a river.

Henderson's study of the Niger town of Onitsha, based on research in 1960–1962, stresses the link with the market, as do Nadel's writings on Nupe. The market queen, the *omu*, and her councillors provide the community with supernatural protection. On occasion, they will take burning firebrands from their homes and throw them onto the inland road or into the river, casting forth accumulated evils and abominations. Witches—sometimes identified as these same women—are thought to meet in the marketplace at night, in the form of birds.[4]

In nineteenth-century mission records, the typical witch among the riverain Igbo was an old widow without children to support and protect her.

IMAGES OF THE WITCH IN THE YORUBA CULTURE SPHERE

In the Yoruba culture sphere, the witch is always a woman. The word *aje* is avoided; they are referred to euphemistically as "Mothers (or Rulers) of the World." In the past, accusations of individuals were rare.[5]

Witchcraft was kept in check by periodic rituals—we have noted Egungun and Gelede, as well as Oro—which on occasion did execute witches and periodically forced women to remain at home. Those close to the witch are most at risk: "If death cannot strike one from within the home, death cannot strike one from without."[6] A woman could become a witch through inheritance from her mother, through choice, or by inadvertently consuming human flesh, thus incurring a debt that had to be repaid. Here, too, witchcraft beliefs are often ascribed to tensions in polygynous households, but whatever its origins, witchcraft has now grown, here and elsewhere, into a far wider-ranging discourse.

Lawal emphasizes that the Mothers are not totally evil, and that their supernatural powers can be harnessed to favorable ends if they are placated—this is the purpose of Gelede. (This contrasts with the other case studies in this chapter, in which the witch or sorcerer is the embodiment of absolute evil.)

According to a verse from the Ifa corpus, God sent two male divinities, Obatala and Ogun, and a female one, to rule over the recently created world. He gave Obatala supernatural power (*ase*), and Ogun control of iron, hunting, and war. The woman asked for her own *ase*, which was given to her in the form of a bird. God warned her not to misuse her power, but this was disregarded. A different Ifa poem attributes the Mothers' powers to Eshu, who insisted that they respect certain objects which individuals could use for their own ritual protection.[7]

The *àjé* stereotype is an old woman who wields astounding telepathic powers. She is thought to conceal the source of her power in a closed calabash containing a bird. Hence her nickname . . . wielder of bird power. At night her soul enters the bird and flies away to attend meetings or to suck the blood of unsuspecting victims, who then eventually die. . . . Because of a mysterious object that lies in her stomach, the *àjé* does not require any other medicine to accomplish her objectives. . . . She can . . . prevent, negate or destroy pregnancy.[8]

It is *okan*, the heart, that travels.

In 1970, Idowu described witchcraft as if it were an empirical social problem: "Do witches exist? I will assert categorically that there are witches in Africa; that they are as real as are murderers." They have a modern bureacratic organization: "Witches form themselves into well organized clandestine cults or guilds on local, regional and interregional levels."[9] Idowu noted the associated fear of poisoning, which is widely documented here and elsewhere.

In Zambia, Archbishop Milingo, quoted in the epigraph to this chapter, believed in the existence of witches and evil spirits, and exorcised them. Morton-Williams writes, in words most Western ethnographers have echoed, "Witchcraft is entirely imaginary. . . . Since witchcraft is impossible, the fear of witchcraft must be symbolic."[10] At least one foreign academic did begin with the assumption that Yoruba witchcraft was an illusion but became convinced of its reality![11] In an earlier chapter, we noted Edith Turner's and Stoller's accounts of supernatural encounters.

IMAGES OF THE SORCERER IN THE CHEWA CULTURE SPHERE[12]

Chi-Chewa speakers were introduced in chapter 16 and were the subject of a further case study in chapter 17. A study of sorcery among the Zambian Chewa, based on research conducted between 1948 and 1953, provides a detailed picture of another model of supernatural evil. The Chewa sorcerer can be either a man or a woman. He or she operates not through innate powers but through magic, usually involving the hair or nail parings of the victim, which is why the term "sorcery" is used in this context.

The Chewa sorcerer was above all a necrophage, disinterring human corpses in order to eat them. To avoid this, a graveyard watch was kept after a death. People avoided cemeteries, lest they be thought sorcerers, which is why a cemetery was a safe place for Nyau members to store large ritual structures. Sorcerers were thought to eat their flesh meals in a coven, and to incur and pay flesh debts: "If someone simply eats the meat killed by his fellows, the latter will tell him, 'You must kill some of your children so that we may partake of them.'"[13]

It is those close at hand who have most to fear: "Sorcerers never attack strangers, they always attack their friends."[14] They have animal familiars, most often a hyena or an owl, but are not shape-shifters.

EXPLAINING MISFORTUNE

The importance of witchcraft as an explanatory model varies, not only from one society to the next but also within a given ethnolinguistic group. Two maps, one published in 1926 and one in 1970, attempted to depict varying degrees of witchcraft belief in southern Nigeria. In the first, the shading ranged from "excessive" to "slight"—one might think that any degree of witchcraft belief was excessive! Except for two coastal enclaves, the Yoruba area was "moderate." The western and riverain Igbo, and those in the hinterland of Onitsha, were labeled "much," and the eastern Igbo interior, "slight." The 1970 map was confined to the Igbo and their neighbors. Witchcraft anxiety among the riverain Igbo (the home of the schoolmaster whose views are quoted above) is "slight to moderate," "negligible" in the eastern Igbo interior, and "intense" among the (non-Igbo) peoples east of the Cross River.[15] Probably no one now would attempt to map shades of anxiety in this way. We are talking of a different cartography, the changing complexities of individual experience. But the regional differences these maps attempted to reflect are real enough.

Not all misfortunes are attributed to witches or sorcerers. Marwick, in his study of the Chewa, investigated 194 cases of serious misfortune and found that a quarter were regarded as acts of God and 55 percent were blamed on sorcerers.[16] Other possible causes of misfortune included an "ancestor" displeased because of neglect. (In a matrilineage, this could be, for instance, a mother's brother.) Ritual or other infringements could prove mortal, not to the offender but to an innocent victim.[17]

In the 1930s, Richards made a very similar list, writing of the Chewa's neighbors, the Bemba (introduced in chapter 19). In their matrilineal organization and their girls' initiations, the two peoples have much in common. Bemba explanations of misfortune included the angry "ancestor," who, in the case of a ruler, may affect the whole land, and the ritual trespasses. Misfortune might be due to a curse or to the avenging ghost of someone who died in unhappy circumstances, neglected or unfairly accused.[18]

Among the Yoruba, misfortune often meant that a divinity was calling the afflicted one to his or her service—divination would reveal this. As we have seen, both Yoruba and Igbo had a concept of personal destiny, chosen before birth (*ori* among the Yoruba, *chi* among the Igbo). Divination and sacrifice could improve this, but not radically change it. In both cultures, misfortune could be caused by a curse or by a ritual trespass. The Igbo believed that someone denied the correct burial rites, because of crimes or a state of ritual impurity, would live on as a lost, malicious spirit, much like its Bemba counterpart.

The expansion of witchcraft beliefs can partly be attributed, paradoxically enough, to the decline of "traditional" religion. This emerges clearly from a study of religious change among the Fipa of southern Tanzania (introduced in chapter 20). In precolonial times, they believed in a remote High God, Indeesa (now replaced by the Christian God, Mungu), and in a variety of nature divinities, each linked with a landmark, such as a lake or mountain, and also in the ongoing power of ancestors to aid or harm. By the 1960s, the cults of nature divinities and of ancestors had apparently disappeared, together with the practice of divination. Witchcraft, which had been one of a number of alternative explanations for misfortune, was left as the only explanation, apart from a new range of harmful spirits that caused disease or insanity. Since witchcraft accusations and ordeals had long been illegal, they took the form of diffused suspicions, sometimes expressed as the fear of poisoning.[19]

CONTROLLING WITCHCRAFT

In precolonial societies, witchcraft was regarded as the greatest of crimes, and often was dealt with at the local level by male masking cults or by individual accusations and ordeals, which frequently took the form of the consumption of poison—the innocent vomited and survived. Knowing that they were not witches, many took the poison willingly. A 1988 ethnographic film on the life of the Baka, hunter-gatherers of the Cameroon rain forests, tells the story of a man accused of sorcery who seeks to prove his innocence by consuming poison, "the truth drug."[20]

In precolonial kingdoms, it was sometimes the ruler who administered ordeals. The loss of this role was one of many factors that eroded rulers' mystique and power.

In colonial times, the poison ordeal was outlawed, and it became a crime to accuse someone of being a witch. There is much evidence from many parts of Africa of a widespread perception that witchcraft, freed from these restraints, had expanded uncontrollably. Sometimes the colonial official was seen as the friend and protector of witches. In Chewa imagery, he provided salt for the sorcerer's meal of human flesh:

> Long ago there were hardly any sorcerers, and you could not find the path to the graveyard, but today it looks like a well trodden road; and this is because of the Europeans. . . . [A]ll they do is give the sorcerer a bag of salt with which to eat his "relish."[21]

Witchcraft is essentially a discourse on inequality; it expresses, in symbolic and elliptical form, a view of the world as a zero-sum game. There is a limited amount of wealth—and other, less tangible goods—in the world, so anyone who has more than his or her share has acquired it at the cost of others. The same view is expressed in a LoDagaa (northern Ghana) account of the life to come, where a rich man suffers for three years, the same period as a witch.[22] In the colonial period, social and economic inequality reached new dimensions, and in turn were dwarfed by the power and opulence of the Big Men of the postcolonial period. The fear of being thought a witch sometimes initially discouraged people from acquiring or spending wealth. In southern Ghana, in the 1950s, it was said:

> It is only since Tingari [anti-witchcraft shrines] and the other protectors came that the rich men in Akwapim have dared to show their riches by building big houses.[23]

WITCHCRAFT ERADICATION: MCHAPE

One response to this dilemma was the widespread creation of movements that sought to eradicate the condition of witchcraft and make its recurrence impossible. Typically, these were movements of young men and women who wore Western dress and used objects such as mirrors and pharmaceutical bottles. They charged fees for their services and were successful entrepreneurs, supplying a commodity that was greatly desired: freedom from witchcraft. Since the evils it was thought to cause did not go away, witchcraft eradication tended to be a recurring phenomenon. Movements as diverse as Maji Maji, Mumbo, and the Lord's Resistance Army also had a strong millennial element. They sought to expel the forces of evil and their various manifestations, such as death, disease, and hunger, and thereby usher in a new age of abundance and happiness.

Mchape ("washing") seems to have originated in Malawi in the 1930s, and spread first to Zambia and then to Zimbabwe, southern Tanzania, and Congo. Its leaders wore Western clothing and worked in the name of a dead and resurrected Malawian called Kamwende. They retailed both protective charms and a drink thought to kill anyone who reverted to witchcraft, which those who feared such accusations welcomed. They said that its power came from the supreme God, Lesa.

Those accused of witchcraft—discerned by the use of mirrors—were told to bring out their evil paraphernalia, and duly gave up the animal horns that were used as receptacles for herbal or magical preparations. Richards, who was living among the Bemba at the time (1934), made a study of 135 of these surrendered horns, and found that only eleven contained substances intended to injure others—the rest were healing remedies or protective charms.[24] Over the next three decades, a series of similar movements followed.[25]

MWANA LESA

Tomo Nyirenda, a Henga from northern Malawi, was a Livingstonia graduate. Like many others, he settled in Zambia. In 1925, he was converted to Watch Tower and became a highly successful preacher, declaring that the end of the world was at hand and that all, including witches, should repent. Among the Lala, western neighbors of the Zambian Chewa, he turned from converting witches to detecting them and then to killing them. He was acclaimed as Mwana Lesa, Son of God. He was captured by the colonial government, and early in 1926 he was tried and executed.

Lipereto came to Mwana Lesa hoping to become a Watch Tower preacher, but was accused of witchcraft and was killed. The pathos of the encounter speaks to us some eighty years later:

> Tomo said to him, "You have come, Lipereto? Today you are going to die." Lipereto said, "All right, if I am a wizard I must die. . . . I have a little horn of jealousy."[26]

WITCHCRAFT ERADICATION: ATINGA

In 1950, a witchcraft eradication movement called Atinga, coming ultimately from the Tingare shrines of Ghana, reached the western borders of the Yoruba culture sphere. Again, the ritual specialists were young people of both sexes, and the victims old women. Older men paid the costs of introducing Atinga—they demanded a substantial initial donation—and reaped some of the financial benefits, another version of witchcraft eradication as capitalist enterprise. Protective medicine was sold, and witches were pointed out by Atinga dancers while in a trance state. The accused could either confess or pay for a test in which a fowl was killed, and guilt or innocence was established by the position in which it ended up. If guilt was established, a cleansing ceremony was required, again at considerable expense. Since no appeal was made to traditional divinities, Christians and Muslims felt able to take part.

Like the dying words of Liporeto, the "confessions" of these old women are eloquent in their pathos:

> A decrepit old woman. . . . All her children were dead. She had never been called a witch before but supposed that as Atinga had caught her, she must have been. . . . She had never owned any bad medicine nor used sorcery against anyone. She had brought her *orisa* [divinities] when she was told to bring her witchcraft properties.[27]

One of the gods whose image she surrended was Orisa Oko, a cult that she had inherited from her mother. As we have seen, this farm god was worshiped by women because of his anti-witchcraft shrine! Those accused in Zambia had produced medicine horns. Those accused in western Nigeria, not knowing what else to do, brought their images of "traditional" gods.

Atinga was initially very popular, and then faded away. It is noteworthy that witchcraft eradication movements in general made no attempt to establish a permanent presence and organization.

CHANGING FORMS OF WITCHCRAFT BELIEF

In popular consciousness, in the course of the twentieth century, ancient stereotypes of the witch were reinvented and took on a life of their own. The idea of the witch as an astral cannibal was a powerful metaphor for the perceived rapacity and violence of the colonial and postcolonial state. The witch feeds on the life force of others to prolong her own existence. Africa's Big Men, who piled up fortunes in Swiss bank accounts, consumed the funds that might otherwise have built schools or hospitals or financed agricultural development. The poor were robbed of resources they needed to survive. The exceptionally long lives of those heads of state who managed to stay in power contrast with the falling life expectancies of their subjects and the high rate of infant mortality. To see the state as cannibal, or as an embodiment of witchcraft, is a "true fiction."[28] Eating is a persistent metaphor for the misappropriation of resources. East Africans call bribes *chai* (tea). Nigerians speak of chopping [pidgin for "eating"] bribes or dividing the national cake.

In eastern Africa, in the colonial period and later, the astral cannibalism of the witch was elaborated, in popular rumor, into elaborate fantasies of vampirism. Often it was the employees of the colonial state—firemen in Nairobi, game wardens in Zambia—who were thought to kidnap people and drain their blood for the benefit of colonial Europeans. On source suggests that the blood was made into pills to prolong their life in the tropics. These rumors were often applied to African Big Men as well. In Kenya, there were stories of red vehicles plying the highway; their occupants kidnapped solitary people and drained their blood for the benefit of wealthy African vampires.[29]

In independent West Africa, witchcraft images have often mutated into urban rumors of blood or money magic that figure regularly in respected newspapers. Victims, often women and children, are thought to be kidnapped and murdered for body parts used in money-making magic.[30] A number of novels deal with this theme—like a contemporary Faust, the perpetrator does not live to be old. These are morality fables, emphasizing that disaster befalls those who seek money at the cost of people.[31]

In studying the changing role of the diviner, I noted the way in which Big Men often surround themselves with ritual specialists. Oppressive rulers are often identified with witchcraft. In the early 1990s, Mobutu's forces were called *les hibous* (owls).[32]

In Equatorial Guinea, the appalling regime of Macias Nguema, its dictator from 1968 to 1979, rested on terror—he killed perhaps a sixth of the population and deliberately built up a reputation for occult power. Toward the end of his regime, Christian services were forbidden and he claimed to be a shape-shifter. After his overthrow, local troops refused to carry out his death sentence, and he was shot by Moroccan guards.

The poor believe that Big Men surround themselves with occult forces. Elite individuals often fear witchcraft at a village level, as emanating from the frustrations and jealousy of the poor. In some cases, including eastern Cameroon, witches have been tried in state courts, and diviners called in as expert witnesses.[33]

CONCLUSION

The quest for healing, the need for a livelihood, and the longing for children are universal. People everywhere ask themselves why, in the words of a famous book on the subject, bad things happen to good people. Many Africans live in adverse ecological environments; they look to ritual to save them from famines, epidemics, or murderous droughts because there seem to be no other forms of protection available.

Neotraditional religion is, as we have seen, insistently this-worldly. The devotee looks for answers to prayer in this life, not for compensation in a life to come. Myth reflects the belief that sickness and death are the result of an act of disobedience in the world of "once upon a time." Misfortune is not part of the natural order of things. If sacrifice and ritual fail, the devotee has several options, which may include a quest for protection against the imagined malice of the witch. I say "imagined" because despite my respect for the writings of those who think somewhat differently, I believe that the malice of the witch is always imagined, a classic instance of religion as false consciousness.

Throughout my life, I have read a great deal of poetry. Remembered fragments weave their way through my thoughts, and when I write of the shadow side of African life, a line from *Othello* is never far from my mind:

Speak of me as I am, nothing extenuate, nor set down aught in malice.

When I think of the state of Africa in general, I think of another line from Shakespeare, though it is perhaps less a description than an aspiration:

But I tell you, my lord fool, out of this nettle, danger, we pluck this flower, safety.

Notes

CHAPTER 1

1. C. Levi, *Christ Stopped at Eboli* (1947), pp. 116–117, cited in A.K. Bowman, *Egypt after the Pharaohs* (Berkeley: University of California Press, 1986), p.185.

2. E.S. Miller, "The Christian Missionary: Agent of Secularisation," *Missiology: An International Review* 1, (1973): 106.

3. J. Janzen, *Lemba 1650–1930: A Drum of Affliction in Africa and the New World* (New York and London: Garland, 1982).

4. P. Gilroy, *The Black Atlantic: Modernity and Double Consciousness* (London: Verso 1993).

5. K.M. Brown, *Mama Lola: A Vodou Priestess in Brooklyn* (Berkeley: University of California Press, 1991).

6. Quoted in N. Bhebe, *Christianity and Traditional Religion in Western Zimbabwe 1859–1923* (London: Longman, 1979), p. 53.

7. R. Horton, "A Hundred Years of Change in Kalabari Religion," in J. Middleton, ed., *Black Africa: Its Peoples and Their Culture Today* (London: Macmillan-Collier, 1970), 195.

8. H.M. Waddell, *Twenty Nine Years in the West Indies and Central Africa* (London: 1863; 2nd ed., London: Frank Cass, 1970), p. 469.

9. R. Horton, "African Traditional Thought and Western Science," *Africa* 37 (1967): 50–71.

10. J. Goody, *The Myth of the Bagre* (Oxford, U.K.: Clarendon Press, 1972), p. 290.

11. R. Horton, "On the Rationality of Conversion," *Africa* 45 (1975): 219–235.

12. O. p'Bitek, *African Religion in Western Scholarship* (Kampala: East Africa Publishing House, 1970). It is important to note that although the "Christian spectacles" approach has been largely abandoned, Idowu's books on Yoruba religion, for instance, contain much excellent information, written as they are by a member of the society studied.

13. E.B. Idowu, *Olódùmarè: God in Yoruba Belief* (New York: Praeger, 1963), pp. 204 and 101–106.

14. R. Horton, "Judaeo-Christian Spectacles: Boon or Bane to the Study of African Religions?" *Cahiers d'Études africaines* 96 *(1984)*: 391–436.

15. J.W. Burton, "Answers and Questions: Evans-Pritchard on Nuer Religion," *Journal of Religion in Africa* 14 (1983): 168.

16. L. Brenner, "Religious Discourses in and about Africa," in K. Barber and P.F. de Moraes Farias, eds., *Discourse and Its Disguises, The Interpretation of African Oral Texts* (Birmingham, U.K.: Birmingham University, African Studies Centre, 1989), pp. 87–103.

17. R. Bagnall, *Egypt in Late Antiquity* (Princeton, N.J.: Princeton University Press, 1993), p. 261.

18. S. Hutchinson, *Nuer Dilemmas: Coping with Money, War and the State* (Berkeley: University of California Press, 1996), p. 31.

19. With the spread of Western education, the reverse is sometimes true. Villagers may avidly study books about their own history and culture, which may then become the raw material of "oral tradition." My own books and articles are much studied in Asaba, and elsewhere in Igboland, so that a contemporary collector of oral tradition may well be reading the *Journal of African History*, at one remove!

20. V. Turner, *The Forest of Symbols* (Ithaca, N.Y.: Cornell University Press, 1967), pp. 19–27.

21. M. Douglas, *Purity and Danger* (London: Routledge, 1966), pp. 173–174.

22. The most readily accessible English version of his work, apart from summaries in secondary works by others, is M. Griaule and G. Dieterlen, "The Dogon," in D. Forde, ed., *African Worlds* (London: Oxford University Press, 1954). M. Griaule, *Conversations with Ogotemmêli* (first published as *Dieu d'Eau: Entretiens avec Ogotemmêli*, 1948; London: Oxford University Press, 1965), is an account of an extended series of conversations with a blind elder.

23. The first edition of B. Ray, *African Religions: Symbol, Ritual and Community* (Englewood Cliffs, N.J.: Prentice-Hall, 1976), devotes eight pages to Griaule's version of the Dogon creation myth (pp. 24–32). It is omitted in the 2nd ed. (2000).

24. T. Robbins, *Half Asleep in Frog Pajamas* (Harpenden, U.K.: No Exit, 2002).

25. W.E.A. van Beek et al., "Dogon Restudied: A Field Evaluation of the Work of Marcel Griaule," *Current Anthropology* 32 (1991): 139. His fieldwork extended over eleven years, and his findings were confirmed by others who had done extended fieldwork among the Dogon. (Responses by J. Bouju, pp. 159–160 and P. Lane, pp. 162–163.)

26. W. Abimbola, *Ifa: An Exposition of Ifa Literary Corpus* (Ibadan, Nigeria: Oxford University Press, 1976).

27. S. Bockie, *Death and the Invisible Powers: The World of Kongo Belief* (Bloomington: Indiana University Press, 1993).

28. All published by the University of Uppsala, Sweden.

29. F. Kramer, *The Red Fez*, trans. M.R. Green (London and New York: Verso, 1993; first published as *Der rote Fes* [Frankfurt am Main, Athenäum Verlag, 1987]).

30. There was also some interaction with Berber peoples living further west, for instance, in Cyrenaica.

31. J. Kamil, *Christianity in the Land of the Pharaohs: The Coptic Orthodox Church* (London: Routledge, 2002), p. 199.

32. Quoted in in A.K. Bowman, *Egypt after the Pharaohs* (Berkeley: University of California Press, 1986), p. 187.

CHAPTER 2

1. Quoted in J. Taylor and D. Lehmann, *Christians of the Copperbelt* (London: SCM Press, 1961), p. 167. For a discussion of some of the abundant literature on the early church in Northern Africa, see the Guide to Further Reading.

2. The biblical references are Isaiah 11:11 and 18:1 (Cush is Nubia, on the Upper Nile); Jeremiah 44; Mark 15:21; Acts 2:5–10, 11:20, 13:1, and 18:24.

3. A recent study questions "gnosticism" as a category. M. Williams, *Rethinking Gnosticism: An Argument for Dismantling a Dubious Category* (Princeton, N.J.: Princeton University Press, 1996).

4. Monoimus, quoted in E. Pagels, *The Gnostic Gospels* (Harmondsworth, U.K.: Penguin, 1982), p. 18.

5. Clement, *Stromateis*, 1.5.28, quoted in W.H.C. Frend, "The Christian Period in Mediterranean Africa," *Cambridge History of Africa*, vol. 2 (Cambridge, U.K.: Cambridge University Press, 1978), p. 416.

6. Gregory of Nyssa, quoted in W.H.C. Frend, *The Rise of Christianity* (London: Darton, Longman and Todd, 1984), p. 636.

7. Tertullian, *Apology*, 40, 2.

8. Some of the Thomas Christians of South India were affiliated to the Jacobite Syrian church.

9. This comes from an extremely obscure source that gives texts and translations of Old Nubian documents preserved in Berlin. F.L. Griffith, *The Nubian Texts of the Christian Period* (Berlin: Königl. Akademie der Wissenschaften, 1913), p. 49.

10. A.F. Walls, *The Cross-Cultural Process in Christian History* (Maryknoll, N.Y.: Orbis, 2002), pp. 30–32, 46.

CHAPTER 3

1. Jalal al-Din al-Suyuti, *Al Jami'al al Saghir*, quoted in M. Ruthven, *Islam in the World* (Harmondsworth, U.K.: Penguin, 1984), p. 157. For the abundant source material on the subject of this chapter, see the Guide to Further Reading.

2. C. Geertz, *Islam Observed: Religious Development in Morocco and Indonesia* (New Haven, Conn.: Yale University Press, 1968), p. 46.

3. A. Ehrenkreutz, *Saladin* (Albany: State University of New York Press, 1972).

4. Al-Zuhri, in N. Levtzion and J.F.P. Hopkins, eds., *Corpus of Early Arabic Sources for West African History* (Cambridge, U.K., Cambridge University Press: 1981), p. 99.

5. Ibn Khaldun, in ibid., p. 331.

6. The one exception is Christian Georgia, which had Turkish slave soldiers.

7. A. Abdul Rahman (pseud. Bint el Shat'e), paraphrased in R. Marcotte, "The Islamic Concept of Women's Emacipation: A Quranic Exegesis of Bint a el Shat'e," paper delivered at the conference of the Australia and New Zealand African Studies Association, Macquarie University, Sydney, Australia, 2002.

CHAPTER 4

1. M. Bello, *Infaq al-Maysur*, trans. E. J. Arnett as *The Rise of the Sokoto Fulani* (Kano: 1922), p. 10. The notes to this chapter refer mainly to primary sources. For secondary sources, see the Guide to Further Reading.

2. Al-Hamdani (d. 945), in N. Levtzion and J.F.P. Hopkins, eds., *Corpus of Early Arabic Sources for West African History* (Cambridge, U.K.: Cambridge University Press, 1981) [henceforth, *Corpus*], p. 29. This invaluable volume makes many of the primary sources readily available.

3. Al-Bakri (d. 1094), in *Corpus*, p. 79.

4. Al-Zuhri (1137–1154), in *Corpus*, p. 98. "Koran" is an older and now disused spelling.

5. D. Conrad and H. Fisher, "The Conqest That Never Was: Ghana and the Almoravids, 1076," *History in Africa* 9 (1982): 21–59.

6. Al-Bakri, in *Corpus*, p. 77.

7. Ibid., pp. 82–83.

8. Ibid., p. 87.

9. Yaqut (1179–1229), in *Corpus*, p. 171.

10. His praise song, translated from Kanuri, is extracted in T. Hodgkin, *Nigerian Perspectives*, 2nd ed. (London: Oxford University Press, 1975), p. 90.

11. The text of the Kano Chronicle can be read in translation in H.R. Palmer, *Sudanese Memoirs* (London: Cass, 1967) pp. 97–132.

12. Ibn Battuta (1304–1368), in *Corpus*, p. 171.

13. Quoted in L. Brenner, "Concepts of Tariqa in West Africa," in D.B. Cruise O'Brien and C. Coulon, eds., *Charisma and Brotherhood in African Islam* (Oxford, U.K.: Clarendon Press, 1988), p. 39.

14. A.A. Batran, "The Kunta, Sidi al-Mukhtar al-Kunti . . . ," in J.R. Willis, ed., *Studies in West African Islamic History*, vol. 1, *The Cultivators of Islam* (London: Cass, 1979); there is a good summary in M. Hiskett, *The Development of Islam in Africa* (Harlow, U.K.: Longman, 1984), pp. 49–51.

15. Quted in D. Robinson, *The Holy War of Umar Tal* (Oxford, U.K.: Clarendon Press, 1985), p. 44.

16. Quoted in D. Robinson, *Chiefs and Clerics: The History of Abdul Bokar Kan and Futa Toro 1853–1891* (Oxford, U.K.: Clarendon Press, 1975), p. 13.

17. *Corpus*, p. 82. For the link of "Banu Naghmarata" with "Wangara," see p. 453.

18. Bello, *Rise of the Sokoto Fulani,*. 3.

19. This theory, called the Hamitic hypothesis, was demolished by, among others, A. Smith, "Some Considerations Relating to the Formation of States in Hausaland," *Journal of the Historical Society of Nigeria* 5 (1970): 329–346.

20. An anonymous text from the end of the tenth or beginning of the eleventh century, in *Corpus*, p. 37.

21. G.S.P. Freeman-Greville, *The East African Coast: Select Documents*, 2nd ed. (London: Rex Collings, 1975), p. 16.

22. Ibid., p. 31.

23. J. Knappert, *Four Centuries of Swahili Verse* (London: Heinemann, 1979), p. 132.

24. G. Shepperson,"The Jumbe of Kota Kota and Some Aspects of the History of Islam in British Central Africa," in I.M. Lewis, ed., *Islam in Tropical Africa* (London: Oxford University Press, 1966), p. 195.

CHAPTER 5

1. J. Hunwick, ed. and trans., *Shari'a in Songhay: The Replies of Al-Maghili . . .* (London: Oxford University Press, 1985), pp. 66–67.

2. E.W. Bovill, ed., *Missions to the Niger,* vol. 2 (Cambridge, U.K.: Cambridge University Press, 1966); Denham's narrative is on p. 478. This passage dates from 1827.

3. J. Greenberg, *The Influence of Islam on a Sudanese Religion* (New York: Augustin, 1946).

4. Quoted in J. Lavers, "Islam in the Bornu Caliphate: A Survey," *Odu* 5 (1971): 21. *Borno* is now the standard spelling.

5. Quoted in B. Barry, "The Subordination of Power and the Mercantile Economy," in R. Cruise O'Brien, ed., *The Political Economy of Underdevelopment: Dependence in Senegal* (Beverly Hills, Calif.: Sage, 1979), pp. 49–50.

6. M. Gomez, *Pragmatism in the Age of Jihad: The Precolonial State of Bundu* (Cambridge, U.K.: Cambridge University Press, 1992).

7. J. Iliffe, *Africans: The History of a Continent* (Cambridge, U.K.: Cambridge University Press, 1995), p. 169.

8. A poem written by Uthman at age twenty, in M. Hiskett, *The Sword of Truth* (London: Oxford University Press, 1973), p. 33.

9. Uthman dan Fodio, in T. Hodgkin, *Nigerian Perspectives*, 2nd ed. (London: Oxford University Press, 1975), p. 249.

10. Ibid., p. 254.

11. B. Mack and J. Boyd, *One Woman's Jihad: Nana Asma'u, Scholar and Scribe* (Bloomington: Indiana University Press, 2000.

12. Muhammad Bello on his father, quoted in Hiskett, *The Sword of Truth*, p. 57.

13. Al Kanemi in Hodgkin, *Nigerian Perspectives*, p. 262.

14. Quoted in Hiskett, *The Sword of Truth*, p. 155.

15. S. Crowther, *Journal of an Expedition up the Niger and Tshadda Rivers . . . in 1854* (1854; 2nd ed., London: Cass, 1970), pp. 157–158.

16. Aliyu, emir of Kano, to *waziri* of Sokoto, in D.J. Muffett, *Concerning Brave Captains* (London: Deutsch, 1964), p. 96.

17. R. Adeleye, "The Dilemma of the Wazir . . . ," *Journal of the Historical Society of Nigeria* 4 (1968): 285–311.

18. There are several versions of his name: Ahmadu (or Hamad), Lobbo, Bari, or Cissé.

19. L. Brenner, *West African Sufi* (Berkeley: University of California Press, 1984), p. 19.

20. Quoted in R.L. Roberts, *Warriors, Merchants, and Slaves: The State and the Economy in the Middle Niger Valley* (Stanford, Calif.: Stanford University Press, 1987), p. 134.

21. H. Barth, quoted in M. Hiskett, *The Development of Islam in West Africa* (London and New York: Longman, 1984), p. 207.

22. L. Sanneh, "Translatability in Islam & in Christianity in Africa . . . ," in T. Blakely et al., eds., *Religion in Africa: Experience and Expression* (London: James Currey, 1994), p. 25. Sanneh was born into a Muslim scholar family but became a Christian when young. He has published extensively on the translation of Muslim and Christian sacred texts.

CHAPTER 6

1. R. Mitchell, *The Society of the Muslim Brothers* (London: Oxford University Press, 1969), p. 229.

2. In the words of a biography of the Mahdi written by one of his followers, quoted here from G.R. Warburg, *Historical Discord in the Nile Valley* (Evanston, Ill.: Northwestern University Press, 1992), p. 43.

3. Quoted in B. Lewis, *The Middle East and the West* (London: Weidenfeld and Nicolson, 1968), p. 33.

4. Ahmad ibn Khalid al-Nasiri, quoted in E. Burke, *Prelude to Protectorate in Morocco* (Chicago: University of Chicago Press, 1976), p. xi.

5. Quoted in T. Mitchell, *Colonising Egypt* (Cambridge, U.K.: Cambridge University Press, 1988), p. 169.

6. Quoted in S.V.R. Nasr, "European Colonialism and the Emergence of Modern Muslim States," in J.L. Esposito, ed., *The Oxford History of Islam* (Oxford, U.K.: Oxford University Press, 1999), p. 563.

7. A. Hourani, *Arabic Thought in the Liberal Age*, 1798–1939 (London: Oxford University Press, 1962), pp. 69, 81. He lived in Paris from 1826 to 1831.

8. Ahmad ibn Khalid al-Nasiri, quoted in Burke, *Prelude to Protectorate in Morocco*, p. 38.

9. Quoted in M. Hiskett, *The Sword of Truth* (London: Oxford University Press, 1973), pp. 164–165.

10. P. von Sivers, "Egypt and North Africa," in N. Levtzion and R. Pouwels, eds., *The History of Islam in Africa* (Athens: Ohio University Press, 2000), p. 31.

11. J. Clancy Smith, "The House of Zainab: Female Authority and Saintly Succession in Colonial Morocco," in N.R. Keddie and B. Baron, eds., *Women in Middle Eastern History: Shifting Boundaries in Sex and Gender* (New Haven, Conn.: Yale University Press, 1991), pp. 254ff.

12. Quoted in J. Clancy Smith, "In the Eye of the Beholder: Sufi and Saint in North Africa . . . 1830–1900," *Africana Journal* 15 (1990): 240.

13. K.S. Vikor, *Sufi and Scholar on the Desert Edge* (Evanston, Ill.: Northwestern University Press, 1995).

14. T. Mitchell, *Colonising Egypt*, p. 42.

15. Quoted in Lewis, p. 46.

16. J. Iliffe, *Africans: The History of a Continent* (Cambridge, U.K.: Cambridge University Press, 1995), p. 164.

17. Quoted in Hourani, *Arabic Thought in the Liberal Age*, p. 226.

18. Quoted in ibid., p. 168; on Abduh, see pp. 130–160.

19. D. Porch, *The Conquest of Morocco* (New York: Knopf, 1983), p. 298.

CHAPTER 7

1. Quoted in C.R. Pennell, *A Country with a Government and a Flag* (Wisbech, U.K.: Middle East and North African Studies Press, 1986), p. 230.

2. There is a considerable literature on the Sayyid, some of it written during the period of Africanist historiography that celebrated resistance. See R. Hess, "The Poor Man of God," in N. Bennett, ed., *Leadership in East Africa* (Boston: Boston University Press, 1968), pp. 63–108; and B. Martin, *Muslim Brotherhoods in the Nine-*

teenth Century (Cambridge, U.K.: Cambridge University Press, 1976), pp. 177–201. The best account is S. Samatar, *Oral Poetry and Somali Nationalism: The Case of Sayyid Muhammad 'Abdille Hasan* (Cambridge, U.K.: Cambridge University Press, 1982).

3. Quoted in Hess, "The Poor Man of God," p. 107; the Khayr were a clerical clan who left the Sayyid and joined his enemies.

4. R. A. Dunbar, "Muslim Women in African History," in N. Levtzion and R. Pouwels, eds., *The History of Islam in Africa* (Athens: Ohio University Press, 2000), p. 404.

5. Pennell, *A Country with a Government and a Flag*, p. 75. This book is my main source for the account that follows.

6. Liberia was never colonized; Ethiopia was invaded by Italian forces in 1935, and the Italians were expelled in 1942.

7. A. Goldschmidt, Jr., *A Concise History of the Middle East*, 7th ed. (Boulder, Colo.: Westview Press, 2002), p. 244.

8. A. Hourani, *Arabic Thought in the Liberal Age, 1798–1939* (London: Oxford University Press, 1962), p. 330.

9. L.C. Brown, "The Role of Islam in Modern North Africa," in L.C. Brown, ed., *State and Society in Independent North Africa* (Washington, D.C.: Middle East Institute, 1966), p. 106.

10. Quoted in T. Hodges, *Western Sahara: The Roots of a Desert War* (Westport, Conn.: Lawrence Hill, 1983), p. 85.

11. Recorded in nineteenth-century Morocco, and quoted in Brown, "The Role of Islam," p. 100.

12. R. Mitchell, *The Society of the Muslim Brothers* (London: Oxford University Press, 1969), p. 30.

13. G.N. Sanderson, "The Nile Basin and the Eastern Horn, 1870–1908," in *The Cambridge History of Africa*, vol. 6, *From 1870 to 1905*, R. Oliver and G.N. Sanderson, eds. (Cambridge, U.K.: Cambridge University Press, 1985), p. 630.

14. Brown, "The Role of Islam," p. 110.

15. Marcel Carret, "Souvenirs," in M. Lings, *A Sufi Saint of the Twentieth Century, Shaikh Ahmad al-'Alawi* (Berkeley: University of California Press, 1961; 2nd ed., 1971), pp. 13–33, see 29.

16. Ibid., p. 20.

CHAPTER 8

1. Al-Kanemi, in T. Hodgkin, *Nigerian Perspectives*, 2nd ed. (London: Oxford University Press, 1975), p. 263. The original uses the older spelling, Bornu.

2. In the case of Egypt, the starting point for this chapter is the army coup of 1952.

3. J.L. Esposito, *The Islamic Threat: Myth or Reality?*, 3rd ed. (Oxford, U.K.: Oxford University Press, 1999), pp. 58–59.

4. L.C. Brown, "The Role of Islam in Modern North Africa," in L.C. Brown, ed., *State and Society in Independent North Africa* (Washington, D.C.: Middle East Institute, 1966), p. 112.

5. Published in a collection of such letters in 1965, and quoted here from M. Ruthven, *Islam in the World* (Harmondsworth, U.K.: Penguin, 1984), p. 143. Al-Shafi'i was the founder of one of Sunni Islam's four schools of law.

6. Quoted in S.J. King, "Economic Reform and Tunisia's Hegemonic Party," in Ali Abdullatif Ahmida, ed., *Beyond Colonialism and Nationalism in the Maghrib* (New York: Palgrave, 2000), p. 187.

7. Lisa Anderson, "Obligation and Accountability: Islamic Politics in North Africa," *Daedalus* 120 (1991): 103; A. Layachi and A. Haireche, "National Development and Political Protest: Islamists in the Maghreb Countries," *Arab Studies Quarterly* (Spring/Summer 1992): 81–82.

8. On this, see the excellent discussion in S.V.R. Nasr, "European Colonialism and the Emergence of Modern Muslim States," in J.L.Esposito, ed., *The Oxford History of Islam* (Oxford, U.K.: Oxford University Press, 1999), pp. 549–600.

9. Quoted in A. Rippin, *Muslims: Their Religious Beliefs and Practices* (London: Routledge, 2001), p. 225.

10. Quoted in Y. Haddad, "Sayyid Qutb: Ideologue of Islamic Revival," in J.L. Esposito, ed., *Voices of Resurgent Islam* (New York and Oxford, U.K.: Oxford University Press, 1983), p. 87.

11. Quoted in ibid., p. 80.

12. Mamun al-Hueibi (b. 1921), in *Al-Majalla*, August 18–24, 1996, trans. Ted Thornton. Available at www.nmhschool.org/thornton/hudevbi.htm.

13. R.S. O'Fahey, "The Past in the Present? The Issue of the Sharia in the Sudan," in H.B. Hansen and M. Twaddle, eds., *Religion and Politics in East Africa: The Period since Independence* (London: James Curry, 1995), pp. 32–33.

14. J.L. Esposito, "Introduction," in J.L. Esposito, ed., *Voices of Resurgent Islam*, p. 11.

15. Marnia Lazreg, "Islamism and the Recolonisation of Algeria," in Ahmida, *Beyond Colonialism and Nationalism in the Maghrib*, p. 148.

16. Gilles Kepel, "Islamism Reconsidered: A Running Dialogue with Modernity," *Harvard International Review* 22 (2000): 22–27.

17. This was after an election, not a coup, but an election in which many reformists were barred from running for office. *The Guardian Weekly*, February 26–March 3, 2004, p. 1.

18. J. Stacher, "Post Islamist Rumblings in Egypt: The Emergence of the Wasat Party," *The Middle East Journal* 56 (2002): 415–432.

19. E.E. Rosander, "Introduction: The Islamization of 'Tradition' and 'Modernity,'" in E.E. Rosander and D. Westerlund, eds., *African Islam and Islam in Africa: Encounters between Sufis and Islamists* (Athens: Ohio University Press, 1997), p. 11.

20. *Osama*, directed by Sidi Barmak (2003). This film won the Golden Globe award for best foreign-language film.

21. Ibn Fartuwa, in Hodgkin, *Nigerian Perspectives*, p. 143.

CHAPTER 9

1. L. Brenner, *West African Sufi* (Berkeley: University of California Press, 1984), p. 1.

2. J.L.Triaud, "Islam in Africa under French Colonial Rule," in N. Levtzion and R.L. Pouwels, eds., *The History of Islam in Africa* (Athens: Ohio University Press, 2000), p. 169.

3. Levtzion and. Pouwels,. *History of Islam in Africa,* chapters 12–16, pp. 251–372. On recent events see especially A. Chaude, "Radicalism and Reform in East Africa," pp. 349–372.

4. M. Hiskett, *The Development of Islam in West Africa* (London: Longman, 1984), p. 281; P. Clarke, *West Africa and Islam* (London: Edward Arnold, 1982), p. 202.

5. I.M. Lewis, ed., *Islam in Tropical Africa* (London: Oxford University Press, 1966), p. 91.

6. W.R. Crocker, *Nigeria: A Critique of British Colonial Administration* (London: Allen and Unwin, 1936), p. 149; S.J. Hogben and A.H.M. Kirk-Greene, *The Emirates of Northern Nigeria* (London: Oxford University Press, 1966), p. 499.

7. Quoted in E.A. Ayandele, *The Missionary Impact on Modern Nigeria 1842–1914* (London: Longman, 1968), p. 149.

8. Hiskett, *The Development of Islam,* p. 124.

9. Quoted in G.O. Gbadamosi, "The Establishment of Western Education among Muslims in Nigeria, 1896–1926," *Journal of the Historical Society of Nigeria* 4 (1967): 114.

10. Quoted in ibid., p. 114, n. 1.

11. From a Hausa poem by Sa'adu Zungur, text and translation in D. Abdulkadir, *The Poetry, Life and Opinions of Sa'adu Zungur* (Zaria, Nigeria: Northern Nigeria, 1974; repr. 1978), p. 97.

12. L. Brenner, ed., "Constructing Muslim Identities in Mali," in *Muslim Identity and Social Change in Sub-Saharan Africa* (Bloomington: Indiana University Press, 1993), pp. 61–62.

13. D.B. Cruise O'Brien, *Saints and Politicians: Essays in the Organisation of Senegalese Peasant Society* (Cambridge, U.K.: Cambridge University Press, 1975), pp. 40–41.

14. For this figure, see ibid., p. 76.

15. Quoted in D.B.C. O'Brien, "Charisma Comes to Town," in D.B.C. O'Brien and C. Coulon, eds., *Charisma and Brotherhood in African Islam* (Oxford, U.K.: Clarendon Press, 1988), p. 149.

16. M. Hiskett, "The 'Community of Grace' and Its Opponents, 'the Rejecters'," *African Language Studies* 17 (1980): 109.

17. J. Paden, *Religion and Political Culture in Kano* (Berkeley: University of California Press, 1973), p. 70.

18. A.R. Mohammed, "The Influence of the Niass Tijaniyya in the Niger–Benue Confluence Area of Nigeria," in Brenner, ed., *Muslim Identity,* pp. 116–118.

19. P. Alexandre, "A West African Islamic Movement: Hamallism in French West Africa," in R.I. Rothberg and A.A. Mazrui, eds., *Protest and Power in Black Africa* (New York: Oxford University Press, 1970), pp. 497–512.

20. R. Otayek, "Muslim Charisma in Burkina Faso," in O'Brien and Coulon, eds., *Charisma and Brotherhood,* pp. 110–111; Alexandre, "A West African Islamic Movement," pp. 508–509.

21. Hausa song, quoted in Hiskett, *The Development of Islam in West Africa,* p. 285.

22. L. Kaba, "Islam in West Africa: Radicalism and the New Ethic of Disagreement," in Levtzion and Pouwels, eds., *History of Islam in Africa,* p. 203.

23. Quoted in Hiskett, "The 'Community of Grace,'" p. 134.

24. A. Gumi, *Where I Stand,* quoted in T. Falola, *Violence in Nigeria* (Rochester, N.Y.: University of Rochester Press, 1998), p. 115. See also R. Loimeier, "Islamic Reform and Political Change: The Example of Abubakar Gumi and the Yan Izala Movement in Northern Nigeria," in E.E. Rosander and D. Westerlund, eds., *African Islam and Islam in Africa* (Athens: Ohio University Press, 1997), pp. 286–307; and M.S. Umar, "Changing Islamic Identity in Nigeria from the 1960s to the 1980s: From Sufism to anti-Sufism," in Brenner, ed., *Muslim Identity,* pp. 154–178.

25. J. Hunwick, "Sub-Saharan Africa and the Wider World of Islam," in Rosander and Westerlund, eds., *African Islam and Islam in Africa,* p. 46.

26. The Aniogulu Tribunal of Inquiry, cited in E. Isichei, "The Maitatsine Risings in Nigeria 1980–85: A Revolt of the Disinherited," *Journal of Religion in Africa* 17 (1987): 194–208. This account is based on this source and on Falola, *Violence in Nigeria,* pp. 137–162.

27. For contrasting viewpoints, see M. Hiskett, "The Maitatsine Riots in Kano, 1980," *Journal of Religion in Africa* 17 (1987): 210–223; P. Lubeck, "Islamic Protest under Semi-Industrial Capitalism: 'Yan Tatsine Explained," *Africa* 55 (1985): 369–389; and A. Christelow, "Religious Protest and Dissent in Northern Nigeria: From Mahdism to Quranic Integralism," *Journal of Muslim Minority Affairs* 6 (1985): 373–390.

28. Kaba, "Islam in West Africa," p. 198.

29. Quoted in ibid., p. 193.

30. Quoted in ibid., p. 197.

31. Mary Smith, trans., *Baba of Karo: A Woman of the Muslim Hausa* (London: Faber, 1954), pp. 118, 131–134.

32. The passage that constitutes one of the three epigraphs of this book comes from his Fulfulde discourses (1933), recorded in French by Amadou Hampate Ba, and quoted in.Brenner, *West African Sufi,* p. 158. The passage on riches is on p. 168.

CHAPTER 10

1. Quoted in R. Gray, *Black Christians and White Missionaries* (New Haven, Conn.: Yale University Press, 1990), p. 54.

2. S. Gobat, *Journal of a Three Years' Residence in Abyssinia,* 2nd ed. (London: Thames Ditton, 1847), pp. 82–83.

3. For a readable account, based on sources in English, of this and other manuscripts preserved in Ethiopia, see E.S. Pankhurst, *Ethiopia: A Cultural History* (Woodford Green, U.K.: Lalibela House, 1955), pp. 201–217. For a more scholarly account, see E. Ullendorff, *Ethiopia and the Bible* (London: Oxford University Press, 1968).

4. Listed in Pankhurst, *Ethiopia,* p. 295.

5. Quoted in Tadesse Tamrat, "Processes of Ethnic Interaction and Integration in Ethiopian History: The Case of the Agaw," *Journal of African History* 29 (1988): 14.

6. R. Beylot, "Estifanos, hétérodoxe éthiopien du xve siècle," *Revue de l'Histoire des Religions* 198 (1981): 281–283; Taddesse Tamrat, "Some Notes on the Fifteenth

Century Stephanite 'Heresy' in the Ethiopian Church," *Rassegna di Studi Etiopici* (Rome) 22 (1966): 110, 111.

7. A. Hastings, *The Church in Africa, 1450–1950* (Oxford, U.K.: Clarendon Press, 1994), pp. 145–146.

8. English text in. Pankhurst, *Ethiopia*, pp. 334–337.

9. J. Lobo, *A Voyage to Abyssinia*, J. Gold, ed., and Samuel Johnson, trans. (New Haven, Conn: Yale University Press, 1985), pp. 53–54.

10. Pankhurst, *Ethiopia*, p. 248.

11. A. Atiya, *A History of Eastern Christianity* (London: Methuen, 1968), pp. 1–145.

12. Mas'udi, extract in J. Kamil, *Christianity in the Land of the Pharaohs: The Coptic Orthodox Church* (London: Routledge, 2002), pp. 237–238.

13. According to B. Sundkler and C. Steed, *A History of the Church in Africa* (Cambridge, U.K.: Cambridge University Press, 2000), p. 17 (no sources given). Atiya, *History of Eastern Christianity*, in a meticulously documented survey (p. 91, n. 1), suggests either forty-five or forty-nine bishops in the eleventh century and sixty-seven in the fourth century.

14. L. Sanneh, "Translatability in Islam & in Christianity in Africa . . . ," in T. Blakely et al., eds., *Religion in Africa: Experience and Expression* (London: J. Currey, 1994), p. 27.

15. Quoted in A.F.C. Ryder, "Missionary Activity in the Kingdom of Warri to the Early Nineteenth Century," *Journal of the Historical Society of Nigeria* 2 (1960): 8.

16. Quoted in ibid., p. 3.

17. J. Adams, *Remarks on the Country Extending from Cape Palmas to the River Congo* (London: Whittaker, 1823; repr. London: Cass, 1966), pp. 124–126.

18. A bishop without a diocese is given a titular see. Henrique's was in Muslim North Africa.

19. Rui d'Aguiar to king of Portugal, May 1516, in G. Balandier, *Daily Life in the Kingdom of the Kongo*, H. Weaver, trans. (London: Allen and Unwin, 1968), pp. 52–53. He adds that he burns traditionalists to death, but there is no other evidence of this.

20. This was at first a proprietary colony, like Virginia.

21. Quoted in G. Bender, *Angola under the Portuguese: The Myth and the Reality* (London: Heinemann, 1978), p. 17.

22. Gray, *Black Christians and White Missionaries*, pp. 11–27.

23. *The Life of Olaudah Equiano*, P. Edwards, ed. (1789; repr. Harlow, U.K.: Longman, 1989), p. 170. It is generally agreed that Equiano wrote this himself— some of his letters survive—but that Cugoano had assistance, possibly from Equiano.

24. J.B. Elliott, *The Lady Huntingdon's Connection in Sierra Leone* (London, 1851), pp. 14–15; extract in C. Fyfe, *Sierra Leone Inheritance* (London: Oxford University Press, 1964), p. 120.

CHAPTER 11

1. Quoted in A.J. Dachs, "Missionary Imperialism: The Case of Bechuanaland," *Journal of African History* 13 (1972): 650–651.

2. The Nestorians differed from both Chalcedonians and Monophysites on Christology. Nestorius, who died in 451, emphasized the difference between Christ's human and divine natures; he said that Mary was the mother of the human Jesus and should not be called Mother of God.

3. D. Livingstone, *A Popular Account of Missionary Travels and Researches* (London: J. Murray, 1875), p. 14.

4. A.M. Falconbridge, *Narrative of Two Voyages to the River Sierra Leone during the Years 1791–1793* (London, 1794; 2nd ed., London: Cass, 1967), pp. 199–200. Horne was a chaplain in Sierra Leone.

5. From a discussion with King William Dappa Pepple of Bonny, in J. Smith, *Trade and Travels in the Gulph of Guinea* (London: Simpkin, Marshall, 1851), pp. 89–95.

6. O. p'Bitek, *African Religions in Western Scholarship* (Nairobi: East African Literature Bureau, 1970), p. 85.

7. *Journals of the Rev. James Frederick Schön and Mr. Samuel Crowther who, with the Sanction of Her Majesty's Government, accompanied the Expedition up the Niger in 1841 on behalf of the Church Missionary Society* (1842; 2nd ed., London: Cass, 1970), p. 48 (Schön's journal, August 26, 1841).

8. D. Livingstone and C. Livingstone, *Narrative of an Expedition to the Zambesi and Its Tributaries* (London: J. Murray, 1865), p. 77.

9. W.H. Bentley, *Pioneering on the Congo,* vol. 1 (London: Religious Tract Society, 1900), p. 194.

10. Quoted in E. Isichei, *The Ibo People and the Europeans* (London: Faber and Faber, 1973), p. 147.

11. Khama in 1879, quoted in A.J. Dachs, "Functional Aspects of Religious Conversion among the Sotho-Tswana," in A.J. Dachs, ed., *Christianity South of the Zambezi,* vol. 2 (Gwelo, Rhodesia: Mambo Press, 1977), p. 156.

12. For more detail on missionaries and the missionary revival, see E. Isichei, *A History of Christianity in Africa* (London: SPCK, 1995), pp. 74–99.

13. There is a rich literature on this subject, including both general books and individual biographies. See W. Williams, *Black Americans and the Evangelization of Africa 1877–1900* (Madison: University of Wisconsin Press, 1982). For an up-to-date bibliography, see D. Killingray, "The Black Atlantic Missionary Movement and Africa, 1780s–1920s," *Journal of Religion in Africa* 33 (2003): 23, n.4 and n.5. The article, on pp. 3–31, is a good summary of the subject.

14. The names are similar and perhaps refer to the same man.

15. H.M. Waddell, *Twenty-nine Years in the West Indies and Central Africa* (1863; 2nd ed., London: Cass, 1970), p. 184.

16. Ibid., p. 208.

17. E. Isichei, ed., "An Obscure Man: Pa Antonio in Lagos," in *Varieties of Christian Experience in Nigeria* (London: Macmillan, 1982), pp. 28–33.

18. G. Prins, *The Hidden Hippopotamus* (Cambridge, U.K.: Cambridge University Press, 1980), p. 201.

19. N. Bhebe, *Christianity and Traditional Religion in Western Zimbabwe 1859–1923* (London: Longman, 1979), p. 30.

20. Ibid., p. 61.

21. W. Colenso, *A Letter to His Grace the Archbishop of Canterbury, upon the Question of the Proper Treatment of Cases of Polygamy,* quoted in J. Guy, *The Her-*

etic: A Study of the Life of John William Colenso 1814—1883 (Johannesburg, South Africa: Ravan Press, and Pietermaritzburg, South Africa: University of Natal Press, 1983), p. 74.

22. N. Etherington, "Mission Station Melting Pots as a Factor in the Rise of South African Black Nationalism," *International Journal of African Historical Studies* 9 (1976): 592–605. The interdenominational sample comprised 177 people in Natal between 1836 and 1885. In addition, 15 percent were joining relatives and 14 percent were drawn by attachment to a missionary.

23. Full text in E. Stock, *The History of the Church Missionary Society . . .*, vol. 2 (London: Church Missionary Society, 1899), p. 105.

24. J.L. Krapf, *Travels, Researches and Missionary Labours* (1860; 2nd ed., London: Cass, 1968), p. 157.

25. R. Oliver, *The Missionary Factor in East Africa* (London: Longman, 1952), p. 184.

26. Quoted in C.P. Groves, *The Planting of Christianity in Africa*, vol. 3 (London: Lutterworth, 1955), p. 157.

27. Public Record Office, London, FO 84/858, Beecroft to Palmerston, April 19, 1851, on a visit eleven years earlier.

28. Bentley, *Pioneering on the Congo*, vol. 1, p. 35.

29. Krapf, *Travels, Researches and Missionary Labours*, p. 122.

30. D. Crummey, *Priests and Politicians: Protestant and Catholic Missions in Orthodox Ethiopia, 1830–1868* (Oxford, U.K.: Clarendon Press, 1972), p. 36.

31. Ibid., p. 46.

32. Ibid., p. 45.

33. For the circumstances surrounding it, see Isichei, *History of Christianity in Africa*, p. 214.

34. H. Watson, *Among the Copts* (Brighton, U.K.: Sussex Academic Press, 2000), p. 8.

CHAPTER 12

1. S. Marks, *Reluctant Rebellion: The 1906–8 Disturbances in Natal* (Oxford, U.K.: Clarendon Press, 1970), p. 357.

2. J.B. Peires, *The House of Phalo: A History of the Xhose People in the Days of Their Independence* (Berkeley: University of California Press, 1982), p. 77.

3. Sechele's brother, Khosilintse, November 22, 1854, in J. Wallis, ed., *The Matabele Journals of Robert Moffat, 1829–1860*, vol. 1 (London: Chatto and Windus, 1945), pp. 377–379.

4. D. Livingstone, *A Popular Account of Missionary Travels and Researches* (London: Murray, 1875), p. 24.

5. R. Moffat, *Missionary Labours and Scenes in Southern Africa* (London: Snow, 1842; New York: Johnson Reprint, 1969), p. 184. The Nama were the Khoi of the Atlantic coast.

6. Peires, *The House of Phalo*, pp. 99ff.

7. From John Knox Bokwe's 1876 translation, in J. Hodgson, *Ntsikana's Great Hymn: A Xhosa Expression of Christianity in the Early 19th Century Eastern Cape* (Cape Town, South Africa: Centre for African Studies, University of Cape Town, 1980), p. 19.

8. J.B. Peires, "Suicide or Genocide? Xhosa Perceptions of the Nongqawuse Catastrophe," *Radical History Review* 46 (1990): 51.

9. C. Bundy, *The Rise and Fall of the South African Peasantry* (London: Heinemann, 1979).

10. P. Landau, *The Realm of the World: Language, Gender and Christianity in a Southern African Kingdom* (Portsmouth, N.H.: Heinemann, 1995), pp. xxvii, 81; the process is documented in chapter 4, pp. 81–112; for cattle herders, see p. 64.

11. L. Thompson, *Survival in Two Worlds: Moshoeshoe of Lesotho, 1786–1870* (Oxford, U.K.: Clarendon Press, 1975), pp. 25, 26. The account that follows comes from this source. Passages quoted subsequently come from pp. 77, 98, and 161.

12. A missionary in 1885, quoted in G. Prins, *The Hidden Hippopotamus* (Cambridge, U.K.: Cambridge University Press, 1980), p. 206.

13. The funds provided by the Lozi king for the venture were entrusted to a South African firm that went bankrupt, but the Barotse National School was founded in 1906.

14. Editorial in the *Sierra Leone Weekly News*, April 8, 1916, quoted in L. Spitzer, "The Sierra Leone Creoles, 1870–1900," in P. Curtin, ed., *Africa & the West* (Madison: University of Wisconsin Press, 1972), p. 100.

15. The title of Miss Tucker's book, *Abeokuta or Sunrise within the Tropics* (London, 1853).

16. E. Isichei, "Christians and Martyrs in Bonny, Ora and Lokoja," in E. Isichei, ed., *Varieties of Christian Experience in Nigeria* (London and Basingstoke: Macmillan, 1982), pp. 63–68.

17. Public Record Office, FO 403/216 (confidential print), "Statement Made by Chiefs after the Meeting of June 10, 1895."

18. I. Schapera, ed., *David Livingstone South African Papers, 1849–1853* (Cape Town: Van Riebeeck Society, 1974), p. 108.

19. C[hurch] M[issionary] S[ociety] Archives, CMS G3A3/1884/20, Crowther to Lang, December 14, 1883.

20. CMS Archives, G3A3/1896/54, Dobinson to Baylis, March 30, 1896.

21. Quoted in B. Sundkler and C. Steed, *A History of the Church in Africa* (Cambridge, U.K.: Cambridge University Press, 2000), p. 424.

22. Quoted in J. de Gruchy, *The Church Struggle in South Africa* (1979; 2nd ed., London: Collins, 1986), pp. 43–44.

23. W. Johnson, "The Africanization of a Mission Church: The African Methodist Episcopal Church in Zambia," in G. Bond et al., eds., *African Christianity: Patterns of Religious Continuity* (New York: Academic Press, 1979), p. 95.

24. Domingo to Booth, 1911, quoted in J. McCracken, *Politics and Christianity in Malawi 1875–1940: The Impact of the Livingstonia Mission in the Northern Province* (Cambridge, U.K.: Cambridge University Press, 1977), p. 216.

25. Quoted in J.D.Y. Peel, *Aladura: A Religious Movement among the Yoruba* (London: Oxford University Press, 1968), p. 296.

26. Bethel was one of the churches founded after the secession from the CMS.

27. Bishop Melville Jones, in 1936, quoted in J.B. Webster, *The African Churches among the Yoruba 1888–1922* (Oxford, U.K.: Clarendon Press, 1964), p. 125.

28. Quoted in A. Omoyajowo, "The Aladura Churches in Nigeria since Independence," in E. Fasholé-Luke et al., *Christianity in Independent Africa* (London: Collings, 1978), p. 110.

CHAPTER 13

1. M. Wilson, *Communal Rituals of the Nyakusa* (London: Oxford University Press, 1959), epigraph.

2. A.F. Walls, "Towards Understanding Africa's Place in Christian History," in J.S. Pobee, ed., *Religion in a Pluralistic Society* (Leiden, Netherlands: Brill, 1976), p. 180.

3. A.F. Walls, *The Cross-Cultural Process in Christian History* (Maryknoll, N.Y.: Orbis, 2002), pp. 63–64.

4. K. Bediako, *Christianity in Africa: The Renewal of a Non-Western Religion* (Edinburgh, Scotland: University of Edinburgh Press, 1995).

5. This figure is constantly cited; it has, however, been pointed out that 12,560 of them are babies born into Christian families. R. T. Coote, "The Numbers Game in World Evangelization," *Evangelical Missions Quarterly* 27 (1991): 121. This article, by an Evangelical, is a most valuable corrective to the "statistics" so easily transferred from publication to publication.

6. *Sunday Times* (London), March 15, 1901, cited in J. Peel, "Gender in Yoruba Religious Change," *Journal of Religion in Africa* 32 (2002): 162, n. 2.

7. A. Hastings, *The Church in Africa 1450–1950* (Oxford, U.K.: Oxford University Press, 1994), p. 420. Walls, *Cross-Cultural Process*, states that no Africans were present. (He informs me that the person mentioned was an African–American.)

8. L. Newbigin, *A Word in Season: Perspectives on Christian World Missions* (Grand Rapids, Mich.: Eerdmans, 1994), p. 98.

9. Quoted in R.W. Strayer, *The Making of Mission Communities in East Africa* (London: Heinemann, 1978), p. 85.

10. An Ewe woman in 1890, cited in B. Meyer, *Translating the Devil: Religion and Modernity among the Ewe in Ghana* (Trenton, N.J.: Africa World Press, 1999), p. 164.

11. M. Nikkel, "Aspects of Contemporary Religious Change among the Dinka," *Journal of Religion in Africa* 22 (1992): 78–94.

12. D. Reeck, *Deep Mende: Religious Interactions in a Changing African Rural Society* (Leiden, Netherlands: Brill, 1976), p. 74.

13. It became Presbyterian because when the Bremen missionaries were interned, Presbyterians from Calabar began to play a limited role among the Ewe.

14. The official report from the Holy Ghost Fathers' mission in eastern Nigeria, for 1892–1894 (French original), quoted in E. Isichei, *Entirely for God: A Life of Michael Iwene Tansi* (1980; 2nd ed., Kalamazoo, Mich.: Cistercian Publications, 1998), p. 12.

15. J.W. Abruquah, *The Catechist* (London: Allen and Unwin, 1965), p. 125.

16. This is available only in French: J. Ki-Zerbo, *Alfred Diban: Premier Chrétien de Haute-Volta* (Paris: Le Cerf, 1983).

17. J. McCracken, *Politics and Christianity in Malawi 1875–1940* (Cambridge, U.K.: Cambridge University Press, 1977), p. 199.

18. T. Beidelman, *Colonial Evangelism: A Socio-Historical Study of an East African Mission at the Grassroots* (Bloomington: Indiana University Press, 1982), p. 68.

19. Holy Ghost Fathers archives, Paris, 191/B/VI, Soul, General Report, August–November 1929. Quoted in Isichei, *Entirely for God*, p. 12.

20. Ngugi wa Thiong'o, *The River Between* (London: Heinemann, 1978), p. 93.

21. Ora oral history, collected by Joseph Eboreime in 1975, in E. Isichei, "Chris-

tians and Martyrs in Bonny, Ora and Lokoja," in E. Isichei, ed., *Varieties of Christian Experience in Nigeria* (London: Macmillan, 1982), p. 75.

22. Quoted in J. Iliffe, *A Modern History of Tanganyika* (Cambridge, U.K.: Cambridge University Press, 1979), p. 224.

23. Filipo Njau, *Aus meinem Leben*, quoted in ibid., p. 225.

24. H. Bley, *South-West Africa under German Rule 1894–1914,* H. Ridley, trans. (London: Heinemann, 1971), p. 143.

25. G. Shepperson and T. Price, *Independent African: John Chilembwe and the Origins, Setting and Significance of the Nyasaland Native Rising of 1915* (Edinburgh, Scotland: Edinburgh University Press, 1958), p. 235.

26. George Mwase's 1932 account, quoted in I. and J. Linden, "John Chilembwe and the New Jerusalem," *Journal of African History* 12 (1971): 632.

27. McCracken, *Politics and Christianity in Malawi*, p. 131.

28. M. Gilbert, "The Cimmerian Darkness of Intrigue: Queen Mothers, Christianity and Truth in Akuapem History," *Journal of Religion in Africa* 23 (1993): 9.

29. I. Linden with J. Linden, *Church and Revolution in Rwanda* (Manchester, U.K.: Manchester University Press, 1977), p. 195. The king was baptized in 1943.

30. A. Hastings, "John Lester Membe," in T. Ranger and J. Weller, eds., *Themes in the Christian History of Central Africa* (London: Heinemann, 1977), p. 187; for Phiri, see p. 183.

31. R. Moore, *Man's Act and God's in Africa* (1940), quoted in R. Gray, "Christianity," in *Cambridge History of Africa*, vol. 7, A.D. Roberts, ed. (Cambridge, U.K.: Cambridge University Press, 1986), p. 178, my source for this paragraph.

32. Byang Kato, *Theological Pitfalls in Africa* (Kisumu, Kenya: Evangel Publishing House, 1975), pp. 180–181.

33. H. Junod, *The Life of a South African Tribe*, 2nd ed. (London: Macmillan, 1927).

34. Archdeacon Walker, quoted in Hastings, *The Church in Africa*, p. 304.

35. Abruquah, *The Catechist*, p. 79; Wole Soyinka, *Ake: The Years of Childhood* (London: Random House, 1981), pp. 11–12.

36. K. Kaunda, *Letter to My Children* (London: Longman, 1973), p. 17.

37. Strayer, *The Making of Mission Communities*, p. 89.

38. The Holiness movement was associated with the Keswick Convention, founded in 1875, and its later offshoot, the Oxford Group, founded by Frank Buchman in 1908, after a transforming religious experience at Keswick. The latter was in turn a formative influence on Alcoholics Anonymous.

39. Josiah Kibira, quoted in Iliffe, *Modern History of Tanganyika*, p. 364.

40. Andrea Kajerero, quoted in ibid., p. 365. "Laodicean" is a reference to Revelation 3:14–22.

41. R. Shorten, "An Anglican Renewal Movement in Relation to Its Zulu Context," *Journal of Theology for Southern Africa* 58 (1987): 34.

42. J. Baur, *2000 Years of Christianity in Africa* (Nairobi: Paulines, 1994), pp. 312–313.

43. A. Hastings, "Were Women a Special Case?", in F. Bowie et al., eds., *Women and Missions Past and Present* (Oxford, U.K.: Berg, 1993), pp. 109–125.

44. Ibid., pp. 114–115.

45. *The African Missionary* (1924): 217.

46. Abruquah, *The Catechist*, p. 71.

47. D. Maxwell, "'Sacred History, Social History': Traditions and Texts in the Making of a Southern African Transnational Religious Movement," *Comparative Studies in Society and History* 43 (2001): 505.

48. bgc.gospelcom.net/emis/1998/cuttingstrings.html.

49. Quoted in J. Burke, "These Catholic Sisters Are All Mamas! Celibacy and the Metaphor of Modernity," in Bowie et al., eds., *Women and Missions*, p. 263.

50. E. Milingo, *The World in Between* (London: Hurst, 1982) p. 73.

51. P. Gifford, "Christian Fundamentalism and Development," *Review of African Political Economy* 52 (1991): 9.

52. Ibid.

53. D. Tutu, *The Voice of One Crying in the Wilderness* (London: Mowbray, 1982), p. 114.

54. J. Ferguson, "De-Moralising Economies: African Socialism, Scientific Capitalism and the Moral Politics of Scientific Adjustment," in S.F. Moore, ed., *Moralising States and the Ethnography of the Present* (Arlington, Va.: American Anthropological Association, 1993), p. 85.

55. Quoted in C. Villa-Vicenzio, "South African Civil Religion: An Introduction," *Journal of Theology for Southern Africa* 19 (1977): 10.

56. Quoted in P. Walshe, "South Africa: Prophetic Christianity and the Liberation Movement," *Journal of Modern African Studies* 29 (1991): 31.

57. A. Luthuli, *Let My People Go* (London: Collins, 1962), p. 46.

58. Ibid., p. 235.

59. R. Elphick and R Davenport, *Christianity in South Africa* (Berkeley: University of California Press, 1997), p. 147.

60. Walshe, "South Africa: Prophetic Christianity," p. 51.

61. J. A. Sampson, *Mandela: The Authorised Biography* (New York: Knopf, 1999), p. 230.

62. J.H. Watson, *Among the Copts* (Brighton, U.K.: Sussex Academic Press, 2000), p. 18. The first chapter of this book, pp. 13–33, is a good source for the monastic revival.

63. Ibid., p. 21.

64. F. Welbourn, *East African Rebels: A Study of Some Independent Churches* (London: S.C.M. Press, 1961). For a more recent account, see S. Hayes, "Orthodox Mission in Tropical Africa," first published in *Missionalia*, www.geocities.com/Athens 7734/orthmiss.htm. Statistics from www.grekorthodox-alexandria.org.

65. J. Peel, "The Christianisation of African Society," in E. Fasholé-Luke et al., eds., *Christianity in Independent Africa* (London: Rex Collings, 1978), pp. 448–449.

66. See, for instance, Newbigin, *A Word in Season*, pp. 115, 125–127.

67. Notably in L. Newbigin, *Foolishness to the Greeks: The Gospel and Western Culture* (London: SPCK, 1986).

68. J. Phillips, "The Mystery of the Seven Murdered Monks," *The Tablet*, May 20, 2000.

CHAPTER 14

1. E. Gunner, *The Man of Heaven and the Beautiful Ones of God* (Leiden, Netherlands: Brill, 2002), p. 8.

2. In some studies, these initials stand for African Independent Churches, African Indigenous Churches, or African Instituted Churches.

3. T. Maluleke, "Theological Interest in AICs and Other Grassroots Communities in South Africa," *Journal of Black Theology in South Africa* 10 (1996): 41.

4. A. Hastings, *The Church in Africa 1450–1950* (Oxford, U.K.: Clarendon Press, 1994), p. 501.

5. J. Lonsdale, in a review of Gunner, *Man of Heaven*, *Journal of Religion in Africa* 33 (2003): 431.

6. R.W. Strayer, *The Making of Mission Communities in East Africa* (London: Heinemann, 1978), p. 86.

7. D. Paulme, "Une Religion Syncrétique en Côte d'Ivoire," *Cahiers d'Études Africaines* 3 (1962): 40–45.

8. Text in C. Irvine, "The Birth of the Kimbanguist Movement in the Bas-Zaire 1921," *Journal of Religion in Africa* 6 (1974): 73–76.

9. M.L. Martin, *An African Prophet and His Church*, D.M. Moore, trans. (Oxford, U.K.: Blackwell, 1975), p. xi. She became the director of their theological training center.

10. Papa Diulangana (1916–2001). He changed the date of Christmas to his own birthday and claimed to be Christ returned.

11. N.H. Ngada et al., *Speaking for Ourselves* (Springs, South Africa: Order of Preachers, 1985), pp. 171–172.

12. J. Comaroff, *Body of Power, Spirit of Resistance* (Chicago: University of Chicago Press, 1985), p. 188.

13. Ibid., p. 200.

14. Arcbishop A. Mhophe, age about ninety, in the early 1980s, in Ngada, *Speaking for Ourselves*, p. 17. Two other Zionist Europeans, Edgar Mahon and Daniel Bryant, also played a formative role in the introduction of Zionism to South Africa.

15. All such figures are well-informed guesstimates, and I have taken them from R. Hoskins's short surveys in C. Partridge, ed., *Encyclopedia of New Religions* (Oxford, U.K.: Lion, 2004). This is also my source for post-Diangienda Kimbanguism and the most recent Shembe developments.

16. Moriah is the hill in Jerusalem where Abraham was willing to sacrifice Isaac.

17. Ngada, *Speaking for Ourselves*, p. 30.

18. B. Sundkler, *Zulu Zion and Some Swazi Zionists* (Gleerups with Oxford University Press, also Studia Missionalia Upsaliensia, 29, 1976) p. 66.

19. Ibid., p. 135.

20. T. Ranger, "Religious Movements and Politics in Sub-Saharan Africa," *African Studies Review* 29 (1986): 23.

21. For a profound reflection on AICs and resistance to the apartheid state, see R. Petersen, "The AICs and the TRC: Resistance Redefined," in J. Cochrane et al., eds., *Facing the Truth . . .* (Athens: Ohio University Press, 1999), pp. 114–125.

22. H. Pretorius and L. Jafta, "A Branch Springs Out: African Initiated Churches," in R. Elphick and R. Davenport, eds., *Christianity in South Africa* (Berkeley: University of California Press, 1997), p. 223.

23. This question is surveyed in J. Thompson, "Shembe Mismanaged? A Study of Varying Interpretations of the Ibandla Lamannazaretha," *Bulletin of the John Rylands Library, University of Manchester* 70 (1988): 185–196. Gunner (*Man of Heaven*, p. 12) points out that six of Shembe's hymns mention Jesus.

24. Sundkler, *Zulu Zion*, p. 198.

25. B. Sundkler and C. Steed, *A History of the Church in Africa* (Cambridge, U.K.: Cambridge University Press, 2000), p. 841.

26. Sundkler, *Zulu Zion*, p. 185.

27. Gunner, *Man of Heaven*.

28. Ibid., p. 79.

29. J. Kiernan, *The Production and Management of Therapeutic Power in Zionist Churches* (Lewiston, N.Y.: Mellen, 1990), p. 44; quoted in Pretorius and Jafta, "A Branch Springs Out," p. 220.

30. Quoted in R.C. Mitchell, "Religious Protest and Social Change: The Origins of the Aladura Movement in Western Nigeria," in R. Rotberg and A. Mazrui, eds., *Protest and Power in Black Africa* (New York: Oxford University Press, 1970), p. 481. This prophet's full name was Moses Orimolade Tunolashe; different sources refer to him as Orimolade or Tunolashe.

31. Isaac Akinyele, in H. Turner, *History of an African Independent Church*, vol. 1 (Oxford, U.K.: Clarendon Press, 1967), pp. 22–23.

32. http://philtar.ucsm.ac.uk/encyclopedia/sub/aladura.html.

33. Interview with Oshoffa in 1980, quoted in J. Olupona, "The Celestial Church of Christ in Ondo: A Phenomenological Perspective," in R. Hackett, ed., *New Religious Movements in Nigeria* (Lewiston, N.Y.: Mellen, 1987) p. 47.

34. The reference is to the People's Temple, a commune founded by Jim Jones in Guyana, which ended in a mass murder/suicide of 900 members in 1978.

35. It began with a woman visionary, Credonia Mwerinde, who received messages from the Virgin Mary. Leadership was taken over by a failed businessman and by a Catholic priest who died in the blaze, Dominic Kataribababo. He had a doctorate in theology and was a former rector of a seminary. C. Onyango-Obbo, "Kanungu Fire: Why Would 500 Be Burnt to Death for a Prostitute?" *The Monitor*, March 22, 2000; Uganda Human Rights Commission Report [on the Kanungu tragedy], 2002.

36. Other churches founded through a split from Catholicism have often been small and ephemeral. They are surveyed in Harold Turner, "African Religious Movements and Roman Catholicism," in *Religious Innovation in Africa* (Boston: Hall, 1979), pp. 147ff.

37. N. Schwartz, "Christianity and the Construction of Global History: The Example of Legio Maria" (based on fieldwork in 1982–1985), in K. Poewe, ed., *Charismatic Christianity as a Global Culture* (Columbia: University of South Carolina Press, 1994), pp. 134, 174. For Aoko's role, see A. Hastings, *A History of African Christianity 1950–1975* (Cambridge, U.K.: Cambridge University Press, 1979), p. 177.

38. J. Fabian, "Jamaa: A Charismatic Movement Revisited," in T.D. Blakely et al., eds., *Religion in Africa: Experience and Expression* (London: James Currey, 1994), pp. 266–274.

39. O. Kalu, "Broken Covenants: Religious Change in Igbo Historiography," *Neue Zeitschrift für Missionswissenschaft* 46 (1990): 307.

40. H Hinfelaar, *Bemba-Speaking Women of Zambia in a Century of Religious Change* (Leiden, Netherlands: Brill, 1994), p. 39.

41. K. Fields, *Revival and Rebellion in Colonial Central Africa* (Princeton, N.J.: Princeton University Press, 1985), p. 7.

42. J.V. Taylor and D. Lehmann, *Christians of the Copperbelt* (London: SCM, 1961), p. 287.

43. C. Perrings, "Consciousness, Conflict and Proletarianisation: An Assessment of the 1935 Mineworkers' Strike on the Northern Rhodesian Copperbelt," *Journal of Southern African Studies* 3 (1977): 50.

44. Fields, *Revival and Rebellion*, pp. 1, 14.

45. K. Wilson, "Cults of Violence and Counter-Violence in Mozambique," *Journal of Southern African Studies* 8 (1992): 558–560.

46. M. Gaiya, "The Pentecostal Revolution in Nigeria," occasional paper of the Centre of African Studies, University of Copenhagen (July 2002), p. 7.

47. *Daily Times* (Lagos), February 16, 1985, p. 11; quoted in F. Mbon, *Brotherhood of the Cross and Star: A New Religious Movement in Nigeria* (Frankfurt, Germany: Lang, 1992), p. 142. This, and Rosemary Goring's account from within, are my major sources. See R. Goring, *Something More Than Gold: A European View of the Brotherhood of the Cross and Star* (Lewes, U.K.: BCS, 1998). Gabriel Amadi, another researcher who joined the movement he was studying, has also published on BCS. G. Amadi, "Healing in the Brotherhood of the Cross and Star," in W. Shiels, ed., *The Church and Healing* (Oxford, U.K.: Blackwell, 1982), pp. 367–383.

48. Mbon, *Brotherhood of the Cross and Star*, p. 80, citing BCS pamphlet literature.

49. Ibid., p. 107.

50. Hymn 68, verse 2, in ibid., p. 117.

51. Hymn 92, verse 3, in ibid.

CHAPTER 15

1. R. Marshall, "'God Is Not a Democrat': Pentecostalism and Democratisation," in P. Gifford, ed., *The Christian Churches and the Democratisation of Africa* (Leiden, Netherlands: Brill, 1995), p. 250.

2. "Charismatic" is often used in Africa, but internationally it refers to Pentecostal movements within older churches (charismatic Anglicans, and so on).

3. A. Anderson and G. Pillay, "The Segregated Spirit: The Pentecostals," in R. Elphick and R. Davenport, eds., *Christianity in South Africa* (Berkeley: University of California Press, 1997), p. 227.

4. P. Pierson, "Non-Western Missions: The Great New Fact of Our Time," in P. Sookhdeo, ed., *New Frontiers in Mission* (Exeter, U.K.: Paternoster Press, 1987), pp. 9–15. The phrase was originally used by the Archbishop of Canterbury in 1942, to refer to the fact that the Christian church had come to exist in some form in almost every country on earth.

5. L. Martz with G. Carroll, *Ministry of Greed: The Inside Story of the Televangelists and Their Holy Wars* (New York: Weidenfeld and Nicolson, 1988).

6. Anderson and Pillay, "The Segregated Spirit," pp. 227–241.

7. P. Gifford, *The Religious Right in Southern Africa* (Harare, Zimbabwe: Baobab, 1988).

8. Gordon Lindsay, "Why the Bible Is the Word of God," quoted in P. Gifford, "'Africa Shall Be Saved': An Appraisal of Reinhard Bonnke's Pan-African Crusade," *Journal of Religion in Africa* 17 (1987): 81.

9. S. Brouwer, P. Gifford, and S. Rose, *Exporting the American Gospel: Global Christian Fundamentalism* (New York and London: Routledge, 1996), p. 155.

10. N.H. Ngada et al., *Speaking for Ourselves* (Springs, South Africa: Order of Preachers, 1985). See also Brouwer et al., *Exporting the American Gospel*, p. 155.

11. G. Moshay, *Who Is This Allah?* (Ibadan, Nigeria: Fireliners International, 1990), cited in Brouwer et al., *Exporting the American Gospel*, p. 174.

12. Brouwer et al., *Exporting the American Gospel*, p. 171.

13. P. Gifford, "Christian Fundamentalism and Development," *Review of African Political Economy* 52 (1991): 15.

14. V. Eto, "Preface," in *Exposition on Water Spirits* (Warri, Nigeria: Shallom Christian Mission, 1983; repr. 1989).

15. R. Marshall, "Pentecostalism in Southern Nigeria: An Overview," in P. Gifford, ed., *New Dimensions in African Christianity* (Nairobi, Kenya: All Africa Conference of Churches, 1992), p. 25.

16. *The News Torch* (Lagos) 1, no. 2, p. 34, quoted in Marshall, "Pentecostalism in Southern Nigeria," p. 25.

17. This paragraph is based on A. Shorter's account of neo-Pentecostalism in Nairobi, "Dangerous Evangelists," *The Tablet*, November 11, 2000.

18. J. Clifton, "Zambian Leader a Crowd Puller," *Sunday Star-Times* (Auckland, New Zealand), September 24, 1995.

19. P. Gifford, "Chiluba's Christian Nation: Christianity as a Factor in Zambian Politics," *Journal of Contemporary Religion* 13 (1998): 363–381.

20. J. Peel, *Religious Encounter and the Making of the Yoruba* (Bloomington: Indiana University Press, 2000), p. 315.

21. Marshall, "Pentecostalism in Southern Nigeria," p. 30, n. 6.

22. Source of Light Ministries, Madison, Georgia, quoted in Gifford, "Christian Fundamentalism and Development," p. 16.

23. There is a detailed and well-documented account in O. Onyinah, "Deliverance as Way of Confronting Witchcraft in Modern Africa: Ghana as a Case History," *Asian Journal of Pentecostal Studies* 5 (2002): 107–134.

24. Matthew Ojo, who has published extensively on the Deeper Life Ministry; is the source for my account of it below. See M. Ojo, "The Contextual Significance of the Charismatic Movements in Independent Nigeria," *Africa* 58 (1988): 175–191; and M. Ojo, "Deeper Christian Life Ministry: A Case Study of the Charismatic Movements in Western Nigeria," *Journal of Religion in Africa* 18 (1988): 141–162. For a recent sympathetic account, see M. Gaiya, "The Pentecostal Revolution in Nigeria," Occasional Paper of the Centre of African Studies, University of Copenhagen (July 2002), pp. 11–23. It is only fair to note that Idahosa also had a good white-collar job in a shoe company.

25. Brouwer et al., *Exporting the American Gospel*, p. 171.

26. D. Maxwell, "Sacred History, Social History: Traditions and Texts in the Making of a Southern African Transnational Religious Movement," *Comparative Studies in Society and History* 43 (2001): 520; my account of Guti comes from this source (pp. 502–524).

27. This account is based on G. Garlock, *Fire in His Bones* (Plainfield, N.J.: Logos International, 1981); and B. Idahosa, *Faith for All Life's Storms* (Eastbourne, U.K.: Kingsway, 1992).

28. Gaiya, "Pentecostal Revolution in Nigeria," p. 14.

29. Ojo calls Deeper Life "charismatic." Marshall considers it a Holiness rather than a charismatic/neo-Pentecostal movement, pointing out that despite the em-

phasis on the Holy Spirit, there is no speaking in tongues or audience participation. "Pentecostalism in Southern Nigeria," pp. 9–10.

30. F.L. Griffith, *The Nubian Texts of the Christian Period* (Berlin: Königliche Akademie der Wissenschaften, 1913), p. 50.

CHAPTER 16

1. K. Barber, "Oriki, Women and the Proliferation and Merging of Orisa," *Africa* 60 (1990): 320.

2. Quoted in E. Isichei, *The Ibo People and the Europeans* (London: Faber and Faber, 1973), p. 146.

3. L. Stevens, "Religious Change in a Haya Village, Tanzania," *Journal of Religion in Africa* 21 (1991): 4.

4. K. Barber, "Discursive Strategies in the Texts of Ifa . . . ," in P. de Moraes Farias and K. Barber, eds., *Self-Assertion and Brokerage: Early Cultural Nationalism in West Africa* (Birmingham, U.K.: Centre of West African Studies, Birmingham University, 1990), p. 222, n. 3. She states that there were 18,000 adults in Okuku in the 1970s.

5. J. Peel, "The Christianisation of African Society: Some Possible Models," in E. Fasholé-Luke et al., eds., *Christianity in Independent Africa* (London: Rex Collings, 1978), p. 452.

6. K. Barber, "How Man Makes God in West Africa: Yoruba Attitudes towads the *Orisa, Africa* 51 (1981) p. 742, n. 5, and p. 743, n. 17.

7. J.D.Y. Peel, *Aladura: A Religious Movement among the Yoruba* (London: Oxford University Press, 1968), p. 94.

8. Oral tradition collected by J. Ejiofor in 1972, in E. Isichei, ed., *Igbo Worlds* (Basingstoke, U.K.: Macmillan, 1977), p. 198.

9. My interpretation of Yoruba religion is greatly indebted to K. Barber's "Oriki, Women and the Proliferation and Merging of Orisa" and "How Man Makes God," and to J.D.Y. Peel, "Gender in Yoruba Religious Change," *Journal of Religion in Africa* 32 (2002): 136–166. My account of Igbo religion relies heavily on my own research, especially in the Niger town of Asaba. Ubah's study of an area near Okigwe yields a strikingly similar picture. C. Ubah, "The Supreme Being, Divinities and Ancestors in Igbo Traditional Religion: Evidence from Otanchara and Otanzu," *Africa* 52 (1982): 90–105.

10. Census data are unreliable and ethnic estimates are highly politicized. These figures give an order of magnitude.

11. L. Brenner, "Religious Discourses in and about Africa," in K. Barber and P.F. de Moraes Farias, eds., *Discourse and Its Disguises: The Interpretation of African Oral Texts* (Birmingham, U.K.: Birmingham University, Centre of West African Studies, 1989), p. 91. The quotation from J. Vansina, *The Tio Kingdom of the Middle Kongo* (London: Oxford University Press, 1973), pp. 226–227, appears here.

12. Brenner, "Religious Discourses," p. 91.

13. J.F. Schön and S. Crowther, *Journals of the Rev. James Frederick Schön and Mr. Samuel Crowther . . . in 1841* (1842; 2nd ed., London: Cass, 1970), p. 50.

14. G.S. Ntloedibe-Kuswani, "Translating the Divine: The Case of Modimo in the Setswana Bible," in M. Dube, ed., *Other Ways of Reading: African Women and the Bible* (Atlanta, Ga.: Society of Biblical Literature, 2001), pp. 78–100.

15. A.B. Ellis, *The Yoruba-Speaking Peoples of the Slave Coast of West Africa* (London: Chapman and Hall, 1894; repr. London: Curzon Books, 1972), p. 41.

16. M. Herskovits, *Dahomey: An Ancient West African Kingdom*, vol. 2 (1938; repr. Evanston, Ill.: Northwestern University Press, 1967), p. 102. The book was based on five months' fieldwork in 1931. There are three distinct pantheons: sky, earth, and thunder. Mawu-Lisa belongs to the first, as does Gu.

17. Peel, "Gender in Yoruba Religious Change," pp. 40–41.

18. W. MacGaffey, "African Religions," in I. Karp and C. Bird, eds., *Explorations in African Systems of Thought* (Bloomington: Indiana University Press, 1980), p. 306.

19. Isichei, *Igbo Worlds,* pp. 176–177 (discussion recorded and translated by Raymond Arazu in 1966). The full text of this interview is the source of the quotation about "government."

20. Ubah, "The Supreme Being, Divinities and Ancestors," pp. 95–96.

21. Isichei, *Igbo Worlds,* p. 100. Oral history collected by N. Nzewunwa in 1973.

22. Ibid., p. 22. Oral tradition collected by M. Onwuejeogwu.

23. It is called Osugbo (gray-haired) among the Ijebu and Egba Yoruba. On Ogboni, see P. Morton-Williams, "The Yoruba Ogboni Cult in Oyo," *Africa* 30 (1960): 362–372.

24. B. Lawal, *The Gelede Spectacle* (Seattle: University of Washington Press, 1996), p. 35. I am much indebted to this valuable account by a Yoruba scholar.

25. See the disapproving account in E.B. Idowu, *Oludumare: God in Yoruba Belief* (London: Longman, 1962), pp. 212–213.

26. Flora Nwapa, *Efuru* (London: Heinemann, 1966).

27. Chinua Achebe, *Anthills of the Savannah* (London: Heinemann, 1988), p. 105.

28. Examples are given in N. Onwu, "Igbo Religion: Its Present Situation," *Africana Marburgensia* 18 (1985): 27.

29. Ulli Beier, *Yoruba Myths* (Cambridge, U.K.: Cambridge University Press, 1980), pp. 6–7; E.B. Idowu, *Oludumare: God in Yoruba Belief* (New York: Praeger, 1963), pp. 59–60.

30. Barber, "How Man Makes God," p. 734; see p. 732 for the manifestations of Soponnan.

31. Ibid., p. 737. Sàngó and Òsun are the correct transcriptions of Shango and Oshun. I have not reproduced Yoruba or any other tonal markings in my own text, except in quotations where they appear. It is one of the signs of the advanced state of Yoruba studies that academic texts reproduce the tones, which is very seldom the case with other (equally tonal) African languages.

32. R. Shaw, "Traditional African Religions," in U. King, *Turning Points in Religious Studies* (Edinburgh, Scotland: Clark, 1990), p. 184.

33. Peel, "Gender in Yoruba Religious Change," pp. 146–148.

34. S. Farrow, *Faith, Fancies and Fetich, or Yoruba Paganism* (London: SPCK, 1926), pp. 53–55. Farrow was a missionary in Abeokuta from 1889 to 1894.

35. For an excellent account of gender and Shango worship, see J.L. Matory, "Government by Seduction: History and the Tropes of 'Mounting' in Oyo-Yoruba Religion," in J. Comaroff and J. Comaroff, eds., *Modernity and Its Malcontents: Ritual and Power in Postcolonial Africa* (Chicago: University of Chicago Press, 1993), pp. 58–88.

36. Herskovits, *Dahomey,* vol. 2, p. 105.

37. A titled man is addressed as Ogbuefi ("cow killer"), referring to the sacrifice made at his installation.

38. S. Barnes, ed., *Africa's Ogun: Old World and New* (Bloomington: Indiana University Press, 1989), pp. 4–6, and, in the same volume, R. Armstrong, "The Etymology of the Word 'Ógún,'" pp. 29–38.

39. For Eshu, and his connections with missionary translations, market transactions, and money, see E. Isichei, *Voices of the Poor in Africa* (Rochester, N.Y.: University of Rochester Press, 2002), pp. 72–73, 229–230. There is a rich literature on Eshu listed in the footnotes of that volume.

40. L. Frobenius, *The Voice of Africa* (1913; repr. New York: Blom, 1968), vol. 1, p. 229.

41. W. Abimbola, *Ifa: An Exposition of Ifa Literary Corpus* (Ibadan, Nigeria: Oxford University Press, 1976), pp. 113–149.

42. Idowu, *Oludumare,* p. 155.

43. From an Ifa divination poem in Abimbola, *Ifa,* p. 115. The list recurs in these texts. A comparable idea is reflected in Igbo personal names such as Onwubiko ("Please, death").

44. Someone seeking sanctuary at a god's shrine became *osu;* sometimes the community offered an individual up as one. *Osu* status was hereditary, and *osu* were endogamous. Chinua Achebe's novel *No Longer at Ease* (London: Heinemann, 1963) gives a moving portrayal of problems caused by *osu* descent in the mid-twentieth century.

45. For a more detailed account of Mami Wata, with line drawings and full references, see Isichei, *Voices of the Poor in Africa,* pp. 188–209.

46. V. Eto, *Exposition on Water Spirits* (Warri, Nigeria: Shallom Mission, 1989), p. 40.

47. J. Murphy, "Oshun the Dancer," in C. Olson, ed., *The Book of the Goddess* (New York: Crossroad, 1983), pp. 190–201.

48. K. Bediako, *Christianity in Africa: The Renewal of a Non-Western Religion* (Edinburgh: Edinburgh University Press, 1995), pp. 18–36. Damuah changed his name to Osofo Okomfo Damuah.

49. M. Wilson, *Rituals of Kinship of the Nyakyusa* (London: Oxford University Press, 1959), p. 18.

50. E. Colson, "Converts and Tradition: The Impact of Christianity on Valley Tonga Religion," *Southwestern Journal of Anthropology* 26 (1970): 147.

51. E. Colson, "A Continuing Dialogue: Prophets and Local Shrines among the Tonga of Zambia," in R. Werbner, ed., *Regional Cults* (London: Academic Press, 1977), p. 128.

CHAPTER 17

1. Quoted in J. Iliffe, *A Modern History of Tanganyika* (Cambridge, U.K.: Cambridge University Press, 1979), p. 227.

2. Compare, for instance, R. Oliver's contribution to the *Cambridge History of Africa,* vol. 3 (Cambridge, U.K.: Cambridge University Press, 1977), pp. 634–636 (which includes a map of the Cwezi state) with the interpretations of C. Wrigley, a leading advocate of the mythical approach, such as "The River-God and the Historians: Myth in the Shire Valley and Elsewhere," *Journal of Religion in Africa* 29 (1988): 367–383 (this discusses both Mbona and the Cwezi).

3. I. Berger, "Fertility as Power: Spirit Mediums, Priestesses and the Precolonial State in Interlacustrine East Africa," in D. Johnson and D. Anderson, eds., *Revealing Prophets* (London: Currey, 1995), p. 74. This chapter (pp. 65–82), and the longer study on which it is based, are my main sources for the Cwezi and Ryangombe. See I. Berger, *Religion and Resistance: East African Kingdoms in the Precolonial Period* (Tervuren, Belgium: Musée Royal de l'Afrique Centrale, 1981). The first published texts of the Cwezi myths in English are readily available. See R. Fisher, *Twilight Tales of the Black Baganda* (1911; 2nd ed., London: Cass, 1970).

4. Berger, "Fertility as Power," pp. 72–73.

5. J. Beattie, "Spirit Mediumship in Bunyoro," in J. Beattie and J. Middleton, eds., *Spirit Mediumship and Society in Africa* (London: Routledge, 1969), pp. 159–170. There is a short account of Cwezi spirit posession in Nkore/Ankole in the same volume: F. Welbourn, "Spirit Initiation in Ankole and a Christian Spirit Movement in Western Kenya," pp. 290–295.

6. Quoted in Iliffe, *Modern History of Tanganyika*, p. 228. My main source here is L. Stevens, "Religious Change in a Haya Village, Tanzania," *Journal of Religion in Africa*, 21 (1991), pp. 6–8.

7. Quoted in Berger, "Fertility as Power," p. 76.

8. Ibid., p. 77.

9. Nyamwezi text, quoted in Iliffe, *Modern History of Tanganyika*, p. 31.

10. H.B. Hansen, "The Colonial Control of Spirit Cults in Uganda," in D. Johnson and D. Anderson, eds., *Revealing Prophets* (London: James Currey, 1995), pp. 146–158. There is a fuller account in J. Freedman, *Nyabingi: The Social History of an African Divinity Period* (Tervuren, Belgium: Musée Royal de l'Afrique Centrale, 1984).

11. The Sena/Tonga, formerly Chikunda, have an interesting history that is outlined in J.M. Schoffeleers, *River of Blood: The Genesis of a Martyr Cult in Southern Malawi, c. AD 1600* (Madison: University of Wisconsin Press, 1992), p. 22.

12. J.M. Schoffeleers, ed., *Guardians of the Land* (Salisbury, Rhodesia: Mambo Press, 1979), p. 220.

13. H.L. Vail, "Religion, Language and the Tribal Myth: The Tumbuka and Chewa of Malawi," in Schoffeleers, ed., *Guardians of the Land*, p. 225; this paper (pp. 209–234) is my source for early Tumbuka religion. For Tunga and Chisumphi, see two articles in the same volume: J.M. Schoffeleers, "The Chisumphi and Mbona Cults in Malawi: A Comparative History," pp. 147–186; and I. Linden, "Chisumphi Theology in the Religion of Central Malawi," pp. 187–208.

14. Schoffeleers, *River of Blood*, p. 31.

15. Schoffeleers, "The Chisumphi and Mbona Cults," p. 159.

16. The main ones are given in Schoffeleers, *River of Blood*, pp. 178–258. There is an earlier version by a colonial official in W. Rangeley, "Mbona—the Rain Maker," *The Nyasaland Journal* 6, no. 1 (1953): 8–27. Schoffeleers studied the cult from 1964 to 1982; his extensive publications on this and allied subjects began in 1971, and over the years, there have been some differences in interpretation. Some of his earlier work is republished in *River of Blood*.

17. Wrigley, "The River-God."

18. M. Daneel, *The God of the Matopo Hills* (Leiden, Netherlands: Mouton, 1970), p. 16.

19. Schoffeleers, "The Chisumphi and Mbona Cults," p. 175; Schoffeleers, *River of Blood*, p. 105.

20. D.N. Beach, *The Shona and Zimbabwe 900–1850: An Outline of Shona History* (London: Heinemann, 1980).

21. The account that follows is based on D. Lan, *Guns and Rain: Guerrillas and Spirit Mediums in Zimbabwe* (London: Currey, 1985); D. Lan, "Resistance to the Present by the Past: Mediums and Money in Zimbabwe," in J. Parry and M. Bloch, *Money and the Morality of Exchange* (Cambridge, U.K.: Cambridge University Press, 1989), pp. 191–208; and K. Garbett, "Disparate Regional Cults and a Unitary Field in Zimbabwe," in R. Werbner, ed., *Regional Cults* (London: Academic Press, 1977), pp. 55–92. Garbett worked in the same area twenty years earlier.

22. A.M. Pacheco (Portuguese source), extract in Lan, *Guns and Rain*, p. 229.

23. Lan, *Guns and Rain*, p. 70.

24. There is a photograph of her, in prison with another medium in 1898, in ibid., facing p. 118.

25. Ibid., pp. 6–7, 217.

26. Ibid., pp. 227–228.

27. N. Bhebe, *Christianity and Traditional Religion in Western Zimbabwe, 1859–1923* (London: Longman, 1979), p. 13. This is my main source here.

28. T. Ranger, *Revolt in Southern Rhodesia* (London: Heinemann, 1967); there is a shorter version in Ranger, "The Role of Ndebele and Shona Religious Authorities in the Rebellions of 1896 and 1897," in E. Stokes and R. Brown, eds., *The Zambesian Past* (Manchester, U.K.: Manchester University Press, 1966), pp. 94–136. The interpretation is critiqued in R. Werbner, ed., "Continuity and Policy in Southern Africa's High God Cult," in *Regional Cults* (London: Academic Press, 1977), pp. 211–214; and in J. Cobbing, "The Absent Priesthood: Another Look at the Rhodesian Risings of 1896–1897," *Journal of African History* 18 (1977): 61–84, and D. Beach, "'Chimurenga': The Shona Rising of 1896–97," *Journal of African History* 20 (1979): 395–420. Clearly there is considerable evidence for Ranger's original view, as is pointed out in Bhebe, *Christianity and Traditional Religion*, pp. 89–97.

29. Ranger, *Revolt in Southern Rhodesia*, p. 385.

30. Werbner, "Continuity and Policy," p. 190. This article (p. 212) is the source for the Kalanga epigraph at the beginning of this book. Daneel, *The God of the Matopo Hills*, p. 16, describes Mwari as a duality, but his main research focus was on independent churches.

31. Werbner, "Continuity and Policy," pp. 187–190.

32. Daneel, *The God of the Matopo Hills*, pp. 77–81; Bhebe, *Christianity and Traditional Religion*, p. 19.

33. Werbner, "Continuity and Policy," p. 214.

34. Collected by R. Werbner and first published in Ranger, *Revolt in Southern Rhodesia*, p. 378.

35. Daneel, *The God of the Matopo Hills*, p. 16.

CHAPTER 18

1. J. Picton, "Masks and the Igbirra," *African Arts* 7 (1974): 38.

2. U. Danfulani, "Factors Contributing to the Survival of the Bori Cult in Northern Nigeria," *Numen* 96 (1999): 429–433. This article (pp. 412–447) is the main source for this account of Bori.

3. A.J.N. Tremearne, *Hausa Superstitions and Customs* (London: Bale & Danielsson, 1913), pp. 111, 534–540.

4. This is an older name for the people now called Gbagyi, but is often used generically in Hausaland to refer to non-Muslim peoples from central Nigeria.

5. A.J.N. Tremearne, *The Ban of the Bori: Demons and Demon Dancing in West and North Africa* (London: Heath, Cranton, and Ousely, 1914; repr. London, Cass, 1968).

6. J. Boddy, *Wombs and Alien Spirits: Women, Men and the Zar Cult in Northern Sudan* (Madison: University of Wisconsin Press, 1989).

7. Ibid., pp. 153–154, 165. For Zar in Somalia, see I.M. Lewis, "Spirit Possession in Northern Somaliland," in J. Beattie and J. Middleton, eds., *Spirit Mediumship and Society in Africa* (London: Routledge, 1969), pp. 188–219.

8. A. Hurskainen, "The Epidemiological Aspect of Spirit Possession among the Maasai of Tanzania," in A. Jacobson-Widding and D. Westerlund, eds., *Culture, Experience and Pluralism: Essays on African Ideas of Illness and Healing* (Uppsala, Sweden: Acta Universitatis Upsaliensis, 1989), p. 139; D. Hodgson, "Embodying the Contradictions of Modernity, Gender and Spirit Possession among Maasai in Tanzania," in M. Grosz-Ngaté and O. Kokole, eds., *Gendered Encounters: Challenging Cultural Boundaries and Social Hierarchies in Africa* (London: Routledge, 1997), pp. 111–129.

9. K. Barber, "How Man Makes God in West Africa: Yoruba Attitudes towards the Orisa," *Africa* 51 (1981): 739.

10. Much has been written on Nyau. See I. Linden with J. Linden, *Catholics, Peasants and Chewa Resistance in Nyasaland 1899–1939* (Berkeley and Los Angeles: University of California Press, 1974), pp. 117–137; and J.M. Schoffeleers, ed., "The Chisumphi and Mbona Cults in Malawi: A Comparative History," in *Guardians of the Land* (Salisbury, U.K.: Mambo Press, 1979), pp. 153, 155, 159; and J. M. Schoffeleers and I. Linden, "The Resistance of the Nyau Societies to the Roman Catholic Missons in Colonial Malawi," in T. Ranger and I. Kimambo, *The Historical Study of African Religion* (London: Heinemann, 1972), pp. 252–276. There are a more recent accounts in D. Kaspin, "Chewa Visions and Revisions of Power," in J. Comaroff and J. Comaroff, eds., *Modernity and Its Malcontents: Ritual and Power in Postcolonial Africa* (Chicago: University of Chicago Press, 1993), pp. 34–57; and J. M. Schoffeleers, *River of Blood: The Genesis of a Martyr Cult in Southern Malawi, c. AD 1600* (Madison: University of Wisconsin Press, 1992). pp. 34–40.

11. I. Linden, "Chewa Initiation Rites and Nyau Societies: The Use of Religious Institutions in Local Politics at Mua," in T. Ranger and J. Weller, eds., *Themes in the Christian History of Central Africa* (London: Heinemann, 1975), p. 40.

12. W. Rangeley, "'Nyau' in Kotakota District," *The Nyasaland Journal* 2 (1949): 36–37.

13. There are photographs and line drawings in Schoffeleers, *River of Blood*, pp. 36–39.

14. Linden, *Catholics, Peasants and Chewa Resistance*, p. 128.

15. Linden, "Chewa Initiation Rites and Nyau Societies," p. 43, n. 47, citing research by Schoffeleers.

16. Linden, *Catholics, Peasants and Chewa Resistance*, p. 120; D. Kaspin, "Chewa

Visions and Revisions of Power," in J. Comaroff and J. Comaroff, eds., *Modernity and Its Malcontents: Ritual and Power in Postcolonial Africa* (Chicago: University of Chicago Press, 1993), p. 49.

17. Kaspin, "Chewa Visions," pp. 48–49.

18. K. Barber, "How Man Makes God in West Africa," p. 729.

19. P. Morton-Williams, "An Outline of the Cosmology and Cult Organisation of the Oyo Yoruba," *Africa* 34 (1964): 256. The northern capital, Oyo Ile, was abandoned in the nineteenth century; the modern city of that name is far to the south.

20. R.F. Thompson, *African Art in Motion* (Los Angeles: University of California Press, 1974), pp. 219–221.

21. W. Abimbola, *Ifa: An Exposition of Ifa Literary Corpus* (Ibadan, Nigeria: Oxford University Press, 1976), pp. 177–179. He fed the witches to satiety on a favorite food and then clubbed them to death.

22. Abimbola, *Ifa*, p. 167.

23. S. Farrow, *Faith, Fancies and Fetich, or Yoruba Paganism* (London: SPCK, 1926), pp. 71–74. He lived in late nineteenth-century Abeokuta.

24. A.B. Ellis, *The Yoruba Speaking Peoples of the Slave Coast of West Africa* (London: Chapman and Hall, 1894; repr. London: Curzon Press, 1974), pp. 44–45.

25. B. Lawal, *The Gelede Spectacle* (Seattle: University of Washington Press, 1996), p. 41. Lawal is my main source for Gelede, which has far more dimensions than can be introduced here.

26. H. Drewal, "Gelede Masquerade: Imagery and Motif," *African Arts* 7 (1974): 8.

27. P. Morton-Williams, "The Atinga Cult among the South-Western Yoruba: A Sociological Analysis of a Witch-Finding Movement," *Bulletin de l'IFAN* ser. B, 18 (1956): 332.

28. W. Abimbola, "The Place of African Traditional Religion in Contemporary Africa: The Yoruba Example," in J. Olupona, ed., *African Traditional Religions in Contemporary Society* (New York: Paragon House, 1991), p. 55.

29. Lawal, *The Gelede Spectacle*, pp. 80–81.

30. J. Peel, "The Christianisation of African Society: Some Possible Models," in E. Fasholé-Luke et al., eds., *Christianity in Independent Africa* (London: Collings, 1978), p. 432. He quotes O. Ogunba, "Ritual Drama of the Ijebu People" (Ph.D. dissertation, University of Ibadan, Nigeria, 1967), p. 320.

31. S. Crowther and J. Taylor, *The Gospel on the Banks of the Niger, 1857–1859* (repr. London: Dawson's, 1968), p. 215. (Crowther's journal)

32. S.F. Nadel, *Nupe Religion* (London: Routledge, 1954), pp. 172–173, 197–201.

33. D. Kohnert, "Magic and Witchcraft: Implications for Democratization and Poverty-Alleviating Aid in Africa," *World Development* 24 (1996): 1349.

34. R. Henderson, *The King in Every Man* (New Haven, Conn.: Yale University Press, 1972), p. 362. His account of the Tall Ghosts (pp. 362–365 and 377–378) is my source here. On Igbo masking in general, see H. Cole and C. Aniakor, *Igbo Arts: Community and Cosmos* (Los Angeles: Museum of Cultural History, UCLA, 1984), pp. 111–215.

35. J. Boston, *The Igala Kingdom* (Ibadan, Nigeria: Oxford University Press, 1968), p. 223.

36. A. Bassing, "Masques Ancestraux chez les Idoma," *Arts d'Afrique Noire* (1973): 6–11 (based on observation in 1959).

37. E. Isichei, "On Masks and Audible Ghosts: Some Secret Male Cults in Central Nigeria," *Journal of Religion in Africa* 18 (1988): 42–70.

38. P.A. Talbot, *In the Shadow of the Bush* (London: Heinemann, 1912), p. 37.

39. T.J. Hutchinson, *Impressions of West Africa* (London: Longman, 1858), p. 143.

40. A number of early twentieth-century publications give lists of *nsibidi* signs; they include J.K. MacGregor, "Some Notes on Nsibidi," *Journal of the Royal Anthropological Institute* 39 (1909): 209–219; E. Dayrell, "Some 'Nsibidi' Signs," *Man* 67 (1910): 112–114; E. Dayrell, "Further Notes on Nsibidi Signs . . . ," *Journal of the Royal Anthropological Institute* 41 (1911): 521–540; Talbot, *Shadow of the Bush*, pp. 447–461.

41. R.F. Thompson, *Flash of the Spirit* (New York: Vintage, 1984), pp. 225–268.

42. On Ekpe today, see R. Hackett, *Religion in Calabar* (Berlin and New York: Mouton de Gruyter, 1989), pp. 182–183.

43. J. Boston, "Some Northern Igbo Masquerades," *Journal of the Royal Anthropological Institute* 90 (1960): 56.

44. D. Bell, *Daughters of the Dreaming* (Sydney, Australia: George Allen & Unwin, 1983), p. 33.

CHAPTER 19

1. E. Turner et al., *Experiencing Ritual* (Philadelphia: University of Pennsylvania Press, 1992), p. 112.

2. T. Rasing, *The Bush Burnt, the Stones Remain* (Leiden, Netherlands: African Studies Centre, 2001), p. 9.

3. For a detailed account of this and other religious changes, see E. Isichei, "Change in Anaguta Traditional Religion," *Canadian Journal of African Studies* 25 (1991): 34–57.

4. National Geographic/WNET (New York), "Love in the Sahel," episode 5 in the series *Africa* (2001). Dama is a masked performance, participation in which marked a young man's formal entry to adult life. This film also depicts the Dogon divination system.

5. A. Richards, *Chisungu* (London: Faber and Faber, 1956). For its form in the late 1990s, see Rasing, *The Bush Burnt*.

6. On linguistic grounds, Hinfelaar suggested that this aspect of girls' initiation originated from a time of contact with "Arab" or Portuguese traders. Cited in Rasing, *The Bush Burnt*, p. 41.

7. Richards, *Chisungu*, p. 13.

8. This was used to weight a digging stick, and is a female symbol.

9. Rasing, *The Bush Burnt*, p. 3.

10. Ibid., p. 53.

11. Turner et al., *Experiencing Ritual*, on her return, and especially Ihamba. Her memoir of 1950s fieldwork is *The Spirit and the Drum: A Memoir of Africa* (Tucson: University of Arizona Press, 1987).

12. A. Jacobson-Widding, *Red-Black-White as a Mode of Thought* (Uppsala,

Sweden: Acta Universitatis Upsaliensis, 1979). On Ndembu color symbolism, see
V. Turner, "Color Classification in Ndembu Ritual: A Problem in Primitive Classification," in V. Turner, *The Forest of Symbols: Aspects of Ndembu Ritual* (Ithaca, N.Y.:
Cornell University Press, 1966), pp. 59–92. This collection of essays also includes a
long account of male circumcision (pp. 151–279) and essays on Ndembu symbolism and liminality and a brief account of Ihamba (pp. 362-370), which is discussed
much more fully in Turner's *The Drums of Affliction* (Oxford, U.K.: Clarendon Press,
1968).

13. E. Turner, "Zambia's Kankanga Dances: The Changing Life of Ritual," *Performing Arts Journal* 30 (1987): 62.

14. From a song for the circumcision ritual, in Turner, *The Spirit and the Drum*,
p. 37.

15. Turner, *Experiencing Ritual*, p. 8. For the emergence of a seen object, extracted by cupping, see pp. 2 and 149.

16. W. Blake, *The Poison Tree*.

17. Documented in detail in Turner, *Experiencing Ritual*, pp. 206–208.

18. G. Lienhardt, *Divinity and Experience: The Religion of the Dinka* (Oxford,
U.K.: Clarendon Press, 1961), p. 257.

19. S. Hutchinson, *Nuer Dilemmas: Coping with Money, War and the State* (Berkeley: University of California Press, 1996), p. 299. She did fieldwork on the eastern and western borders of the Nuer culture sphere.

20. M. Nikkel, "Aspects of Contemporary Religious Change among the Dinka,"
Journal of Religion in Africa 22 (1992): 85–87. His research was among the Bor
Dinka.

21. W. Bosman, *A New and Accurate Description of the Coast of Guinea* (1705;
repr. London: Cass, 1967), p. 232. For a Nri oral text on bloodshed, see E. Isichei,
Igbo Worlds (Basingstoke, U.K.: Macmillan, 1976), pp. 21–28, interview by M.
Onwuejeogwu.

22. M. Herskovits, *Dahomey: An Ancient West African Kingdom*, vol. 2 (repr.
Evanston, Ill.: Northwestern University Press, 1967), p. 203.

23. S.F. Nadel, *Nupe Religion: Traditional Beliefs and the Influence of Islam in
a West African Chiefdom* (New York: Schocken Books, 1970), p. 54.

24. W. Abimbola, *Ifa: An Exposition of Ifa Literary Corpus* (Ibadan, Nigeria: Oxford University Press, 1976), pp. 199–200.

25. Herskovits, *Dahomey*, vol. 2, pp. 203, 209.

26. Ibid., pp. 218–222.

27. K. Barber, "Discursive Strategies in the Texts of Ifa and in the 'Holy Book
of Odu,'" in P. Farias and K. Barber, eds., *Self-Assertion and Brokerage: Early Cultural Nationalism in West Africa* (Birmingham, U.K.: Birmingham University, Centre of West African Studies, 1990), p. 199. As she points out (p. 223, n. 6), not all
the texts are memorized; each poem has eight parts, only four of which must be rendered word for word. As she also notes, printed versions tend to edit accounts of
Oldumare so that they are compatible with Christian ideas of God (p. 205).

28. Ibid., pp. 211–222; the passage referred to is on p. 220.

29. For Afa among the Igbo, see H. Cole and C. Aniafor, *Igbo Community and
Cosmos* (Los Angeles: University of California, 1984) pp. 72–74; John Umeh, *After God Is Dibia* (London: Karnak, 1997 and 2000). Umeh is an Igbo professor of
Estate Mangement who grew up in a dibia family and is now part of the international "traditional" healer/shaman network, to which, for instance, some Hawaiian

kahuna practitioners also belong. Like some Yoruba intellectuals of an earlier day, he seeks to establish similarities between Igbo and ancient Egyptian religion. See also A. Shelton, "The Meaning and Method of Afa Divination among the Northern Nsukka Ibo," *American Anthropologist,* 67 (1965): 1441–1455.

30. R. Armstrong, "The Use of Linguistic and Ethnographic Data in the Study of Idoma and Yoruba History," in J. Vansina, ed., *The Historian in Tropical Africa* (London: Oxford University Press, 1964), pp. 136–139; the relevant word lists are on p. 139. Armstrong began this research project with Ray Bradbury, an Edo specialist; it seems to have been given up after Bradbury's untimely death.

31. R. Burton, *A Mission to Gelele King of Dahomey* (1864; repr. London: Routledge, 1966), p. 195.

32. W. van Binsbergen, "Regional and Historical Connections of Four-Tablet Divination in Southern Africa," *Journal of Religion in Africa* 36 (1996): 25, n. 16. Burton, *Mission to Gelele*, p. 195, also mentions a nineteenth-century popular work on the subject, *Napoleon's Book of Fate.*

33. L. Brenner, "Histories of Religion in Africa," *Journal of Religion in Africa* 30 (2000): 153–162. There is more on sand writing in van Binsbergen, "Regional and Historical Connections," pp. 16–18.

34. Nadel, *Nupe Religion*, pp. 38–67.

35. B. Reynolds, *Magic, Divination and Witchcraft among the Barotse of Northern Rhodesia* (Berkeley: University of California Press, 1963), p.102 (based on research in 1956–1957). There is an unsourced reference to human sacrifice by the apprentice basket diviner in E. Zuesse, *Ritual Cosmos* (Athens: Ohio University Press, 1979), p. 215. My main source for Four Tablet divination is the article by van Binsbergen (note 32) and his "Four-Tablet Divination as Trans-Regional Medical Technology in Southern Africa," *Journal of Religion in Africa* 25 (1995): 114–140. He established the Shona origins of *hakata* (which other evidence also suggests) by cluster analysis.

36. Van Binsbergen, "Regional and Historical Connections," depicts the Shona tablets on p. 11 and the Tswana on p. 3.

37. Ibid., p. 17.

38. Reynolds, *Magic, Divination and Witchcraft*, p. 102.

39. Turner, *The Spirit and the Drum*, pp. 121–122.

40. H.A. Junod, *The Life of a South African Tribe*, vol. 2, 2nd ed. (London: Macmillan, 1927), p. 571.

41. E. Evans-Pritchard, *Witchcraft, Oracles and Magic among the Azande* (Oxford, U.K.: Clarendon Press, 1937), p. 270.

42. Herskovits, *Dahomey*, vol. 2, p. 203.

43. P. Stoller, "Eye, Mind and Word in Anthropology," *Homme* 24 (1984): 93. His own experience with sorcerers is summarized on pp. 94–101. See also P. Stoller and C. Olkes, *In Sorcery's Shadow* (Chicago: University of Chicago Press, 1987).

44. Evans-Pritchard, *Witchcraft, Oracles and Magic*, pp. 238–239.

45. Evans-Pritchard, *Nuer Religion* (Oxford, U.K.: Clarendon Press, 1956), p. ix.

46. S. Feierman, "Therapy as a Sytem-in-Action in Northeastern Tanzania," *Social Science and Medicine* ser. B, 15 (1981): 355.

47. S. Ellis and G. ter Haar, "Religion and Politics in sub-Saharan Africa," *Journal of Modern African Studies* 36 (1998): 189, for these examples.

48. Admiral Didier Ratsiraka, who was head of state from 1975 to 1993. Kaunda's adviser was Dr. Ranganathan.

49. R. Hackett, "Close Encounters of the Third Kind: Spiritual Technology in Modern Nigeria," paper presented at the International Association for the History of Religions Conference, Sydney, 1985. There is some information about Okopedi in Hackett's *Religion in Calabar* (Berlin and New York: Mouton de Gruyter, 1989), pp. 184 and 208, n. 9.

50. E. Turner, "Philip Kabwita, Ghost Doctor: The Ndembu in 1985," *The Drama Review* 30 (1986): 12–35.

CHAPTER 20

1. "The Forgotten Country," a poem, written with others in an exercise book, by an anonymous soldier in the Lord's Resistance Army, in 1987. It breaks off abruptly. It is given in full in H. Behrend, *Alice Lakwena and the Holy Spirits: War in Northern Uganda, 1985–97* (London: Currey, 1999), pp. 166–170; the passage quoted is on p. 166.

2. W. MacGaffey, "The Religious Commissions of the Bakongo," *Man* 5 (1970): 31.

3. R. Hackett, *Religion in Calabar* (Berlin: Mouton de Gruyter, 1989), p. 183.

4. T. Rasing, *The Bush Burnt, the Stones Remain: Female Initiation Rites in Urban Zambia* (Münster, Germany: Lit, 2002), p. 53.

5. Ibid.; A. Richards, *Chisungu: A Girls' Initiation Ceremony among the Bemba of Northern Rhodesia* (London: Faber and Faber, 1956).

6. Rasing, *The Bush Burnt*, p. 252.

7. For a fuller account of the history of Benin, Oyo, and Igala, with references, see E. Isichei, *A History of Nigeria* (Harlow, U.K.: Longman, 1983), pp. 132–141, 182.

8. A Nuer informant cited in G. Lienhardt, *Divinity and Experience: The Religion of the Dinka* (Oxford, U.K.: Clarendon Press, 1961), p. 301. Lienhardt discusses the question of these live burials on pp. 298–319.

9. E. Krige and J. Krige, *The Realm of a Rain-Queen* (London: Oxford University Press, 1943), p. 13. This is the source of my account; recent events come from press reports. Their fieldwork was done between 1936 and 1938, with some shorter earlier visits.

10. Ibid., p. 1.

11. Ibid., p. 167.

12. Ibid.

13. R.S. Rattray, *Ashanti* (Oxford: U.K.: Clarendon Press, 1923), p. 84.

14. He worked in an area that had few earth priests. E. Evans-Pritchard, *Nuer Religion* (Oxford, U.K.: Clarendon Press, 1956). See the interpretation of T. Beidelman, ed., "Nuer Priests and Prophets," in *The Translation of Culture* (London: Tavistock, 1971), pp. 375–415.

15. My main source for Ngungdeng and Gwek is D. Johnson's exemplary study, *Nuer Prophets* (Oxford, U.K.: Clarendon Press, 1994), pp. 73–125, 174–200.

16. D. Johnson, "The Prophet Ngungdeng and the Battle of Pading," in D. Johnson and D. Anderson, eds., *Revealing Prophets* (London: James Currey, 1995), p. 211, quoting an interview with Ngungdeng's grandson.

17. Photographs taken by Coriat, the official who destroyed the mound, and others are reproduced in Johnson, *Nuer Prophets*, facing p.1 and pp. 89, 196.

18. Johnson, "The Prophet Ngungdeng," p. 218.

19. Ibid. For a photograph, see Johnson, *Nuer Prophets*, p. 206.

20. Beidelman, "Nuer Priests and Prophets," pp. 391–392.

21. Quoted in S. Hutchinson, *Nuer Dilemmas: Coping with Money, War and the State* (Berkeley: University of California Press, 1996), p. 338.

22. Ibid., pp. 342–343.

23. E. Isichei, *Igbo Worlds* (Basingstoke, U.K.: Macmillan, 1977), pp. 179–182, 192–197.

24. T. Shaw, *Igbo-Ukwu: An Account of Archaeological Discoveries in Eastern Nigeria,* 2 vols. (London: Faber and Faber, 1970). For a summary of its significance, see E. Isichei, *A History of the Igbo People* (Basingstoke, U.K.: Macmillan, 1976), pp. 10–16.

25. R. Waller, "Kidongoi's Kin," in D. Johnson and D. Anderson, eds., *Revealing Prophets* (London: Currey, 1995), pp. 28-64; and J. Bernsten, "Maasai Age-Sets and Propetic Leadership 1850–1910," *Africa* 49 (1979): 134–146.

26. Waller, "Kidongi's Kin," p. 29.

27. Isichei, *Igbo Worlds,* p. 198. There were several different accounts of Ewenihi's predictions, only one of which was published in this anthology.

28. This theme is explored in E. Isichei, *Voices of the Poor in Africa* (Rochester, N.Y.: University of Rochester Press, 2002), pp. 170–173.

29. R. Willis, "Kaswa, Oral Traditions of a Fipa Prophet," *Africa* 40 (1970): 248–255.

30. Isichei, *Voices of the Poor*, p. 172.

31. Quoted in J. Iliffe, *A Modern History of Tanganyika* (Cambridge, U.K.: Cambridge University Press, 1979), p. 169.

32. Ibid. Sayyid Said was a sultan of Zanzibar who died in 1856.

33. Iliffe, *Modern History of Tanganyika*, p. 200, citing G. Gwassa's estimate of African casualties. Iliffe notes, cautiously, "and he may be right."

34. J. Nyerere, *Freedom and Unity* (London: Oxford University Press, 1967), p. 2.

35. J. Nyerere, "Statement to the U.N. Fourth Committee," December 1956, in ibid., p. 41.

36. P. Nowroejee, "Maji Maji" (1973), text in M. Wright, "Maji Maji: Prophecy and Historiography," in D. Johnson and D. Anderson, *Revealing Prophets* (London: Currey, 1995), p. 140, n. 6.

37. He belonged to the Kakwa, a small ethnic group in northern Uganda. Idi Amin was a member of this group.

38. J. Middleton, "The Yakan or Allah Water Cult among the Lugbara," *Journal of the Royal Anthropological Institute* 92 (1963): 91.

39. The most plausible explanation is based on the fact that in Swahili, *ka* is a diminutive prefix, and *ma* its opposite; as in many African languages, repetition intensified the meaning. The Kenya Africa Union was called Kau. The name Mau Mau embodies a claim to be much greater than Kau. J. Lonsdale, "Mau Maus of the Mind: Making Mau Mau and Remaking Kenya," *Journal of African History* (1990): 393, n. 2, citing T. Colchester.

40. J. Lonsdale, "The Prayers of Waiyaki: Political Uses of the Kikuyu Past," in

D. Johnson and D. Anderson, eds., *Revealing Prophets* (London: Currey, 1995), p. 269. He states that the words usually translated "land and freedom" really mean "self-mastery through land." This article is an outstanding study of the changing ways in which "prophets" are remembered.

41. Ibid., p. 272. For the missionary clause, see S. Weigert, *Traditional Religion and Guerrilla Warfare in Modern Africa* (Basingstoke, U.K.: Macmillan, 1996), p. 25: "I shall never help the missionaries in their Christian faith to ruin our traditional and cultural customs."

42. Quoted in ibid.

43. E.S. Odhiambo, "The Movement of Ideas: A Case Study of Intellectual Reponses to Colonialism among the Liganua Peasants," in B.A. Ogot, ed., *History and Social Change* (Nairobi, Kenya: Hadith 6, 1976), p. 179.

44. D.L. Barnett and K. Njama, *Mau Mau from Within* (London: Macgibbon & Kee, 1966), p. 335. In this source, academic analysis from the first author and the memoirs of the second are printed alternately.

45. Ngugi wa Thiong'o, *Devil on the Cross* (London: Heinemann, 1982), p. 39.

46. These grievances are summarized in J. Penvenne, "Mozambique: A Tapestry of Conflict," in D. Birmingham and P. Martin, eds., *History of Central Africa: The Contemporary Years since 1960* (Harlow, U.K.: Longman, 1998), pp. 254–255.

47. See K. Wilson, "Cults of Violence and Counter-Violence in Mozambique," *Journal of Southern African Studies* 18 (1992): 527–553.

48. This account is based on ibid., pp. 560–580; for Mungoi, see pp. 555–557.

49. The main source here is Behrend, *Alice Lakwena and the Holy Spirits.* She did fieldwork in 1989. Her earlier articles contain further information, notably "The Holy Spirit Movement and the Forces of Nature in the North of Uganda 1985–1987," in H. Hansen and M. Twaddle, eds., *Religion and Politics in East Africa* (London: Currey, 1995), pp. 59–71. See also T. Allen, "Understanding Alice: Uganda's Holy Spirit Movement in Context," *Africa* 61 (1991): 370–399.

50. The full text of this eloquent and moving document is given in Behrend, *Alice Lakwena,* pp. 163–170.

51. J. Lonsdale, "When Did the Gusii (or Any Other Group) Become a Tribe?" *Kenya Historical Review* 5 (1977): 122–133.

52. This version appeared in an anonymous article by a colonial official, and is quoted here from A. Wipper, *Rural Rebels: A Study of Two Protest Movements in Kenya* (Nairobi, Kenya: Oxford University Press, 1977), p. 35. This study is the main source for this account, supplemented by B. Shadle, "Patronage, Millennialism and the Serpent God Mumbo in South-West Kenya 1912–1934," *Africa* 72 (2002): 29–54.

53. Wipper, *Rural Rebels,* p. 35.

54. William Ochieng, "Genesis of Abagusii Grudge against the Narc Government," *Daily Nation,* November 30, 2003.

CHAPTER 21

1. T. Beidelman, *Moral Imagination in Kaguru Modes of Thought* (Bloomington: Indiana University Press, 1986) epigraph.

2. M.D.W. Jeffries, "The Umundri Tradition of Origin," *African Studies* 15 (1956): 122–123.

3. E. Evans-Pritchard, *The Nuer* (Oxford, U.K.: Clarendon Press, 1940), p. 49.

4. N. Berdyaev, quoted in J. Irwin, *An Introduction to Maori Religion* (Bedford Park, South Australia: Australian Association for the Study of Religions, 1984), p. 8.

5. J. Fernandez, "African Religious Movements," *Annual Review of Anthropology* 7 (1978): 221–222.

6. G. Lienhardt, *Divinity and Experience: The Religion of the Dinka* (Oxford, U.K.: Clarendon Press, 1961), pp. 171–176, 188–193; D.H. Johnson, *Nuer Prophets* (Oxford, U.K.: Clarendon Press, 1994), pp. 41–43.

7. Ulli Beier, *Yoruba Myths* (Cambridge, U.K.: Cambridge University Press, 1980), pp. 7–14; E.B. Idowu, *Oludumare: God in Yoruba Belief* (New York: Praeger, 1963), pp. 19–21.

8. R. Fisher, *Twilight Tales of the Black Baganda* (1914; 2nd ed., London: Cass, 1970), p. 65. This book (pp. 69–76) is my source for this account, together with B. Ray, *Myth, Ritual and Kingship in Buganda* (New York: Oxford University Press, 1991), pp. 55–56.

9. Wrigley points out that in luGanda, Kintu can mean "thing," but in the Ganda legend outlined below, it means "man." (Ki is an honorific prefix.) It is possible that the name of the Nyoro rebel against God needs this kind of exegesis. C. Wrigley, *Kingship and State, the Buganda Dynasty* (Cambridge, U.K.: Cambridge University Press, 1996), p. 89.

10. B. Ray, *Myth, Ritual and Kingship in Buganda* (New York: Oxford University Press, 1991), p. 59.

11. A. Roberts, *A History of the Bemba* (Madison: University of Wisconsin Press, 1973), pp. 39ff.

12. Lienhardt, *Divinity and Experience,* pp. 34–35.

13. The word for "God" in the original text is an Asante one, "Onyankopon." R.S. Rattray, *Ashanti Proverbs* (Oxford, U.K.: Clarendon Press, 1916), pp. 20–21.

14. E. Isichei, *A History of Nigeria* (London: Longman, 1983), p. 284 (citing the Plateau History Project, Waya collection).

15. F.M. Deng, *Africans of Two Worlds: The Dinka in Afro-Arab Sudan* (New Haven, Conn.: Yale University Press, 1978), pp. 57–58. The Garden of Eden stories are on pp. 52–57. Deng (b. 1938) comes from the Ngok Dinka; these stories were collected in the 1970s. There are several more in Lienhardt, *Divinity and Experience,* pp. 34–35.

16. H.A. Junod, *The Life of a South African Tribe,* vol. 2, 2nd ed. (London: Macmillan, 1927), pp. 350–351. The people of southern Mozambique whom he calls Thonga were previously known as the Tonga, and now are called either Tsonga or Shangaan.

17. Text in M. de P. Neiers, *The Peoples of the Jos Plateau, Nigeria: Their Philosophy, Manners and Culture* (Frankfurt am Main, Germany: Lang, 1979), pp. 174–175.

18. Lienhardt, *Divinity and Experience,* p. 36, quoting a text first published in 1949.

19. Frobenius, quoted in H. Abrahamsson, *The Origin of Death: Studies in African Mythology* (Uppsala, Sweden: Studia Ethnographica Upsaliensa, 1951), p. 68.

20. For a fuller account of this theme, with detailed references, see E. Isichei, *Voices of the Poor in Africa* (Rochester, N.Y.: University of Rochester Press, 2002), pp. 175–178, 180–182.

21. R. Armstrong, "The Etymology of the Word 'Ògún,'" in S. Barnes, ed., *Africa's Ogun: Old World and New* (Bloomington: Indiana University Press, 1989), pp. 29–38.

22. S. Bockie, *Death and the Invisible Powers: The World of Kongo Belief* (Bloomington: Indiana University Press, 1993), pp. 36–38.

23. W. Bosman, *A New and Accurate Description of the Coast of Guinea* (1705; 2nd ed., London: Cass, 1967), p. 147.

24. W.F.P. Burton, *The Magic Drum: Tales from Central Africa* (London: Methuen, 1961), p. 85.

25. R. Finnegan, *Limba Stories and Story-Telling* (Oxford, U.K.: Clarendon Press, 1967), pp. 261–263.

26. For an excellent collection of essays on the Trickster, see R.D. Pelton, *The Trickster in West Africa: A Study of Mythic Irony and Sacred Delight* (Berkeley : University of California Press, 1989).

27. P. Fraenkel, *Wayaleshi* (London: Weidenfeld and Nicolson, 1959), pp. 14–15. The quotation about Eshu (Esu in original) comes from B. Belasco, *The Entrepreneur as Culture Hero: Pre-Adaptations in Nigerian Econcomic Development* (New York: Bergin, 1980), p. ix.

28. S. Crowther and J.C. Taylor, *The Gospel on the Banks of the Niger* (1899; repr. London: Dawson's, 1968), pp. 447–451. The original translations are given here. Reprinted in E. Isichei, *Igbo Worlds: An Anthology of Oral Histories and Historical Descriptions* (Philadelphia: Institute for the Study of Human Issues, 1978), pp. 281–285.

29. C. Wrigley, "The River-God and the Historians: Myth in the Shire Valley and Elsewhere," *Journal of Religion in Africa* 29 (1988): 372.

30. T. Beidelman, *Moral Imagination in Kaguru Modes of Thought* (Washington, D.C.: Smithsonian Institution Press, 1993), p. 210.

CHAPTER 22

1. E. Milingo, *The World in Between* (London: Hurst, 1982), p. 36.

2. G. Parrinder, *Religion in Africa* (London: Pall Mall, 1969), p. 65.

3. E. Evans-Pritchard, *Witchcraft, Oracles and Magic among the Azande* (Oxford, U.K.: Clarendon Press, 1937), pp. 21, 387.

4. R. Henderson, *The King in Every Man* (New Haven, Conn: Yale University Press, 1972), p. 310. The ritual is very similar to the Asaba one described earlier.

5. P. Morton-Williams, "The Atinga Cult among the South-Western Yoruba: A Sociological Analysis of a Witch-Fnding Movement," *Bulletin de l'IFAN* ser. B, 18 (1956): 331. This article, based on fieldwork among the Egbado Yoruba in 1950, is an invaluable source.

6. Proverb quoted in ibid., p. 326.

7. B. Lawal, *The Gelede Spectacle* (Seattle: University of Washington Press, 1996), pp. 31–32.

8. Ibid., p. 32.

9. E.B. Idowu, "The Challenge of Witchcraft," *Orita* 4 (1970): 3–16.

10. Morton-Williams, "The Atinga Cult," p. 327.

11. R. Prince, "Indigenous Yoruba Psychiatry," in A. Kiev, ed., *Magic, Faith and Healing* (New York: Collier-Macmillan, 1964), pp. 84–120. See also E. Turner et

al., *Experiencing Ritual* (Philadelphia; University of Pennyslvania Press, 1992; and P. Stoller, "Eye, Mind and Word in Anthropology," *Homme* 24 (1984) pp. 94–101.

12. My account is based on M. Marwick, *Sorcery in Its Social Setting: A Study of the Northern Rhodesian Cewa* (Manchester, U.K.: Manchester University Press, 1965).

13. Ibid., p. 79.

14. Ibid., p. 3.

15. P.A. Talbot, *The Peoples of Southern Nigeria*, vol. 2, (London: Oxford University Press, 1926), p. 201; G.I. Jones, "A Boundary to Accusations," in M. Douglas, ed., *Witchcraft Confessions and Accusations* (London: Tavistock, 1970), p. 322.

16. Marwick, *Sorcery in Its Social Setting*, table I, p. 16. Smaller percentages were attributed to various forms of human agency, including suicide, and to spirits. Many of the cases he studied were deaths, for which "serious misfortune" may be an understatement!

17. Ibid., pp. 64–68. For example, a woman may die if her husband commits adultery when she is pregnant.

18. A. Richards, "A Modern Movement of Witch-Finders," in M. Marwick, ed., *Witchcraft and Sorcery: Selected Readings* (Harmondsworth, U.K.: Penguin, 1970), pp. 171–172. As among many other peoples, there is a distinction between the "good" ancestor with a grievance and the perennially hostile and embittered ghost.

19. R. Willis, "Changes in Mystical Concepts and Practices among the Fipa," *Ethnology* 7 (1968): 144–145.

20. Phil Aglund, director and writer, *Baka: People of the Rain Forest*, DJA River Films, Channel 4 (1988).

21. Quoted in Marwick, *Sorcery in Its Social Setting*, p. 93.

22. Jack Goody, *Death, Property and the Ancestors* (London: Tavistock, 1962), p. 373.

23. M. Field, *Search for Security: An Ethno-Psychiatric Study of Rural Ghana* (London: Faber and Faber, 1960), p. 112.

24. Richards, "A Modern Movement," pp. 168–170.

25. Bwanali was founded in Malawi in 1947. Its eponymous founder seems to have seen himself as a healer, and did not ask for payment. Kamcape (a form of mchape?) was documented in Ufipa in 1964; apparently it was instituted by another dead and resurrected founder, called Icikanga. See M. Marwick, "The Bwanali-Mpulumutsi Anti-Witchcraft Movement," and R. Willis, "The Kamcape Movement," in Marwick, *Sorcery in Its Social Setting*, pp. 178–183 and 184–198, respectively. Both are abridged versions of articles that originally appeared in *Africa*. There was a real diviner in northern Malawi, active from 1956 to 1964, with the nickname Chikanga (Courage). A. Redmayne, "Chikanga: An African Diviner with an International Reputation," in M. Douglas, ed., *Witchcraft Confessions and Accusations* (London: Tavistock, 1970), pp. 103–128.

26. T. Ranger, "The Mwana Lesa Movement of 1925," in T. Ranger and J. Weller, *Themes in the Christian History of Central Africa* (London: Heinemann, 1975), pp. 45–75. The quotation is on p. 59.

27. Morton-Williams, "The Atinga Cult," p. 322.

28. This theme is discussed in detail in E. Isichei, *Voices of the Poor in Africa* (Rochester, N.Y.: University of Rochester Press, 1972), pp. 89–256.

29. Ibid., pp. 111–125.

30. Ibid., pp. 143–150.

31. L. Oyegoke, *Cowrie Tears* (Harlow, U.K.: Longman, 1982); Buchi Emecheta, *Naira Power* (Basingstoke, U.K.: Macmillan, 1982); A. Babarinsa, *Anything for Money* (Basingstoke, U.K.: Macmillan, 1985).

32. F. De Boeck, "Postcolonialism, Power and Identity . . . ," in R. Werbner and T. Ranger, eds., *Postcolonial Identities in Africa* (London: Zed, 1996), p. 102, n. 9.

33. P. Geschiere, "Domesticating Personal Violence: Witchcraft, Courts and Confessions in Cameroon," *Africa* 6 (1994): 323–337.

Glossary

Unless otherwise specified, these words are Arabic.

Amir. Commander.

Ansar. Helper. Also refers to the Medina Muslims who assisted the Islamic community after the *hijra*.

Baraka. Blessedness, charisma.

Cerno (Fulfulde). Title for a learned man, similar to *mallam* in Hausa.

Emir (Hausa). Ruler of one of the Sokoto caliphate's constituent states; see *Amir*.

Fatwa. An authoritative, formal legal opinion issued by a mufti.

Fayda. Overflowing. Refers to God's gifts, and hence is sometimes translated as "grace."

Hadith (pl., *ahadith*). Traditions of the Prophet; not in the Quran, but recorded by those who knew him. The Quran and the hadith are the basis of the Sunna, together with consensus and analogy.

Hijra. The emigration of the Prophet and his supporters from Mecca to Medina.

Imam. Leader of prayer in the mosque. Sometimes refers to the head of an Islamic state. Among Shi'ite Muslims, it refers to a succession of early heads of the Islamic community, descended from Muhammad through Fatima and Ali through Husein and Ali Zain. After the death of the sixth imam in 765, interpretations of the succession diverge.

Itjihad. Independent analysis of Islamic traditions or laws.

Jahiliyya. Age of ignorance. Applied to pre-Islamic Arabia and, by contemporary Islamists, to flawed Muslim governments and societies.

Jama'a. Islamic Community.

Jihad. Struggle. Generally used for wars waged in the name of Islam. (A jihad of the sword is *jihad al-sayf.* A preaching jihad is *jihad al-qawl.*

Khalifa, caliph (literally, "deputy"). Originally, the head of the worldwide Muslim community; also used in smaller states whose rulers claim the title, such as Sokoto and Morocco. *Khalifa* also refers to the regional head of a Sufi order.

Madrasa. College where advanced Islamic subjects, such as jurisprudence, are taught.

Mahdi. The Rightly Guided One who will appear before the end of the world.

Makhzan. Government (literally, "treasury").

Mallam (Hausa). A learned man.

Mamluk ("owned"). Elite Muslim soldiers in Islamic states, recruited from enslaved Christian children.

Marabout (French, from *murabit*). Popular term in francophone Africa for a Muslim Sufi or teacher/scholar.

Mawali. Clients.

Mufti. An expert on Sharia law, qualified to give *fatwa,* or rulings.

Mujaddid. The Renewer. Thought to appear in every Islamic century.

Mulid. Celebration of the festiva of Muslim saints (the same word is used by the Copts for festivals of Christian saints).

Mullah (Turkish, absorbed into English). A member of the *ulama.*

Murabitun (from *ribat*). Originally men of the *ribat,* or fortification. It later came to refer to Muslim Sufis and ascetics; see also *marabout.*

Qadi. A judge in a *sharia* court.

Quran (literally, "recitation"). The sacred text of the revelation dictated to Muhammad. Also spelled *Qran* and, in older books, *Koran.*

Ribat. Originally a fort on an Islamic frontier; later a Sufi residential community, similar to *zawiya.*

Salaf. Ancestor (*salafiyya*).

Sayyid. Lord; a descendant of the Prophet, especially though Husein ibn Ali; see *sharif.*

Sharia. The laws of Islam.

Sharif (pl., *shurfa;* literally, "noble"). A descendant of the Prophet, especially though al-Hasan ibn Ali.

Sheikh. A highly esteemed scholar or Sufi.

Shia (literally, "party"). Originally those who supported Ali's claim to the caliphate. A minority grouping in Islam, distinct from Sunni. It now has many branches.

Shurah. Consultation.

Sidi. See *Sayyid*.

Sufi. A mystic; often a member of a *tariqa*.

Sultan. Man of power.

Sunna. The Customs of Muhammad, recorded in the Hadith, and, together with the Quran, the basis of Islamic law.

Sunni. The larger Muslim grouping; its members owe allegiance to one of the four law schools.

Tariqa (pl., *turuq*). Way; a Sufi order.

Ulama (sing., *alim*). Scholars learned in Islamic studies, such as Quranic studies, *sharia*, and theology.

Umma. Community.

Wird. The litany of a particular Sufi order, additional to the prayers required of all Muslims.

Zawiya (pl., *zawaya;* literally, "corner" or "nook"). A communal Sufi residence and training center.

A Guide to Further Reading

In many cases, the sources for a particular subject are given in the notes to each chapter, and this guide does not attempt to duplicate this material. Chapters 2 and 3 were lightly noted, since I felt that the vast literature lent itself better to bibliographic entries. Chapter 4 is based mainly on printed primary sources; the secondary literature is introduced here.

The Journal of Religion in Africa is an invaluable resource. Regular reference to new issues is probably the best way of keeping up to date with the subject, especially for neotraditional religion and Christianity. Excellent material also appears regularly in the journal *Africa*. Many valuable articles relevant to neotraditional religion have appeared in *African Arts*.

CHAPTER 1: THE STUDY OF "TRADITIONAL" RELIGION

Religion 20 (1990). The whole October issue was devoted to the methodology of the study of African traditional religion.

L. Brenner, "Religious Discourses in and about Africa," in K. Barber and P.F. de Moraes Farias, eds., *Discourse and Its Disguises: The Interpretation of African Oral Texts* (Birmingham, U.K.: University of Birmingham, African Studies Centre, 1989), pp. 87–105.

On Seeing "Traditional" Religion through "Christian Spectacles"

R. Horton, "Judaeo-Christian Spectacles: Boon or Bane to the Study of African Religions?" *Cahiers d'Études Africaines* 96 (1984): 391–436.

Okot p'Bitek, *African Religion in Western Scholarship* (Kampala: East Africa House, 1970).

The following articles by Robin Horton are still frequently cited:

"African Traditional Thought and Western Science," *Africa* 37 (1967): 50–71.
"On the Rationality of Conversion—Part 1," *Africa* 45, no. 3 (1975): 219–235.
"African Conversion," *Africa* 41 (1971): 85–100.
This is also true of J. Fernandez's contributions on typology and methodology, such
as his "African Religious Movements," *Annual Review of Anthropology* 7
(1978): 195–234.

Ancient Egypt

There is a vast literature on religion in ancient Egypt, including the following:

J.H. Breasted, *Development of Religion and Thought in Ancient Egypt* (New York:
Harper & Row, 1959).
A.R. David, *The Ancient Egyptians' Religious Beliefs and Practices* (London:
Routledge, 1982).
S. Quirke, *Ancient Egyptian Religion* (London: British Museum, 1992).
R. Wilkinson, *The Complete Gods and Goddesses of Ancient Egypt* (New York: Thames
and Hudson, 2003), which has an up-to-date bibliography and is well illus-
trated.
A.K. Bowman, *Egypt after the Pharaohs* (Berkeley: University of California Press,
1986), particularly good on religious change in the later period.

CHAPTER 2: THE EARLY CHURCH IN
NORTHERN AFRICA

There is a vast literature here, too. A good start is:

Philip F. Esler, ed., *The Early Christian World*, 2 vols. (London and New York:
Routledge, 2000), an encyclopedic thematic study, full of excellent contribu-
tions by specialists, each with an up-to-date bibliography. Those especially
relevant to this book are all in volume 2:
W.H.C. Frend, "Martyrdom and Political Oppression," pp. 815–839.
A. Logan, "Gnosticism," pp. 907–928.
J. Alexander, "Donatism," pp. 952–974.
D. Rankin, "Arianism," pp. 975–1004.
F. Norris "Origen," pp. 1005–1026.
D. Wright, "Tertullian," pp. 1027–1047.
R. Kaemer and S. Lander, "Perpetua and Felicitas," pp. 1048–1068.
C. Stewart, "Anthony of the Desert," pp. 1088–1101.
D. Brakke, "Athanasius," pp. 1102–1127.
C. Harrison, "Augustine," pp. 1205–1227.
Henry Chadwick, *The Church in Ancient Society: From Galilee to Gregory the Great*
(Oxford, U.K.: Oxford University Press, 2001), is a masterly and recent sur-
vey. Since it is arranged in 61 chapters, it is easy to find the sections relevant
to Africa.
W.H.C. Frend, *The Rise of Christianity* (London: Darton, Longman and Todd,
1984), is another fine, but somewhat older, survey.
A concise and still valuable version can be found in W.H.C. Frend, "The Christian

Period in Mediterranean Africa," in *Cambridge History of Africa*, vol. 2 (Cambridge, U.K.: Cambridge University Press, 1978), chap. 7, pp. 410–489.

On the gnostics, see E. Pagels, *The Gnostic Gospels* (Harmondsworth, U.K.: Penguin, 1982), and later works by the same author.

The prison journal of Perpetua of Carthage is widely available, for instance, in E. Petroff, *Medieval Women's Visionary Literature* (New York: Oxford University Press, 1986), pp. 70–77.

J.E. Salisbury, *Perpetua's Passion: The Death and Memory of a Young Roman Woman* (New York: Routledge, 1997).

Peter Brown, *Augustine of Hippo: A Biography* (London: Faber and Faber, 1967), is a classic, as is his *Religion and Society in the Age of Saint Augustine* (London: Faber and Faber, 1972).

G. Bonner, *St. Augustine of Hippo: Life and Controversies,* rev. ed. (Norwich, U.K.: Canterbury Press, 1986).

W.H.C. Frend, *The Donatist Church: A Movement of Protest in Roman North Africa,* 3rd ed. (Oxford, U.K.: Clarendon Press, 1985). First published in 1952, this book is influential, controversial, and much debated. For a recent, up-to-date, and concise account, with bibliography, see Alexander's contribution in Esler (above).

Roger S. Bagnall, *Egypt in Late Antiquity* (Princeton, N.J.: Princeton University Press, 1993), an outstanding work, thematically arranged; the section on religion is on pp. 251-309.

Norman Russell, *Cyril of Alexandria* (London and New York: Routledge, 2000).

Nubia

W.Y. Adams, *Nubia: Corridor to Africa* (Princeton, N.J.: Princeton University Press, 1977), chaps. 14 and 15, pp. 433–506.

J. Spaulding, "Medieval Christian Nubia and the Islamic World, . . . " *International Journal of African Historical Studies* 28 (1995): 577–594.

Ethiopian Christian History

The best introduction to Ethiopian Christianity from its origins until the end of the nineteenth century is in the relevant chapters of Adrian Hastings, *The Church in Africa 1450–1950* (Oxford, U.K.: Oxford University Press, 1994).

E.Ullendorff, *Ethiopia and the Bible* (London: Oxford University Press, 1968), and *The Ethiopians: An Introduction to Country and People,* 3rd ed. (Stuttgart: Steiner, 1990).

S. Kaplan, "Ezana's Conversion Reconsidered," *Journal of Religion in Africa* 12 (1982): 166–186.

S. Kaplan, *The Monastic Holy Man and the Christianization of Early Solomonic Ethiopia* (Wiesbaden, Germany: Franz Steiner Verlag, 1984).

Taddesse Tamrat, *Church and State in Ethiopia 1270–1527* (Oxford, U.K.: Clarendon Press, 1972).

M. Abir, *The Era of the Princes: The Challenge of Islam and the Re-Unification of the Christian Empire* (New York: Praeger, 1968).

D Crummey, *Priests and Politicians, . . . 1830–1868* (Oxford, U.K.: Clarendon Press, 1972).

Coptic Christianity

The classic study of Coptic Christianity, by a Copt, is Aziz Atiya, *A History of Eastern Christianity* (London: Methuen, 1968), pp. 1–145.

Islam: Some Good General Introductions

These works do not focus mainly on Africa, but provide excellent background for those unfamiliar with Islamic history, religion, and culture.

M. Ruthven, *Islam in the World* (Harmondsworth, U.K.: Penguin, 1984).

K. Armstrong, *Islam: A Short History* (London: Phoenix, 2000).

J.L. Esposito, ed., *The Oxford History of Islam* (Oxford, U.K.: Oxford University Press, 1999), a beautifully illustrated thematic book with good bibliographies.

I. Lapidus, *A History of Islamic Societies* (Cambridge, U.K.: Cambridge University Press, 1988).

A. Goldschmidt, Jr., *A Concise History of the Middle East*, 7th ed. (Boulder, Colo.: Westview Press, 2002), good on Egypt and on the Near and Middle East, with which Egypt's history is closely linked.

The Life of Muhammad and the Dawn of Islam

F.E. Peters, *Muhammad and the Origins of Islam* (Albany: SUNY Press, 1994).

H. Kennedy, *The Prophet and the Age of the Caliphates* (London: Routledge, 1986).

Islam in Africa: General

N. Levtzion and R.L. Pouwels, eds., *The History of Islam in Africa* (Athens: Ohio University Press, 2000), a large collection of regional and thematic essays, mainly on sub-Saharan Africa. Each essay has a full and up-to-date bibliography.

M. Hiskett, *The Course of Islam in Africa* (Edinbugh, Scotland: Edinburgh University Press, 1994), concise (200 pages), with a regional approach.

CHAPTER 3: THE SPREAD OF ISLAM IN NORTHERN AFRICA TO 1800

Some of these books also cover a later period.

J. Abun-Nasr, *A History of the Maghreb in the Islamic Period* (Cambridge, U.K.: Cambridge University Press, 1987).

The relevant chapters of the *Cambridge History of Africa* (Cambridge, U.K.: Cambridge University Press, 1977) are still an excellent introduction:

M. Brett, "The Arab Conquest and the Rise of Islam in North Africa," *Cambridge History of Africa,* vol. 2, chap. 8, pp. 490–555, and in the same volume, chap. 10, Brett's "The Fatimid Revolution (861–973) and Its Aftermath in North Africa," pp. 589–636.

H. Fisher, "The Eastern Maghrib and the Central Sudan," *Cambridge History of Africa,* vol. 3, chap. 4, pp. 232–330.

P.M. Holt and M.W. Daly, *A History of the Sudan from the Coming of Islam to the Present Day*, 4th ed. (Harlow, U.K.: Longman, 1988).

M. Brett, *The Moors: Islam in the West* (London: Orbis, 1980), has beautiful photographs by W. Forman and also includes Spain.

R. Le Tourneau, *The Almohad Movement in North Africa* (Princeton, N.J.: Princeton University Press, 1969).

M. Brett, *The Rise of the Fatimids* (Leiden, Netherlands: Brill, 2001).

Yusuf Fadl Hasan, *The Arabs and the Sudan: From the Seventh to the Early Sixteenth Century* (Edinburgh: Edinburgh University Press, 1967).

R. S. O'Fahey and J. Spaulding, *Kingdoms of the Sudan* (London: Methuen, 1974), on three sultanates in the southern Sudan: Sennar, Wadai, and Darfur.

CHAPTER 4. THE GROWTH OF ISLAM IN SUB-SAHARAN AFRICA

N. Levtzion and J.F.P. Hopkins, eds., *Corpus of Early Arabic Sources for West African History* (Cambridge, U.K.: Cambridge University Press, 1981), is a precious resource, with primary source material in translation and much interpretative material.

N.Levtzion has made invaluable contributions to this area, including his "The Sahara and the Sudan from the Arab conquest of the Maghrib . . . ," in *Cambridge History of Africa*, vol. 2, chap. 11, pp. 589-636, and more recently, "Islam in the Bilad al-Sudan to 1800," in N. Levtzion and R.L. Pouwels, eds., *The History of Islam in Africa* (Athens: Ohio University Press, 2000), pp. 63–91.

N. Levtzion, *Ancient Ghana and Mali* (London: Methuen, 1973), is still the standard account of these empires.

M. Hiskett, *The Development of Islam in West Africa* (London and New York: Longman, 1984).

J.R. Willis, ed., *Studies in West African Islamic History*, vol. 1, *The Cultivators of Islam* (London: Cass, 1979).

Articles on Islam in Africa are often published in general books which are predominantly concerned with the Middle and Far East. N. Levtzion, ed., *Conversion to Islam* (New York: Holmes and Meier, 1979), chaps. 9–13, is an example.

The following are important articles:

H.J. Fisher, "Conversion Reconsidered: Some Historical Aspects of Religious Conversion in Black Africa," *Africa* 43 (1973): 27–40.

D. Conrad and H. Fisher, "The Conquest That Never Was: Ghana and the Almoravids, 1076," *History in Africa* 19 (1982): 21–59.

J. Hunwick, "Secular Power and Religious Authority in Muslim Society: The Case of Songhay," *Journal of African History* 37 (1996): 175–194.

L. Kaba, "The Pen, the Sword and the Crown: Islam and Revolution in Islam Reconsidered," *Journal of African History* 24 (1984): 241–256.

J. Lavers, "Islam in the Borno Caliphate," *Odu* 5 (1971): 27–53.

The Swahili Coast

There is abundant primary material in the following:

G.S.P. Freeman-Greville, *The East African Coast: Select Documents,* 2nd ed. (London: Rex Collings, 1975).

Jan Knappert, *Four Centuries of Swahili Verse* (London: Heinemann, 1979).

D. Nurse and T. Spear, *The Swahili: Reconstructing the History and Language of an African Society, 800–1500* (Philadelphia: University of Pennsylvania Press, 1985).

The present book does not cover Islam in eastern Africa or southern Africa after 1800, for reasons of space. For a good history of the former that ends in 1900, see R. Pouwels, *Horn and Crescent: Cultural Change and Traditional Islam on the East African Coast* (Cambridge, U.K.: Cambridge University Press, 1987).

N. Levtzion and R.L. Pouwels, eds., *The History of Islam in Africa,* includes substantial coverage of eastern and southern Africa chaps. 12–16, pp. 251–372. Note R. Pouwels, "The East African Coast, c. 790 to 1900 C.E," pp. 251–272.

CHAPTER 5: NEW STATES IN THE WESTERN SUDAN

There is an abundant literature on the jihadist states. Older "Africanist" works tend to idealize them and to see them as exemplars of state formation, and, where appropriate, of resistance to colonialism. More recent studies show a greater awareness of the social costs in war and enslavement.

A good recent survey, with a good bibliography, is D. Robinson, "Revolutions in the Western Sudan," in N. Levtzion and R.L. Pouwels, eds., *The History of Islam in Africa* (Athens: Ohio University Press, 2000), pp. 131–152.

N. Levtzion, *Islam in West Africa: Religion, Society and Politics* (Aldershot, U.K.: Variorum, 1994), is a collection of reprinted and new articles. See chaps. 6–9: "Rural and Urban Islam," "The Eighteenth Century: Background to the Islamic Revolutions in West Africa," "Eighteenth Century Renewal and Reform: The Role of Sufi Turuq . . . ," and "Notes on the Origins of Islamic Militancy in the Futa Jallon."

The second of these articles is reprinted from a collection edited by N.Levtzion and J. Voll, *Eighteenth Century Renewal and Reform in Islam* (Syracuse, NY: Syracuse University Press, 1987), which also includes a chapter by L. Brenner on Uthman dan Fodio, and one by F. de Jong on the Khalwatiyya in Egypt.

P. Curtin, "The Jihads of West Africa: Early Relations and Linkages," *Journal of African History,* 22 (1971): 11–24.

D. Robinson, "The Islamic Revolution of Futa Toro," *International Journal of African Historical Studies* 8 (1975): 185–221.

M. Hiskett, *The Sword of Truth* (Oxford, U.K.: Oxford University Press, 1973), an excellent life of Uthman dan Fodio.

B. Mack and J. Boyd, *One Woman's Jihad: Nana Asma'u, Scholar and Scribe* (Bloomington: Bloomington, Indiana University Press, 2000.)

M. Last, "Reform in West Africa: The Jihad Movements of the Nineteenth Century," in J.F. Ajayi and M. Crowder, eds., *History of West Africa*, vol. 2 (London: Longman, 1974), pp. 1–29.

D. Robinson, *The Holy War of Umar Tal* (Oxford, U.K.: Clarendon Press, 1985).

J. Abun-Nasr, *The Tijaniyya: A Sufi Order in the Modern World* (Oxford, U.K.: Oxford University Press, 1973).

B. G. Martin, *Muslim Brotherhoods in Nineteenth Century Africa* (Cambridge, U.K.: Cambridge University Press, 1976), which includes chapters on dan Fodio, Abd al-Qadir (Algeria), al-Hajj Umar, the Sanusiyya (Libya), and the Sayyid (Somalia).

Much of the material on Hamdullahi is in French, but see the following:

M. Johnson, "The Economic Foundations of an Islamic Theocracy: The Case of Masina," *Journal of Religion in Africa* 17 (1976): 481–495.

Yves Person wrote a vast three-volume study of Samori in French. For a short, accessible account in English, see his "Samori and Islam," in J.R. Willis, ed., *The Cultivators of Islam* (London: Cass, 1979), pp. 259–277.

CHAPTER 6: NORTHERN AFRICA IN THE NINETEENTH CENTURY

P. Holt, *The Madhist State in the Sudan,* 2nd ed. (Oxford, U.K.: Clarendon Press, 1970).

S. Samatar, *Oral Poetry and Somali Nationalism: The Case of Sayyid Muhammad 'Abdille Hasan* (Cambridge, U.K.: Cambridge University Press, 1982).

K.S. Vikor, *Sufi and Scholar on the Desert Edge* (Evanston, Ill.: Northwestern University Press, 1995), on al-Sanusi.

R. O'Fahey, *Enigmatic Saint: Ahmad ibn Idris and the Idrisi Tradition* (Evanston, Ill.: Northwestern University Press, 1990).

R. Danziger, *Abd al-Qadir and the Algerians* (New York: Holmes and Maier, 1977).

J.C. Vatin, "Religious Resistance and State Power in Algeria," in A. Cudsi and A. Dessouki, eds., *Islam and Power* (Baltimore: John Hopkins Press, 1981), pp. 119–157.

J. Clancy-Smith, "Saints, Mahdis, and Arms: Religion and Resistance in Nineteenth-Century North Africa," in E. Burke and I. Lapidus, eds., *Islam, Politics and Social Movements* (Berkeley: University of California Press, 1988), pp. 60–79.

A. Hourani, *Arabic Thought in the Liberal Age 1798–1939* (London: Oxford University Press, 1962), an influential book of lasting value.

N. Keddi, *Sayyid Jamal ad-Din "al-Afghani"* (Berkeley: University of California Press, 1972).

M.A.Z. Badawi, *The Reformers of Egypt* (London: Croom Helm, 1976), a study of al-Afghani, Muhammad Abdu, and Rashid Ridha.

The following are concerned with political rather than religious history, but still have varying degrees of relevance to the latter.

J. Ruedy, *Modern Algeria: The Origins and Development of a Nation* (Bloomington: Indiana University Press, 1992).

M. Morsy, *North Africa 1800–1900* (London: Longman, 1984).

P. Vatikiotis, *The History of Egypt from Muhammad Ali to Sadat,* 2nd ed. (London: Weidenfeld and Nicolson, 1980).

CHAPTERS 7 AND 8: NORTHERN AFRICA IN THE TWENTIETH CENTURY

The following are valuable, wide-ranging articles:

S.V.R. Nasr, "European Colonialism and the Emergence of Modern Muslim States," in J.L.Esposito, ed., *The Oxford History of Islam* (Oxford, U.K.: Oxford University Press, 1999).

Nikki Keddie, "The Revolt of Islam, 1700 to 1993: Comparative Considerations and Relation to Imperialism," *Comparative Studies in Society and Religion* 63 (1994): 463–487.

On Northern Africa

Lisa Anderson, *The State and Social Transformation in Tunisia and Libya, 1830–1980* (Princeton, N.J.: Princeton University Press, 1986).

C.H. Moore, *Politics in North Africa: Algeria, Morocco and Tunisia* (Boston: Little, Brown, 1970).

Jamil Abu-Nasr, "The Salifiyya Movement in Morocco," *Middle Eastern Affairs* 6 (1963): 90–105.

On Islamism

The literature is vast and growing daily; some of it deals specifically with Egypt and the Maghrib, and some has a global focus.

For a valuable and concise overview, see Lisa Anderson, "Obligations and Accountability: Islamic Politics in North Africa," *Daedalus* 20 (1991): 93–112.

Gilles Kepel is an influential commentator on "re-religionisation." See his *Jihad: The Trail of Political Islam*, A.F. Roberts, trans. (Cambridge, Mass: Harvard University Press, 2002), and "Islamism Reconsidered: A Running Dialogue with Modernity," *Harvard International Review* 22 (2000): 22–27.

Richard Mitchell, *The Society of the Muslim Brothers* (London: Oxford University Press, 1969; repr. 1993, with new introduction).

J.L. Esposito, ed., *Voices of Resurgent Islam* (New York: Oxford University Press, 1983), see especially Y. Haddad, "Sayyid Qutb: Ideologue of Islamic Revival," pp. 67–98; L. Anderson, "Qaddafi's Islam," pp. 134–149; and Hassan al-Turabi, "The Islamic State," pp. 241–251.

J.L. Esposito and J. Voll, *Makers of Contemporary Islam* (Oxford, U.K.: Oxford University Press, 2001), see chapters on Hasan Hanafi (Sudan), pp. 68–90; Rashid Ghannoushi (Tunisia), pp. 91–117; and Hasan al-Turabi (Sudan), pp. 118–149.

Ali Abdullatif Ahmida, ed., *Beyond Colonialism and Nationalism in the Maghrib* (New York: Palgrave, 2000).

J.L. Esposito, *The Islamic Threat: Myth or Reality?*, 3rd ed. (Oxford, U.K.: Oxford University Press, 1999).

Jamal Benomar, "The Monarchy, the Islamist Movement and Religious Discourse in Morocco," *Third World Quarterly* 10 (1988): 539–555.

A. Layachi and A. Haireche, "National Development and Political Protest: Islamists in the Maghrib Countries," *Arab Studies Quarterly* 14 (1992): 69–91.

CHAPTER 9: WEST AFRICA SINCE 1900

There is a rich literature on the Mourides:

D.C. O'Brien, *The Mourides of Senegal: The Political and Economic Organisation of an Islamic Brotherhood* (Oxford, U.K.: Clarendon Press, 1971).

D.C. O'Brien, *Saints and Politicians: Essays in the Organisation of Senegalese Peasant Society* (Cambridge, U.K.: Cambridge University Press, 1975).

For a more recent examination, see D. Robinson, "Beyond Resistance and Collaboration: Amadu Bamba and the Murids of Senegal," *Journal of Religion in Africa* 21 (1991): 149–171.

There is also a rich literature on the interactions between Sufis and "reformists" and Islamists.

See especially D. Westerlund and E. E. Rosander, eds., *African Islam and Islam in Africa: Encounters between Sufis and Islamists* (Athens: Ohio University Press, 1997); and Lansiné Kaba, "Islam in West Africa: Radicalism and the New Ethic of Disagreement," in N. Levtzion and R.L. Pouwels, eds., *The History of Islam in Africa* (Athens: Ohio University Press, 2000), pp. 189–208.

L. Brenner, ed., *Muslim Identity and Social Change in Sub-Saharan Africa* (Bloomington and Indianapolis: Indiana University Press, 1993), which is wider in scope.

There is a substantial literature on Islam in contemporary or near contemporary Nigeria, notably:

Toyin Falola, *Violence in Nigeria* (Rochester, N.Y.: University of Rochester Press, 1998), which contains full bibliogaphic references.

There is a considerable literature on Maitatsine listed in Falola. It includes E. Isichei, "The Maitatsine Risings in Nigeria 1980–85: A Revolt of the Disinherited," *Journal of Religion in Africa* 17 (1987): 194–208; and M. Watts, "Islamic Modernities? Citizenship, Civil Society and Islamism in a Nigerian City," *Public Culture* 8 (1996): 251–289.

There is a useful bibliography on Islam in Nigeria (earlier period through the present) produced by the African Studies Centre, Leiden, Netherlands at http://asc.leidenuniv.nl/library/webdossiers/dossiernigeriaandislam.

L. Brenner, *West African Sufi* (Berkeley and Los Angeles: University of California Press, 1984), is a notable biography of a Sufi saint.

Christianity in Africa

There are three standard histories of Christianity in Africa.

Elizabeth Isichei, *A History of Christianity in Africa* (London: SPCK, 1995), is the most accessible and concise (but still 420 pages!), and covers the period from the dawn of Christianity to the 1990s. It gives a much fuller—but somewhat older—account than is possible here. The literature on neo-Pentecostalism and my thinking on the subject have moved on.

Adrian Hastings, *The Church in Africa 1450–1950* (Oxford, U.K.: Oxford University Press, 1994), is much longer (706 pages) and covers a shorter period. It is both learned and insightful. Inexplicably, Hastings omits the Copts. This can be supplemented by his earlier work, now somewhat out of date:

A. Hastings, *A History of African Christianity, 1950–1975* (Cambridge, U.K.: Cambridge University Press, 1979).

B. Sundkler and C. Steed, *A History of the Church in Africa* (Cambridge, U.K.: Cambridge University Press, 2000), is longer still (1,232 pages!) and is best used as a reference work. It attempts to cover the period since 1920, country by country.

See also A.F. Walls, *The Cross-Cultural Process in Christian History* (Maryknoll, N.Y.: Orbis, 2002), insightful essays, with a great deal of overlap between them.

CHAPTER 10: CHRISTIANITY FROM CA. 500 TO CA. 1800

There is an extremely rich literature on Christianity in the Kongo kingdom.

J. Thornton, "The Development of an African Catholic Church in the Kingdom of Kongo, 1491–1750," *Journal of African History* 25 (1984): 147–167.

J. Thornton, *The Kingdom of Kongo: Civil War and Transition, 1641–1718* (Madison: University of Wisconsin Press, 1983).

A. Hilton, *The Kingdom of Kongo* (Oxford, U.K.: Clarendon Press, 1985).

R. Gray, *Black Christians and White Missionaries* (New Haven, Conn.: Yale University Press, 1992), pp. 11–58.

G. Balandier, *Daily Life in the Kingdom of Kongo*, H. Weaver, trans. (London: Allen and Unwin, 1968).

S. Axelson, *Culture Confrontration in the Lower Congo* (Uppsala, Sweden: Studia Missionalia Upsaleinsia, 1970), which includes the nineteenth century.

Alan Ryder is the authority on Christianity in Warri. His work is most readily accessible in his "Precursors," in Elizabeth Isichei, ed., *Varieties of Christian Experience in Nigeria* (London: Macmillan, 1982), pp. 10–27.

CHAPTERS 11 AND 12: CHRISTIANITY IN NINETEENTH-CENTURY AFRICA

Southern Africa

N. Etherington, "Recent Trends in the Historiography of Christianity in Southern Africa," *Journal of Southern African Studies* 23 (1993): 201–219, is a good start.

Nineteenth-century mission history was one of the first fields on which historians of Africa concentrated, in the 1960s and 1970s, and many relevant studies resulted. On southern Africa they included the following:

N. Bhebe, *Christianity and Traditional Religion in Western Zimbabwe 1859–1923* (London: Longman, 1979).

J. McCracken, *Politics and Christianity in Malawi 1875–1940* (Cambridge, U.K.: Cambridge University Press, 1977), on the making of the Livingstonia elite, and the role they played.

Books that do not focus explicitly or exclusively on religion are often very relevant. This is true of:

L. Thompson, *Survival in Two worlds: Moshoeshoe of Lesotho 1786–1870* (Oxford, U.K.: Clarendon Press, 1975).

G. Prins, *The Hidden Hippopotamus* (London: Longman, 1979; Cambridge, U.K.: Cambridge University Press, 1980), on Lozi history.

J.B. Peires, *The House of Phalo: A History of the Xhose People in the Days of Their Independence* (Berkeley: University of California Press, 1982), esp. chap. 5. Peires has published widely on religious themes. See, for instance, the following:

J.B. Peires, "Suicide or Genocide? Xhosa Perceptions of the Nongqawuse Catastrophe," *Radical History Review* 46 (1990): 47–57, and "The Central Beliefs of the Xhosa Cattle Killing," *Journal of African History* 28 (1987): 43–64.

More recent works tend to emphasize language and gender, and source material produced by African Christians.

P. Landau, *The Realm of the Word: Language, Gender and Christianity in a Southern African Kingdom* (Portsmouth, N.H.: Heinemann, 1995), is a deservedly highly regarded book on the Ngwato Tswana.

There is a rich literature on the Xhosa prophets, including a two-part article by J. Hodgson, "A Study of the Xhosa Prophet, Nxele," in *Religion in Southern Africa* 6 (1985): 11–36, and 7 (1986): 2–23.

J. Hodgson, *Ntsikana's Great Hymn: A Xhosa Expression of Christianity in the early 19th Century Eastern Cape* (Cape Town, South Africa: Centre for African Studies, University of Cape Town, 1980), is valuable.

For a recent introduction to the history of Christianity in South Africa before 1900, without a bibliography (but densely footnoted), see R. Elphick and R. Davenport, *Christianity in South Africa* (Berkeley: University of California Press, 1997), part 1, pp. 1–134.

East Africa

R.W. Strayer, *The Making of Mission Communities in East Africa* (London: Heinemann, 1978).

F. Welbourn, *East African Rebels* (London: SCM Press, 1961); chap. 5 discusses Spartas.

There is a substantial literature on the nineteenth-century history of Christianity in Buganda, including D.A. Low, *Religion and Society in Uganda 1875–1900* (Kampala: East African Institute of Social Research, 1955); C. Wrigley, "The Christian Revolution In Buganda," *Comparative Studies in Society and History* 2 (1959): 33–48; J. Rowe, "The Purge of Christians at Mwanga's Court," *Journal of African History* 5 (1964): 55–72; J. Brierley and T. Spear, "Mutesa, the Missionaries and Christian Conversion in Buganda," *International Journal of African Historical Studies* 21 (1988): 601–618.

West Africa

In West Africa, too, Africanist historians of the 1960s and 1970s often focused on nineteenth-century mission history. Well-known examples include the following:

J.F.A. Ajayi, *Christian Missions in Nigeria, 1841–1891* (London: Longmans, 1965).

J.B. Webster, *The African Churches among the Yoruba 1888–1922* (Oxford, U.K.: Clarendon Press, 1964).

A recent classic, making use of the many written sources emanating from Yoruba Christians in CMS employ is J. Peel, *Religious Encounters and the Making of the Yoruba* (Bloomington: Indiana University Press, 2000), which is valuable on "traditional" religion as well.

Here, too, books not ostensibly concerned with Christianity often include a good deal on its history. This is true of E. Isichei, *The Ibo People and the Europeans* (London: Faber and Faber, 1993), which includes a detailed study of the Niger Mission, and of C. Fyfe's monumental *A History of Sierra Leone* (London : Oxford University Press, 1962).

E. Isichei, ed., *Varieties of Christian Experience in Nigeria* (London: Macmillan, 1982) is a collection of short biographies; most are of nineteenth- and twentieth-century Christians, some of whom were members of mission churches, and others, of AICs.

CHAPTER 13: CHRISTIANITY IN THE TWENTIETH CENTURY: THE OLDER CHURCHES

R. Gray, *Black Christians and White Missionaries* (New Haven, Conn.: Yale University Press, 1992), pp. 59–117.

A recent collection with a twentieth-century emphasis and full references is T. Spear and I. Kimambo, eds., *East African Expressions of Christianity* (London: James Currey, 1999).

R. Elphick and R. Davenport, *Christianity in South Africa* (Berkeley: University of California Press, 1997), part 2, pp. 124–241.

J. de Gruchy, *The Church Struggle in South Africa* (1979; 2nd ed., London: Collins, 1986).

J. Cochrane et al., *Facing the Truth: South African Faith Communities and the Truth and Reconciliation Commission* (Athens: Ohio University Press, 1999).

See also T. Beidelman, *Colonial Evangelism* (Bloomington: Indiana University Press, 1982).

I. Linden with J. Linden, *Church and Revolution in Rwanda* (Manchester, U.K.: Manchester University Press, 1977).

J. Iliffe, *A Modern History of Tanganyika* (Cambridge, U.K.: Cambridge University Press, 1979), not primarily "about religion," but it discusses Christianity (and Islam and "traditional" religion) with learning and humanity.

E. Fasholé-Luke et al., eds., *Christianity in Independent Africa* (London: Rex Collings, 1978), a large collection of essays.

Elizabeth Isichei, *Entirely for God: A Life of Michael Iwene Tansi* (1980; 2nd ed., Kalamazoo, Mich.: Cistercian Publications, 1998), a grassroots biography of an Igbo Catholic priest, based largely on oral sources.

There is a rich literature on *jamaa*:

J. Fabian, *Jamaa: A Charismatic Movement in Katanga* (Evanston, Ill.: Northwestern University Press, 1971), and "Jamaa: A Charismatic Movement Revisited," in T.D. Blakely et al., eds., *Religion in Africa: Experience and Expression* (London: Currey, 1994), pp. 266–274.

W. de Craemer, *The Jamaa and the Church* (Oxford, U.K.: Clarendon Press, 1977).

On Milingo, see E. Milingo, *The World in Between* (London: Hurst, 1982); and G. ter Haar, *Spirit of Africa: The Healing Ministry of Archbishop Milingo of Zambia* (London: Hurst, 1992).

Paul Gifford, *African Christianity: Its Public* Role (Bloomington: Indiana University Press, 1998), presents case studies of Ghana, Uganda, Zambia, and Cameroon.

Paul Gifford, ed., *The Christian Churches & the Democratisation of Africa* (Leiden, Netherlands: Brill, 1995).

B. Meyer, *Translating the Devil: Religion and Modernity among the Ewe in Ghana* (Trenton, N.J.: Africa World Press, 1999).

For a short version, see B. Meyer, "If You Are a Devil, You Are a Witch . . .," *Journal of Religion in Africa* 22 (1992): 98–131.

CHAPTER 14: AFRICAN INITIATED CHURCHES: THE PROPHETIC MODEL

There is a vast literature here, much more extensive than on the older churches, and there is room here only for a selection.

Jean Comaroff, *Body of Power, Spirit of Resistance* (Chicago: University of Chicago Press, 1985), a highly regarded study of religious change among the southern (South African) Tswana; it includes good material on "traditional" religion as well as on the Zion Christian Church.

E. Gunner, *The Man of Heaven and the Beautiful Ones of God* (Leiden, Netherlands: Brill, 2002), wonderful material from Shembe and his followers.

T. Ranger, "Religious Movements and Politics in Sub-Saharan Africa," *African Studies Review* 29 (1986): 1–68, widely cited but now rather out of date.

N.H. Ngada et al., *Speaking for Ourselves* (Springs, South Africa: Order of Preachers, 1985), an account of Zionism from within.

B. Sundkler, *Zulu Zion and Some Swazi Zionists* (Uppsala, Sweden: Studia Missionalia Upsaliensia, 1976), especially valuable because of his intimate, first-hand knowledge of past Zionist prophets and their churches.

J. Thompson, "Shembe Mismanaged? A Study of Varying Interpretations of the Ibandla Nazaretha," *Bulletin of the John Rylands Library* 70 (1988): 185–196.

The standard (and different) accounts of Harris are the following:

D. Shank, *Prophet Harris: The Black Elijah of West Africa* (Leiden, Netherlands: Brill, 1994).

G. Haliburton, *The Prophet Harris* (New York: Oxford University Press, 1973).

On Kimbangu and other Kongo prophets, compare M.L. Martin, *An African Prophet and His Church,* D.M. Moore, trans. (Oxford, U.K.: Blackwell, 1975), with various accounts by W. MacGaffey, such as his "Kimbanguism and the Question of Syncretism in Zaire," in T. Blakely et al., eds., *Religion in Africa* (London: Currey, 1994), pp. 241–256, and *Modern Kongo Prophets* (Bloomington: Indiana University Press, 1983).

J. Janzen and W. MacGaffey, *An Anthology of Kongo Religion* (Lawrence: University Press of Kansas, 1974), is a rich source on AICs and "traditional" religion.

The best account of Alice Lenshina and the Lumpa Church is in H. Hinefelaar, *Bemba-Speaking Women of Zambia in a Century of Religious Change* (Leiden, Netherlands: Brill, 1994), which includes much on "traditional" Bemba religion and lists earlier studies.

J.D.Y. Peel, *Aladura: A Religious Movement among the Yoruba* (London: Oxford University Press, 1968).

H. Turner, *History of an African Independent Church,* 2 vols. (Oxford, U.K.: Clarendon Press, 1967), a pioneering study of the Church of the Lord (Aladura).

R. Hackett, ed., *New Religious Movements in Nigeria* (Lewiston, N.Y.: Edwin Mellen, 1987).

G. Bond et al., *African Christianity: Patterns of Religious Continuity* (New York: Academic Press, 1979), part 1, by S. Harris, is on the Harrist Churches, and part 4, by B. Jules-Rosette, is on the Maranke Apostles.

Bennetta Jules-Rosette, *African Apostles: Ritual and Conversion in the Church of John Maranke* (Ithaca, N.Y.: Cornell University Press, 1975).

On Masowe, see C. Dillon-Malone, *The Korsten Basket Makers* (Manchester, U.K.: Manchester University Press, 1978).

CHAPTER 15: THE GLOBAL AND THE LOCAL: NEO-PENTECOSTALISM

Gifford's voluminous but hostile accounts of neo-Pentecostalism have done much to shape perceptions. They include the following:

P. Gifford, *Christianity and Politics in Doe's Liberia* (Cambridge, U.K.: Cambridge University Press, 1993).

Steve Brouwer, Paul Gifford, and Susan Rose, *Exporting the American Gospel: Global Christian Fundamentalism* (New York and London: Routledge, 1996), chaps. 7 and 8.

P. Gifford, *New Crusaders: Christianity and the New Right in Southern Africa* (London: Pluto Press, 1991).

P. Gifford, ed., *New Dimensions in African Christianity* (Nairobi: All Africa Conference of Churches, 1992).

P. Gifford, "'Africa Shall Be Saved': An Appraisal of Reinhard Bonnke's Pan-African Crusade," *Journal of Religion in Africa* 17 (1987): 63–92.

P. Gifford, "Prosperity: A New and Foreign Element in African Christianity," *Religion* 20 (1990): 373–388.

P. Gifford, "Christian Fundamentalism and Development in Africa," *Review of African Political Economy* 52 (1991): 9–20.

P. Gifford, "Chiluba's Christian Nation: Christianity as a Factor in Zambian Politics," *Journal of Contemporary Religion* 13 (1998): 363–381.

Marshall-Fratani is more sympathetic; her more recent work includes the following:

R. Marshall, "'Power in the Name of Jesus': Social Transformation and Pentecostalism in Western Nigeria 'Revisited,'" in T. Ranger and O. Vaughan, eds., *Legitimacy and the State in Twentieth Century Africa* (Basingstoke, U.K.: Macmillan, 1993), pp. 213–246, and R. Marshall-Fratani, "Mediating the Global and the Local in Nigerian Pentecostalism," *Journal of Religion in Africa* 28 (1998): 278–315.

A. Corten and R. Marshall-Fratani, eds., *Between Babel and Pentecost: Transnational Pentecostalism in Africa and Latin America* (London: C. Hurst, 2000), parts 1 and 3.

See also the following:

Matthews Ojo, "The Contextual Significance of the Charismatic Movements in Independent Nigeria," *Africa* 58 (1988): 175–191, and "Deeper Christian Life Ministry: A Case Study of the Charismatic Movements in Western Nigeria," *Journal of Religion in Africa* 18 (1988): 141–162.

The work of David Maxwell has added significant new dimensions:

D. Maxwell, "'Sacred History, Social History': Traditions and Texts in the Making of a Southern African Transnational Religious Movement," *Comparative Studies in Society and History* 43 (2001): 502–524, and several rejoinders to Gifford:

"Delivered from the Spirit of Poverty? Pentecostalism, Prosperity and Modernity in Zimbabwe," *Journal of Religion in Africa* 28 (1998): 350–373, and "In Defence of African Creativity," *Journal of Religion in Africa* 30 (2000): 468–481.

See also Maxwell's "'Catch the Cockerel before Dawn': Pentecostalism and Politics in Post-Colonial Zimbabwe," *Africa* 70 (2000): 249–277.

Neotraditional Religion

B. Ray, *African Religions: Symbol, Ritual and Community,* 2nd ed. (Upper Saddle River, N.J.: Prentice-Hall, 2000), is a useful introductory study. It is based on contemporary ethnographic studies, and does not adopt a historical approach.

Jean Comaroff and John Comaroff, eds., *Modernity and Its Malcontents: Ritual and Power in Postcolonial Africa* (Chicago: University of Chicago Press, 1993), is a valuable collection of studies of contemporary religious change, with good material on spirit possession, masks, and witchcraft.

There are many collections of essays on neotraditional religion; some also include Christianity and/or Islam in Africa.

T. Blakely et al., eds., *Religion in Africa* (London: Currey, 1994), includes chapters on both Christianity and "traditional" religion.

Other well-known collections include W. Arens and I. Karp, eds., *Creativity of Power: Cosomology and Action in African Societies* (Washington, D.C.: Smithsonian Institution Press, 1989); and I. Karp and S. Bird, *Explorations in African Systems of Thought* (Bloomington: Indiana University Press, 1980).

J. Olupona, ed., *African Spirituality Forms: Meanings and Expressions* (New York: Crossroad, 2000), is best on "traditional" religion, though it includes chapters on Christianity and Islam, among them one by L. Brenner on Sufism (pp. 324–349).

R. Hackett, *Religion in Calabar* (Berlin: Mouton de Gruyter, 1989), surveys the various forms of religious practice, both Christian and neotraditional, in a Nigerian city.

R. Werbner, ed., *Regional Cults* (London: Academic Press, 1977).

Robin Horton, "A Hundred Years of Change in Kalabari Religion," in John Middleton, ed., *Black Africa: Its Peoples and Their Cultures Today* (London: Macmillan, 1970).

CHAPTER 16: DIVINITIES

The Igbo Case Study

There is valuable primary material in E. Isichei, *Igbo Worlds* (Basingstoke, U.K.: Macmillan, 1977).

C. Ubah, "The Supreme Being, Divinities and Ancestors in Igbo Traditional Religion: Evidence from Otanchara and Otanzu," *Africa* 52 (1982): 90–105.

R. Henderson, *The King in Every Man* (New Haven, Conn.: Yale University Press, 1972), a superb study of the Niger Igbo town of Onitsha.

S. Jell-Bahlsen, "The Lake Goddess Uhamirri/Ogbuide . . . ," in Olupona, ed., *African Spirituality*, pp. 38–53.

The Yoruba Case Study

B. Lawal, *The Gelede Spectacle* (Seattle: University of Washington Press, 1996), an exemplary account by a Yoruba scholar that sheds light on much besides Gelede.

Barber's work on Yoruba culture is always of great value.

K. Barber, "How Man Makes God in West Africa: Yoruba Attitudes towards the Orisa," *Africa* 51 (1981): 724–745.

K. Barber, "Oriki, Women and the Proliferation and Merging of Orisa," *Africa* 60 (1990): 313–335.

B. Belasco, *The Entrepreneur as Culture Hero: Pre-Adaptations in Nigerian Economic Development* (New York: Bergin, 1980), an interesting work that is underused, perhaps because of its title, in which the exploration of themes such as Eshu is not apparent.

S. Barnes, ed., *Africa's Ogun: Old World and New* (Bloomington: Indiana University Press, 1989).

The writings of P. Morton-Williams, though older, are of lasting value:

"The Atinga Cult among the South-Western Yoruba: A Sociological Analysis of a Witch-Finding Movement," *Bulletin de l'IFAN* ser. B, 18 (1956): 315–344.
"An Outline of the Cosmology and Cult Organization of the Oro Yoruba," *Africa* 34 (1964): 243–260.
"Yoruba Responses to the Fear of Death," *Africa* 36 (1966): 34–40.
"The Yoruba Ogboni Cult in Oyo," *Africa* 30 (1960): 362–373.

See also:

J. Pemberton, "Eshu-Elegba: The Yoruba Trickster God," *African Arts* 9 (1975): 20–27, 66–70.
J. Wescott, "The Sculpture and Myths of Eshu-Elegba, the Yoruba Trickster," *Africa* 32 (1962): 336–354.
J. Peel, "Gender in Yoruba Religious Change," *Journal of Religion in Africa* 32 (2002): 136–166.
Joseph Murphy, "Oshun the Dancer," in C. Olson, ed., *The Book of the Goddess Past and Present* (New York: Crossroad, 1983), pp. 190–201.

There is a rich literature on Mami Wata:

For a recent account, with references and line drawings, see E. Isichei, *Voices of the Poor in Africa* (Rochester, N.Y.: University of Rochester Press, 2002), chap. 14, "Mami Wata: Icon of Ambiguity," pp. 188–209.
K. O'Brien Wicker, "Mami Wata in African Religion and Spirituality," in J.K. Olupona, ed., *African Spirituality* (New York: Crossroad, 2000), pp. 198–222.
H. Drewal, ed., *Sacred Waters: Mami Wata and Other Water Spirits in the African-Atlantic World* (Los Angeles: Fowler Museum, 2005).

CHAPTERS 17 AND 18: ANCESTORS AS DIVINITIES AND POWERS EMBODIED

The extensive literature on which my account is based, is detailed in the notes. See also:

C. Wrigley, *Kingship and State: The Buganda Dynasty* (Cambridge, U.K.: Cambridge University Press, 1996).
J. Beattie and J. Middleton, eds., *Spirit Mediumship and Society in Africa* (London: Routledge, 1969).
J. Boddy, "Spirit Possession Revisited: Beyond Instrumentality," *Annual Revue of Anthropology* 23 (1994): 407–434.
H. Behrend and U. Luig, eds., *Spirit Possession: Modernity and Power in Uganda* (Oxford, U.K.: Currey, 1999).
M. Grosz-Ngate and O. Kokole, eds., *Gendered Encounters* (New York: Routledge, 1997), an extremely valuable collection; see the contributions by J. Rosenthal on spirit posession among the Ewe and D. Hodgson on the same phenomenon among the Masaai.
J. Rosenthal, *Foreign Tongues and Domestic Bodies: Personhood, Possession, Gender and the Law in the Ewe Gorovvodu Order* (Charlottesville: University Press of Virginia, 1997).

CHAPTER 19: RITUAL AND DIVINATION

Ritual: The Ndembo Case Study

Victor Turner's works are the indispensable starting point; see the following:

V.Turner, *The Forest of Symbols: Aspects of Ndembu Ritual* (Ithaca, N.Y.: Cornell University Press, 1966), and *The Drums of Affliction* (Oxford, U.K.: Clarendon Press, 1968).

They should be compared with Edith Turner's lively reflexive account of the same place and time, *The Spirit and the Drum: A Memoir of Africa* (Tucson: University of Arizona Press, 1987), and of her 1985 visit, *Experiencing Ritual* (Philadelphia: University of Pennsylvania Press, 1992).

W. van Binsbergen, *Religious Change in Zambia* (London: Kegan Paul, 1981), emphasizes change and regional cults, a contrast with Victor Turner's approach. His paper "Mukanda" is an interesting study of change in a male cirumcision ritual among the Nkoya of Zambia. It appeared in J.P. Chrétien et al., eds., *L'Invention Religieuse en Afrique* (Paris: Karthala, 1993), pp. 49–103.

Divination

P. Peek, ed., *African Divination Systems: Ways of Knowing* (Bloomington: Indiana University Press, 1991), a collection of case studies, all different from the ones used in this book; the sources for Ifa and other forms of divination discussed in the text are given in footnotes.

CHAPTER 20: ROYALS, PRIESTS, AND PROPHETS

Sacred Kings and Queens

G. Feeley-Harnick, "Issues in Divine Kingship," *Annual Review of Anthropology* 14 (1985): 273–313, an excellent discussion with a good bibliography up to the time of publication.

M Young, "The Divine Kingship of the Jukun: a Re-Evaluation of Some Theories," *Africa* 36 (1966): 135–152.

J. Vaughan, "A Reconsideration of Divine Kingship," in I. Karp and C.S. Bird, eds., *Explorations in African Systems of Thought* (Bloomington: Indiana University Press, 1980), pp. 120–142.

Prophets

The indispensable starting point is in D. Johnson and D. Anderson, eds., *Revealing Prophets* (London: Currey, 1995).

Maji Maji

There is a large literature here, to which M. Wright, "Maji Maji: Prophecy and Historiography," in D. Johnson and D. Anderson, *Revealing Prophets* (London: Currey, 1995), is a good guide.

The Kaguru Case Study

For an excellent ethnography, see T. Beidelman, *Moral Imagination in Kaguru Modes of Thought* (Washington, D.C.: Smithsonian Institution Press, 1993).

The Nuer and Dinka Case Studies

The classic ethnographies are the following:

E. Evans-Pritchard, *Nuer Religion* (Oxford, U.K.: Clarendon Press, 1956).
G. Lienhardt, *Divinity and Experience: The Religion of the Dinka* (Oxford, U.K.: Clarendon Press, 1961).

Evans-Pritchard, in particular, generated a vast number of reinterpretations, such as:

T. Beidelman, "Nuer Priests and Prophets," in T. Beidelman, ed., *The Translation of Culture* (London: Tavistock, 1971).
D. Johnson, *Nuer Prophets* (Oxford, U.K.: Clarendon Press, 1994), an outstanding study of religious change.
D. Johnson, "Foretelling Peace and War: Modern Interpretations of Ngungdeng's Prophecies in the Southern Sudan," in M. Daly, ed., *Modernization in the Sudan* (New York: Barber Press, 1985), pp. 121–136.
M. Nikkel, "Aspects of Contemporary Religious Change among the Dinka," *Journal of Religion in Africa* 22, no. 1 (1992): 78–94.
S. Hutchinson, *Nuer Dilemmas: Coping with Money, War and the State* (Berkeley: University of California Press, 1996), an excellent example of contemporary reflexive ethnography.

On Nuer/Dinka identity, see also:

A. Southall, "Nuer and Dinka Are People: Ecology, Ethnicity and Logical Possibility," *Man* 11 (1976): 463–491.

Mau Mau

There is a vast literature on Mau Mau, but the indispensable starting point is:

B. Berman and J. Lonsdale, *Unhappy Valley: Conflict in Kenya and Africa* (London: Currey, 1992), part 5, pp. 225–460.

See also:

J. Lonsdale, "Mau Maus of the Mind: Making Mau Mau and Remaking Kenya," *Journal of African History* 31 (1990): 393–421.
L. White, "Separating the Men from the Boys: Constructions of Gender, Sexuality and Terrorism in Central Kenya 1939–59," *International Journal of African Historical Studies* 23 (1990): 1–25.
On the links between wars in independent Africa and "traditional" religion, see S. Weigert, *Traditional Religion and Guerrilla Warfare in Modern Africa* (Basingstoke, U.K.: Macmillan, 1996).

Alice Lakwena

The sources are listed in the notes to my account. See also H. Behrend, "Power to Heal, Power to Kill . . . in Northern Uganda (1986–1994)," in H. Behrend and U. Luig, eds., *Spirit Possession* (Madison: University of Wisconsin Press, 1999), pp. 20–34, which contains rather more on Kony.

New Religious Movements

The case study in this book is the Mumbo cult (sources in notes to text), but there are other well-studied comparable movements. Several of the case studies in R. Hackett, ed., *New Religious Movements in Nigeria* (Lewiston, N.Y.: Mellen, 1987), belong to this category.

J. Fernandez, *Bwiti: An Ethnography of the Religious Imagination in Africa* (Princeton, N.J.: Princeton University Press, 1982), is a classic (and vast, 731 pages) study of a religious movement among the Fang of Gabon, based on fieldwork in 1959–1960.

For a shorter version of this and an account of an additional movement see Fernandez's "The Affirmation of Things Past," in R. Rotberg and Ali Mazrui, eds., *Protest and Power in Black Africa* (New York: Oxford University Press, 1970), pp. 427–457.

On the Arathi movement among the Kikuyu, see D. Sandgren, *Christianity and the Kikuyu* (New York: Lang, 1989), chap. 7, pp. 121–136.

CHAPTER 21: MYTHOLOGY AND PROVERBIAL WISDOM

R. D. Pelton, *The Trickster in West Africa: A Study of Mythic Irony and Sacred Delight* (Berkeley: University of California Press, 1989).

On proverbs, see D. Bieybuyck, *Lega Culture* (Berkeley: University of California Press, 1973), which includes an account of Bwami, a society of initiated members associated with a vast collection of proverbs, as well as with works of art.

C. Wrigley, *Kingship and State: The Buganda Dynasty* (Cambridge, U.K.: Cambridge University Press, 1996), offers daring interpretations from a structuralist point of view. Wrigley was profoundly influenced by the works of the Belgian scholar Luc de Heusch., especially *The Drunken King*, R. Willis, trans. (Bloomington: Indiana University Press, 1982).

V. Görög-Karady has published extensively on the myth of a cosmic choice, and the white and black brothers, in French. See also T. Beidelman, "A Kaguru Version of the Sons of Noah," *Cahiers d'Études Africaines* 3 (1963): 474–490; and M. Bourdillon, "Gleaning, Shona Section from Biblical Myth," in W. James and D. Johnson, eds., *Vernacular Christianity* (Oxford, U.K.: JASO, 1988), pp. 120–130.

CHAPTER 22: SUFFERING AND ITS INTERPRETERS

Witchcraft

Older studies that, like many such, are still of value, include the following:

M. Douglas, ed., *Witchcraft Confessions and Accusations* (London: Tavistock, 1970).

M. Marwick, ed., *Witchcraft and Sorcery: Selected Readings* (Harmondsworth, U.K.: Penguin, 1970).

The contemporary reinterpretation of witchcraft is a major theme in the following:

J. Comaroff and J. Comaroff, eds., *Modernity and Its Malcontents* (Chicago: University of Chicago Press, 1993).

E. Isichei, *Voices of the Poor in Africa* (Rochester, N.Y.: University of Rochester Press, 2000), part 2, pp. 89–255, explores the way in which ancient idioms of witchcraft have been reinvented in the poetics of rumor, and critique oppressive social structures. Various chapters deal, among other themes, with vampire, zombie, and shape-shifter rumors, and blood/money magic and with the way in which ancient stereotypes of the dangerous woman find a new vitality in the age of AIDS.

The following articles offer a variety of significant insights:

R. Shaw, "The Production of Witchcraft/Witchcraft as Production: Memory, Modernity and the Slave Trade in Sierra Leone," *American Ethnologist* 24 (1997): 856–876.

J. Brain, "Witchcraft and Development," *African Affairs* 81 (1982): 371–384.

S. Drucker-Brown, "Mamprusi Witchcraft: Subversion and Changing Gender Relations," *Africa* 63 (1993): 531–549.

A. Gottlieb, "Witches, Kings and the Sacrifice of Identity . . . ," in W. Arens and I. Karp, eds., *Creativity of Power* (Washington, D.C.: Smithsonian Institution Press, 1989), pp. 245–272.

D. Kohnert, "Magic and Witchcraft: Implications for Democratization and Poverty-Alleviating Aid in Africa," *World Development* 24 (1996): 1347–1355.

T. McCaskie, "Anti-Witchcraft Cults in Asante: An Essay in the Social History of an African People," *History in Africa* 8 (1981): 125–153.

Cameroon

Peter Geschiere has written important studies of contemporary witchcraft beliefs in Cameroon.

P. Geschiere, *The Modernity of Witchcraft: Politics and the Occult in Postcolonial Africa* (Charlottesville: University Press of Virginia, 1997). He has also written articles on the subject, sometimes in collaboration with C. Fisiy.

P. Geschiere, "Domesticating Personal Violence: Witchcraft, Courts and Confessions in Cameroon," *Africa* 64 (1994): 323–341.

C. Fisiy and P. Geschiere, "Judges and Witches, or How Is the State to Deal with Witchcraft? . . ." *Cahiers d'Études Africaines* 118 (1990): 135–156.

C. Fisiy and P. Geschiere, "Sorcery, Witchcraft and Accumulation . . . ," *Critique of Anthropology* 11 (1991: 251–278.

Eric de Rosny, a Catholic priest, trained as a *nganga* and wrote a book that gives valuable insights into witchcraft beliefs in Cameroon: *Healers in the Night*, R. Muir, trans. (New York: Orbis, 1985).

A Tiv Case Study

There is interesting material on witchcraft and witchcraft eradication among the Tiv of central Nigeria (not covered in this book). Compare the ethnographic account in Laura Bohannan and Paul Bohannan, *The Tiv of Central Nigeria* (London: International African Institute, 1953), pp. 81–93, with a reflexive (and inappropriately titled) "anthropological novel" by Laura Bohannan that, significantly, first appeared under the pseudonym Leonore Smith Bowen: *Return to Laughter* (1954; New York: Doubleday, 1964), based on fieldwork in 1949–1953.

A classic account from within is Akiga Sai, (trans. R. East), *Akiga's Story*, R. East, trans. (1939; London: International African Institute/Oxford University Press, 1965).

J. Tseayo, *Conflict and Corporation in Nigeria* (Zaria, Nigeria: privately printed, 1975), is an account by a Tiv academic with interesting material on anti-witchcraft movements.

There is an ever-growing body of material on witchcraft accusations in southern Africa. This includes:

I. Niehaus, "Witch-Hunting and Political Legitimacy: Continuity and Change in Green Valley, Lebowa, 1930–91," *Africa* 63 (1993): 498–530.

C.B. Yamba, "Cosmologies in Turmoil: Witchfinding and AIDS in Chiawa, Zambia," *Africa* 67 (1997): 200–223.

E. Bähre, "Witchcraft and the Exchange of Sex, Blood and Money among Africans in Cape Town, South Africa," *Journal of Religion in Africa* 32 (2002): 300–334.

Index

About the Author

ELIZABETH ISICHEI taught at African Universities for sixteen years, nine of which were spent as Professor of History at the University of Jos, Nigeria. She is currently Professor of Religious Studies at the University of Otago, New Zealand. She has written many titles on African history and religion, including *The Ibo People and the Europeans* (1973), *A History of Christianity in Africa* (1995), and *Voices of the Poor in Africa* (2002).

DATE DUE

April '10   08

APR 2 2 2008